D1562659

UNDER THE DRONES

Modern Lives in the Afghanistan-Pakistan Borderlands

EDITED BY
Shahzad Bashir
Robert D. Crews

HARVARD UNIVERSITY PRESS

Cambridge, Massachusetts / London, England / 2012

This book was made possible in part by a grant from Carnegie Corporation of New York. The statements made and views expressed are solely the responsibility of the authors.

Library of Congress Cataloging-in-Publication Data
Under the drones : modern lives in the Afghanistan-Pakistan borderlands / edited by Shahzad Bashir, Robert D. Crews.
    pages : maps ; cm
  Includes bibliographical references and index.
  ISBN 978-0-674-06561-1 (alkaline paper)
 1. Afghanistan—Relations—Pakistan. 2. Pakistan—Relations—Afghanistan.
3. Afghanistan—Boundaries—Pakistan. 4. Pakistan—Boundaries—
Afghanistan. 5. Borderlands—Afghanistan. 6. Borderlands—Pakistan.
7. Afghanistan—Politics and government. 8. Pakistan—Politics and
government. 9. Islam and politics—Afghanistan. 10. Islam and politics—
Pakistan. I. Bashir, Shahzad, 1968– II. Crews, Robert D., 1970–
  DS357.6.P18U53 2012
  958.104'71—dc23   2011044605

Contents

Afghanistan and Pakistan

The Af-Pak frontier

Introduction

Shahzad Bashir and Robert D. Crews

Glancing at the front page of any major Western newspaper nowadays, one is likely to see a story about Afghanistan or Pakistan. Such stories tend to engage the same topics over and over: terrorism, militancy, suicide bombings, counterinsurgency operations, corruption, mistreatment of women, and occasional triumphs by heroic Afghans and Pakistanis in the face of nearly impossible odds. Journalistic descriptions primarily privilege the present, seen through the interests and perspectives of Western observers, as the ultimate vantage point for what occurs along the boundary between these two modern nation-states. The people who populate these stories seem to be stuck in a kind of time warp of unchanging "tribal" traditions, eternally isolated since time immemorial and only now coming face to face with realities the rest of the planet takes for granted as part of the modern world. The Taliban, the region's most potent sociopolitical force of recent times, is referred to as "medieval" without anyone batting an eye, even though the social formations that comprise the group have their origins in the 1980s. On the rare occasion when a historical perspective is invoked, it has only a few oft-repeated markers: Alexander the Great, the "great game" between the Russian and British empires in the late nineteenth and early twentieth centuries, and the Soviet invasion of 1979 and its consequent civil war. People who live there would seem to become historical subjects only when acted upon by outsiders, most recently by the Americans and their NATO allies. The most striking image of this engagement with the inhabitants of the region is that of the drone aircraft, piloted from Nevada or Florida, conducting high-altitude aerial surveillance of this rugged borderland and periodically unleashing lethal fire on suspected militants below in what many commentators have understood as a contest between the sophisticated technology of the modern, civilized West and the savagery of a backward foe. In the absence of such intervention, these populations are portrayed as living without any sense of change, eternally wallowing in a world of barbarity, which if left to itself would ultimately strike out against the security of the West.

This book challenges this portrayal of the Afghanistan-Pakistan borderlands and seeks to provide an alternative to thinking about the region that is narrowly framed by Washington's shifting conceptions of security. Drawing away from descriptions predicated on global politics alone, we wish to illuminate aspects of the rich social and cultural worlds that are opaque to cameras mounted on drones flying many thousands of feet above this terrain. Beginning in 2008, policymakers in the United States began to use the neologism "Af-Pak" to denote the territory that the late former UN ambassador Richard Holbrooke characterized as a single "theater of war." Frustrated by the expansion of the Taliban insurgency in Afghanistan and the persistence of "safe havens" for militants on Pakistani territory, Holbrooke, President Barack Obama's special representative to the region, called for an integrated approach to Afghanistan and Pakistan. In 2009 the Obama administration not only shifted resources from Iraq to the region but, under General David Petraeus, expanded a counterinsurgency strategy that in turn hinged upon particular conceptions of society, politics, and culture in Afghanistan and Pakistan.

Now imagined as a continuous war zone, Af-Pak appeared to be inhabited by populations governed by primitive and archaic norms. Drawing on the authority of social scientists and various contractors and informants under the Pentagon's Human Terrain System Project, this way of envisioning the region promised a scheme for making these populations legible. The experience of the Iraq war had alerted experts to the problem of sectarian politics, but it was their encounter with "tribes" that suggested a grid of identification that could be exported to this theater. The inhabitants of Af-Pak seemed to be wholly defined by the immutable categories of tribe and ethnicity. Paradoxically, military planners and their civilian advisors seized upon the idea of tribe as the essential key to Afghan and Pakistani identities at a time when the concept had long been abandoned by most anthropologists and scholars in related fields. From the late 1960s, researchers began to question the utility of a term that commonly assumed the timeless existence of closed social units with clear biological boundaries and fixed membership occupying a lower stage of human development. Instead they pointed to the malleability, flexibility, and even dynamic modernity of societies where people maintained meaningful genealogies that interacted in complex ways with other social and political identities.[1] But the search for a "tribal strategy" in planning for Af-Pak was more than an academic skirmish. Tribal identity was thought to determine the political loyalties of entire populations. Moreover, tribes appeared to furnish hierarchical mechanisms of social control as well as civilian groups who could be recruited to fight on behalf of U.S. and NATO forces. When the Taliban emerged in southern Afghanistan in 1994 and seized Kabul in 1996, Western media tended to describe them as fundamentalist zealots. In combating the neo-Taliban resurgence a decade later, however, U.S. military intelligence officers and their advisers had come to highlight the "martial character of Pashtun tribes." David Kilcullen, the most influential theorist behind the new counterinsurgency doctrine developed in response to the Iraq and Afghan wars, contrasted the two theaters by asserting that "it is a rare Iraqi who loves the fight itself," whereas "Afghans do: they like to win, and are certainly not averse to killing, but what they really love is the fight, *jang* (battle), for its own sake."[2]

As the geographic focus of American strategy shifted to the 1,600-mile frontier across which Afghan insurgents retreated to mountain sanctuaries in Pakistan, the Pashtuns residing on both sides of the border came to dominate debates about counterinsurgency. Insurgents fighting the Kabul government and U.S. and NATO forces in Afghanistan were drawn from this group, and in 2007 a similar movement, the Tehrik-e Taliban, emerged among the Pashtuns in Swat in northwestern Pakistan, pressing for the implementation of Islamic law in a manner resembling that of the Afghan Taliban. At the same time, Western intelligence agencies concluded that the "tribal" region of northwestern Pakistan also served as a refuge for al-Qaida. Thus the "Pashtun belt" came to be defined by multiple insurgencies and fierce military campaigns waged from the air and on the ground. Meanwhile, the latest counterinsurgency doctrine called for the urgent mapping of Pashtun tribes and customs. The study of the Pashto language, which was offered in only one or two universities in the United States and a handful of military schools, was less a priority than the hiring of Pashtun translators, who could earn $200,000 a year or more by deploying to the field with NATO forces. Given this language deficit and the increasing inaccessibility of actual Pashtun populations, military intelligence and contractors looked to past research, most of which was conducted decades ago and before the dislocations of the Afghan revolution and Soviet war. This scholarship in turn drew heavily on the ideas and language of British colonial administrators who had themselves resorted to ethnography as a strategy to rule this space.

Yet this engagement with the British colonial record reflected many of the contradictions of Af-Pak strategy. Military planners and advisors rejected the notion that the United States acted as an empire, but they freely adopted policies based on their reading of examples from this imperial past. More important, they tended to adopt colonial representations of the Pashtuns and the mythology of a "wild" frontier that imbued British writing about the region. Similarly, media portrayals of these borderlands stressed their "lawlessness" and the ferocity of the supposedly war-loving population that lived there. First identified as one of the "martial castes" by British administrators after the revolt of 1857 in India, the Pashtuns regularly appeared in colonial literature as perennially armed and spoiling for bloody combat with the "infidels"; and frequent revolts, often inspired by mullahs, led British officials such as the young Winston Churchill to conclude that this was "a land of fanatics [where] common sense does not exist."[3] If Afghanistan was "the graveyard of empires," as many war critics insisted, the frontier was an unconquerable fortress guarded by frenzied tribal warriors.

As many chapters in this book seek to show, the excessively warlike images of the borderland have been based on a very partial and tendentious reading of history. It is true that Pashtuns have expressed pride, including in poetry and song, about the martial prowess of their ancestors, but deeper engagement with the historical record reveals that they were to be found not only sniping at British soldiers from craggy mountain passes but, at least as frequently, serving the queen in the Indian Army and fighting and dying in British campaigns throughout the empire. In the 1820s, for example, local communities rejected calls for jihad that other regions of India found compelling.[4] A century later in the North West Frontier of India they also formed a mass movement, the Khudai Khidmatgars, under the leadership of a "Frontier Gandhi" who was committed to a nonviolent campaign of civil disobedience to unify the Pathans or Pakhtuns (as they were known in India) and oppose British rule.[5] The arena in which these varied politics took shape, the frontier, has been a place of war but also one of commercial, cultural, and intellectual exchange linked to global flows of people, commodities, and ideas. If it has appeared "unruly" or "lawless" at various moments in its modern history, this is not only because men have taken up the gun to resist some kinds of external authority but also because regional governments, imperial powers, and even local inhabitants have at certain times identified their interests with maintaining a particular political regime there.

Even the border that cuts through this space, the famed Durand Line of 1893, has played a distinctive role that has evolved over time. Whereas militants, religious activists, and migrants often disregard its existence, this line has taken on real significance for traders and truckers, as Gilles Dorronsoro shows in Chapter 2, because it brings profit to those who move differently valued goods across it. The borderland is a place of transnationalism, but also of the intensification of national politics. Indeed, the history of this borderland, as many of our authors show, is the history of dynamic interconnections, mobile populations, and religious and ethnic heterogeneity and change. From the late nineteenth century on, a succession of great powers have jockeyed for influence in the region, but those external forces are not the sole shapers of the region's contemporary history. The inhabitants of the region have interacted with empires, nation-states, and transnational actors in a variety of ways beyond the blinkered reading of counterinsurgency theory.

If the social sciences and history represented one key to unlocking the opaque politics of the Afghan-Pakistan borderlands, aerial surveillance has been another. With the complicity of local governments, unmanned drones and other aircraft offered a vantage point that permitted commanders to surmount vast distances and difficult terrain—including the borders of the state of Pakistan—to render visible the enemies below. By the end of April 2011, the Obama administration had approved roughly 240 drone missile strikes in Pakistan alone. Following the killing of Osama bin Laden in the Pakistani town of Abbottabad by U.S. Navy Seals on May 2, drone attacks in Pakistan continued and even increased in frequency. Answering critics who charged that these missile strikes were often based on faulty intelligence and that they killed indiscriminately, the CIA asserted in August 2011 that its drone campaign had not killed a single noncombatant since May 2010. But a growing number of eyewitness accounts of civilian deaths and psychological trauma among villagers (and their animals) who had survived attacks, often to be targeted again as rescuers or funeral attendees, called into question security officials' claims about the technological precision that allowed them to decipher the identities of the inhabitants that they had marked for death under the drones.[6]

To the architects of the new American counterinsurgency doctrines, the struggle to master and pacify Af-Pak was more than a contest between backward tribesmen and modern science: it also entailed a mission that was defined as both humanitarian and political, the fight for "hearts and minds." Inspired by Greg Mortenson's *Three Cups of Tea* and the work of other Western activists in the region and armed with selected insights from British colonial counterinsurgency, policymakers set out to make the promotion of development, education, and health essential parts of the military project in Afghanistan. In pursuing these efforts to transform Afghan society, the Pentagon could largely bypass the government in Kabul, but in Islamabad it had to contend with multiple and competing state institutions with uneven control over Pakistani territory.

Like other military strategies, the "hearts and minds" campaign reveals an understanding of the societies of the region that is skewed by

American security concerns. Perhaps most important, it has rested on the insistence that these populations remain loyal or at least apolitical. Recipients of humanitarian assistance are thus expected to be not just grateful but acquiescent to U.S. forces and their local allies in all circumstances. American authorities have asked Afghan civilians to accept apologies and compensation payments for injuries and deaths caused by American forces (in 2010, reportedly about $2,900 apiece to wounded individuals, and $4,800 apiece to the families of those killed). The government of Pakistan has promised similar amounts of compensation to victims of drone attacks in some cases. At the same time, American authorities have regularly dismissed critiques of air strikes and raids that have caused civilian casualties or, especially in the case of Pakistan, objections to the violation of national sovereignty. Moreover, when several million civilians were uprooted by fighting between the Pakistani Taliban and military in 2009, and by massive floods in 2010, precipitating one of the worst refugee crises in modern times, drone strikes and other counterinsurgency operations continued, while the vast resources of the United States and NATO alleviated the plight of very few Pakistanis. Indeed, over the past four years civilian deaths related to armed conflict in the region have increased yearly. In 2010 these numbered 2,777 in Afghanistan and more than 3,000 in Pakistan. Although various observers attribute roughly 75 percent of these deaths to insurgents, the growing rates of civilian casualties caused by U.S. and allied forces, particularly as a result of drone warfare, suggest the extent to which the ideas that underpin Af-Pak as an uninterrupted war theater are deeply flawed.

The chapters in this book contest the prevailing discourse on the region, which we find to be simplistic, inaccurate, and alarmingly dehumanizing. Singly and together, the chapters aim to subvert existing paradigms by restoring a sense of history to the region, in two ways. First, the authors of the chapters engage various aspects of recent history through detailed analyses that document intellectual and social formations and their evolutions. We contend that the social and historical complexity discussed in this vein should be taken as entirely normal for the region, as it is for the rest of the world. And second, we seek to show that the static and ahistorical image of the region itself has a particular history that is connected to the interests of the empires, kingdoms, nation-states, and ruling elites that have exerted their influence over the area from the nineteenth century to the present.

We seek to investigate this space as a modern borderland where lives have historically been framed, on the one hand, by state boundaries and, on the other, by mobility and an expansive geographic imagination linking the region to distant trading, religious, and other centers. The chapters in this volume critically engage with the prevalent use of nation-state as the ultimate unit of scholarly analysis. With its distinctive politics and historical trajectory, the region has fitted poorly into universalizing theories of development and counterinsurgency. As in many borderlands, the Afghan-Pakistan frontier has not been thoroughly colonized by modern state institutions. But this does not mean that its politics are not "modern." From the "great game" of Anglo-Russian colonial rivalry to the Cold War and the post-9/11 era, these communities have interacted with political actors and movements near and far. And although this border is one of the most porous in the world, integration into two very distinct nationalist projects has had real consequences regarding formation of communal identities and participation in economic and sociopolitical networks that prevail in the two countries. Indeed, contrary to prevailing discourses, nationalism rather than religion has a greater role in the formation of the region's modern politics. We seek to understand the transnational dynamics of this border while remaining attentive to the unique historical imprint made by states that have claimed control over this territory and its inhabitants.

The arrangement of chapters in this volume aims to convey the reader through clustered engagements with major issues we must consider to carry forward with the project of rethinking the Afghanistan-Pakistan borderlands. In the first two contributions, Amin Tarzi and Gilles Dorronsoro highlight historical and contemporary nuances that need to be kept in mind to understand the way the region in question has functioned as a borderland since the nineteenth century. Tarzi's chapter is both a historical survey of Afghan and Pakistani attitudes toward the boundary and a concrete policy-oriented prescription for transcending the mistrust that has haunted the dealings between the two countries for more than sixty years. Challenging one of the central tropes about the border, Tarzi highlights the centrality of the Durand Line to nationalist politics in both states and reveals how this boundary—often dismissed by observers as a meaningless fiction—has in fact been critical to elite conceptions of sovereignty and nationhood. Tarzi suggests that political elites in both states need to confront the way governments in their country have used the border to delegitimize or undermine the governments in the other. Without such reorientation, which requires a courageous acknowledgment of the relevant history, Afghanistan and Pakistan are unlikely to develop a healthier relationship as neighbors.

the border

Complementing Tarzi's perspective, Gilles Dorronsoro analyzes the border as a malleable and porous structure that carries particular opportunities and limitations while also being affected by local and international developments. He shows how the boundary represents the essential condition of possibility underlying the definition of ethnic, political, and religious affiliations of the people who have lived on either side. Here we witness the complex roles played by peoples identified as Pashtuns, Baloch, Taliban, tribal chiefs, and mullahs. Providing a counter-narrative to the dominant views, this chapter shows the border as a place of incessant change and movement, physical as well as intellectual.

In Chapters 3 and 4 we move from an overall conceptualization of the frontier to the details of lives and literary expression that go across the boundary line. In Chapter 3, Sana Haroon discusses the conjunction between religion and politics by considering the activities of Islamic religious scholars in Afghanistan, British India, and Pakistan. Following trails left by various Deobandi scholars shows that Afghanistan acted as a refuge as well as an advantageous employment zone for Indian scholars during the first half of the twentieth century. During the 1980s, in contrast, the Soviet occupation of Afghanistan provided a unifying cause to religious scholars in Pakistan, raising their political profile on the national level. Haroon's analysis shows that religious scholars' prominence on today's political stage derives from a history that has crisscrossed the Durand Line for more than a century. Quite significantly, this history of border crossing by religious scholars is inflected at least as much by pragmatism and nationalism as by religious ideology.

Perhaps the two factors that most unite the populations that sit astride the Afghanistan-Pakistan boundary are religion and the Pashto language. While religious linkages have been subject to much scholarly and policy analysis, little effort has been put into understanding the Pashto-speaking arena as a zone imbued with particular modes of literary and folk expression that can be actualized in multiple forms. In Chapter 4, James Caron addresses this gap by focusing on the *talib* (singular for Taliban) as a literary and social symbolic figure with a long history. Caron locates the Taliban's political appeal for local populations through an analysis of literary motifs found in modern Pashto literature. Providing insight into a topic hardly ever invoked, Caron's chapter illuminates the conjunction of language, politics, and aesthetics in this region that has deep roots in South Asian social and literary history. Caron's chapter provides us with a sense of the interplay between formal literature, folk literature, and new media such as videos uploaded to the Internet from locales in the Afghanistan-Pakistan borderland.

The notion that tribal and ethnic affiliations are the key to understanding Afghanistan has by now come to be seen as an obvious fact by journalists and policy analysts. This surety masks complicated histories and present circumstances that we would do well to investigate, whether for academic or policy considerations. Chapters 5, 6, and 7 attempt to do this by considering paradoxes and biases in the way we conceptualize Afghanistan as a place as well as the way this question has figured into the country's politics since 2001. In Chapter 5, Shah Mahmoud Hanifi examines the brittle narratives that have characterized Afghan nationhood since the nineteenth century. Particularly significant in this regard is Hanifi's discussion of the disconnect between ideologies of the state, on the one hand, and, on the other hand, a lack of investment in political and social programs that usually underlie modern state-building projects. Through Hanifi's discussion we come to understand the rhetoric and reality of Afghanistan as a modern political entity constructed at the intersection of the interests of those living within as well as those living beyond the boundaries that appear on contemporary world maps. Hanifi's work goes beyond academic critique and historical overview: he suggests that constructing a successful nation-state for the future requires that Afghans engage in substantive discussions about the way they construct their past. An open-ended discussion of such questions is a first step toward imagining the nation in a way that is both equitable and sustainable.

Chapters by Thomas Ruttig and Lutz Rzehak bring us analyses of the way notions regarding tribe and ethnicity play out in today's Afghanistan.

In Chapter 6, Thomas Ruttig comments on perhaps the most consequential questions for the region's political future: What defines the Taliban as a group? How can we assess the history of their Pashtun and religious identities? And what are the possible implications of this story for a political settlement that might at last bring an end to a war that has raged for more than thirty years? Ruttig shows that, rather than presuming that terms like *tribal* and *Islamist* have stable meanings, we must attend to the histories of people's affiliations and self-representations. This endeavor reveals a sociopolitical world in rapid motion, transforming as well as being transformed by factors both local and global.

In Chapter 7, Lutz Rzehak looks at the politics of ethnicity in the region, examining the negotiations among different kinds of Baloch, as well as between Baloch representatives and other groups in the country, in the context of the creation of a new Afghan constitution after the fall of the Taliban in 2001. Here we see the connection as well as the disjunction between ethnic identity and language, both of these being consequential for group interactions that take place in the "national" space of a country of immense internal diversity. These explorations of the malleability of ethnicity and the varied ways of being "Pashtun" or "Baloch" challenge Af-Pak strategists' attempts to utilize ethnic and tribal labels as instruments of political control and instead show them to be multivalent, situational, and always in dynamic tension with other frames of identification.

Chapters 8 through 11 take us from Afghanistan to discussions of specific events, developments, and modes of expression in Pakistan. In Chapter 8, Faisal Devji provides a concise but trenchant analysis of a 2007 incident in which Pakistani armed forces stormed an Islamabad mosque complex associated with religious radicals, killing about two hundred people. Far from being a group longing for a return to premodern religious norms, the religious radicals in question were media-savvy propagandists who articulated their message in the language of civil-society activists. Devji argues that paying close attention to rhetoric for and against denizens of the Red Mosque complex reveals the fundamentally pluralistic and fractured nature of Islamic militancy in contemporary Pakistan. Devji's assessment implies that policies constructed on the presumption of monolithic militancy are fundamentally misplaced and unlikely to form the basis of long-term solutions to problems faced by Pakistan's government and society.

Devji's interpretive critique is complemented in Chapter 9 by the work of economists Tahir Andrabi, Jishnu Das, and Asim Ijaz Khwaja, who demonstrate that concrete data from Pakistan refute the notion that the country has been overrun by religious schools that are breeding grounds for religious militancy. This chapter is especially valuable for demonstrating that significant aspects of the conventional wisdom associated with the conceptualization of Af-Pak as a single theater of culture and war have no basis in concrete research. In Pakistan, overall as well as in areas adjacent to the Afghan border, the story of development and expansion of educational opportunities seems to have little connection to war or religious militancy. The representation of Pakistan as a place full of religious schools that are churning out hordes of militants is thus based on generalizing from exceptions; it is a concomitant of presumptions driven by Western military and security agendas rather than systematic observation and analysis.

Broadening from considerations of particular events and institutions, in Chapter 10 Farzana Shaikh takes up the question of Sufism, a type of Islam that local elites and foreign think tanks alike have put forth as an antidote to militancy in Pakistan. Shaikh contextualizes this prescription with respect to the history of Pakistan, both as an idea in the British period and a reality since 1947. This historical survey underscores Sufi actors' ambivalent position in Pakistani state endeavors, adding a cautionary note to recent rhetoric emanating from American think tanks such as the Rand Corporation. Shaikh's chapter is especially valuable for showing that, contrary to the isolating portrayal dominant in the West, we must understand socio-intellectual trends in Afghanistan and Pakistan as resulting from constant interaction between national and international arenas.

Finally in the consideration of Pakistani specifics, in Chapter 11 Jamal Elias concentrates on expressions of identity displayed in the "moving murals" that ply the country's highways. Elias highlights the potential of truck decoration to act as an index for cultural themes that predominate among the Pashtun and Punjabi ethnic groups. By registering both readable structures and change over time, Elias illuminates truck decoration as an especially valuable site for the apprehension of vernacular aesthetics as well as sociopolitical identities. As presented by Elias, the vivacity as well as aesthetic, economic, and ideological complexity of truck decoration in Pakistan should give us pause before making any easy generalizations about the country. It should also help us see the thorough interpenetration between religion and nationalism that is as much a part of the scene in Pakistan and Afghanistan as in other parts of the world.

The book's last two chapters attempt to convey aspects of the lived experience of Afghanistan by alternating between macro and micro perspectives. In Chapter 12, Nushin Arbabzadah presents the history of Afghanistan's media, from the first newspapers printed in the late nineteenth century to the numerous television channels operating in the country since 2001. Arbabzadah emphasizes the necessity of taking a long historical view of the evolution of Afghan media in order to see the connections between sociopolitical developments and the evolution of broadcasting contents and means. As with articles concerned with other spheres, the story of the mediascape encompasses highly significant change over time and a current situation marked by opportunities, limitations, and predictable as well as unexpected contradictions.

Chapter 13, by Fariba Nawa, is a poignant case for what we see as this volume's ultimate purpose: to restore local human agency to the discussion of Afghanistan, Pakistan, and the contested borderland that they share. Nawa's subjects are Afghan women involved in the drug trade that currently forms an essential pillar of the Afghan economic and sociopolitical scene. While abstraction and theorization are a necessity in the academic trade, the stories presented in this chapter display the concreteness of lives constantly being constructed, broken, and reconstructed in the midst of brutality as well as opportunity.

The coverage of topics related to the Afghanistan-Pakistan borderlands in this volume is neither encyclopedic nor exhaustive. We are aware that many more aspects of the subject could be included in a collection such as this. For pragmatic as well as conceptual reasons, we have limited ourselves to assessment of issues that interconnect the two countries. In addition to the chapters that explicitly crisscross the boundary (Tarzi, Dorronsoro, Haroon, Caron), treatments that cover only one of the two countries are directly relevant for the other country. Thus, issues that Hanifi,

Ruttig, Rzehak, Arbabzadah, and Nawa raise regarding Afghanistan bear thinking about in the context of Pakistan. And chapters by Devji, Shaikh, Elias, and Andrabi, Das, and Khwaja reflect on matters equally relevant for discussing contemporary Afghanistan. Our hope is that, individually and together, these treatments will act as beginnings of longer conversations in which Afghanistan and Pakistan are treated in a single frame, not as a unified theater of war but as contiguous modern nation-states whose complex situations overlap and frame each other's realities.

We realize also that comprehensive discussions of both Afghanistan and Pakistan have facets that go beyond the matter of overlap between the two. Afghanistan's lengthy boundaries with Iran, Turkmenistan, Uzbekistan, and Tajikistan implicate distinctive sets of political and cultural issues that deserve attention beyond the purview of this volume. Most poignantly, full-scale discussions of ethnic and religious identities in Afghanistan require looking at social formations that cross over to these other states. Similarly, Afghanistan has a long history of engagements with regional and world powers, including India, Russia, Saudi Arabia, the United Arab Emirates, the United Kingdom, and, most recently, the United States. From the period of the Soviet invasion, Afghan populations have been major foci of international aid and humanitarian organizations, and the country's engagement with a long list of NGOs has intensified since the American-led NATO invasion of 2001. Provisions and entanglements produced by the state's many relationships with agencies as well as other governments have placed Afghanistan in a complex web of financial arrangements involving the world monetary system. It is tendentious and overly simplistic to depict the Afghan state as a hub of corruption, as recent journalistic reports have tended to do. Afghan patterns pertaining to financial matters need to be contextualized in light of the way international agencies and other governments have incentivized the functioning of local transactions based on their own political and social agendas.

Pakistan's historical and social complexities also far exceed the matter of the country's relationship with Afghanistan. Most notably, throughout the country's history, Pakistani military and political elites have defined their priorities relative to the border with India rather than Afghanistan. Moreover, Pakistani politics have been defined by the country's status as a successor state to British India and its early alignment with the United

States against the Soviet Union. These factors are in part responsible for a history dominated by military coup d'états. The Pakistani state has also had close relationships with China, Saudi Arabia, and the United Arab Emirates, underwritten by security concerns as well as flows of migrant workers. In the policy context, Pakistan's involvement with Afghanistan has been contingent on these other involvements and historical burdens that have lives much larger than the issue of the boundary to the west. In the social arena, Pakistan's map of ethnic groups has involved numerous continually evolving formations whose relationships to the national state and predominant cultural ethos have precipitated events ranging from the creation of Bangladesh in 1971, a constant agitation in Balochistan since the 1970s, and urban violence in the city of Karachi since the 1980s. None of these identity-based "insurgencies" in Pakistan are susceptible to monocausal explanations; they require historicization with respect to particular local, national, and international circumstances that have affected various parts of Pakistan at different times. If the Pakistani state is to be defined by a history of insurgency and counterinsurgency, it proves the rule for postcolonial states rather than providing any kind of an exception. This is so particularly for South Asia, where India has faced insurgencies since the moment of independence and civil wars have been the central defining features of the recent histories of Sri Lanka and Nepal.[7]

These brief comments may be thought of as a synopsis of a constantly expanding circle of issues that begin to arise as we consider Afghanistan and Pakistan beyond matters that connect the study of the two countries. While the essays in the volume do not traverse this wider terrain, we do wish to point out that the kind of engagements with particular matters that are to be found in the following pages represent a replicable overall perspective. As we have emphasized throughout the introduction, this volume aims not only to inform on topics that do not make it to newspapers but also to suggest ways in which the overall discussion of places such as Afghanistan and Pakistan needs to change in order to provide better coverage and solutions than the ones currently available.

The chapters in this volume are penned by individuals whose primary identifications vary between being humanists, social scientists, journalists, and experts on political and security matters. Some have origins in Afghanistan and Pakistan; others come from Europe and the United

States. They write in varying registers, their discourses impelled by questions of quite different origins and ultimate ends. As the volume progresses, the focus shifts between international, national, and local issues, addressed in varying levels of specificity and generality and sometimes even arguing opposing positions. We consider this diversity of voices and scopes to be a core value of the collection as a whole. When brought to bear on the essential task of reimagining how we understand the connections as well as separations between Afghanistan and Pakistan, differences among perspectives represented here can work to demolish the monolithic picture that continues to be projected incessantly in the mainstream of journalistic and policy-oriented discussions. This, we believe, is a task that needs urgent attention as a matter of academic as well as political praxis.

1 / Political Struggles over the Afghanistan-Pakistan Borderlands

Amin Tarzi

Since the drawdown of the United States military presence in Iraq in 2009, Afghanistan and, by extension, Pakistan have become the main immediate military and political challenges not only for Washington but also for a large number of allies of the United States. The primary reason Afghanistan and Pakistan have become the focal point of much of the Western world's military and political involvement is because this region harbors terrorist organizations with international reach, such as al-Qaida, as well as local groups such as the Taliban. These local groups, while more inward-looking, have hosted international terrorists and continue to have links with al-Qaida and a host of other terrorist outfits. A victory by groups such as the Taliban in Afghanistan or the Tehrik-e Taliban-e Pakistan (TTP) in Pakistan not only could allow al-Qaida-type organizations to incubate with ease in the territory of Afghanistan and Pakistan, but also, in the case of the latter country, might lead to a nuclear-weapons-capable radical regime. Since the start of hostilities in Afghanistan in 2001, a healthy relationship between Kabul and

Islamabad has been considered a prerequisite for success in the West's attempt to dismantle al-Qaida and also to deny it and organizations of its type a foothold in the Afghanistan. This was further "officialized" by the administration of U.S. President Barack Obama when it became a core part of its policy to succeed in Afghanistan. In his speech establishing his administration's policies for Afghanistan, President Obama said that the United States would "act with the full recognition" that success in "Afghanistan is inextricably linked" to U.S. partnership with Pakistan.[1] Since that speech, many organizations within the U.S. government and those supporting it have formed their Af-Pak groups and task forces in order to better accommodate the new Afghanistan policy, which has formally recognized Pakistan as an integral part. While the policy of connecting the Afghan problem, and therefore the solution to that problem, to Pakistan can only be regarded as overdue by eight years, this chapter briefly reviews the historical and geopolitical reasons this is a significant obstacle and suggests a possible path forward to common ground.

At the core of the current conundrum between Afghanistan and Pakistan is both countries' refusal to accept the viability of the other as a state with full sovereignty within their current internationally accepted boundaries. From the dawn of the formation of Pakistan as a separate state in 1947, Afghanistan has regarded its southeastern neighbor as an illegitimate usurper of Afghan territory. Pakistan, on the other hand, has tried to defuse the irredentist claims of its northwestern neighbor through a series of intrigues designed to keep Afghanistan weak and dependent on Pakistan, while working on replacing Afghanistan's nationalism with a more Pakistani-controlled pan-Islamism, thus rendering Afghan nationalistic territorial claims irrelevant.

While one can argue that the current Afghan-Pakistani deadlock is not solely a result of the two countries' boundary dispute, the border issue is like the eight-hundred-pound gorilla in the room. At the height of tensions between the two countries, Afghanistan, with a much weaker military and economy, was never a serious threat to Pakistan's sovereignty; however, as argued by Pakistani scholar and diplomat Husain Haqqani, Afghanistan's claims on Pakistan's territory led to an "overall feeling of insecurity" within Pakistani leadership and "became part of the combination of perceived security threats that required" military buildup and

historical suspicion

the forging of alliances.[2] Beginning in the mid-1970s, the use of Islam to curtail Afghanistan's ambitions gradually gained currency among Pakistani strategists. This Islamization policy became much more rigorous after the victory of the leftist People's Democratic Party of Afghanistan (PDPA) in 1978 and the subsequent invasion of Afghanistan by the Soviet Union a year later.[3] The fervor of Afghanistan's claims on Pakistan territory has lessened significantly when one compares the official rhetoric of Kabul since the 1990s to what was prevalent in the three decades after Pakistan's formation. Nevertheless, in this chapter I argue that unless the narrative attached to the Durand Line—as the Afghan-Pakistani border is popularly referred to—is debated between Kabul and Islamabad, and both sides orient on finding a mutually respectful solution, for the foreseeable future the pendulum of affairs between Pakistan and Afghanistan most likely will remain in the zone of mistrust, swinging between indirect conflict and periods of fake friendship. In this state, the pendulum will not move toward the center where the two states would regard each other as equal partners working toward harmonization of their policies toward groups such as al-Qaida and the neo-Taliban.[4] Thus, a cloud of uncertainty resides over both countries, with potentially dire consequences for Afghanistan and Pakistan but also with global repercussions—as in the terrorist attacks in 2001 in the United States, in 2004 in Madrid, in 2007 in London, and in 2008 in Mumbai, to name a few.

The Durand Line

The "Durand Line," arbitrarily drawn by the British Raj in India with the formal acquiescence, if not total satisfaction, of the Afghan ruler, Amir Abdul Rahman (r. 1880–1901), to clearly demarcate the two sides' sovereign authorities, served immediate national interests but functioned only as a paper exercise in governance. The treaty negotiated between the amir and Sir Henry Mortimer Durand, the foreign secretary of the British Raj, was signed on November 12, 1893, though Abdul Rahman never relinquished his desire to bring under his control the Pashtuns living in the semiautonomous tribal lands on the Indian side of the border. He nevertheless was keenly aware that his country served as a curtain *(hijab)* between British India and Russian Central Asia. Exploiting

"Anglo-Russian rivalries to further his political objectives," the amir had chosen to befriend the former. He believed that Russian plans called for total occupation of the Afghan territories, while Britain simply desired to protect their imperial rule over India.[5] Thus, Abdul Rahman sought to secure his own territory and worry about the Pashtuns in India later or leave that for his successors. According to Malcolm E. Yapp, although the amir told Durand in 1893 that he "wanted a wall around his country so that he might know exactly where he was," he had a longer-term agenda that he chose not to disclose at that time. Yapp continues,

> Equally and plainly, however, he regarded the relinquishment of his claims to the tribal territories on the north-western frontier of British India—the area to which he referred as Yaghistan, although the term sometimes has a wider application—as temporary concessions of a nature similar to that which he had been obliged to make in order to secure British recognition [of his amirship] in 1880. Without doubt the Amir hoped that in the course of time Islamic or Afghan rule—the distinction was to become much more important than he realized— would be extended over these tribal areas and Afghanistan would gain an outlet to the sea. But in the circumstances of 1893 there was no way in which he could realise his ambitions.[6]

To contain any Afghan ambitions on India's northwest frontier region, after the death of Abdul Rahman in 1901, the British concluded a treaty with his son and successor, Amir Habibullah (r. 1901–1919), in 1905, affirming British India's control over the new amir's foreign policy dealings. Following his assassination in 1919, his son Amanullah (r. 1919–1929) acceded to the throne as the ruler of Afghanistan. After a brief armed conflict known as the Third Anglo-Afghan War, in which Kabul tried to incite Pashtuns in the tribal areas of India, Afghanistan and British India concluded a treaty of peace in August 1919, resulting in Afghanistan's full independence; however, Amanullah was unable to gain control of the tribal areas and reluctantly accepted the Indo-Afghan frontier (the Durand Line) as it had been accepted previously by his father and grandfather.[7] This point was reaffirmed two years later in 1921 when the two countries established normal diplomatic relations as sovereign states.[8] The Afghan official stance regarding the territories and peoples across the

Indo-Afghan frontier remained, for the most part, static until the formation of Pakistan as an independent country in 1947.

Pashtunistan/Pakhtunistan Policy

The concept of an independent homeland for the Pashtuns in what was then the North West Frontier Province (NWFP) and the tribal regions adjoining the Afghan border in India was first raised by the Khudai Khidmatgar organization with the support of the All India National Congress. This homeland would serve as a countermeasure to attempts by the All India Muslim League to partition the subcontinent into a Muslim majority state of Pakistan and a Hindu majority state of India. Although almost 100 percent Muslim, the Pashtun Khudai Khidmatgar leadership, fearful of domination by Punjabis in a postpartition state, supported Congress's initial stance on keeping India whole. After the Congress and Muslim League agreed on the partition plan, the main leader of the Khudai Khidmatgar movement, Abdul Ghaffar Khan, told Mohandas Gandhi—his close personal friend—that by choosing partition, Congress had thrown the Pashtuns "to the wolves," and therefore, having been "disowned" by India, Pashtuns opted not to participate in a referendum to join India or Pakistan, but rather would decide on creating a "Pakhtunistan or Pakistan."[9]

With the Muslim League and Congress agreeing on a partition plan in mid-1947, Afghan authorities felt left with a fait accompli, partially due to Kabul's lack of understanding of or involvement in the partition process. As a result, they began their multipronged quest to demand a voice in the future of the Pashtuns living in both the NWFP and the tribal regions adjoining the Afghan border.[10] Afghanistan announced its "Pashtunistan" or "Pakhtunistan" policy by casting the sole negative vote in September 1947 at the United Nations General Assembly on the question of Pakistan's admission to the United Nations. Although Kabul recanted its negative vote, the stated Afghan policy was to "wholeheartedly" support the "principles on which the claim for an independent Pakhtunistan is based."[11] The geographical limits of the state imagined by the Afghan side extended from the "Pamir massif to the shores of the Arabian Sea and the Iranian frontier," covering an area of more than 190,000 square miles and including "all the territory between the River Indus, which is the natural and historical frontier of the Indian sub-continent, and the Afghan border."[12] In other words, the state envisaged by Kabul included all of the current Khyber Pakhtunkhwa and Balochistan provinces in addition to the Federally Administered Tribal Areas (FATA) of Pakistan.

The historical rationale for including Balochistan as part of Kabul's concept of a Pashtun homeland is not precisely clear. However, as the Pashtunistan policy progressed, the Baloch were included as part of the people whose cause Afghanistan would champion. Kabul's claim to Balochistan may have been based on a brief period of rule in the seventeenth century by the Afghan ruler Ahmad Shah Durrani over the Khanate of Kalat. The Baloch, despite having greater grievances with the Pakistani state than with the Pashtuns and despite supporting armed struggles for independence, did not seem inclined to become part of a greater Pashtun state supported by Afghanistan, itself dominated by the Pashtuns.[13] For Kabul, the unstated rationale of inclusion of Balochistan in the Pashtunistan scheme was to gain access to the open seas.

Thus, the policy's major strategic rationale—in addition to sentimental and historical links with the Pashtuns—was to allow for the pursuit of a policy of confrontation with its new neighbor.[14] Though Kabul's stated policy did not explicitly demand the annexation of Pakistani territory west of the Indus River, the Afghan National Assembly in 1949 repudiated all treaties, conventions, and agreements concluded between Afghanistan and British India, thus nullifying the terms of the Durand Agreement and subsequent Afghan pledges of noninterference in the affairs of tribes residing on the opposite side of the Durand Line. Furthermore, in 1955, after West Pakistan became a unified province under the One Unit policy, a *loya jirga* (grand assembly) held in Kabul rejected the inclusion of Pashtun areas as part of Pakistan.[15]

Through the 1970s, Afghan policies toward Pakistan ranged from hostile to lukewarm, with periods of limited armed conflict along their mutual border and attacks on diplomatic missions. Until the victory of the People's Democratic Party of Afghanistan in 1978, the Pashtunistan issue formed a major component of Afghan foreign policy and drained much of that country's meager resources and most of its political capital. According to some Afghan historians, the pursuit of the Pashtunistan policy enabled Afghan rulers, especially Muhammad Daud, who served as prime minister from 1953 to 1963 and the country's first president from 1973 to 1978, to curtail minimal freedoms and usher in a more dictatorial system.[16] Seemingly unable to alter or abandon the Pashtunistan option, successive Afghan governments have pursued the policy of hostility toward their neighbor; the notion that the border between Afghanistan and Pakistan was illegitimate became—and has remained to date—a significant part of the Afghan national narrative and, indeed, of that country's identity.

Initially, Pakistan did not regard Afghanistan's position as a direct threat to its territorial integrity, deeming it manageable.[17] However, while Afghanistan pursued its hostile policies toward Pakistan, the latter was not able to "concentrate all its resources and attention on the Kashmir front." As such, the Afghan policies were regarded by Pakistan as a "diversionary tactic" benefiting India.[18]

Pakistan's threat perception toward Afghanistan was linked to Kabul's close ties with the Soviet Union and also to India. By not recognizing the border, Afghanistan was laying claim to more than half of Pakistani territory and supporting Pashtun and Baloch nationalism inside Pakistan. Soviet support for the Pashtunistan policies of Kabul showed up in official Moscow statements, such as a 1960 speech by the First Secretary of the Communist Party of the Soviet Union, Nikita S. Khrushchev, in which he said that "historically Pushtunistan has always been a part of Afghanistan."[19] Islamabad regarded Kabul's demand for Pashtunistan as part of a larger Soviet policy of encroachment on its territory. To curtail Afghan nationalistic demands, Pakistan relied on a policy that promoted Afghan Islamist groups and personalities as a tool to gain leverage inside Afghanistan and eventually provide Islamabad with a friendly and nonintrusive client government in Kabul. From the 1960s onward, Pakistani intelligence agencies encouraged their country's Islamist parties to seek ideological allies inside Afghanistan, as only "Afghans convinced of Islamic ideology, and Pakistan's special place in the revival of Islam's glory, would transform their country into Pakistan's allies."[20]

With the PDPA victory in Kabul and the subsequent invasion of Afghanistan by the Soviet forces a year later in 1979, Islamabad's perceived threats became an international concern. Pakistan's allies among Afghanistan's Islamist personalities rushed across the border to form the anticommunist resistance under the leadership of Pakistan. The decade-long occupation of Afghanistan by the Soviet Union, coupled with the reliance of the Afghan resistance (the *mujahedin*) on Pakistani support, not only enabled Islamabad to enter the Afghan political scene as never before but also altered the nature of Afghanistan's leadership. The elite evolved from a nationalist group based on Afghan exclusivity to a non-statist Islamist group that felt as comfortable in Pakistan as they did in Afghanistan. The royal government of Afghanistan—as well as Muhammad Daud's republic—had regarded itself as the vanguard of Pashtun nationalism and thus regarded the creation of Pakistan as an affront to Afghanistan's very nature as the land of the Pashtuns. The PDPA leadership, while split between international Marxists and those keen on Afghan nationalism, still regarded Afghanistan as a country that had obligations, not only to bring equality and justice to its own people, but also to redress the needs of the Pashtun and Baloch people across the border in Pakistan. Islamabad hoped that the mujahedin leadership, in contrast, would support the notion of an Islamic nation in which ethnicity and borders would be secondary to the unity of the community. Afghan leaders with such a vision would render Afghanistan's claims on Pakistani territory irrelevant and would make Pakistan—a country created on the basis of Islamic identity rather than nationalism—the dominant power not only in Afghanistan but in the region. In sum, according to Haqqani,

> The prospects of Afghanistan, with Indian backing, stirring the ethnic cauldron in Pakistan became part of the list of challenges that the country's leaders had to deal with to forge Pakistan's identity as an independent state. Pakistan's Afghan policy was fitted into the over-reaching policy tripod. Pakistan emphasized its Islamic ideology with the hope of blunting the challenge of ethnic nationalism supported by Afghanistan, tied Afghan aspirations for a Pashtunistan to an India plan to break up Pakistan, and sought U.S. assistance in pursuing an agenda of regional influence.[21]

Pakistan's support of the Afghan resistance against the Soviets and their allied PDPA regime in Kabul provided Islamabad with the opportunity to once and for all eliminate the dangers of being squeezed between the pincers of two enemies, Afghanistan in the west and India in the east.

Indeed, during the final days of the PDPA regime in Kabul in the early 1990s, Pakistani officials repeatedly asserted that they did not accept the burden of, and risks associated with, being a front-line state in the war against Soviets in Afghanistan for the sole purpose of "merely hav[ing] an Afghanistan like the one that preceded the conflict."[22] According to Marvin Weinbaum, in 1991 Pakistan looked forward to securing a "strategic depth" in a friendly Afghanistan vis-à-vis the Indian threat. "A conflict inside Afghanistan that ended favorably," Weinbaum argued, "could provide the kind of friendly regime, expectedly an Islamist one . . . that would enable Pakistan to avoid traditional insecurity or at least neutralize its western tribal borderlands and avoid future Afghan governments with strong links to New Delhi."[23]

To Islamabad's dismay, its goal of installing an Islamabad-friendly, Islamist ally in Kabul after the last PDPA government fell in 1992 failed because the Afghan side began a protracted civil war. Islamabad's influence to realize its vision of establishing a client state in Kabul faded. Some of the personalities reared by Pakistan since the mid-1970s to serve as Islamabad's policy implementers in Afghanistan turned against their old masters, mostly not for ideological reasons but rather for simple political expediency. The border issue lay dormant and unresolved, and increasingly the new rulers of Kabul accused Pakistan of interfering in the internal affairs of their country and turned to alternative allies, including Islamabad's archenemy, India.

However, seen from another perspective, with the demise of PDPA the objectives of the Islamabad-backed insurgency were partially achieved, with Pakistan becoming the main external player in the Afghan political game. From the early 1990s until the demise of the Taliban regime at the end of 2001, Pakistan's position on the political process in Kabul either directly dictated the results or became the most significant determinant of the outcomes. Frustrated with the inability of its clients in Afghanistan—led by Gulbuddin Hekmatyar, leader of a branch of the Hizb-e Islami—to consolidate their myriad positions and cement their rule as a unified Afghan government, and exceedingly worried about India's reach into and influence within Afghan affairs, Pakistan supported an alternative to the mujahedin in a movement sprung from within ranks of Afghan seminary students studying in Pakistan, namely the Taliban.

By the mid-1990s "Pakistan had de facto control of most of Afghanistan through their proxy Taliban."[24] However, even the subservient Taliban would renege on the issue of the legitimacy of the Afghan-Pakistan border. According to Ahmed Rashid, while the Pakistani military "assumed that the Taliban would recognize the Durand Line" and would "curb Pashtun nationalism in the NWFP," in practice the "opposite occurred," with the Taliban refusing to drop claims to parts of Pakistani territory. "The Taliban fostered Pashtun nationalism, albeit of an Islamic character."[25]

The combination of conservative Pashtunism and radical Islamism made the Taliban an increasing international and internal liability for Pakistan. In September 2001 this dual nature of the Taliban regime enabled al-Qaida to carry out devastating attacks on U.S. soil from its sanctuaries in Taliban-controlled Afghanistan, prompting Islamabad to make a quick turnabout and abandon its proxy in favor of joining in a strategic partnership with the United States. However, from the beginning this partnership had an "asterisk," as explained by Haider A. H. Mullick, that Pakistan would pursue al-Qaida but would "selectively target—and in later years abet—the Afghan Taliban in the hope of rekindling strategic depth vis-à-vis India under the blanket of its strategic spread."[26]

Revival of the Border Issue

In Islamabad's calculation, post-Taliban Afghanistan presented a step backward in its grand strategic scheme of having an Islamist-oriented and Pakistan-dependent government in Kabul that would also preferably be hostile or at least lukewarm to India. The realities in Afghanistan were in most cases the opposite, and with Western backing, Kabul found new life to exercise its dormant dreams of a "greater Afghanistan," with a greater number of Afghans linking overall insecurity and the inability of their country to move forward to schemes—some real, others imagined—orchestrated by Pakistan. While the issue of legitimacy of the international border between Afghanistan and Pakistan has not been formally discussed as an issue itself in any great detail, the very fact that the border remains contested should be great cause for concern. In 2007, after Pakistan announced that as a countermeasure to cross-border activities by insurgents it would construct a fence along designated portions of its boundary with Afghanistan, authorities in Kabul reacted with disdain. Afghan officials remained more diplomatic about the reasons for Kabul's rejection of planned fencing of the border; however, the government-owned Kabul daily, *Anis*, published an editorial accusing Pakistan of knowingly "acting against an absolute right of the Afghans" and vowed that "one day when Afghans are mighty, they will surely reclaim that part of their territory."[27] In Pakistan's threat perception, regardless of the actual ability of Afghanistan to endanger its territorial integrity, the reopening of the Pashtunistan question is surely a major step backward from the 1990s when Islamabad relished the thoughts of dominating its neighbor to the west. Kabul, on the other hand, regards Pashtunistan as the only trump card in its position in a game where Pakistan—at least in Afghanistan's perception—holds most, if not all, of the other cards. The stance by the Afghan government has been supported by some of its Western allies as well, providing more credence to Kabul's irredentist stance. Writing in 1991, Weinbaum had envisaged that the Pashtunistan issue could be reopened at a future date as "an Afghan counterweight to a Pakistan that was perceived as asserting too strong an influence."[28]

With the U.S.-led efforts to bring security and stability in Afghanistan still not achieved, greater emphasis has been placed on an Afghanistan-Pakistan solution to curtail the spread of al-Qaida-type terrorism in both countries and beyond. However, "Pakistan-Afghanistan collaboration cannot take place as effectively" until the disputed Durand Line border is officially recognized and its security becomes a collaborative effort by both states.[29]

Conclusions

Pakistan and Afghanistan have coexisted as neighbors since 1947, and although they share historical, cultural, and commercial ties, the two neighbors have failed to regard one another as fully legitimate states. Instead, Afghanistan has set out to undermine Pakistan's territorial integrity, and Pakistan has aimed at thwarting Afghanistan's political independence. At the core of these policies lies the Durand Line. Even though solving the border issue and rendering the Durand Line irrelevant might not solve all

of the grievances—based on the real or imagined actions of either party—
that have become part of the operating narratives and strategic calcula-
tions of both Kabul and Islamabad, a mutually agreed-upon border with
joint responsibility over its security and commercial potentials has to be
regarded as a great step forward, not only in reassuring both parties of the
other's goodwill but also in changing the omnipresent policies of negativ-
ity to one with a positive outlook. To the skeptics, the European experience could serve as a good model, albeit with stark differences between
the two cases. Europe has illustrated that borders that once divided can
indeed unite. *EU, west thalia*

On the Pakistani side, an initial step to legitimize the border would
be the incorporation of FATA into Pakistan proper. This step would stop
Afghan claims that Pashtuns living in FATA are not full Pakistani citizens, thereby fueling Kabul's long-standing claim of stewardship of these
people. Also, a fully integrated FATA would make it more difficult for the
insurgents and terrorists to incubate in the region. Writing seven years
after Pakistan's formation, Major General M. Hayaud Din recommended
that his country within twenty to twenty-five years strive to replace the
agencies composing FATA with administrative districts. "For obvious
geographical and political reasons the anomaly of our Frontier must be
re-adjusted,"[30] he added. Similar suggestions have been put forth in more
recent times, with Shuja Nawaz recommending that Pakistan end the
"treatment of FATA as a buffer zone between Afghanistan and Pakistan
and treat the Durand Line as a true border . . . [with] Afghan recognition
of the Durand Line as a de jure border."[31]

As the party disputing the legitimacy of its border with Pakistan,
Afghanistan ought to make a bold move to turn the page in relation to
not only its neighbor but also itself. A reversal of the Pashtunistan narrative along with efforts to render the border irrelevant through connecting communities on either side of the Durand Line via commerce and
projects would not only benefit those communities, but would also go a
long way in binding the people of both countries beyond the historical
claims and counterclaims. However, observers of Afghanistan note that
recognition of the Durand Line by Kabul as a de jure border would be
tantamount to political suicide for any particular Afghan government. To
avoid such a political and stability risk, perhaps the voice of the Afghan

people should be made the deciding factor through a loya jirga, of course after a thorough awareness campaign on the benefits of such a move.

As part of the solution, Pakistan would be expected to abandon its desire to overly influence the future makeup of the Afghan political system, provided Kabul neither harbors any territorial ambitions on Pakistani territory nor allows its own territory to be used for fomenting anti-Pakistan elements. Afghanistan should also expect to be given access to a Pakistani port on preferential arrangements. Construction of a limited railway inside Afghanistan and connecting that to the Pakistani railroad network would be an added bonus for both countries. Islamabad should also abandon its policy of trying to shut India out of the Afghan commercial and political scene.

According to an unnamed Western diplomat, Pakistan has fears, perhaps legitimate, that if it stopped playing the card of supporting the neo-Taliban, Pashtunistan "as an issue will come back" to dominate the relations between Islamabad and Kabul, as it did prior to the 1990s. The diplomat suggested that both Afghanistan and Pakistan "need to stop political games," adding that "Pakistan needs to stop seeing Afghanistan as a stalking-horse for India" while "Afghans have to stop holding over Pakistan the Sword of Damocles" in the form of Pashtunistan.[32] Indeed, not only for Afghanistan and Pakistan, but for NATO-led efforts under way in Afghanistan, a rearrangement of Pakistan-Afghanistan bilateral relations, beginning with resolving the difficult question of the common boundary between the two states, seems a necessary ingredient for success.

2 / The Transformation of the Afghanistan-Pakistan Border

Gilles Dorronsoro

S ince the Soviet invasion of 1979, the Pakistan-Afghanistan border has been one of the most unstable and strategically important places in the world. Although certain uses of the border—such as providing sanctuary—have persisted over time, in other significant ways its political economy has changed dramatically. Over the last three decades, the war in Afghanistan and political transformations in Pakistan have prompted a reorganization of the border area in both scope and importance. The main players were the Pashtun tribes living on both sides of the international border.[1] In Pakistan, the British-inherited indirect rule has come to a de facto end with the penetration of the Pakistani army, while the Afghan state is mostly absent from the border area. Despite repeated military operations, both Afghanistan and Pakistan have lost control of a large part of the border area, where the dominant forces are now jihadist groups, opposed both to the state and to the tribal system. In addition, since the late 1970s the Pashtun tribes have lost their monopoly on smuggling. The level of contraband traded across the border has risen exponentially, with billions of dollars illegally exchanged every year.[2] Commercial networks developed a wider geographic range due to the presence of refugees in the Arab Gulf. Pashtun refugees in Karachi began playing a major part in the transportation business. Finally, madrasas have played an active role in building networks on both sides of the border and have gained political influence in a way that amounts to a social revolution. In addition, Arab individuals and countries have heavily financed specific strains of Islam, mostly Salafist, in Pakistan and Afghanistan.

This chapter gives a framework to explain the sociological and political upheaval of the border that has occurred since the late 1970s through a redefinition of the "border" as a transnational space. First, I seek a reimagining of the Afghan-Pakistan border that moves away from envisioning it simply as a line on a map. At least in this part of the world, the international border doesn't separate people and limit transactions. On the contrary, the border is often the main reason why people interact. The intensification of exchange comes from the fact that resources and capital have different values on each side of the border. Custom duties come easily to mind for material goods, but one can also consider the security of a sanctuary or the value of social capital like religious education or tribal affiliations as reasons people and goods are moving incessantly across the border.[3]

This approach tends to emphasize the importance of geography and space against a deterritorialized notion of "globalization" and the irrelevance of borders and territories.[4] Contrary to popular belief, the lack of state control of the international border and the increase in exchanges (economic, cultural, and so on) is producing more-complex, more-differentiated territories. In particular, the areas that lie along both sides of the border can be conceptualized as constituting a transnational space characterized by specific rules of interaction. It could then be seen as a modality of regionalization or local autonomy produced by an international border. The similarities with the Kurdish area between Iraq and Turkey are especially striking.

Last, I want to contribute to this debate by conceptualizing this transnational space as the result of the interplay of multiple fields.[5] The goods and the resources reallocated on both sides of the border, as well as the actors involved, are different in nature. From an analytical point of view, the transnational space is therefore the result of the combination of three major fields: tribal, political, and religious. Each field has different stakes, rules of interaction, geographic scopes, timelines, and institutions, which do not always overlap.

Building on this conceptualization, I examine the changes in the Afghanistan-Pakistan borderland and their causes. These changes occurred along several general lines: in the geographic scope of what constitutes this transnational space; in the intensity of exchanges across and along the border; and in the rules of the game between players. Then I suggest the centrality of three dynamics: the weakening of the old institutional framework, the intensification of exchanges, and the nationalization *and* radicalization of "border politics."

1. The traditional political order of the border was defined by indirect rule in Pakistan and, to a certain extent, in Afghanistan: tribes were both autonomous and encapsulated. But the tribal system has been weakened by the rise of the religious men and the emergence of jihadist groups. The notables have lost their influence because they are no more the main interlocutors of the state.

2. The rapid increase in exchanges (of goods, refugees, fighters, religious students, and, on another level, ideas) is more than a consequence of "globalization"; it is directly linked to the weakening/ disappearance of the Afghan state and the consequences of Pakistani policies. Characteristics generally associated with the borderland in a narrow geographical sense (lawlessness, autonomy from the state) are now pervasive in a much larger area.

3. The lack of state control facilitated the emergence of a transnational political field of jihadist parties. But this phenomenon doesn't imply the end of the border. In fact, the nationalization of politics is the central trend and reinforces the role of the border. There are no transnational political actors (in terms of recruitment or agenda). Only the madrasas have a real ability to go beyond citizenship, but they play quite different roles in the two countries.

The Emergence of a Transnational Jihadist Field and the Nationalization of Politics

In the 1980s the emergence of Pakistani and Afghan jihadist parties operating on both sides of the border created a field of cooperation (and sometimes competition) around security issues and a common political discourse. But far from becoming irrelevant, the border's strategic and political value was enhanced. Significantly, no transnational parties emerged; the Afghan and Pakistani political spheres remain distinct to this day. First, the border (the sanctuary) is a key resource for players, which constrains their agenda vis-à-vis the host country. Second, politics is both more national (less parochial) and more radical. In an apparent paradox, the retreat of the state allows more participation in national politics. Therefore, the growing influence of armed groups in the border area is part of the nationalization of politics and, especially in Pakistan, a twisted "mainstreaming" of the periphery through radical groups. The national dimension of politics, which must be distinguished from the influence of the state, is reinforced because it is part of the disintegration of indirect rule. I will explain first the emergence of jihadist parties as a product of Pakistani policies, then their limited autonomy.

State policies, especially those of Pakistan, were indeed a key element in the formation of the transnational jihadist field. Pakistan has been a sanctuary for different Afghan parties since the 1970s; Afghanistan has been a sanctuary on a much more modest scale, mostly for Pashtun and Baloch nationalists. The continued support to some Afghan parties is fundamentally linked to Pakistani national interests as defined mostly by the military elites: competition with India and search for a "strategic depth."[6] The Pakistani sanctuary is a key resource for Afghan political parties fighting in Afghanistan, and it allows the Pakistani military to shape the Afghan political field, eliminating the leftist nationalist or conservative Afghan parties and supporting the more Islam-oriented movements.

As early as the 1970s the Pakistani state supported Islamist movements in Afghanistan. In particular, the ISI (Inter-Services Intelligence) helped the failed Islamist coup in 1975 as a way to put pressure on then prime minister Daud, who—from the Pakistani perspective—appeared too close to Iran and the Soviets and unwilling to renounce Afghan claims on the Pashtun area on the Pakistani side of the border. On the other side of the border, the Afghan government supported Baloch training camps in 1978 in the south of Afghanistan. The chief of the Marri tribe, who was in overt conflict with the Pakistani state between 1973 and 1977, and Khan Abdul Ghaffar Khan, the leader of the Khudai Khidmatgars, were frequently in Kabul. Khan was buried in Afghanistan in 1988.

In the 1980s, Afghan Sunni political parties were created in Pakistan, and a Pakistani general was present at every meeting of the Afghan parties in Peshawar. In the 1990s the emergence of the Taliban was linked to Pakistani policy, notably the search for a proxy in Afghanistan. The initial objective of the Pakistan government was to establish a land link to Turkmenistan in order to open up Central Asia to Pakistan's economic and political influence. In the spring of 1994 the Taliban movement crossed the border and started its dramatic conquest of Afghanistan with the direct involvement of the Pakistan military.

In addition, the Pakistani jihadist movements, largely born from the Kashmir policy of Pakistan, had a sanctuary in the border areas, mostly in Pakistan but also in some parts of Afghanistan during the 1990s. The origin and the evolution of the fundamentalist movements in Pakistan are then clearly autonomous from the Afghan crisis, and the sectarian violence in Pakistan is neither an effect of the Afghan war nor a by-product of the emergence of the Taliban. After the fall of the Kabul regime in 1992, the transfer to Afghanistan of jihadist groups fighting in Kashmir supported by Islamabad was a way to avoid international pressure, especially from India and the United States. One of the consequences of this transfer was the growing connection with fundamentalist Pashtun movements on the border. The military wing of the Jama'at-e Islami, the Hizb al-Mujahedin, the Harakat al-Ansar (also known as Harakat al-Mujahedin), and other transnational groups such as bin Laden's al-Qaida, are or have been in Afghanistan. After 2001 these radical movements started a frontal fight against the Pakistan army.

The Pakistani policy facilitated the formation of a complex set of relationships between Afghan and Pakistani parties. The Afghan Islamist parties were connected with the Pakistani Jama'at-e Islami since the emergence of political parties in Afghanistan in the 1970s. Jama'at-e Islami has been a model for the Afghan Sazman-e Jawan-e Musulman (Organization of the Young Muslim), and its offshoot, the Hizb-e Islami. Although the Hizb-e Islami took inspiration from the same organizational model, this does not mean that the two movements had the same type of recruits, nor the same strategy. The Afghan students were looking for a strong model of organization that could compensate for the weakness of their social integration (most of them were from poor and provincial families); the Jamaʻat-e Islami, on the other hand, is a party of the petite bourgeoisie and socially better integrated. During the Soviet occupation, the connections between Afghan jihadist parties in exile and their Pakistani counterparts grew closer, since most of the Afghan parties were in exile in Peshawar, Pakistan. The Pakistani religious movements served as a pro-jihad, pro-Afghan advocate on the Pakistani political scene, with ideological and personal affinities playing a role in the depth and duration of the complex connections. The relationship between the Hizb-e Islami and the Jamaʻat-e Islami were extremely strong during the 1980s, and in fact until 1994, when the Taliban marginalized the Hizb-e Islami. Later the Taliban had well-known connections with the Jamʻiyat-e ʻUlama-e Islam, which built up support among the Pashtun tribes in North West Frontier Province (NWFP; today Khyber Pakhtunkhwa) and Balochistan during the 1990s. The Jamʻiyat al-ʻUlama supported the government of Benazir Bhutto, and this connection facilitated the support of the military. Maulana Fazlur Rahman, the leader of this party and himself a Pashtun, is a former chairman of the Foreign Affairs Commission of the Parliament and was close to Benazir Bhutto.

Beyond organizational links, jihad and the Islamic state are common themes on both sides of the border. The Afghan jihad, on a par with Kashmir, is an important element in the discourse of the Pakistani parties, both the illegal jihadi and legal fundamentalist ones. The latter are known for their difficulty gaining significant support during the elections, and they try to mobilize individuals with highly emotional issues, especially in relation to the Kashmir and Afghan jihads. The Afghan jihad is still popular in Pakistan because it plays well with the strong anti-American feelings of the population. But despite a relatively common ideology and practical cooperation, there is no trend toward a fusion or even a close coordination between Afghan and Pakistani parties, for both strategic and sociological reasons. The limited exception is al-Qaida, the only movement without a national or territorial-based agenda. Even in North Waziristan, where the cooperation between Afghan and Pakistani militants is arguably the closest, the Haqqani network has objectives that are different from those of the Pakistani movements. Two elements explain this situation: the nationalization of politics in the border area and the strategic constraints.

Political parties tend to be organized on a national base. Contradictory dynamics explain why one can see increasing national integration in Pakistan and at the same time the growing autonomy of the border area. In Pakistan, the integration of Khyber Pakhtunkhwa (earlier North West Frontier Province) in the Pakistani state has been growing since the 1950s with the presence of Pathan officers in the army (generals Adam, Afridi, Khatak, Nasrullah Babar). Under Zia ul-Haq, a significant part of the military elite was coming from the Army Belt (Peshawar, Attok, Rawalpindi, Jhelum). This was not true for Balochistan Province, which is more deeply alienated from the state. The war in Afghanistan has accelerated the integration of Khyber Pakhtunkhwa and the FATA (Federally Administered Tribal Areas) in Pakistan. The Urdu language is becoming dominant, at least in the cities, where most of the newspapers are in Urdu. In comparison, the Pashto language doesn't give access to modern culture. In madrasas, the language of study is traditionally Pashto, but another language (Urdu or Arabic) is generally compulsory. The presence of a large number of refugees was not conducive to a renewal of Pathan nationalism and the emergence of an irredentist movement. On the contrary, the difference between refugees and Pakistani citizens is quite clear, and Pakistani parties have used anti-refugee rhetoric since the 1980s. The war in Afghanistan and the presence of jihadist movements on the border have directly challenged traditional institutions. The army is penetrating the FATA, which is no longer dealt with by British-style indirect governance. On the Afghan side of the border, the Taliban are a national insurgency (as opposed to a local or Pashtun insurgency). Even though the majority of their recruits are Pashtun, they also fight in non-Pashtun areas of the north. Furthermore, the Taliban's objective of a sharia-oriented state is clearly national, not internationalist. In addition, Pashtun ethnicity cannot easily cement a new transnational movement, because in both countries the recruitment is larger than the Pashtun community. The jihadist parties on the border are increasingly linked to radical groups operating in Punjab, which tend to use the border area as a sanctuary against the Pakistani state. The growing integration of these groups into national politics is contentious and leads to more violence.

Finally, strategic constraints limit the level of cooperation, at least in the short term. There is no military solidarity now between the Afghan and Pakistani Taliban; the Pakistan army is careful to focus its offensive on the local militants, such as those in South Waziristan. The Pakistan army is able to launch large-scale offensives against the Pakistani Tehrik-e Taliban and still supports the Afghan Taliban. Even in the absence of day-to-day control by the state, the border is quite real in the political order, because the political agenda and the necessities of recruitment make it impossible to build a common base.

The Rise of the Madrasa

In both countries the madrasas have become more influential and deeply involved in politics in the last decades as a consequence of the civil war in Afghanistan and Pakistani state policies. Due to the long-term weakness of the educational system in Afghanistan, Afghan students are crossing the border to be trained in Pakistani madrasas. Some of them return to Afghanistan after a few years with a strong impact on social norms and Islamic teachings.[7] This transnational network of madrasas extends far beyond the border area: from Karachi to Peshawar and, in Afghanistan, beyond the Pashtun belt, even if the majority of the students are Pashtun.

The increase in the number of madrasas since the 1980s has had a tremendous impact at a political and societal level. In Afghanistan, the rise of fundamentalism, which is not limited to the Taliban movement, had revolutionary consequences. Indeed, the emergence of a clerical state goes against the entire political history of Afghanistan, where religious leaders were relatively marginal, except in a few circumstances like the revolt in 1929.[8] In Pakistan the jihadist movement is not predominantly controlled by ulama, and the Jam'iyat-e 'Ulama (with its religious leadership) is relatively marginal. Still, the Taliban are offering a revolutionary model, more appropriate than Iran because they are Sunnis, to the jihadist movements in Pakistan. The "talibanization" of Khyber Pakhtunkhwa and Balochistan provinces, with the diminishing cultural freedom and a severe drop in the demand for female education, is at least partially a consequence of the growing influence of the madrasa.

The rise of fundamentalist madrasas in the border regions is a long-term process linked both to the preaching of the fundamentalist movement Tablighi Jama'at and to Pakistani state policies. Since the 1950s, the Tablighi has penetrated these areas, and local values such as honor and revenge have been reinterpreted and reinforced to respond to larger changes in Pakistani society that are seen as a threat to the social order. In the 1980s, Pakistan saw a spectacular development of its network of madrasas. This situation is largely due to Zia ul-Haq's policy of Islamization (1977–1988). Universities' recognition of diplomas received from madrasas and the compulsory tax *(zakat)*, part of which goes to the madrasas, have been the main factors underpinning this phenomenon. Furthermore, Zia ul-Haq encouraged the building of madrasas in the NWFP to help the Afghan jihad, which is why the number of madrasas there is growing more rapidly than in the rest of the country.

In addition, those madrasas belong to different religious schools: Deobandi, Barelwi, Ahl-e Hadith. Some of those madrasas have a national influence, notably the Jam'iyat al-'Ulum al-Islamiyah, created by Allama Yusuf Binori in Binori Town (near Karachi), educating eight thousand students (with its twelve affiliated madrasa). The Dar al-'Ulum Haqqaniyya madrasa in Akora Khattak (Peshawar district), created in 1947, has educated one-third of the Deobandi ulama in Pakistan, even if today it has less influence, or at least a smaller proportion of students. In addition, Saudi Arabia has financed the new Jam'iyat Imam Bukhari madrasa in Peshawar, officially opened in June 1999 in the presence of Muhammad Abdul Rahman from the Saudi ministry of religious affairs. The director of this madrasa is close to the Ahl-e Hadith movement and belongs to the Jama'at al-da'wa al-Quran wa al-sunna, a movement active in Kunar Province of Afghanistan in the 1990s.

With the current war, the proportion of Afghan students in Pakistani madrasas has noticeably increased. In 1982 approximately 9 percent of the Taliban in the NWFP were Afghans, and this proportion has rapidly increased. Between 1960 and 1983, the number of Taliban increased from 7,897 to 78,439 in the NWFP. For example, the majority of the 750 students of the Jam'iyat Imam Bukhari madrasa that we mentioned earlier are Afghans. Likewise, 15 percent of the students of the Dar al-'Ulum Haqqaniyya madrasa were Afghans in 1960, while in 1985, 60 percent were Afghans. The Afghan students have generally joined the Deobandi madrasas because of the historical links between the Afghan ulama and the Dar al-'Ulum Deoband madrasa in India, even if today the relationship between this madrasa and the Pakistani Deobandi movement is limited. But under the generic term *Deobandi,* one finds in fact different kinds of discourses, and one should not overestimate the education of those ulama and the coherence of their ideology.

The madrasas' deep ties to political parties is a new phenomenon that will have a long-term impact on the role of religious leaders in the area. For example, the leader of the Dar al-ʿUlum Haqqaniyya madrasa, Maulana Sami al-Haq, is the secretary-general of the Jamʿiyat al-ʿUlama,. Other madrasas, belonging to the Ahl-e Adith current or linked to Jamaʿat-e Islami, are more open to modernity, at least in a technological sense (there are English-language and computer skills classes). The Jamaʿat-e Islami has opened a lot of madrasas in Khyber Pakhtunkhwa (forty-one madrasas, a third of the new ones in the province, and nineteen after the Soviet invasion), even if the Deobandi are still the majority in the province. Besides the presence of Afghan Taliban, the Pakistani madrasas are directly linked to the Afghan war because participation in the jihad is seen as the natural extension of schooling. Most of the volunteers are Afghans, but some Pakistani citizens are also participating in the jihad, generally originating from the NWFP and Balochistan, and less often from Sindh or Punjab. The Dar al-ʿUlum Haqqaniyya madrasa, led by Maulana Sami al-Haq (leader of a splinter faction of the Jamʿiyat-e ʿUlama-e Islam after 1986), has provided thousands of recruits for the Afghan jihad.

Most of the Taliban ulama have been educated in the ex-NWFP and Balochistan during the war. In particular, the Dar al-ʿUlum Haqqaniyya in Akora Khattak has trained some of the most important cadres of the movement.[9] There are strong links of solidarity between the ulama trained in the same madrasa and their students. The ulama, who are part of the Taliban movement, have a strong group consciousness, even if, as in any other organization, they also have conflicts. The key experience shared by the group was the education of its members in the Pakistani madrasas in the 1980s. From the Dar al-ʿUlum Haqqaniyya madrasa at Akora Khattak came Hajji Ahmad Jan, minister of mines; Mawlawi Qalamuddin, head of the religious police; and Mawlawi Arifullah Arif, deputy minister of finance. One of the few former commanders to become a leader of the movement, Mawlawi Haqqani, a former commander from Hizb-e Islami (Khales), also spent several years at the madrasa Dar al-ʿUlum Haqqaniyya, first as a student and then as a teacher.

The Weakening of the Tribes

The tribes are part of a dual system of interaction: with the state and with other tribes on both sides of the border. The border defines the place of the tribes as specific in the administrative system, in the form of indirect rule. Historically the FATA in Pakistan, or to a lesser extent the special status of border tribes in Afghanistan, created a distinct political and social organization in the two countries. There is a striking parallel with the Ottoman Empire and the use of the Kurdish tribes against internal and external (perceived) threats. In both cases the very existence or survival of a tribal organization is directly linked to its geographical position and state policies. In addition, the different tribes on both sides of the border constitute a field with complex rules of competition and collaboration (contraband, family relationship, solidarity in case of exile, and so forth). Here the border is a key resource, because the tribes are able to exploit economic opportunities and gain protection from their national governments by crossing the border. The tribal system initially had a strong territorial component and was relatively limited in its scope, but massive migrations since the 1980s have extended that scope.

The tribal system and norms are less relevant in a region now dominated by radical groups and fundamentalist madrasas. The tribes are no longer the central players and natural interlocutors of the state. In particular, the traditional model of uprising against the state—the uneasy alliance between the tribes and the mullah (the "mad mullah," as described by British sources) has disappeared. The causes of the marginalization of the tribes are somewhat different on the two sides of the border, but the role of the state and the emergence of religious political leaders are the key factors.

On the Pakistani side of the border, tribal leaders have lost their position in the political system, and jihadist parties have waged a war against such traditional elites, sometimes with the support of the Pakistani state. The indirect rule of the tribal area through political agents in the FATA has de facto disappeared. The army is occupying part of the tribal areas, notably South Waziristan and Bajaur, and is under pressure from the United States to extend its operations. Current Pakistani military operations in the border area have forced hundreds of thousands of tribesmen to relocate. Pashtun tribesmen are now living in Karachi or even in the

Gulf, extending considerably the tribe's economic and political tribal network. The tribal field is now more transnational, but also less territorial.

On the Afghan side of the border, the Taliban have marginalized the tribes in the east. The tribes still play a role in commercial networks and migrations, but they are no longer a central political player on both sides of the border. The tribal system is weak in most parts of Afghanistan: the Pashtun generally have a tribal identity, but it is not the most frequent base of mobilization. One should not confuse tribal identity, a rather flexible and open notion, and tribal institutions that place enforceable obligations on the members of a tribe. The concept of "tribe" is often misunderstood, because it covers two different situations. The tribes in the south were dominated by aristocratic families and large landowners connected to the state since its origin. Political entrepreneurs, especially in Kandahar, can use tribal identity as a way to build patronage, but tribal institutions are generally not functioning. In the east the tribes were more protected from the penetration of state administration, but functioned in practice as a means to relay state action. Paradoxically, the more institutionalized the tribes are (as in the east), the more local and enmeshed they are in state structures. In both cases, far from being exterior to state structures, the tribes were a relay and part of the political system. This is why the tribes were not an alternative to the state, as demonstrated after 1979 in the countryside, where the commanders, and not the tribes, became the basic political structures.

The rise of the Taliban is one of the causes of the political marginalization of the tribes. The Taliban movement is ideologically opposed to tribal politics or Pashtun nationalism as a matter of principle. Within the movement, local solidarities were a stronger mobilizing force than affiliation to a Pashtun ethnicity as such. For example, Mullah Omar is from Tarin Kot, in the province of Oruzgan, and Mullah Omar's countrymen, such as Mullah Abbas, held positions of authority. In addition, Mullah Omar is a Ghilzai Pashtun Hotak, a group that was overrepresented in the Taliban government. There were other solidarity networks, such as networks of mujahedin who had previously served under the same commander, such as Mawlawi Jalaluddin Haqqani, formerly of Hizb-e Islami (Khales). The Taliban managed to build transtribal groups (even between tribes that are normally opposed). In some cases they have killed or frightened elders who opposed them. The tribes who try to resist have seen their ability to move outside their territory significantly limited. The Taliban let the tribes get money from Provincial Reconstruction Teams (PRTs), but these tribes do not oppose Taliban groups that cross their territory, and members of the tribes are individually joining the Taliban. In addition, the Taliban are trying, with a fair amount of success, to build transtribal groups of fighters, particularly in the eastern provinces. The process is close to what happened during the last few years in Waziristan, where the jihadist parties were able to marginalize elders and built a movement strong enough to supersede the tribal system. In a few places the local tribe favors the government but is not in a position to actively oppose the Taliban (Popolzai in Kandahar, Karokhel in Sarobi and Khaki-Jabar districts southeast of Kabul, Jaji in Khost).

The new leaders in the tribal areas have a specific profile, quite different from the old elites. First, most of the aristocratic families in the south have lost their influence. After 2001 a few pro-American families gained a central role in local politics (the Karzai family in Kandahar), but they are in no way representative of the old elites and they are acting basically as jihadist commanders, very different from the prewar notables. Second, the tribal war, as a way of fighting centered on individual prowess with limited casualties, has disappeared. The new military elites are using their ability to get resources from abroad and their connections to larger networks to reinforce their local strength.[10]

Finally, the mullahs, who before 1979 had a limited place in the tribal universe, have seen their prestige and their power increase because of the civil war. The mullahs were able to give a credible narrative, the jihad, to insurgents. In addition, they were able to provide a relatively straightforward judicial system to people in the countryside after the disappearance of the state. The increasing power of the mullahs is in no way traditional. The emergence of religious leaders to mediate between tribes in time of crisis is not a new phenomenon in the border area. The "mad mullahs" of the British literature were in fact charismatic figures able for some time to coordinate tribes in the name of the jihad. The current situation is radically different. The mullahs are not short-term figures but are part of strong institutions, madrasas, and political parties, able to mobilize much more resources than any tribes.

The second element that explains the transformation of the tribal universe is the decline of its institutions. In the east of Afghanistan, the fighters are often from the same tribe, but this doesn't imply that their ideology or their organization is tribal. One cannot confuse the logic of recruitment and the modality of organization. For example, the Haqqani network is recruiting at least initially on a tribal base. But its extension of the network to other tribes (and beyond to individuals not belonging to a tribe) cannot be explained without taking into account the ideological drive of the insurgents. In addition, the war has changed the fighters and the tribes. The commanders leading the fighters were dependent on external resources from political parties (based in Pakistan or in Iran). The influx of money and resources made them more professional and distinct from the tribal population in general. In consequence, the commanders were largely outside the normal functioning of a tribal system. The *Pashtunwali* and even the sharia were largely ignored by the most powerful leaders. The local conflicts were not settled by negotiations in a traditional way, notably because they had political implications and because the state was not there to limit the intensity of the fights. In addition, the mullahs were able to impose sharia against tribal norms more often. Islam has always been a central element of the tribal identity, although with some ambiguity because a large part of tribal norms run directly counter to the sharia as interpreted by the mullahs.

Finally, the Karzai administration and the United States have tried to use the tribes against the Taliban, but what could have been an empowerment of the tribal institutions is in fact a further step toward their disintegration. For example, the decision to pay *arbaki* (the tribal militia, which normally recruits unpaid volunteers) has destroyed their legitimacy. Experience shows that the tribal militias were accepted locally insofar as they were seen to be independent from the state and limited to the intratribal (nonpolitical) conflicts. Conflicts between tribes or political parties (like the Taliban) necessitate bigger mediators (such as the state).

Conclusions

State policies are at the root of the transformation of the border area and the changed relationship between the center and the periphery. The growing importance of madrasas since the 1980s and the new institutional order on the Pakistani side of the border are direct products of decisions made in Islamabad and in Kabul. For example, the Sipah-e Sahaba (Anjuman Sipah-e Sahaba), created in 1989 under the leadership of Maulana Azam Tariq and pushing the Pakistani state to declare the Shia to be non-Muslim, is most probably a consequence of the instrumentalization of Islam by the Pakistani government under Zia ul-Haq. Its militants have fought in Afghanistan, especially at the battle in Mazar-e Sharif, where in 1998 they massacred hundreds of Shiite Hazaras and some Iranian diplomats. In Afghanistan, the revolution started with the ill-directed effort by the communists to redefine the relationship between the state elites and the population. But the idea that the states can undo the result of its policies is misleading. In both Islamabad and Kabul, the limited power of the center is the most striking feature of the current political situation.

The facts that state control has lessened and the transmission of contraband goods has risen should not be seen as endangering the existence of the border. In the current international order, the failure of a state doesn't threaten its territorial integrity, contrary to the realist (unrealistic) theory; borders are more stable than states. There is no disappearance of the border, because its existence is still fundamental in the exchanges, but there is an extension of the transnational space affected by it and a growing autonomy vis-à-vis the states. But a redrawing of the border could be envisioned if Afghanistan were to be partitioned between Pashtun-dominated areas and the rest of the country, as has been suggested.[11]

In the long run, there is the possibility of a reconstruction of an Afghan state with the Taliban, as shown in the 1990s. If it happens through negotiations or military victory, the border on the Afghan side will be again under state control, at least partially. The situation in Pakistan is fundamentally different: there is no clear prospect of a return of the state in the border areas, despite the current military operations. The stabilization of Afghanistan could help, at least if Afghanistan does not become a sanctuary for jihadist groups targeting the Pakistani state, but the weakening of state institutions in Pakistan in general is a more profound problem, reflecting the corruption of the elites and a worldview (competition with India through proxies) that endangers the very survival of the country.

3 / Religious Revivalism across the Durand Line

Sana Haroon

In the early twentieth century Afghanistan became a rallying point for anticolonial nationalists in British India, and between 1985 and 2001 it again became a rallying point, this time for Pakistani religious politics. In both cases, religious scholars (ulama) who called themselves Deobandi were engaged in projects in Afghanistan constructing a moral and authoritative framework that drew on the pedagogies of Sunni revivalist Islam in an attempt to co-opt the moral legitimacy of the faith for the state. Spanning almost a century, the events that I describe in this chapter demonstrate, not so much a consistency of intent among the ulama east of the Durand Line or of the governments of Afghanistan, but instead the ways in which Afghanistan and Pakistan have shared a history and a political economy of Islamic revivalism that is definitively anti-imperialist in its motivations.

The Deobandi Ulama in Afghanistan

Through the early twentieth century, the religious elites of Afghanistan worked in an uneasy accord with the government in Kabul.[1] Afghan rulers attempted alternately to subordinate and appease the many religious figures whose own authority derived from localized influence.[2] One consistent strategy employed by all these rulers of Afghanistan was to try to absorb and control discourses of Islamic teaching, learning, and jurisprudence as educational management and lawmaking processes were centralized and regularized. However, the state periodically used the clergy as autonomous actors who could represent the will of the state outside Kabul, whether to forge consensus or to rally armed retinues.[3] On the Indian side, the early twentieth century was a period of intense nationalist writing and activity alongside pan-Islamic leanings. Several ulama trained at the Deoband school in Uttar Pradesh conceived of a plan to free India of colonial control by mobilizing the northwest frontier Pashtun "tribes" as an army of liberation. The movement was called the Jama'at-e Mujahedin in a self-conscious linking with an earlier jihad against the Sikhs in the same region in 1831. When the plan was discovered in 1916, several of the conspirators based in the Pashtun frontier region of British India moved across into Afghanistan. Among the Jama'at-e Mujahedin were Fazl Ilahi, Fazl Rabbi, and Saif al-Rahman (1859–1949), all of whom had studied at the Dar al-'Ulum Deoband.[4] The movement has been rightly understood as rooted in antipathy toward the British government in India and in a claim to political spaces within which the ulama could establish government and law on an Islamic model. But we should add to this rationale that the ulama who went to Afghanistan were not otherwise employed, had few chances for great social and economic success in India, and were highly educated and impassioned. After completing a grueling seven- to ten-year course of study, the ulama had been trained at Deoband in the Arabic language and sometimes in Persian, and in Quranic science, philosophy, and logic. They were writers, legal thinkers, and translators with scholarly and religious obligations to painstakingly establish the lines of authority of any argument they might make. This was a time when Islamic religious knowledge and training could no longer get a man a job in a colonial education system that drew on English linguistic skills, Western-style scientific and mathematical training, and British jurisprudential practices.

In Afghanistan, by contrast, Dar al-'Ulum Deoband's institutional reach was an important avenue of the Jama'at-e Mujahedin's contact with the government. Deoband's reputation, and the absence of an equivalent madrasa in Afghanistan itself, meant that Deoband-educated ulama were brought into the state negotiation of Islam. Obaidullah Sindhi, an Indian scholar, along with two compatriots, arrived in Afghanistan in 1915 and presented himself at the court of Habibullah Khan in a meeting arranged by Hajji Abdul Razzaq, a Deoband-educated scholar and a member of Amir Habibullah's parliament, who had lived in Afghanistan well prior to the arrival of the Jama'at-e Mujahedin. Abdul Razzaq had also become a judge in Habibullah's government, in charge of the administration of sharia, and taught at the Madrasa-e Shahi, the state madrasa producing an official compilation of fatwas, or points of legal interpretation, in several volumes.[5] These ulama taught in the madrasas and served as authoritative commentators on points of law and interpretation. During its early years Amir Habibullah Khan's Habibiyya College, the first institution of higher education in Afghanistan, largely recruited teachers educated in India.[6] Meanwhile, Sindhi set up what he called the Provisional Government of India in Exile, representing a number of revolutionary parties, including the Jama'at-e Mujahedin as well as other Indian nationalists and socialists. The express purpose of the mission was to see through a "scheme" for the invasion and liberation of India from the historic northwestern route.[7]

British pressure to decrease Afghan involvement across the Durand Line and to control the Indian revolutionaries, the Jama'at-e Mujahedin, at his court suggested to Habibullah that he should take control of these relationships himself. Concurrently, his increasingly insecure position at the court forced him to rethink his domestic policy. Although he had initially appeared ambivalent toward the pan-Islamists at his own court, Habibullah silenced Mahmud Tarzi in his denouncements of British policy.[8] However, in 1917 Habibullah had several of the Indian mujahedin, including Obaidullah Sindhi and Maulana Saif al-Rahman, placed under house arrest and removed Hajji Abdul Razzaq from government service.[9] But the Jama'at-e Mujahedin came back into official favor in the Kabul court after Habibullah was assassinated in 1919 and his son Amanullah Khan took over. In April Amanullah declared in front of the British agent to Kabul that Afghanistan was thereafter "as independent a state as other states and powers of the world . . . [and that] no foreign power will be allowed to interfere internally and externally with the affairs of Afghanistan."[10] On May 4, Afghan troops moved into Bagh, on the British side of the border. Framed as a direct response to the British as they pushed forward into northwest India to establish garrisons in Waziristan, this mobilization was part of Amanullah's move to overturn the protectorate status accorded to Afghanistan under previous Anglo-Afghan treaties.[11] Amanullah then immediately returned to traditional Afghan military policy, rallying the Pashtun tribes under the Afghan flag and using the Jama'at-e Mujahedin to mobilize the Pashtuns across the Durand Line against the British Government of India.[12]

When Amanullah formally recognized the delimitation of the modern Afghan state at the Durand Line after 1923, a new period of modernizing and regularizing systems of government, defense, and education began in Afghanistan that engaged the Indian ulama in different ways. They remained socially distinct, living as a small diasporic community in Afghanistan, but contributed to the world of print, education, and jurisprudence in ways that continued to shape Islamic practice there. Maulvi Bashir stayed on to try to establish contact with the Russian consul in Afghanistan, possibly trying to solicit Bolshevik money and support for the "revolutionary bases" and providing services as an informer for the Kabul regime until his death in 1934.[13] Fazal Ilahi and Saif al-Rahman also remained in Kabul, the former working as a teacher and the latter as a judge and advisor to the government in the field of jurisprudence.

As he began consolidating power, Amanullah aimed to appropriate the irrefutability of Quranic logic for the state. In addition to formalizing a legal code and administrative practices, the Ministry of Justice printed and circulated state-sanctioned curricula for legal studies.[14] A curriculum was also laid down for teaching religion in schools with the stated objective of communicating principles of personalized, disciplined religious practice with an emphasis on teaching the singularity of God, observance of regular prayers, fasting in the month of Ramadan, charitable giving, and the obligation of Hajj.[15] It encouraged a highly personalized and internalized practice of faith by an Afghan citizenry and allowed the state the autonomous use of Islamic principles as content for a national, state-administered legal system.

As he regularized and created consensus over state-controlled administration, legal practice, education, and the military, Amanullah needed allies who not only could create curricula and law but could contribute

to the creation of institutions—whether press, schools, or parliaments—
that would reinforce the state's prerogative over lawmaking and law
enforcement. He turned to Hanafi theological discourse, which had been
influential in the Kabul area since 1858 and had been reaffirmed in the
compilation of Afghan laws under Habibullah.[16] The Indian ulama were
uniquely suited to this project, communicating fluently in Persian in
addition to Arabic and Urdu and often some English.[17] It is important
to note, however, that this involvement was not necessarily reflected in
the nationalistic discourse of Amanullah's Afghanistan. In 1925 the editors of the newspaper *Ittehad-e Mashriqi* (mostly migrants from India)
printed an announcement that the Afghan Publication Law stated that
"only Afghan subjects may edit newspapers and proprietors and editors
must be Afghans of a good character."[18] In the edicts of 1927 Amanullah
stated that only Afghan nationals could run schools.

The personal records of one Indian scholar describe his engagement
with the state and Islamic practice in Afghanistan at a variety of levels—not necessarily impinged upon by the laws intended to regularize
educational and administrative practices. Maulana Saif al-Rahman, a
Pakhtun from Mathra, north of Peshawar, who had studied under Maulana Mahmud al-Hasan at the Dar al-ʿUlum Deoband, was instructed
by his teacher to perform *hijrat*—to migrate out of India as a mark of
rejection of colonialism.[19] He moved to Jalalabad, where he was invited to
stay with the Afghan finance minister and began to receive an allowance
from Habibullah Khan.[20] He then began to teach at "various madrasas"
in Afghanistan, and shortly before Habibullah's assassination in 1919 he
was appointed as a judge of the military court.[21] On Amanullah's accession, Saif al-Rahman promised that he and other Indian ulama would "of
course participate and contribute . . . religious, political and official service" in Afghanistan.[22] During the 1923-24 Loya Jirgas and constitutional
debates, Saif al-Rahman was appointed advisor as a member of the high
council of state. He was also ostensibly charged with encouraging consensus among the ulama and fostering support for Amanullah's political
reforms. Saif al-Rahman's papers include a series of notes written in Arabic quoting and explaining hadith (sayings attributed to the Prophet) and
Quranic verses on the need for community building and consensus. Jot-
ted alongside these hadith is a draft of a statement of agreement between

different ulama reached at a "grand gathering." These personal notes constitute Saif al-Rahman's core arguments to the forum of the Loya Jirga. They demonstrate the extent to which his knowledge of and authoritative use of Hanafi "authenticated" hadith and interpretations were fashioned as a basis for a wider political authority and participation in the Loya Jirgas of 1923–24.[23]

Clearly highly regarded for his religious training, Saif al-Rahman was invited to participate in the process of fashioning a regular, state-monitored religious curriculum. First he was invited to the Ministry of Education to serve as an examiner for graduating judges.[24] Later he was asked back to discuss the appropriate syllabus for training judges and to participate in discussions over the appropriate syllabus for a school of sharia.[25] Saif al-Rahman's authoritative knowledge of Hanafi pedagogy was being appropriated by state-sponsored institutions. This made him a man of great significance in the relatively small Afghan world of teaching and learning of legal practice. He attended dinners at the private residence of the Minister of the Royal Office of the King[26] and fast-breaking parties thrown by the Ministry of Education in Ramadan.[27]

Once the principles of Amanullah's constitution of 1923 had been decided, it was up to the *qazis* (judges) of different districts to enforce them. Saif al-Rahman remained involved in the central administration and oversight over legal practice, again applying his own expert knowledge of Hanafi jurisprudence to work out inconsistencies or contradictions that arose in the application of a central legal code. In one instance this involved conducting an investigation into three separate jail sentences—for ten years, three years, and four years, for identical crimes—handed down in Shinwari, Jalalabad, and a third location.[28] In another case, Saif al-Rahman worked through Hanafi law to come up with an absolute age of puberty for application in cases where the age of maturity was of relevance.[29] Mechanisms of centralization defined the role that Saif al-Rahman would play through at least 1936, when the number of official requests for his intervention decreased.

During Amanullah's reign, Saif al-Rahman had the state's authority as an interlocutor outside of Kabul.[30] Like Abdul Razzaq, Amanullah Khan's deputy in Waziristan from 1919–1923, Saif al-Rahman was not part of the system of tribally organized alliance to the state, and his involvement in matters of government, like the involvement of Abdul Razzaq, suggests a parallel system of checks and balances. That the Afghan amir would use a scholar born and trained in India to serve as an intercessionary with his own population is an insight into how Amanullah attempted to overcome some of the restrictions of the tribal alliance systems and tradition as he created systems of state governance.

Like Amanullah, Nadir Shah (r. 1929–1933) reinforced the preeminence of sharia and Hanafi jurisprudence in the 1931 constitution and continued to assert the state's prerogative over lawmaking. A number of madrasas imparting training in Hanafi law were created between 1929 and 1960, beginning with the Madrasa Dar al-ʻUlum-e Arabi, which was established in Kabul near the end of Amanullah's reign. These were followed by the Abu Hanifa school in Bagram, Fakhr al-Madaris and Madrasa Jami in Herat, Madrasa Asadia in Mazar-e Sharif, and Najm al-Madaris in Jalalabad.[31]

However, Nadir Shah was far less reliant on individual scholars, instead using systems of religious consensus created by his predecessor and building on constitutional agreements reached at the loya jirgas held by Amanullah. Almost immediately after taking control, he created the Jamʻiyat al-ʻUlama Afghanistan, a state-convened religious advisory council, and the 1931 constitution included a stipulation that Hanafi law and interpretation would be used to define Afghan law.[32] The principal of the state-run madrasa Jamiʻa ʻArabiyya was nominated as an ex-officio member of the Jamʻiyat al-ʻUlama, and the body was mandated with the work of managing a religious studies curriculum in Afghanistan, forging continuity between Amanullah's policies and those of Nadir Shah.[33]

During Nadir Shah's reign, Saif al-Rahman and other Indian ulama drew on their own networks of authority and fraternity based on friendship and patronage. Saif al-Rahman supported at least a few young Pashtun students to study in Afghanistan during his time in Kabul.[34] He maintained close personal ties with Qazi Sayyid Mujaddid, governor of Shinwar, and with other members of the government, including a Mufti Jan Muhammad with whom Saif al-Rahman's son received an appointment for a short time.[35] And using his own connections in Peshawar, he began to engage in trade. At the same time, he became more reliant on his sons, one of whom began teaching English in a local Kabul high school. Another son Abdul Aziz, who began to be referred to as *maulvi* (someone with authoritative knowledge about Islam) managed some of the family trade.[36]

With the accession of Zahir Shah (r. 1933–1973), the influence of the Indian ulama within the Afghan state was clearly on the decline and the salaries and privileges granted by Amanullah expired and were not renewed.[37] Saif al-Rahman's 1930 petition to allow his sons to inherit his land was not answered, and his repeated requests to Zahir Shah's government asking that he be allowed to sell the lands were eventually refused outright.[38] The influence of the Indian ulama within Afghanistan's "Islamic bureaucracy," institutionalized by Nadir Shah as the Jam'iyat al-'Ulama, gradually declined while the state continued to try to centralize, regularize, and monitor religious discourse.[39] In later years the arena for this project moved to the faculty of Islamic law and the faculty of theology at Kabul University.[40] But despite the state's engagement with Islam and disengagement with the Indian ulama, the revivalist discourse was inherently self-sustaining and autonomous, because the markers of religious accomplishment and authority were based in knowledge of Arabic language and classical texts—not just in academic accreditations received through the Jam'iyat or at the university.

Saif al-Rahman, like other ulama, was aware of this autonomy and maintained his connections to an Arabic linguistic world. He subscribed to Arabic journals, ordered classical and contemporary Islamic texts on hadith, jurisprudence, and Islamic history from the Arabian Peninsula, used his own connections to call on King Abdul Aziz at the Riyadh court when he went on Hajj, and tried to initiate contact between the Afghan court and the anticolonial Sheikh al-Sanusi, whose religious movement had reverberations in the trans-Saharan region.[41] Saif al-Rahman used his links with the Arab world to engage in a debate about a translocal Muslim politics. In his letter to the editor of *Shuban al-Muslimin,* an Arabic journal published out of Mecca, Saif al-Rahman said, "I request you to add articles on political issues to its content for most countries and nations need to know appropriate politics. This is one of the most necessary areas [for comment]; most important and beneficial to alert men and awaken them."[42] In this carefully worded suggestion, Saif al-Rahman demonstrated his enduring concern with rationalizing a politics based on religion and led by the ulama—the position that had brought him to Afghanistan in the first place.

Deobandi Ulama and Sharia in Pakistan and the Afghan Jihad

After decolonization and partition of the Indian subcontinent in 1947, certain Deobandi ulama who found themselves on the Pakistan side of the border attempted to create local madrasas that would impart the Hanafi curriculum taught at Deoband, and hence continued to call themselves and their students Deobandi. They were the most organized of the ulama in Pakistan, and from early on have occupied a central position in religious politics. However, these politics were and are contended and complemented by other groups, including Islamists who are not ulama such as the Jama'at-e Islami, by ulama from competing scholarly traditions such as the Barelvis and the Shafi'is, and by other pedagogies such as that of the Tablighi Jama'at, which encourages a personalized practice irrespective of scholarly training, and the Ahl-e Hadith. Like many other new citizens, the ulama who found themselves in Pakistan in 1947 waited for the violence, migrations, and border adjustments to end before they reembarked on postcolonial religious projects. These included Maulana Maududi of the Jama'at-e Islami and Shams al-Haqq Afghani, a Pashtun from Khyber Pakhtunkhwa and a former student of Obaidullah Sindhi, who was also minister for education in the princely state of Kalat. Abdul Haqq, a student at Deoband who could not return to India, set up a madrasa in the outskirts of Peshawar around 1952. In 1954 Maulana Yusuf Binori established the madrasa Jam'iyat al-'Ulum al-Islamiyah in Karachi. Mufti Muhammad Shafi', another Deobandi, established the madrasa Dar al-'Ulum Karachi in 1951 and went on to become a member of the Constituent Assembly.

In 1951 Pakistan's ulama signed a twenty-two-point declaration that stated that law and the constitution must not contradict Islamic principles—a position that was reiterated sporadically and eventually ratified in the 1973 constitution.[43] However, Pakistani approaches to law and legislation, Islamic and otherwise, were deeply ambivalent. This had much to do with the country's inability to create a constitution and stable legislative bodies, and the fact that Pakistan retained (and still retains) a great number of laws made during the colonial period. Sharia was significant only in determining the outcome of cases relating to "inheritance, marriage and caste and other religious usages and institutions," as under the colonial definition of "Personal Law."[44] There were few Islamist parliamentarians in Pakistan who were interested in nurturing exclusivist religious discourses on social authority, law, and legislation. The authority of the Sunni Hanafi ulama over the definition of a political Islam was also contested by other Islamist groups—most notably by Maulana Maududi, who held strongly that the ulama did not have a place in politics.[45]

Deobandis' combined pedagogic and societal objectives of creating an Islamic framework of knowledge for a wider Pakistani public were initially expressed through reprints of classic Deobandi texts on the role of the ulama in politics, in fatwas related orally and reported in the press, and in mosque sermons. In 1957 Mufti Mahmud and other Deobandi ulama set up a national curriculum for Islamic primary and secondary schools. Creation of an Islamic system of schooling set the stage for the organic evolution of an Islamic society that received and interpreted information through the framework of the Arabic language, Quranic knowledge, and the early history of Islam as an example of an ideal societal and social order. These schools became a system of patronage of the pedagogies of Islamic teaching and learning, creating jobs for the ulama graduating from the madrasas, and extending an Arab linguistic, Islamic historical, and Quranic moral framework as the basis for all historical inquiry.

The Pakistani ulama's discovery of a legitimate politics that knitted their religious interpretative authority with a mandate to govern began again with the jihad in Afghanistan. During the 1970s and 1980s some textual expositions on the logic and divinity of the Quranic revelation were published for a wider public.[46] Only after 1983, a year marked by little more than occasional calls by mujahedin for the help and advice of Pakistani ulama, did the concept of jihad become widely introduced in a Pakistani public religious discourse.[47] After this time, the politics of jihad in Afghanistan became pivotally linked to the still-nascent discourse on sharia in Pakistan.

The 1985–1986 parliament, which included members of the Jam'iyat-e 'Ulama and Jama'at-e Islami, was presented with the Nifaz-e Shariat

Bill—a constitutional amendment that required that *all* Pakistani laws be brought into conformity with Islam in order to "protect the sharia." Passage of the shariat bill would have privileged the ulama as the determinants of which laws were Islamic and which were not. In rallying a base of support for the Nifaz-e Shariat Bill, the Deobandis of Khyber Pakhtunkhwa (then called North West Frontier Province) created the organization Tehrik-e Nifaz-e Shariat-e Muhammadi, which organized conferences through the cities and towns of the Pakhtun northwest in 1985–1986.[48] Great public resistance to the passage of the bill was posed by more secular-minded groups and also religious groups such as the Sunni Ahl-e Sunnat wa al-Jama'at, whose own differences with the Deobandis meant that the passage of the bill would have excluded them from mainstream definitions of Islamic law. As a result, the passage of the bill was prevented at the national level.

At exactly the same time, between 1985 and 1987, the ulama of Pakistan decided that they must come out in material and military support of the Afghan mujahedin. In schools and mosques, Deobandi ulama began calling for Pakistanis to join in the jihad. In a speech to a gathering of members of Dar al-'Ulum Haqqaniyya in 1986, Abdul Haqq said the following:

> Now our country is in a fragile state and we are trapped between two issues. The first is the government's hypocrisy as it battles us with delaying tactics in passing the shariat bill. In fact now there is open opposition to us. On the other hand the socialist group has come back to life and the powers of those without religion have come to life. . . . May God keep the Afghan mujahed alive and keep him steadfast and give him victory. If these people were not here then the Frontier and Balochistan would have been in the grip of Russia. And if the Afghan mujahedin are fighting for the freedom of Afghanistan today, then on the other hand they are also fighting for the time that it is Pakistan's time for war. . . . The way all of you have achieved laureates and wondrous accomplishments in the field of education, don't fall behind now in the battle field of jihad. Our struggle and efforts will not be to bring strength to any religion-less powers, nor for western democracy nor for governing power. Our effort should be purely for shariat. . . .

Now we want that the ulama should unite and for the sake of the way of shariat put their hands on the collar of the government and make them agree to the shariat bill.[49]

The politics of militancy, as demonstrated in Afghanistan, came to be seen as the solution to the impasse reached by the Deobandi ulama and specifically the Jamʻiyat al-ʻUlama in the world of participatory politics in Pakistan. They pointedly engaged with the politics of jihad as a politics of eventual governmental and authoritative reorganization of Pakistan.

Radicalization of ulama politics was not limited to Haqqaniyya in the northwest. It extended as far as Karachi. In 1988 Mufti Muhammad Rahman of Madrasa Binoriyya visited Jalaluddin Haqqani and other mujahedin leaders in Afghanistan, telling them that he wanted his students to learn the "mindset of jihad." Haqqani was reportedly very pleased at this offer and sent Fazl al-Rahman Khalili to Karachi to invite people there to jihad. Hence, "in the yearly vacations of 1988, large numbers of students from Binoriyya town went to training to Afghanistan and participated in the *jihad*." Among those students who joined the jihad at this time was Maulana Masud Azhar, who took "sixty days of training instead of the required three days." Azhar then established the group Jaish-e Muhammad, which has been under scrutiny since 2001 for its links to al-Qaida.[50]

The jihad progressed and the Afghan mujahedin reclaimed Afghanistan. With the withdrawal of Soviet troops in 1989 and the slow emergence of the Taliban, the Pakistani ulama were excited by the success of jihad as a model for creating a new system of authority—pedagogic, jurisprudential, and representative. In 1991 a slim volume was published at Haqqaniyya called *Islamic Revolution and Its Philosophical Underpinnings,* a text explaining the necessity of complete revolutionary reorganization of society, which also argued that Afghanistan was the "point of entry of a worldwide Islamic revolution" because it represented a moral order that, by virtue of being based on sharia, would bring peace to a world otherwise torn apart by the warfare created by Western imperialism.[51]

Since 1986 the politics of Pakistani Islam have rejected the restrictions of a participatory arena of postcolonial politics that still privilege feudal elites and colonial law. Religious literary production and primary and secondary education became the mainstay of the ulama's activities in Pakistan. The number of registered religious schools grew to over twelve thousand by 2008.[52] Publishing activity also increased dramatically as part of the ulama's conscious imperative to expand the base of religiously inspired discourses. Journals edited by Deobandi ulama but intended for a wider circulation, such as *al-Haqq* in Akora Khattak,[53] *al-Khair* in Multan, *al-Balagh* and *Beenat, Khatam-e Nabuwwat* in Karachi, *Haqq* in Lahore, and *Talim al-Quran* in Rawalpindi, began to be published.[54] Commentaries, articles and sermons were published in popular editions.[55]

Older works by Deobandis who had been part of the Jama'at-e Mujahedin movement were reprinted by madrasa presses and independent publishers and discussed as classic interpretations of the religious-political imperative of an anticolonial regional Islam. Letters and writings of Obaidullah Sindhi about Afghanistan, the Jama'at-e Mujahedin, and the jihad that they had emulated, that of Sayyid Ahmad Shaheed, were republished in Lahore, Peshawar, and Karachi.[56] Maulana Masud Azhar's sermons included references to the hazraat (respected people) of Deoband who had migrated to Afghanistan as a gesture of disgust with the British government of India. In these texts, the narrative of jihad based in Afghanistan was rationalized morally, intellectually, and historically.

Conclusions

Much has been made of the jihadis from the east crossing over into the Pakhtun northwest to fight jihads in the eighteenth and nineteenth centuries and then again in the twentieth. To do so with a sense of unique insight and in search of a conspiracy is unnecessary because the Deobandis themselves created the historical narrative of these three jihads. At both the beginning of the nineteenth century and at its end, the ulama east of the Durand Line felt they could have no impact on the definition of state and law in their own countries without overturning a moral and political order first. Afghanistan gave them a base from which to do that. Those who went across in 1914 rationalized their jihad with reference to the nineteenth-century movement, while those of 1985 looked back to an institutional history from Deoband to justify their position.

Unlike the early nineteenth century, however, there is little to suggest that the Afghan mujahedin or the Taliban engaged the Pakistani ulama in a serious debate over the form and implementation of sharia in Afghanistan but looked to the latter only to rally military and diplomatic support for their position. Unlike Amanullah in the early twentieth century, the mujahedin worked across the Durand Line, negating the border and, with it, a geographically circumscribed politics. But precisely like their involvement in the creation of an Afghan legal code derived entirely from Hanafi jurisprudence, involvement in the Afghan jihad made it possible for the ulama to challenge the investment of power and authority in Western knowledge systems and colonial and postcolonial elites.

In the autonomous and fluid world of public discourses, the interpretative particularities of the Deobandi position become less relevant, and we can see the extent of the impact that Afghanistan's recent Islamist politics have had for Pakistan. Religiously motivated involvement in the Afghan jihad and in the post-jihad Taliban regime has received wide vocal support from a Pakistani public. This support is vocalized as anti-imperialist sentiment, which scholars and contemporary commentators have taken at face value as misguided expressions of solidarity with a global Muslim unity. In fact the empathy is related always to the present state of disenfranchisement in Pakistan itself, where the pedagogies imparted at a few particular elite institutions or in the West, the privileges conferred by a few genealogies, and the links of a very few to the export economy have concentrated wealth and power in a domain that is inaccessible to those educated in underfunded and poorly managed government schools and universities.

With a newfound legitimacy after the mujahedin victory over the Soviets, the ulama pushed the sharia bill through the Pakistan parliament in 1991. It created a constitutional amendment that privileged "shari'a as laid down in the Quran and Sunna as the supreme law of Pakistan," and required now that shari'a and the Arabic language be taught in universities.[57] In 1996 the Tehrik-e Nifaz-e Shariat-e Muhammadi gained new strength with the movement for the implementation of sharia in Swat led by Sufi Muhammad. Sufi Muhammad emulated the emerging Taliban regime in Afghanistan by creating vigilante militias who would oversee a public morality in the Swat area.[58]

There has been a gradual disavowing of militancy by Pakistani ulama subsequent to the international vilification of al-Qaida and the regularizing of the religious schools by the government through curriculum reform and oversight. Pakistan's Islam is once more being brought back into a mainstream of participatory politics. But Pakistan's politics is a politics changed by the work of the ulama in a discursive and pedagogic sphere, and it is absorbing the moral and intellectual frameworks of Islamic enquiry, so passionately and forcefully expounded by the ulama.[59]

4 / Taliban, Real and Imagined

James Caron

T his chapter is an exploratory genealogy of the interplay between religious student—*talib*—as a folk symbol in Pashto expressive arts, and talib as social actor. It particularly seeks to draw out older cultural roots of the symbol *talib* that may be overlooked in non-Pashtun public images of the idea, but that remain part of the contested perceptions related to "taliban" for many who are integrated into Pashto-speaking publics in both Afghanistan and Pakistan—particularly those clustered around the northern zone between Jalalabad and Peshawar, and the southern zone between Kandahar and Quetta. Beyond the realm of ideas and symbols, this chapter points out earlier variations on a social institution—variations that have also been underappreciated in historical and social science literature. That is, there had long been a social institution of semi-itinerant bands of grassroots intellectuals known as taliban, perhaps operating on local circuits linked to particular shrines, mosques, and groups of villages, but integrated across considerable distances via networks that cut across tribes and even (to a lesser extent) administrative boundaries. It is this cultural history that at least some activists in contemporary movements have consciously recalled, even if direct institutional links to present-day Taliban do not exist. This chapter also traces some of the interplay over time between grassroots intellectuals; the social and political discontent that interfaces with them; and the states that have ruled the populations on either side of the Afghanistan-Pakistan border.

Let us begin with a paradox: the simultaneous disunity and unity of Taliban organizations on either side of the mountains that make up the Afghan and Pakistani frontiers. For several years since 2005, numerous new and unrelated factions arose in Pakistan across a linguistically and culturally heterogeneous territory, building on the brand established by an older and also unrelated set of actors in 1990s Afghanistan. The name was also applied as a catchall to multiple unrelated organizations in Afghanistan. Yet it is precisely this brand name *Taliban* that ties together disparate local struggles in the perceptions of both wider society and of the activists themselves. More importantly, it demarcates a growing awareness of, and participation in, an imagined countercultural commonality.

I argue that multiple Pashto public domains on either side of the border have been fragmented, yet are still interlinked through local literary traditions as well as new media. Further, I argue that the idea of "Taliban" is a collective persona that political activists (that is, *the* Taliban) are able to inhabit and control—but only to some extent. A constraint to this control lies in the visions that societies at large create about them, visions that they are unable to fully control. Perhaps for this reason the official communications of a resurgent Afghan Taliban speak of "the mujahedin," or simply the parallel "government" of the "Islamic Emirate of Afghanistan." Those constraining visions differ according to the long-term administrative and cultural legacies of the two states that seek to structure and reorient domestically the Pashto-language publics that straddle their frontiers. Paying attention to the histories of popular cultures that share certain tropes and themes, despite and against the elite fragmentation of the contemporary nation-state system, grants us a historical perspective that narrow attention to discrete political organizations alone cannot.

After some remarks on the current content and context of this loaded word, *talib,* I will discuss the sources available for reconstructing the evolution of the symbol *talib* from the early twentieth century until now, across eastern Afghanistan and the Peshawar Valley in particular. I will then look at interactions between grassroots action and elite discipline that contoured the *talib* symbol during the 1980s and 1990s war periods: elite discipline that flowed from transnational elite scholars temporarily located in the urban center of Quetta in Pakistan, to the Kandahari trenches across the border, and then to the nascent Taliban government in Afghanistan that consciously sought to transcend intra-Pashtun cultural specificity. After addressing post-2001 trends in Pakistani and Afghan Pashto-language constructions of *taliban* as symbol and Taliban as actors, from several very different degrees of distance, I will conclude with some notes on new forms of media—media that render uniquely visible the ambivalence in grassroots interactions with the brand-name *Taliban*.[1]

Taliban and the World of Pashto Language and Literature

In the process of fleshing out these narratives and these themes, my aim is to wed two universes—one profoundly longue-durée and strategic in scope, and the other very local, particularistic, tactical. Our primary question may be phrased thus: Where do these local countercultural movements fit into the idea of long-term histories of state formation, ones that now articulate a sort of national universality in addition to deeper, extracolonial roots of cultural legitimacy and continuity? What are they "countercultural" against?

Shah Mahmoud Hanifi makes a point regarding continuity in Afghanistan's modern history, arguing that cosmopolitan registers of Persian supply the fixity of documentation, reining in mobile populations and capital; and, we might add, organizing solidarities of potential resistance into manageable tribal units.[2] At the same time, we may argue alongside Muzaffar Alam and Rosalind O'Hanlon, among others, that many genres of elite Persianate literature—*adab*—supplied a moral discipline that reinforced political orders in most regional states prior to European colonialism.[3] This cultural aspect of dominance was articulated not only through state action but also through conscious interaction of individuals in a self-defined Persianate "Republic of Letters" that bridged culturally distinct regions. These publics of shared cultural consumption and production were effective at assimilating local cultures into themselves, even while maintaining a separation of cross-ethnic imperial society from its hinterlands.

In monarchic Afghanistan, a new dynastic territory carved out of earlier Safavid and Mughal territories, Pashto was treated as a semifavored stepchild by the government since the 1800s, to the extent that it was engaged at all. Since the 1930s, its literary tradition had been championed as the heritage of the monarchic state, which nonetheless continued to rule through the edifice of Persian bureaucracy that it had inherited from its Mughal and Safavid forerunners. Older Persianate genres such as the *Nizam-nama* (an administrative edict) reinforced traditional ideals of imperial rule over, and dynastic distance from, less powerful Pashtuns and non-Pashtuns alike. Meanwhile innovative genres such as formal passports, private property deeds, and updated forms of mortgaging added to the state's repertoire of rule through textual discipline of society.

In the North West Frontier, British imperial society also built on an inherited bifurcation between cosmopolitan state and provincial vernacular culture—overlaying it, deepening it, and rendering it more complex rather than doing away with it. Through the 1920s, sons of rural notables still studied didactic Persian classics that claimed universality in their scope, texts like *Gulistan* and *Bustan,* alongside Urdu and English texts that articulated new imperial cosmopolitanisms. Meanwhile, the ethnography of colonial administration, like trends in counterinsurgency today, helped reinforce "tribal" or localized geographic consciousnesses at the expense of wider political awarenesses. The mobile and itinerant talib, long a fixture of rural society, did not sit easily in this fragmenting, localizing world. And let us now invert our view, from the top-down to the bottom-up, with particular reference to only one symbol of resistance among many.

What are the earliest local literary sources we have for a social perception of talib as counterculture? Proverbs and two-line folklore snippets tied to variations on a longer folktale, the *qissa* (story) of "Talib Jan and Gulbashara," use the basic Pashto word for "student" *(talib)* in the context of a specific romantic countercultural social type—as opposed to the more general use of that word as a bare reference to a student. The first printed elaboration of the story with which I am familiar appears in

Muhammad Gul Nuri's collection of folk stories, *Milli Hindara (Mirror of the Nation)*, vol. 2, published in Kabul in 1945. It contains a number of short poetic phrases related to talibs that circulated through rural society earlier, and links them through a quasi-nationalist narrative possibly reconstructed by Nuri himself.

Here, in the older folk fragments as well as in Nuri's prose story, the talib is depicted as an outsider lover, a traveler in an itinerant yet morally respectable occupation related to affairs of the mind and the heart, whose life represents an opposition to the mundane material and political fixity of settled life. These sources are generally dateless and anonymous folklore refractions; and by the time such snippets were preserved in printed folklore anthologies like Nuri's, they were remade to operate in essentialized or abstracted worlds, in the realm of pure trope and social archetype, without any cues that would foster historical specificity.

Apart from what people said about them in folklore and in nationalist literature, taliban were not only passively represented. Part of the reason Pashtun religious students' persona has been imagined as a distinct social type, to an apparently greater extent than in neighboring regions of Pakistan and Afghanistan, is related to their own activities in carving out something of a youth "counterpublic." This taliban subculture was an adjunct to scholastic networks and institutions, but was conceptually autonomous to some extent, as we shall see. Since at least the middle of the twentieth century and probably much earlier, taliban had created their own real institutions that backed up the world of ideas—that is, through cross-regional mediation and social networking.

Explicit reports of this sort of activity come through in a few biographical directories *(tazkiras)*, and in some secondary Afghan-language literature in disciplines such as folklore and ethnomusicology. The researcher Muhammad 'Arif Gharwal, working in 1980s Khost, Afghanistan, has traced a 1943 reference by the Afghan folklorist Muhammad Gul Nuri to *taliban's atans* (a type of popular dance) as differing from their mainstream counterparts "in all Pashtun regions" to varying degrees. This reference, printed in the Olympian, national-scale print culture of midcentury Kabul, suggests something of a top-down awareness of a similarly nonlocalized, yet non-elite, subculture in development. And by the time Gharwal wrote, a good deal more scholarship had developed for him to cite, on either side of the Afghanistan-Pakistan border, regarding separate forms of poetry and of dancing that were particular to taliban parties.[4]

But the best source for reconstructing this milieu is memoir and recollection. These kinds of sources are most directly telling for our purposes—and at the same time, the least forthcoming of all. This empirical gap makes a close reading of tropes and symbols in folklore all the more important, if less than precise as a historical method. This method cannot aid in geographically specific, rooted history that illustrates the diverse experiences of Pashtun societies. But it can at least illuminate some aspects of ideology in a hybrid oral and literate Pashto-language public sphere that have been shared across regions in a common cultural-historical patrimony. And the very fact of this decontextualized cultural history—in which geographical and temporal specificity are hard to come by—is itself a form of historical evidence. From it, we must infer a type of cultural sharing that overcame much administrative structuring and acted against (perhaps in reaction to) a localizing of people's social frames of reference.

We should reiterate that the majority of references to Pashtun "taliban" in secondary literature in Afghan languages point merely to (largely rural) students in a traditional situation, where individual students would apprentice themselves to a teacher and learn as much as possible, sometimes memorizing and mastering ideas in extraordinarily complex Arabic texts before moving on to another teacher.[5] Students could travel quite widely in this quest for ever more stimulating texts and ever more connected teachers. In the eastern provinces of Afghanistan, biographical directories as well as secondary literature tell us that local scholarly networks often converged on a center of gravity in the outskirts of Jalalabad, Afghanistan, in the intellectual and spiritual networks forged by the Sahib of Hadda in the late nineteenth century. But this was by no means the only such center of gravity. Kandahar city and its environs formed another notable locus, as attested to by ample entries in Muhammad Wali Zalmay's *Notables of Kandahar*.[6] Meanwhile the higher institutions of the Peshawar Valley and especially the Indus and Gangetic plains seem in many of the sources to have held the greatest regional cachet.[7] In these middle and upper educational registers, the hard-to-recover world of the marginal Pashtun talib begins to shade into the far-better-documented universe of Urdu-language religious education.

However, we should also note a continuum between those "serious" students whose stories have made it into history books as individual intellectuals, and some of the other practices fostered by educational networks and young men's search for all that mobile education could bring in addition to knowledge. Could it be subsequent historiography, rather than actual experience, that has separated sober youth scholasticism from the romanticized lifestyle of the wandering talib band of exuberant young Pashtun men in the mid-twentieth century? The two are certainly not so easily separated in literary imagination even to this day. Note, for example, the most detailed account I have seen of an early twentieth-century wandering talib band—this recollection, like Nuri's cryptic footnote, relates to 1943 or thereabouts. It dates to the time that its author, Ajmal Khattak, was serving in the shrine village and traditional center of rural learning in Ziarat Kaka Sahib, Nowshera district, in present-day Pakistan. It is worth quoting at length:

> Ghwaye Mullah was from the village Dandoka, of the Yusufzai tribe [probably in Swabi district, in the Peshawar Valley]. He was a renowned jokester, and had oral and extemporaneous poets traveling with him too. He was trained in the traditional education of the time, and in his body and physique looked to be a severe and sturdy Pashtun. At all times he had twenty to thirty students along with him, and wherever they were, when the time for the lesson came, he would also teach them. But usually it was exuberant carefree (*mast*) students who would travel with him, of the sort who just studied so that they could say they were students. Their real job was joking, buffoonery, exuberant acting out, *atan* dancing, and eating the ready-made food that people gave them (*tayar-khori*).
>
> From his external appearance no one would have guessed this; and looking at him one would get the impression of a great scholar (*'alim*). But the mouth on him was such that if anyone approached him, he would ridicule the person to such an extent that no one else would have the temerity to take his attention. His thing was that he'd go with his students from village to village. They'd take payment from the *khans, maliks,* and respectable people of the village and amuse them with jokes and buffoonery, and with insulting poems about those who

opposed them. And if anyone didn't give them payment, they would shame them in village after village. . . .

Ghwaye Mullah would stand with the students in a field, and a student would begin beating on a barrel drum, a frame drum, or a clay pot, while the rest would make sounds on hand drums. Mullah Ghwaye himself would tell jokes and sing poems, while the students behind him would let out cries, thrash their heads, or dance the *atan*. And all the villagers would sit and watch, laughing. It is worth emphasizing that [the mullah] did this work not in order to earn money, but rather for pleasure. This was one feature of how they spent their time. They would spend their own time in exuberant carefree happiness, and would also make the people happy.[8]

Besides Ajmal Khattak's empirical recollections outlined above, he gives more insight into how society viewed the persona, if not the person, of the talib in a well-known 1960s poem of his. In contrast to other social actors' material concerns, the talib's thoughts of paradise are taken from the imagery of the half-religious, half-folk-romance chapbook tale he is reading:

I asked a *mullah,* what do you think Paradise is like?
He ran his fingers through his beard and said
"Fresh fruits and rivers of milk"
A *talib* was sitting nearby
I asked him, what do you say?
He put aside the book of Zulekha he was reading, and said
"Beautiful women with (tattooed) green dots on their cheeks"
A *khan* (rural leader) raised his head from a lengthy *sajda* (prostration
    in prayer)
What is your opinion, Khan Sahib? I asked
He adjusted his turban and said
"Luxuriously furnished and perfumed mansions"
Nearby, a labourer stood in his tattered clothes
I asked him, do you know what Paradise is?
He wiped the sweat from his brow and said
"It's a full stomach and deep slumber."[9]

Talibs' liminality—their interaction with, yet separation from, ordinary society—perhaps allowed society to superimpose a sense of abstraction onto the persona of the talib, as a young man inhabiting a dreamlike landscape of fantasy. The two types of account—talib as actor and talib as trope—are blended in Zakariya Mlatar's rather more poetic account of talib life, in the preface to his highly fascinating *tazkira* of Pashto poets who chose the pen name "Talib" for themselves. Mlatar applies the following generally to the eastern provinces of Afghanistan, particularly Nangarhar and Kunar, Laghman, Logar, and Paktia/Khost; more specificity than this, especially of time period, is not forthcoming:

> Before, when educational programs didn't have their current form, education could only be had in the *madrasa* and the mosque, and this was the only route to literacy. Students would go to distant countries for knowledge, and would bring back with themselves treasuries of knowledge and information, and various types of books and diwans. . . .
>
> *Talibs* have one part in each year for travel and recreation which they spend in *melas* [outdoor festivals] and *atans,* and they gather up money for themselves which they call *sobat.* Pashtuns view talibs with respect; in order to make the case, here are a few *landays* [two-line poems] from Pashto folk literature which praise the talibs:
>
> > The *taliban* have come, parties and parties of them / But the *talib* of my heart has not come; I shall die! . . .
> >
> > Don't make *taliban* into lovers, God / And add the suffering of love onto the suffering of knowledge! . . .
> >
> > The *taliban* have climbed up into the country / But myself, my beloved's eyes have struck me down so I stayed. . . .
>
> The reason why *talibs* are so praised in *landays* is that they would spend many years gone and out of their homeland *(wrak aw jula watan).* Pashtun girls would depict this long journey of theirs in the form of *landays.* And sometimes, from among them, true love would find the form it takes in the folkloric legend of Talib Jan and Gulbashara.[10]

The above account feels rather more fanciful than that in Ajmal Khattak's memoir. Is there any reason to try and separate the fanciful from the factual, though? This romanticism, as well as its usefulness as a type of social critique, benefits from a willing decontextualization. It operates in the field of abstract schematic morality, rather than the fixity of precise contingent description; and it thus becomes applicable to multiple contexts. It seems instructive at the very least to note the romance of the persona as well as the fun imagined as part of the lifestyle, and to highlight the authors' own schematic, antihistorical perceptions and presentations of a fluid masculine youth counterculture standing in opposition to the rigid voice of sober authority. In this discussion, I draw on Asef Bayat's important work on fun and youth culture, among that of other social scientists. Here, though, is a case different from those that Bayat describes: the "displays of spontaneity and joy and the pursuit of everyday pleasures," as he puts it, are not in opposition to any "Islamist moral paradigm" as they are in his case studies of late twentieth-century Egypt and Iran.[11] These early twentieth-century Pashtun talibs actually presented their own "Islamic" moral paradigm. The fun of living a talib subculture during the recreational season, and the pleasure that audiences got from their performances, came from the fact that it was an alternative to a different set of established norms, that of purely secular landed power.

In most iterations of the folk romance "Talib Jan," the romance generally takes place between Talib Jan and a king's or a landowner's daughter, maximizing the scandal value as well as a symbolic contrast between marginality and power. But beyond this sort of symbolic token, it would seem that the fluidity and mobility of taliban in the mid-twentieth century on either side of the mountains would run directly counter to an accelerated social and economic process of rooting in territory. In Afghanistan, where colonial and monarchic politics meant that everyday people were increasingly cut off from the global economy since the 1930s, there was a concomitant upswing in investment in landed power and ties to the monarchy for prestige as well as for a link to the outside world. This was accompanied by a solidification of landed, reflexively Pashtun values of gravitas, sobriety, and intermediary lordship on the grassroots level. In this case, the analysis of talib parties' activities would be roughly similar to Asef Bayat's reading of Victor Turner: as "carnivalesque," as "extending the politics of joy . . . into struggles against structures of hierarchy at large."[12]

We get a direct glimpse of this "politics of fun" in an institutional sense, too, in Ajmal Khattak's account above. By virtue of their mobility, talibs began to carve out a public zone of antihierarchical speech. It would not be easy to criticize or lampoon local power in a local setting; but by extending their activities across wide swaths of the countryside, transcendent of local control, Mullah Ghwaye and his troupe were able to insulate themselves from repercussions and give voice to local criticisms of local khans, maliks, and others.

Further, in the British imperial territory of the 1930s that Khattak's account relates to, we also see talibs disrupting another form of hierarchy. Even as the nationalist movement in the North West Frontier Province (NWFP) resisted both British imperial power and the large provincial landowners who served as adjuncts to empire, the Khudai Khidmatgar movement in particular rested on a castelike division of "officers" and "mass" members and demanded that the socially marginal subsume their agency into its own. Further, the primary nationalist movements in the NWFP were geographically rooted in terms of their structures in the same centers of gravity that sustained empire—new market towns and the villages in their orbit. Taliban activity, rooted not in imperial centers but in older interlinked geographies of shrine villages and rural centers of traditional Persianate learning, disrupted the hierarchies and the rootedness of both empire and the nationalist movement, which by that time was well-entrenched. Ajmal Khattak, himself a nationalist activist, recalls at a different point in his memoir with some ironic bemusement how the bawdy humor of Mullah Ghwaye's party disrupted a traditional folk festival in Ziarat Kaka Sahib, a festival that had been appropriated by nationalist activist poets over the early 1940s.

Given the current associations of the word *Taliban* in Pashtun society, it seems odd to cast taliban in the role of the fun-loving rural youth escaping social discipline. Of course, in the contemporary situation, this intuition is not far from the mark. This is indicative of the changing role of taliban in the social imagination, as well-funded networks of a new type of religiously identifying political actor came to appropriate the label. Nonetheless, they appropriated a label that was rich with preexisting connotations, and that continued to be larger than a single political movement; and they were not unaffected by either the possibilities or the constraints imposed by these external ideas.

From Evasion to Mobilization and Domination

Is there a connection between these older images of people referred to as "talibs" and the Taliban that dominate our current perceptions of the word? In an institutional sense, not at all (or at most only very tenuously). But in the world of social imagination beyond their exclusive control, Taliban insurgents since the 1990s have come to inhabit certain aspects of this older persona whether they want to or not, especially the trope of the passionate outsider youth that the traditional persona of "talib" articulated. This has had effects on rank-and-file talibs, regardless of what Islamist ideologues in the movements would prefer. Consider, for example, the highly romanticized set of Taliban self-portrait photographs published by Thomas Dworzak, in which young Taliban fighters highlight their beauty as they pose with flowers and eyeliner against garden and alpine backdrops. Such an aesthetic comes into much sharper focus through this lens.[13]

Through this type of imagery, as well as songs related to Taliban political movements, we can also get a view of self-construction in talib-related media—both by actual taliban and by poets who are sympathetic to the movement. While conducting unrelated field research in Peshawar in 2005, I was informed that although the (original) Afghan Taliban had banned music, they benefited from a transnational rise in popular cassette songs performed by both men and women that celebrated them. Some of these, produced mostly in Pakistan for the transnational Afghan market, took the form of martyrdom songs; but others were composed in feminine voice, addressing the talib warrior as a lover. Longing and the separation of travel, traditional tropes in talib lore, took on new significances. Romanticism of talib itinerancy became successfully welded with discourses of honorable masculinity prominent in the genres of jihad poetry described by David Edwards, among others.[14]

Along with the moral self-alignment involved in composing such works, there is also the moral self-alignment involved in actively consuming such works, in an era where consumers have a wide selection of songs to buy and listen to, or, nowadays, to seek out on the Internet. Continued and cumulative interaction with the talib brand, by non-talib individuals' consumption and compositions, continues to determine the character of that brand over time in the late twentieth-century public domain.

This is especially true in elite counter-narratives that pulled the persona of talib closer to authoritative respectability. Of course, romance and fun are not the only genealogical thread worth tracing in this account of talib as persona. The thread of sincerity, earnestness, and morality is worth tugging on, when explaining why this countercultural persona was adopted by those who would rule; and why at least some people would have a stake in its respectability that extends beyond the rational calculation of security. A parallel rhetoric in elite literary Pashto, especially of Afghanistan, was built up around the Afghan talib persona in the last decade of the twentieth century. This new rhetoric sublimated youth agency and passionate love of the talib trope into a sort of pious heroism, or into the abstract world of courtly love poetry, or both. This discourse assimilated the idea of the romanticized countercultural talib, the subject of the descriptions above (and perhaps more common as trope than as fact), into the equally marginal yet far more mundane, far more disciplined reality of the stationary village student talib of 1960s and 1970s Afghanistan, particularly of the southern provinces centered on greater Kandahar. This milieu has been described by former Afghan Taliban official Mullah Zaeef in the beginning of his autobiography, among other sources.[15]

On the revolutionary side of the Taliban movement, much poetry composed by higher-ranking ideologues in the Afghan Taliban regime, as it consolidated itself, took pains to disavow the romanticized persona of talib:

> I write poetry, but I won't write poetry in love of my lover
> I won't write about my beloved's little red lips or cheeks
> Neither about the coquetry of the beloved, or the wretched state of the
>   lover
> I won't write about the mysteries of love, or the adornments of
>   freewheeling girls[16]

We should temper this view with that of Mullah Zaeef, again, whose narrative includes visions of romance, in a pure and Platonic yet no less obsessive form, as permeating the everyday life of the movement's original core, during the 1980s:

> May God be praised! What a brotherhood we had among the *muja-hedeen!* We weren't concerned with the world or with our lives;

our intentions were pure and every one of us was willing to die as a martyr. When I look back on the love and respect that we had for each other, it sometimes seems like a dream.[17]

Zaeef notes the everyday engagement with poetic forms of self-expression that helped constitute the persona of early movement leaders at the time. As reported by Zaeef, one night in the late 1980s after a clash with Soviet forces, at a party of poetry and singing on the very day he lost his eye, Mullah Muhammad Omar himself sang *ghazals* in the classical vein: "My illness is untreatable, oh, my flower-like friend / My life is difficult without you, my flower-like friend."[18]

By the time the Taliban formed a government in Kabul and began ruling a country, complex negotiations were involved in integrating romantic persona into hierarchical discipline—negotiations in poetic genre and in actual life. Negotiations in the world of genre are illustrated by various aspects of an admittedly more complex work, a poetry collection entitled *Da Patsun Zhagh,* or *Voice of the Uprising,* printed in Quetta in 1997. It was written by a non-Taliban religious scholar and poet named Haqyar, originally of Kandahar though based in Quetta, in a consciously classical Persianate style:

> Who is this that refuses love?
> I don't know whether they're Muslim or an infidel
> This lamp-flame of love is very ancient
> It's been a tradition since eternity . . .
> Poetry and *mulla*-ism are not opposed
> I, Haqyar, am both *mawlana* and poet.

Another poem:

> In you, Mahmud of Ghazni grew up
>   You raised so many great scholars
> You raised Mirwais and Abdali
>   You raised so many strong youths
> You are the home of the saints of Kabul
>   And countless shrines
> You are the home of mystics and holy men
>   Many renowned personalities

You are a minaret of learning and art
    O, cradle of sacrificing heroes!
You are the minaret of Allahu Akbar!
    O, cradle of the strong and the brave
O, homeland of the Amir al-Mu'minin
    Now too you have many strong children
O, beautiful and colorful homeland of Haqyar
    Thank God you have lovely *taliban!*

Here the idealized talib has been partially assimilated to the very civilizational narrative that he once stood in opposition to. But it is not only—not even primarily—the poetry that disciplines, in this literary collection. The author dedicated his work to the memory of the Pakistan-trained, Kandahar-based Deobandi intellectual and renowned teacher of Afghan religious students, Abdul Ghaffar "Bariyalai." Bariyalai was himself an accomplished poet in the *sabk-e hindi* style, which uses passionate lyric in a highly abstract and stylized fashion, and it appears that Haqyar followed this courtly style in emulation of him. Bariyalai additionally appears, at least in the 1990s, to have enjoyed some status as a spiritual grandfather of the elders of the original, Kandahar-based Afghan Taliban movement, whether this ancestry was real or fictive. Second, the poetry collection was also "presented in the service of" a young talib who "took over from that elder," who "is spending the years of his youth in the reform of society," and who is recognized as "well-bred" because the "traces of his father and forefathers are present in him": Mawlawi Wakil Ahmad Mutawakkil, the Taliban government's soon-to-be foreign minister. I suspect that the dedication was made by the author, an intellectual who was cautiously supportive of the Taliban movement but hoped that his (occasionally impressive) poetry might help to humanize and enrich the Taliban leadership, and discipline it before more experienced religious authority, as much as to inspire it. But certainly in the selections above, alongside a territorial religious nationalism claiming the energies of countless youths for itself in the latter poem, and the framing in the dedication that subsumes talib youth within the hierarchies of patriarchal lineage, we still see a celebrated ideal of youthful passion dressed in pious clothing.

Why was this a useful persona for Taliban supporters to appropriate, adapt, and lionize? Perhaps because traditional taliban life, as narrated by multiple sources in a coalescing, cross-regional "conventional wisdom," was a countercultural force with revolutionary potential, and this ideology was useful to the actual revolutionary movement. The earlier talib persona was permeated with a romantic, transgressive flavor of freedom that carved out an autonomous public zone divorced from state or even local control by virtue of its transregional, anti-local mobility. Indeed, this is one of the reasons it is difficult to grant greater geographic specificity to the sources presented here. And as part of this fluidity, the content of the talib persona was also flexible. This freedom and horizontality were easily adaptable into a contrast to the hierarchies created and contested by local predatory militia leaders, as much as earlier manifestations of landed power. It was easily adoptable for new actors.

The most widely known origin tale of the original Afghan Taliban movement was narrated by the BBC in 1994, and is echoed by Mullah Zaeef in his memoir. In essence, once the Soviet military withdrew from Afghanistan and external financial support for the seven militant factions dried up, the lower ranks of those factions in Afghanistan began forcibly extracting resources from the rural poor and from each other in its place. The countryside fragmented into shifting, overlapping territorial units of depredation, especially in the comparatively hierarchical south—Kandahar, Helmand, Oruzgan—that formed the heartland of the original Taliban. The English word *warlordism* tells us less about local perceptions of this period than two interrelated Pashto words: *topak-salari* and *patak-salari,* or "rule by the rifle" and "rule by the checkpoint."[19] In his narration, Mullah Zaeef tells us that the initial taliban activism in 1994 mobilized older bands of talib fighters who used to work for the Sayyaf mujahedin faction. He narrates that the mobilization came in response to both these trends, trends that drastically circumscribed mobility and eroded the dignity and honor of everyday people, and that accentuated the political economy of localized, territorial warrior patriarchy to a degree unprecedented in contemporary Afghan historical memory.[20]

The usefulness of the talib trope for the original Afghan movement was this: it allowed them to brand a new faction of activists, supported by Pakistani intelligence, to bring security and stability to neighboring

Afghanistan, as a movement of resistance to this fragmentation and local hierarchization of social life. This was possible because of two things: the cross-regional, nonterritorial nature of religious learning (whether in countercultural or regular student experience), and traditional ideologies about talibs (whether or not those ideologies reflected most current talibs' experience). The traditional construction of the talib was not only about fun, it was about marginality as an alternative expression of masculinity and social morality that did not depend on competition and domination. The talib was already often construed as a sincere and powerless ascetic in contrast to the rapacious khan—and by extension, the *qomandan* or *topaki* (militant commander or foot soldier). As Haqyar's poetry and his dedication to Mutawakkil illustrate, the talib's romanticized yet domesticated passion contributed to supporters' ability to describe them as sincere in motivation and pursuing a politics of reform. This was in conscious opposition to the politics of exploitation.

At the same time as an ideal of youthful passion was disciplined and channelized into a political-military movement by the hierarchies of urban and (locally) cosmopolitan Deobandi scholarship, it was still valuable as popular persona. In periods of Taliban mobilization, both during the 1990s and in the post-2001 resurgence, these alternate constructions have been cast not only as "different," as in times past, but as morally superior. And the marginality of talib social habits that did not seek aggrandizement over those of rural poor Pashtuns was successfully integrated into a narrative of populism. This is part of the continued sticking power of the talib persona—as opposed to the actual experience of situations in which Taliban movements have extended their hegemony. In this connection, a contemporary Pakistani Pashto refashioning of the "Talib Jan" story is worth exploring in greater depth.

The Romance of Rejection and Martyrdom

A ten-rupee chapbook folk romance between Talib Jan and an eponymous "Pashtana" (the character's name is merely the feminine of "Pashtun") in part represents an updated retelling of the folk tale, printed in Peshawar in the first decade of the 2000s.[21] It also, I suspect, represents an allegorical adaptation of the story, to serve as a literary image of the moral dimensions of how "Pashtun society" related to Taliban in the period of Afghanistan during and after their rule. In so doing, it re-adapts the talib persona to a post-rule situation.

The story exists in a curious hybrid of realistic and idealized, almost abstracted, context. Descriptions of modern material culture seem designed to place it in a context relevant to present-day readers. There are no more kings and such; here there are electric lights and government schools. The lexicon appears consciously "Afghanized" by an author who otherwise writes in colloquial Peshawari Pashto. Some cues date the story to a period "after the fall of Dr. Najib," who was the communist leader of Afghanistan until 1992. Yet there is little to no other mention of political rule. The primary social frame of the story could better be described as "village society", and temporality operates not in historical time but, rather, in relative time: "before" as opposed to "now." The story begins with Pashtana's father telling his daughter that "before," people were genuine. They helped each other out at harvest; it was not a society like "now," where "each Pashtun lies in wait, thirsty for each other's blood."

Early in the story, Pashtana receives an anonymous note from a boy in class, slipped into one of her books and declaring his love for her. When Pashtana reads the letter, she is highly offended by the presumption and thinks: "Dear God! If I'm not wrong, this looks like the work of a *khan*. And there's that flirtatious boy in our classroom!" She is furious, and writes him a shaming letter ("even selling your sister in the bazaar would be better than this action of yours!").

This episode does not arise again, and seems intended primarily as a way of postulating a khan morality in direct opposition to talib morality. Some few days later, a talib party arrives at Pashtana's home, which, as the home of a wealthy landowner, hosts them and feeds them. Talibs being pious and harmless, and pure in motivation, there is no impropriety in Pashtana bringing them their tea and food; but as their leader, Talib Jan, blesses her with a hand on the head, she falls for him instantly. It is she, this time, who writes the love letter, this time passed on through a younger child talib who functions as message carrier. As in the much older Talib Jan story in Muhammad Gul Nuri's 1945 publication of Pashto folktales, most of the story takes the form of delayed gratification, as Talib Jan is torn between his love for itinerant learning and his love for the girl. Eventually after a long period of patience and longing, with Talib Jan playing hard to get, they decide to marry, in defiance of all social conventions related to khans' daughters and talibs alike.

In the contemporary story, though, conflict arises not only from the deceit of maids and the class disparity of the girl and a talib, as in older versions. In this one, a passionate but weak Pashtana allows herself to be seduced by thoughts of marriage to her cousin, a young khan whose match has been arranged for her by her brothers in London, and who everyone tells her is both handsome and suitable. Eventually, while Talib Jan is out on his travels with the talib party, she decides to marry that young khan, and rejects Talib Jan through a cruel exchange with the young messenger. The sincere Talib Jan is crushed by this betrayal. He falls into illness and never recovers, dying in a hospital in the presence of the messenger, his younger brother. The doctor tells the brother to take Talib Jan away because there is nothing that can be done. His younger brother weepingly protests that being itinerant talibs, they have no one, and nowhere to go. The story ends with the narrator telling us that it is not just a folktale at all; rather, he heard it from Talib Jan himself on his deathbed near Jalalabad. Revisiting the scene, he has discovered that Talib Jan's grave is now venerated as that of a martyr to love. Even Pashtana's expatriate brothers visit it to pay their respects.

Several points are important to note. There is a very clear distinction here between khan morality and talib morality, which is more explicitly and schematically articulated as such than in nearly any other talib-related media that I have seen. It hinges on an opposition of talib passion as "sincerity," as opposed to the "desire to use, exploit" inherent in the way that Pashtana saw the young khan's pursuit of her. The gentle passive romance of the talib is, for the purposes of this story, the opposite of the romance of the khan, a predatory male persona who actively pursues what he wants. Then there is the conclusion, in which Pashtana ends up married to a khan after all, through the intervention of her brothers in London.

For me, this feels like an echo of the idea of talib passion as true or superior morality in opposition to rapacious naked power, which we saw in Mullah Zaeef's Taliban origin narrative. By the ending, the simplicity and the mildness of the modern talib is established as being congruent with the more general ingenuousness and sincerity of times past. In the undefined, traditional "old days," everyone was better; but that was before the rise of rapacious politics. "Now," only the talib preserves this unshaking and uninfluenceable devotion, a love that is pure and lust-free.

Is this quasi-allegorical reading a stretch? Possibly, though even if so, it still represents a continued engagement with passionate and itinerant talib as a trope in conscious opposition to that of the khan. But in favor of an allegorical reading, why else would the female protagonist "Gulbashara" inexplicably be renamed "Pashtana," the generic word for "female Pashtun" and not a given name in Pashtun society? Even "Talib Jan" has a name, Mullah Abdul Ghaffur. And why would it end in this sort of personal betrayal, unlike earlier versions? The story seems intended to play upon the familiar folkloric persona of Talib Jan as a way to convey a historiographical vision: what is, for the author, the heartbreaking rejection of sincere talib morality by Karzai-era Afghan Pashtuns, and their "marriage" to khan-ism through the intervention of foreign brothers. The martyrdom of Talib Jan in the story carries additional layers of meaning in this context as well. And there can be no doubt that contemporary media about the Taliban, as well as actual Taliban propaganda, both play upon the same sorts of tropes as above.

A celebration of the Taliban's purported obsessive passionate devotion to homeland and to Islam, and the motifs of passionate self-sacrifice and martyrdom that emerge in this narration, build upon earlier constructions of the talib trope. The martyrdom, or other form of absence of the passionate talib lover, appears a common trope in contemporary poetry composed for or by Taliban and performed without musical accompaniment. A short number of excerpts from Taliban poems, taken from the streaming video site youtube.com, may serve to illustrate this point. Of the vast number of Taliban lyrics currently available, a sizable percentage rely on romantic imagery as part of martyrdom. Consider the following lines, intended as the *nara* (call and response phrases) for a Taliban *atan* dance:

> Once more, my poor heart breaks out into *naras*
>> The Taliban come to my memory like flowers
> Oh Lord, what happened to those red and white birds?
>> The Taliban come to my memory like flowers

Much time has passed, my dear, since our meetings ended
    The Taliban come to memory like flowers[22]

The *naras* go on to describe the sufferings of the young Taliban as they were massacred in northern Afghanistan by the Northern Alliance, among other less-specific topics. Meanwhile, other Taliban songs are less focused on the pathos of martyrdom, yet still express traditional tropes of romantic obsession and self-sacrifice, deploying poetic vocabulary that recalls older rural poetry from *tazkiras*. For example, *sati* (a poetic appropriation of the image of a wife's ritual immolation on her husband's funeral pyre), and the moth incinerated by its love for the flame, are arresting enough tropes in traditional Pashto folk poetry due to their extremity. The effect is all the more jarring when combined, in contemporary poems, with youth militarism and the potentially ominous promise of a meeting as in the following:

Death, my dear, when you look for me, look on the front lines
    I am a falcon of the homeland, look for me in the high mountains
My dear, ask the eagles and the birds
    Look for me among the leaders of the deserts and wastelands . . .
I am a *sati* in the fire; I am alight with my own religion
    I am a moth, look for me in the flame of the Qur'an
Tortured by love, I am still faithful to my beloved
    Look for me in sobs in the deserts and wastelands
I'll come to you on foot, in hopes of a meeting
    My friend, look for me in prayers and in *khatms* [a ritual Quran recital in memory of the dead].[23]

Conclusions

It should be clear that a historical account of romanticization in the content of media need not imply an uncritical romanticization on the part of the consumer, as opposed to a considered, ambivalent, tactical one. As illustrated above, romanticization has served Taliban interests at times, but has also been a tool of non-Taliban elite discipline, as in the poetry of Maulawi Haqyar. A final view, that of mass discipline of those who would inhabit the symbolic value of "talib," might be gained through another intellectual named Haqyar, a blind poet-entertainer of southern Afghanistan who performed taliban songs for rural audiences. As of 2010 he was no longer limited to the world of contingent improvisation. Alongside the polished propaganda videos officially released by Taliban organizations, the current series of conflicts gripping Afghanistan and northwestern Pakistan alike have also spawned new forms of networked media, with informal cell-phone video sharing being particularly noteworthy. In one such video posted to youtube.com, recorded in a village notable's meetinghouse *(hujra)*, we find not an elite disciplining of Taliban message, but ambivalent discipline by non-elite concerns; and we are finally confronted with the stark materiality underlying the discontent that propels people's engagement with the talib as symbol and actor alike.

Beginning with a view of tribal society as fractured and (locally?) self-interested, Haqyar posits Taliban morality as both more expansive and superior: "Don't name those Pashtuns as real Pashtuns, O Lover / Pick up a rifle and be honorable / Don't fight in your home like jackals. . . . Weep at the task presented to all Afghans / If God is present, then go ahead and remake History anew. . . . The Taliban may take pride in their name, no? / The streets and alleys are full of foreigners."[24]

In video, the contingency of recording allows for more nuanced readings of the transcendental romanticization of taliban than other media would allow. Here we find the talib as a passionate hero who operates on the strategic scale of egalitarian national history, and even potentially on the universal and metaphysical scales of divine and human history. Yet the poem's lyrics take on fuller meanings from the circumstances presented in real-time moving imagery—a beleaguered, impoverished performer, commandeered by high-handed and half-dismissive rural landowners to sing for them in their *hujra,* in the heart of the resurgent Taliban's sphere of influence. The egalitarian national belonging that the Taliban promise in romanticized theory—much like the deliverance from "foreign" dominance based in monarchic Kabul, late-colonial and post-colonial London, or present-day Islamabad, Kabul, and Washington—stands for Haqyar as just that: a promise, one that remains unfulfilled. The song clearly praises and underscores the trope, even as it points out the contradiction of abstract ideal persona and real-life, tactical actor. Haqyar's negotiation between sarcasm and idealism is vague enough to chip away at multiple hierarchies at once, without reprisal. In varying degrees of directness he delegitimates rural power, the Afghan government, and its NATO allies. Most importantly, though, he also critiques a cross-regional Taliban authority that now occupies a subsection of the very domain of strategic cultural power that an ideal talib as symbol, and taliban as actually occurring actors, once both militated against.

With the increasingly globalized Afghan wars of the late twentieth and early twenty-first centuries, as well as the increasing crisis of legitimacy of the Pakistani state in its northwestern regions, however, this zone of strategic power is less informed by any one hegemonic cultural stream than it has been at any point since the 1500s. The bureaucratic legacies of post-Persianate dynastic and colonial imperialism not only jostle against nation-state ideals of citizenship. They also collide with late twentieth-century ideals of universality, ideals represented in the phrase *international community* that can also marginalize expressions of localism. And they currently also collide against a particular brand of locally decontextualized Islamic universalism: an ideological product of local social history, at least in part, but one that actively downplays and marginalizes its localness. In the increasingly complex interplay of resistance and power in the fractured polities straddling the Afghan-Pakistan border, cell-phone sharing and streaming Internet videos have strengthened the phenomenon of cross-border mediation, interacting in all these anti-localisms simultaneously.

Let us consider one ironic symptom of this increasingly complex mediascape: for some of Daud Haqyar's audiences, at least, a decontextualized, imagined talib that served as an *ideal* symbol of antistructural resistance has come to be pitted not only against postimperial states, but against real-time taliban, who are themselves a new form of structure-creating actor. It is perhaps too early to predict the long-term outcomes of this ongoing public, participative history.

5 / Quandaries of the Afghan Nation

Shah Mahmoud Hanifi

Epistemology is basically the study of how something came to be known. It helps us to identify the parameters, or the combination of possibilities and limits, of how Afghanistan is understood and acted upon. My interest here is to use the intellectual tools of epistemology as a means to revitalize a shared, polyethnic sense of Afghan nationalism at a moment in history when we may very well be witnessing Afghanistan's disintegration. The epistemological orientation of this paper will identify "intellectual fault lines" in our knowledge about Afghanistan. We can all benefit from new ways of knowing and acting on Afghanistan, and the critical tone of this chapter represents a major plank of an admittedly revisionist platform. In my view, the foundation of Afghan nationalism requires reinforcement along intellectual seams where three sets of questions arise, regarding (a) movement and migration within, to, and from the country; (b) local attachments and inter-regional relations within Afghanistan; and (c) connections of Afghan elites to external resources and worldviews.

Allow me to briefly elaborate each of these points. To better under-stand how diverse Afghan communities relate to each other and to oth-ers, much more critical attention to the history of mobility among these populations is needed. Wherever Afghans are found, they retain link-ages to and memories of other places, making it incumbent to reckon with both territorialism and extraterritoriality among them. As a pre-ponderantly rural society, migrations between rural localities as well as urban–rural relations in Afghanistan, including both urbanization and ruralization processes, deserve more analytical attention. A full under-standing of cities in Afghanistan also requires attention to each major city's primary market connections with urban locations across interna-tional borders, including Kabul's intimate relationship with Peshawar, which cumulatively undermine the formation of national markets in the county. The historical pattern of elites in Afghanistan sharing some form of diaspora experience before, after, or both before and after their periods of rule significantly affects national politics. Among the cul-tural consequences of those diasporic experiences, new language acqui-sition is arguably most significant. The extraterritorial experiences of political elites also tend to generate financial dependencies and ideo-logical transformations that simultaneously structure and destabilize national politics.

The narrative below will briefly trace the genealogy of "Afghanistan" and knowledge about it. Colonial knowledge formation is the focus of the following outline of Afghanistan's intellectual architecture wherein I will present three inter-related arguments. The first is that Afghani-stan as currently understood is a British colonial construction in both material and ideological terms. The second is that Afghan elites have uncritically absorbed and reproduced colonial frameworks of reckon-ing about themselves and their homeland. We will see this effect mainly through a national imagery anchored in Aryanism, Kabul, and jihad. The capstone or "take away" position adopted here is that until Ameri-can and other neocolonial actors in the country today become cogni-zant of and transcend the contradictions and inconsistencies of classic colonial forms of knowledge, their projects in and visions of Afghani-stan will remain literally and practically unrealistic and unrealizable.

Introductory Problems of Knowing Afghanistan

In any epistemological inquiry the question of data is determinant and inescapable. And it is important to be clear from the start about how comparatively scant the cultural and historical database is for Afghanistan, but, more importantly, how that scarce information is subject to extreme political manipulation. Take, for example, the population of the country, which is currently estimated in the U.S. *CIA World Factbook* at nearly 29 million, reduced from an earlier 33 million estimate. Either estimate of the current total population of the country stands in stark contrast to the 13 million figure officially registered for Afghanistan's population 1979, that is, before the large-scale casualties and exodus of multiple millions of refugees from the country.[1]

It is difficult to reconcile the Afghanistan population estimates of 1979 and 2010 without reference to the steadily increasing global humanitarian and military funding streams leading to Afghanistan that need to be bureaucratically justified by higher body counts of living and dead people in the country. Numeric and visual representations of ethnicity and ethnic distribution within the country are even more problematic than the cumulative total population in estimates, once the methodology behind the statistics and cartography are considered. The deployment of ethnic maps and ethnic statistics by the international community in its attempts to manage local and national political processes in the country perpetuates a number of problematic predicates for knowing and acting on Afghanistan.

The relatively limited data for Afghans and Afghanistan feel more cavernous due to the low scale of the qualitative analysis brought to bear on them. Social science concepts such as state, nation, ethnicity, and tribe, with deep intellectual lineages that have spawned sub-branches of literature across a number of academic disciplines, are generally not applied and interrogated with any substantial rigor in analyses of Afghanistan. A primary index of this scholarly marginality is that academic literature about the Afghan nation-state and its constituent tribes and ethnicities is generally insulated from work within particular disciplines and interdisciplinary writings organized around these key concepts. Basic, but important, questions about nationalism, class, and urban–rural relations, for additional examples, have not been asked in and of Afghanistan. Most important among these questions are those interrogating the ongoing *relationships between* the tribal, ethnic, and national levels of identity in Afghanistan, which are anything but discrete and hermetically sealed off from one another. In some ways Afghanistan appears trapped in an intellectual black hole.

There are a number of problematic features common to a majority of writings about Afghanistan that explain the contours of the metaphorical black hole or Bermuda Triangle that "absorbs much and produces little," as Afghanistan scholarship is so prone to do. The first is the historiographic problem of determining what precisely is meant by the term *Afghan*. Through time and across space and languages, there are considerable ambiguities attached to the word *Afghan*, with complications becoming particularly acute when Afghans are considered in relation to Pashtuns and Pathans.[2] In addition to shifting and inconsistent meanings of the word *Afghan*, the word *Afghanistan* is also invoked by different authors at different historical moments between 1747 and 1893. Perhaps of most consequence is the fundamental misreading of the historical record insofar as the explicitly Persianate state of Afghanistan is misconstrued as being dominated by the Pashtun ethnic group. We will return to this important issue at various times below.

To conclude these introductory comments, I invite the reader to contemplate this question: Given the global attention Afghanistan has received, how is it that the unique and important cultural and historical configuration of Afghanistan has generally escaped critical attention from, and failed to exert tangible influence upon, the academy at large and the social sciences in particular? One possible answer is that Afghanistan is so unique that academic literature about it can only be consumed by country specialists. However, in this regard we do not find the relatively few scholars of Afghanistan having a shared set of unique skills, regarding local languages for example, that would confine them to reading each other's work and engaging in internal debates about the grammatical structure of Pashto, to continue with the example of specific local language expertise. To condense an argument about the dire intellectual straits Afghanistan faces, I would say that a combination of limited data, weak theory, and overt politicization has kept the scholar-ship on Afghanistan not only insulated from the wider academy but also disaggregated on its own terms.

These features of Afghanistan scholarship are impediments to growth on its own terms and expansion in comparative terms, and they need to be surmounted. The body of this chapter will scrutinize some of the normative canonical understandings of Afghanistan while also offer-ing conceptual and historiographic antidotes to the malaise of orthodox scholarship on the country. I will first review the biography of the founder of the Afghan state, then turn to the crucial colonial period before mov-ing to consider features of Afghan nationalism and the intellectual his-tory of U.S.–Afghan relations. Along the way, I will address various forms of migration, Kabul-centrism, and externalities.

Reconsidering the Origin of the State

The origins of Afghanistan are critical, and understanding the processes at work as Afghanistan emerged can be used creatively to build a multi-ethnic sense of nationalism in Afghanistan. Toward that end it is worth reviewing the biography of the founder of the polity. It is commonly understood that Ahmad Shah (1723–1773) unified the Pashtun tribes and founded Afghanistan in 1747.[3] As the founding father of the country, he is known as Ahmad Shah Baba. The standard narrative relates that, upon his coronation, Ahmad Shah changed his name, and that of his tribe, from Abdali to Durrani.[4] A final component of the master narrative of Afghanistan's origin is that Ahmad Shah wrote poetry in Pashto, a fact that partisans of a particular vision of the Afghan past cite to validate his Pashtun identity.[5]

This abbreviated foundational narrative of the country is often invoked but rarely elaborated upon, and to my knowledge it has not been academi-cally interrogated. Cursory examination of the available evidence raises a number of theoretical questions and destabilizes the dominant narra-tive about Afghanistan's origins and cultural constitution. In the first instance, Ahmad Shah was born in Multan, a province of Sind in Mughal India. His family subsequently moved to the region between Herat and Mashhad in Safavid Khorasan. Ahmad Shah entered the service of Nadir

Shah Afshar, the Turco-Persian ruler who terminated Ghilzai Pashtun rule in Iran and the territory that is now Afghanistan and established a fifth school of Jafari law that synthesized elements of Shia and Sunni Islam.[6] Upon Nadir's death, Ahmad Shah intercepted a caravan of booty from Nadir's conquest of Delhi that was moving toward Persia. This interception occurred near Kandahar, where he was coronated through the agency of a Sufi master named Sabir Shah. Ahmad Shah's official history is modeled on Nadir Shah's, and all of Ahmad Shah's known correspondence with the Ottomans and the British in India is written in Persian.[7] Ahmad Shah continued Nadir Shah's pattern of invading India to sustain the world's last nomadic conquest empire. Ahmad Shah is buried in Kandahar, and his son and successor, Timur Shah (1748–1793), moved the capital of the polity to Kabul to be closer to the Shia Qizilbash community Nadir Shah had transferred there (in the Chindawul section of the city) as a "rear guard" during his invasion of the Mughal empire in India.[8]

A few additional details compromise the clarity and demonstrate the fragility of the founding narrative of Afghanistan as it is commonly transmitted. In the first geographic instances, Ahmad Shah's birth in Multan, his rearing and political maturation in Persia, and his coronation and burial in Kandahar are difficult to fit within typical Kabul-centric territorial conceptions of Afghanistan.[9] Ahmad Shah's portrayal as a staunchly Sunni unifier of the Pashtun tribes become less clear the more one considers his political attachment to Nadir Shah, whose polity was imbricated with Shias and Shiism, and recalls that both Ahmad and Nadir Shah engaged in sustained hostilities with Ghilzais. A conspicuous claim, then puzzling abandonment, of cultural substance is reflected in the general lack of celebration and circulation of Ahmad Shah's collection of Pashto poetry. Similarly, Ahmad Shah's name change from Abadali to Durrani cries out for critical analysis in lieu of the near-hagiographical acceptance it has thus far been accorded.

Even this most rudimentary expansion and rereading of Ahmad Shah's biography raises a number of questions about mobility, territoriality, cultural complexity, tribal dynamics, Islamic diversity, external relations, the relationship between the Persian and Pashto languages, and the so-called ethnic constitution of Afghanistan. These are in principle theoretical questions about an easily expanded data set that carry political implications, whereas the prevailing practice is to de-theorize and hyperpoliticize interpretations of limited information about Afghanistan. The tendency to overly Pashtunize Ahmad Shah's biography comes at the expense of fully appreciating the full range of his cultural experiences and interactions and embracing the historic reality of his fluidity of movement across geographic and cultural boundaries. This intellectual posture toward Afghanistan has its origins in British colonialism. Indeed, the word *Afghanistan,* which was absent in Ahmad Shah's lexicon and worldview, comes to us primarily as an enduring effect of British colonialism.

As a general rule, colonialism works toward the standardization of certain interpretations of local populations over less-persuasive or less-marketable ones. This happens in a large number of ways, including through the production and deployment of hegemonic texts about the group or area in question. In the case of Afghanistan's colonial encounter, one book set the intellectual parameters for knowing the country from Kabul-centric and Pashtun-centered viewpoints when in fact Kabul is the most exceptional, most unique, and least typical location in the country, and the caricatures of Pashtuns that are conspicuously devoid of Pashtun views and voices *mutatis mutandis* deny and/or distort the breadth of their interactions with other populations.[10]

Contrary to the long-held flippancies about the fundamentally inconsequential impact of British colonialism on Afghanistan, it is becoming increasing clear that the British exerted a formative impact on Afghanistan in territorial, economic, political, demographic, and intellectual terms.[11] To fully appreciate the range and depth of the colonial impact on Afghanistan, one must abandon the untenable assumption that failed colonial wars leave inconsequential legacies on societies subjected to and left behind by them. The epistemological impact of British colonialism determined the categories used to understand Afghanistan, the rules for how the categories operate in their own right and in relation to each other, and how those categories can and should be acted upon. To demonstrate these aspects of colonial knowledge formation, we will briefly examine the telescoping of geographic conceptualizations and the shifting engagements of Afghan languages before outlining the American appropriation of those British models of colonial conduct toward Afghanistan.

The first written communications between the British and Ahmad Shah occurred in 1760–1761. Henry Vansittart (b. 1732), the officer who handled this Persian-language correspondence for the British East India Company, was also responsible for first bringing the Pashto language to the formal institutional attention of the colonial authorities.[12] In 1784 he submitted an abridged Persian translation of a Pashto-language text, wherein Pathans are identified as Afghan "sects" in India, and a separate, shorter sample of the Pashto language to Sir William Jones (1746–1794), the founder of the Asiatic Society of Bengal. Vansittart described the combined history of Afghans and Pathans and the usage by those groups of the Pashto and Persian languages. The history of these Pashto-speaking, Persian-writing Afghans and Pathans conveyed a description of their descent from one of the lost Jewish tribes, a feature of the narrative that piqued Jones's interest.[13]

Jones was an accomplished philologist who commanded multiple languages. Based upon the similarities he identified between languages, including Greek, Latin, Arabic, Persian, and Sanskrit, Jones developed the idea of a common, ancestral Indo-European language from which those distinct languages evolved. The Indo-European idea and his multiyear engagement with Pashto and other Indian-language materials, including lexicographical works and narrative genealogical histories, allowed Jones to hypothesize in 1790 an Afghan connection to, or rather descent from, the lost Israelite tribes through the Chaldaic language. The Indo-European idea generally, and the Jewish descent theory specifically, were organizing ideas for a large body of subsequent scholarship on Afghans, Pathans, Pashto-speakers, and their migrations and interactions with other linguistic communities across a great deal of time and space.

In many ways the cultural and historical complexity that marked the communities inhabiting this space was organized, simplified, and standardized by Mountstuart Elphinstone (1779–1859), whose book *An Account of the Kingdom of Caubul* (1815) positioned Pashto speakers as the original Afghans who speak Pashto, a language said to have limited literary value, but who use Persian in spoken and especially in written form.[14] Elphinstone understood that the rulers of Kabul were Persian speakers who did not use Pashto, and the widespread use of interpreters and translators throughout his extensive entourage may help explain why linguistic conduct did not feature into Elphinstone's evaluation of identity and its politics in this environment. As the first diplomatic emissary from the East India Company to the Durrani court, Elphinstone's portrait of a Kabul-centered Afghan polity dominated by Persian speakers claiming Pashtun identity was officially sanctioned even before the book's publication. Elphinstone's view received wide circulation and made a deep and permanent institutional impact in the context of the first Anglo-Afghan war when it was reprinted and mass-circulated to serve as a military handbook for the invading Army of the Indus and the immense and growing global imperial apparatus that produced and sustained it.

Elphinstone's understanding remains intact and unassailable until today, and in that sense his work established the epistemological parameters within which Afghanistan has been and can be understood.[15] Elphinstone portrayed the Durrani elite as urbanized, culturally Persianized, and somehow tame, while the majority "primordial" (my word) inhabitants of the kingdom in the rural zone that dominated the landscape were not only Pashto speakers but also practitioners of a normative tribal code of conduct known as *Pashtunwali*. Social and cultural relations and political hierarchies in this context were conceptualized through the Indo-European idea, with its genealogical idiom that rationalized Elphinstone's understandings and glosses of similarities and distinctions among Afghans and Pashtuns. The intellectual legacy of Elphinstone is a stultifying tautology of Afghanistan where Pashtuns rule but can't be ruled, and where a Kabul-centered Afghan-Pashtun state exists in a permanent condition of discord with a rural Pashtun-Afghan nation. Elphinstone's version of the Kabul Kingdom came through the Persian language and translations of it; he demonstrated no knowledge of, and did not express the need or desire to know, Pashto. It simply was not necessary for knowing the country.

Henry George Raverty (1825–1906) was the colonial official who took the Pashto language most seriously and gained the greatest competency with it.[16] Raverty's career reveals a trend toward the military monopolization of Pashto language instruction and the market for printed Pashto texts during the nineteenth century. The British military co-optation of the Pashto language was motivated in part by a desire to issue orders to large and growing numbers of Pathan regiments under colonial command that were used to gain strategic footholds throughout South Asia, indeed across the entire British imperial world system until it collapsed in the 1940s. British military needs marginalized the academic and intellectual questions and priorities concerning the colonial engagement of Pashto.

Afghanistan began to appear consistently on maps in the 1860s and 1870s, but it was not until after the second Anglo-Afghan war (1878–1880), during the reign of Abdul Rahman (r. 1880–1901), that all of its borders were established. Abdul Rahman was enabled by and dependent upon British money, weapons, and technical expertise to execute his internally aggressive form of rule. The colonial subsidies Abdul Rahman received annually amounted to approximately 15 percent more than the revenue base generated by the Afghan state prior to accepting his British appointment as the amir of Kabul. There was a drastic reconfiguration of the human, animal, and commodity traffic flows between Afghanistan and British India during that time, becoming far more limited in volume, much more restricted to the Khyber Pass corridor between Kabul and Peshawar, and subject to substantially more surveillance by the Afghan and British Indian states. Far from celebrating Pashtunness of any sort, Abdul Rahman used coercive means attained through colonial subsidies to concentrate considerable violence upon Pashtuns (not just during the Ghilzai Rebellion of 1896–1897) and other groups (not limited to the Shia Hazaras, who were branded as heretics, and non-Muslim Kafir populations, who were forcibly converted in the 1890s). Abdul Rahman emphasized and invoked Sunni Islamic rhetoric and sharia courts—not Pashtunwali—as a way to manage the linguistic and tribal identities that were reconfigured as the country took shape.[17] By the turn of the twentieth century, Afghanistan had assumed its now-familiar position as an impoverished economic dependency on the margins of the global capitalist system where state coercion alienated wider society.[18] Despite a brief, third Anglo-Afghan war in 1919, the British continued to engage Afghanistan diplomatically and economically and employ Pathans militarily through the World Wars and until they formally relinquished their colonies in South Asia and the Middle East in 1947 and 1948, respectively.

The British colonial construction of Afghanistan occurred on many levels: cartographically, diplomatically, economically, and through actual and fictional historical narratives. In rudimentary terms, the territorial mobility, multilingualism, cultural dynamism, and heterogeneity Vansittart and Jones encountered in the late eighteenth century were homogenized, simplified, and standardized by Elphinstone a generation later in the early nineteenth century. Elphinstone's Kabul-centered and Persianized views of Afghans were theoretically hinged on the unified structure of Pashtun genealogies that in practice masked a number of tensions and contradictions insofar as the Pashto language and identities packaged around it are concerned. In terms of state engagement as measured by resources expended, British India and its heir Pakistan have acted with far greater consequence than Afghanistan in providing institutional frameworks for the cultivation of Pashto language study, teaching, and printing, again in large measure for military application.[19]

Whereas Vansittart, Jones, and Raverty emphasized migration and the Pashto language as routes to understanding Afghans, Elphinstone established a Kabul-centered Persian discourse for Afghanistan that elided the place of Pashto and the complications of that language's relationship to Persian. Elphinstone's simplified treatment of Afghans and Afghanistan, curiously purged of, but still haunted by, Pashto and Pashtuns, was officially institutionalized and popularly circulated during the period of British colonialism in South Asia.

In the twentieth century the influence of Elphinstone's views was amplified and standardized through their adoption by Afghan officials and intellectuals between the World Wars and American academics and policymakers in the Cold War era. In many ways the impact of Elphinstone's Kabulized and Persianized treatment of Afghans and Afghanistan, and his tautological reasoning about Pashtuns both dominating state politics and successfully resisting the state, are directly evident today in both Afghanistan and the United States. The most ironic gaps in the colonial rendition of Pashtun-dominated Afghanistan are the Pashto language and Pashtun voices, but also routinely edited out of this view are non-Pashtuns generally; minority groups such as Hindus, Sayyids, Qizilbash, and other Shia communities; and Sufis and Sufi orders, in particular.

Nationalism, Cold War Anthropology, and Neocolonial Knowledge

In the twentieth century the Afghan state undertook a number of domestic initiatives to cultivate a sense of an Afghan nation. These activities included archaeological investigations, museum displays, and military parades. State-sponsored writing was particularly significant in this regard, and some of the government texts that promoted Afghan nationality were the annual *Salnama* series, the newspapers *Anis* and *Islah,* and school textbooks. Newspapers, schoolbooks, and other techniques and formats for locating and narrating the nation in Afghanistan were in large measure inspired and mediated by nationalist movements in the Middle East and South Asia that were in turn imbricated within the global historical course of colonialism.

The traditions invented by the Afghan state for the Afghan nation include three colonial apparitions that assumed particular appeal during the period between the two World Wars. The first was the idea of Afghans as Aryans, which was adopted as the primary means by which to surmount the increasingly apparent ethnic distinctions in Afghanistan. The Aryan idea was excavated in practice using the science of archaeology, itself a field of study that carries a weighty colonial heritage. In Afghanistan state-sponsored minds intellectually situated the Aryan idea within the Indo-European framework of historical reasoning that Jones developed.[20] The Afghan National (Kabul) Museum was established in 1919, and in keeping with classic colonial principles, a number of foreign archaeologists, including French, German, Italian, and Japanese teams, led the way on digs that unearthed objects of Afghan national historic value at a number of sites between the 1920s and 1940s.[21] Later in the century, Russians, Americans, and other international actors, such as the Agha Khan Institute, have sponsored excavations and renovations and funded exhibitions to provide the Afghan state a sense of its own pre-Islamic archaeological past.[22] The second identity marker for the Afghan nation developed by the state was that of a community of Muslims historically united in the service of jihad against non-Muslims, particularly against Hindus and Christians. Abdul Rahman used the rhetorical tool of jihad against external powers but also against internal dissidents and heretics.[23] And of course we cannot forget that the trope of Islamic jihad and fanaticism was also diligently cultivated and craftily deployed by the British in India and elsewhere in their global empire.[24] The punch line here is that the Afghan state, and Abdul Rahman in particular, capitalized both rhetorically and materially on a discourse of jihad that was in many, but not all, ways colonially produced and marketed. The third way in which the Afghan state reproduced colonial visions of itself was through a nearly exclusive focus on Kabul, as first propounded in the title of Elphinstone's foundational imperial digest. In many ways Kabul represents the Afghan state, and vice versa, a near-symmetrical reflection induced to a great extent by colonial power.[25]

The Afghan state also took episodic steps to relabel administrative divisions, state medals, and civil and military titles using Pashto terms.[26] The state at least once compelled government officials to undergo Pashto language training.[27] The efforts to Pashtunize titles and labels met with some durable, if limited, successes, but they also resulted in both linguistic inconsistencies and social hostilities of the type that caused some projects, such as civil servant language tutorials, to be abandoned shortly after implementation. In the twentieth century, Pashto had a precarious place in the Afghan state structure, and in the twenty-first century, despite some developments that may be seen as "advances," the Afghan state structure and key segments of its elite remain alienated from large numbers of the Pashto-speaking base of the Afghan nation. This situation can be remedied with an inventive redeployment of historical ammunition. The first step on that remedial agenda is to recognize the fundamental problem, namely, the blind acceptance of the baseless delusion that the Afghan state is dominated by Pashtuns, when in fact the overwhelming weight of the historical evidence clearly indicates that the Afghan state is at its core a Persianate construct on the margins of which, yes, there is also evidence of Pashtuns and Pashto. The point here is that those exceptional, limited, and episodic appearances of Pashto and Pashtuns in the Afghan state prove the rule of it being historically dominated by Persianate structures and actors. One could go a step further and convincingly argue that Afghan state authorities and institutions have in fact spent much of their time and resources trying to keep Pashtuns out of the system!

The American academic and political engagement of Afghanistan is fully nested within Cold War politics and U.S. intelligence gathering.[28] Louis Dupree, a World War II veteran and, it is very important to note, a trained archaeologist who studied under the physical anthropologists Carleton Coon and Earnest Hooton at Harvard, became the point person or new colonial "man on the spot" for the American global project that was emerging out of the British one. As indicated by "The Inward Looking Society," chapter 12 of his important book, *Afghanistan* (1973), Dupree was particularly adept at eliding internal movement and external connections in Afghanistan that served well in perpetuating exotic portrayals of an isolated, violent, and xenophobic mountain people.[29] Despite the obvious distinctions between the two, there are a number of important similarities between Louis Dupree and Mountstuart Elphinstone.[30] These include a decidedly Kabul-centric view of Afghanistan, an extremely weak or total lack of command of the Persian language, and nearly complete inattention to the Pashto language. Dupree's *Afghanistan* is encyclopedic in scope and as such resembles Elphinstone's holistic account of the Kabul kingdom. Just as a number of variables conspired to have Elphinstone set the standard for British colonial ways of knowing Afghanistan, as the first fully credentialed American academic emissary, dedicated Cold Warrior, and confirmed "lover" of the country, Dupree was considered the first and last word of expertise and authoritative knowledge about Afghanistan in American policymaking circles.[31]

Perhaps predictably, in one of the last publications before his death Dupree paid tribute to Elphinstone by stating that anything said about Afghan society after him (Elphinstone) is merely a "footnote."[32] Dupree's legacy lives on through his widow, Nancy, the Honorary Grandmother of Afghanistan according to the Afghan Embassy in Washington, and a number of intellectual protégés such as David B. Edwards and state intelligence agents such as Milton Bearden.[33] The influence of Dupree is very strong in the Human Terrain System teams that are at present among the lynchpins of the U.S. government's reinvigorated militarized policy in Afghanistan.[34]

Elphinstone and Dupree appear as two panes of the same colonial window on Afghanistan. Through the binoculars their writings and careers jointly form, it becomes clear the American imperial apparatus has reproduced much of the British colonial mindset toward Afghanistan across a wide range of public and private institutions and organizations. It is particularly interesting to note the historic resemblance between the American sequestration and monopolization of Pashto language training at military institutions, particularly the Defense Language Institute at Monterey, and the British structuring of Pashto language training through an examination hierarchy within its army officer training programs at military colleges in the Punjab Province after its establishment in 1849 and in the North-West Frontier Province after its creation in 1901.[35]

A Call for More Evidence and Alternative Reasoning

Readers will benefit from a speedy review of how the instability of eighteenth-century colonial knowledge about Afghans was regimented during the nineteenth-century construction of Afghanistan, then reified by the Afghan state in the twentieth century, and is now intellectually underpinning the American project in the country in the twenty-first century. Early British Indian thought about Afghans involved sophisticated forms of knowledge informed by local language competency and detailed attention to linguistic interaction that was organized to help explain the history of human migrations across Eurasia. We have seen how Jones's Indo-European theorizing and the body of scholarship it formed was displaced in colonial knowledge structures about Afghans by Elphinstone and the diplomatic and scholarly mission he led. The work of the Elphinstone team simplified and stabilized a complex and moving body of knowledge and resulted in the institutionalization of a partial, inconsistent, and contradictory set of claims and positions about Afghans and their languages and polity.

Abdul Rahman exploited the ambiguities of colonial formulae about Afghans, particularly regarding the place of Durrani dynastic authority in conceptions of Pashtun tribal dynamics, while also capitalizing on colonial paranoia about the potential for jihad among the North-West Frontier Pathan tribes. In the first half of the twentieth century, Afghan state officials adopted and implemented mainstream colonial views of themselves in a number of national identity-making projects, while also relying on multiple foreign governments to fund research into its own archaeological history. During the Cold War, American academic production and, through it, U.S. government policy appropriated and thus reinforced British colonial paradigms. American perpetuation of British colonial forms of knowledge continues today in many ways. So, too, in the international network of nongovernmental organizations, one encounters British colonial ideas uncritically received and acted upon by parasitic swarms of old experts and new specialists on Afghanistan operating and profiting under America's watch.

The durable power of colonial scholarship on Afghanistan is reflected today by its wholesale adoption and full immunity from critique by Afghans, Americans, and other international actors. The failure of British and subsequent imperial projects in Afghanistan has been predicated on the fault lines of colonial forms of knowledge about the country. More importantly, the failure of the Afghan state to intellectually engage its colonial inheritance has impeded it from successfully articulating a coherent and durable national identity.

Put differently, colonialism created an Afghan state, but the format of the polity and discourse about it has left this state unable to fabricate an effective sense of nation. Contrary to the course of other, more successful nationalist movements in the colonial world, many of which certainly reproduced colonial structures in the postcolonial era, the Afghan state and its nationalism have neither consciously embraced and expanded upon its colonial predicates, nor rejected them in the process of formulating original, autonomous, and distinct narratives of its own history, culture, society, and polity. In Afghanistan the colonial period as a whole remains a largely unknown time. As such the many important economic, cultural, and ideological transformations accompanying the colonial period have been denuded of influence and made taboo within Afghan society, on the one hand, while simultaneously, on the other hand, the Afghan state was appropriating and reproducing highly militarized and racialized colonially constructed visions of itself. This historical contradiction needs an intellectual resolution.

The primary colonial inheritance and impediment to the Afghan state's ability to nurture an inclusive and effective nationalism is the idea of Pashtun dominance. As we have seen, the Pashtun domination thesis is a trope, a tautological colonial construction, insofar as it traps explanations of the successes and failures of the state and local resistance to its influence in a box of circular reasoning about Pashtuns. In summary retort to established predicates, I ask: How could the Afghan state be both dominated and undermined by Pashtuns? Any answer to this rhetorical and practical question should at the very least prompt inquiries about how the state and tribes understand and practice Pashtunwali differently. But yet even basic questions about the presence of Pashtunwali or elements comprising it in the state structure have never been asked. Notwithstanding some notable exceptions, such as James Caron, Lutz Rzehak, and others in this volume, it still remains generally the case that the majority of Afghan and foreign scholars have yet to transcend colonially essentialized and caricatured versions of who the Pashtuns are and what motivates them to do what they do.

A first step in the critique of colonial, national, and international forms of knowledge about Afghanistan is to ask the following questions: In what contexts and in what ways has the Durrani elite of Afghanistan practiced Pashto linguistically or otherwise, and how have Afghan state institutions historically incorporated Pashto and Pashtuns? How has the Afghan state been articulated to serve the collective interests of Pashtuns? When did the Afghan state and its personnel speak, practice, or otherwise engage Pashto, and how were Pashtuns as a whole involved in those activities and efforts? Answers to these basic questions regarding the Afghan state's Pashto credentials immediately flounder and soon sink the colonially constructed intellectual battleship that is counterproductively floated on and firing against the idea of Pashtun domination of Afghanistan.

Conclusions

Rethinking the postulates behind the faulty colonial predicate of Pashtun domination of Afghanistan draws attention to the functions of territoriality, mobility, and the boundaries of identity in the national discourse. A logical starting point to apply this "rethinking of boundaries" agenda is with the founder of the polity, Ahmad Shah. In an epistemological spirit, then, it is useful to ponder the consequences of creatively using Ahmad Shah's non-Kabul and non-Pashtun experiences to make him, not a Pashtun first and an Afghan secondarily, but an Afghan first and someone who appreciated Pashto and Pashtuns as an additional feature of identity. Such an incorporative rather than exclusionary cultural disposition is surely possible, but the political feasibility of such daring intellectual maneuvers remains an open question to say the very least. The fact remains that to fully and realistically embrace Ahmad Shah entails reckoning with his birth in Multan, his political maturation in Persia, his military service in a polity highly inflected by Shiism, his personal relationship to Nadir Shah, his Sufi connections, and his ties to Kandahar, at least. The intellectual and political move toward an expanded and more detailed appreciation of Ahmad Shah should not be seen as diluting his Pashtun-ness but rather as broadening his Afghan-ness. This is one important example of how epistemology can be a powerful tool in the service of a new nation-building project that works against the ineffectual, exclusionary, and colonially inspired versions of Afghan nationality and state building.

It has long been common intellectual practice to lump together the categories Afghan, Pashtun, and Pathan. However, once data-driven, historically, and theoretically informed questions about the relationships among Afghans, Pashtuns, and Pathans are asked, the house of cards that is their unison begins to collapse. What becomes apparent in their stead are questions about the external experiences and connections rulers of Kabul bring with them to power. Historically Ahmad Shah was tied to the world beyond whatever the nonexistent "Afghanistan" could have meant for him. Further consider the period 1839 to 2001: Shuja's reinstatement, Abdul Rahman's appointment, Nadir Shah's return, Zahir Shah's migrations, and Hamid Karzai's biography. Does not the connection to and dependency on external resources undermine the political legitimacy of colonially propagated personalities and regimes in Kabul, at least in principle, for ordinary Pashtuns and Afghans, at any time?

This question should be of interest not only to Afghan nationalists but to academics interested in Afghanistan. It arises from a combination of historical realities in Afghanistan involving migration, local urban–rural relations, and interactions with the wider regional and global environment. Any answer to this rhetorical question should draw attention to the most elementary and important hermeneutic rules: Afghanistan is interactive, not isolated; dynamic, not stable; diverse, not homogeneous; and dependent on, rather than autonomous from, its surroundings. One practical implication of this ontology is that until those positioned as Afghan elites can consistently and publicly recognize and engage their personal identities and external dependencies, the traditional Pashtun bogeyman will, as Hollywood dictates, continue to jump out of the village closet and terrify the urbanites so the United States and its allies can continue to bomb in horror. Afghanistan may be on the brink of extinction. It is time to ask difficult questions as to what it was, is, and can yet still be "of, by and for" the Afghan people, constitutionally and otherwise.

6 / How Tribal Are the Taliban?

Thomas Ruttig

Recent developments in Afghanistan have underscored that there is still an immense lack of understanding—and even of interest—with regard to the nature of the Taliban movement. As a result, there is considerable confusion as to whether the largest and most influential insurgent movement is mainly driven by ethnic, religious, or political motives. In this chapter I aim to clarify the often complex forces that shape the Afghan Taliban movement. I explore several central questions, including this: Are the Taliban a Pashtun tribal or even nationalist force, or are they, as they claim to be, supra-ethnic Islamists who do not acknowledge tribal, ethnic, and linguistic differences but "only recognize Muslims"? In addition, I discuss the place of tribes and their institutions within Afghan society; distinguish between what is real and what is myth, as constructed by Afghans and also by foreign observers; and then discuss the origins of the Taliban movement, the (limited) role of Islamist ideology, the extent to which it can be considered a Pashtun nationalist movement, and whether the Taliban have morphed into a "Neo-Taliban" movement.

Even though the complex issues of reconciliation and reintegration in Afghanistan are currently being discussed and even shaped into program, there is an immense lack of understanding regarding the Taliban. Claims made in the context of psychological warfare have taken precedence over real analysis—for example, that the Taliban are simply "terrorists" or linked with the drug economy, or that most of their foot soldiers are in it primarily for the money. This lack was reflected in Western governments' approach at and after the international Afghanistan conference in London in January 2010, when the still-underdeveloped "Afghanistan Peace and Reconciliation Program" (APRP) of the Afghan government received political approval and even some financial commitments. It continued in the mainly welcoming response from Western capitals with regard to the June 2010 National Consultative Peace Jirga in Kabul. But it also was evident at the Afghan-led discussions at the jirga itself. President Hamid Karzai reflected on the outlines of the APRP—which was presented to the London conference and to parts of the donor community in Kabul—in his opening speech to the delegates of the jirga. But the document was not presented to or distributed among them. In this major government document, although still a draft, the criteria for political accommodation with the insurgents had not yet become clear. This reflects the still-enormous lack of understanding of who the insurgents (and their main composite element, the Taliban movement) are and what aims they pursue. Alternately, perhaps, it reflects the view that a differentiated analysis is not necessary for the implementation of the program, of which President Karzai's Western partners have unambiguously adopted only the reintegration side.

The National Consultative Peace Jirga, as well as the wave of arrests of Afghan Taliban leaders in Pakistan in January and February 2010, shows that motives of power and control still dominate the "peace and reconciliation" agenda.[1] No interest was shown in how common ground can be created at either the national or the regional levels. Discussions about whether there exist "moderate" Taliban (that is, Taliban interested in talking or negotiating) have overshadowed deeper questions about the character of the movement and how it affects prospects for political accommodation. The answers to these questions have important implications for the debate on reconciliation and reintegration, as they provide an indication of whether and under which circumstances the Taliban may be ready to join a political process and what they would want to get out of it.[2] The question of how "tribal" the Taliban are is also significant in the debate on whether and how so-called "tribal" or "community defense" forces can or should be used to push back the influence of the Taliban in certain areas of Afghanistan.

Pashtun Tribes, between Myth and Reality

Much has been written about the Pashtunwali, the code of conduct and way of life of the Pashtuns. But much of it has been mystified, both by Afghans and by foreign observers, not least because—in the light of more than thirty years of conflict—the past radiates a golden light of nostalgia. To understand which roles tribes and their institutions are playing today, a lot of rubble has to be cleared away. Although Pashtunwali is often described in its ideal form and as static, it actually evolves and differs in time and space. Individuals have started to dominate institutions that originally were the embodiment of collective interests. With its core principles of "honor" and "courage" (*nang* and *tora*), "hospitality" (*melmastia*), "seeking shelter by submission" and "revenge" (*nenawata* and *badal*), "a moratorium on a conflict and the deposit to guarantee it"(*tiga* and *baramta*), its tribal institutions like the "the tribal leader and the village elder" (*khan* and the *malek*), the tribal assembly and its reinforcement instrument (*jirga* and the *arbakai*), as well as the Pashtuns' notorious fragmentation, embodied in the principle of *tarburwali* (the enmity between "cousins"), Pashtunwali is a complicated—and unwritten—system. The knowledge of it is preserved by the whitebeards (*spingiri*) and the *jirgadar,* those "who have [the knowledge about] the jirga."[3] It is not secret knowledge and is transferred to the younger generations by example: young boys are supposed to be present at jirgas and see how the elders do it.

Already in the 1970s, Christian Sigrist used the terms *acephalous* and *segmented societies* for this kind of social organization, with its hierarchy of loyalties between relatives from the level of the family (*kor,* in Pashto, "house") on the bottom up to the level of nation (*mellat*), country (*mamlakat*), or fatherland (*watan*).[4] Loyalty is extended only when the particular level on the hierarchy pyramid is externally threatened. For example, if some *kor* of one tribe would be in latent conflict with other *kor* of the same tribe in one particular area—about land, forest, or water use—these *koruna* would stick together and defend themselves with a higher level of loyalty when threatened by an outside group. On the topmost ("national") level this would mean that when all Afghan ethnic groups are threatened by outside aggression, they cooperate with each other. This was proven during the Soviet occupation in the 1980s.

The Pashtuns are one, if not the largest, of the world's tribal societies. Kinship as a principle of social organization, nevertheless, is nothing special to the Pashtuns. Most of what is said, for example, about the Somalis would make sense for the Pashtuns as well:

> All Somalis are born into this social structure and because it defines a person's relationship to other Somalis and non-Somalis, kinship is a critical source of an individual's identity. Knowledge of a person's clan can enable one to identify their elders, deduce where they reside and whom they are likely to vote for in an election. . . . Kin groups form alliances, divide and realign in response to internal and external events and processes. The clan or sub-clan that a person identifies with (or is identified with) will depend on the prevailing context and issue at hand, such as access to environmental resources, the control of real-estate, competition for political office or a collective response to security threats. The tradition of exogamous marriage means that Somalis can have relatives in several clans dispersed over large geographical areas. . . . Clans and genealogies are therefore dynamic social constructs that can be subject to different interpretations and are used to describe and validate changing social and political relationships. They are, as Luling has described, "not only good to fight with (or play politics and do business with) but good to think with.". . . . In the context of state collapse and in the absence of state institutions and other forms of political organisation the kinship system provide[s] a structure for inter-group relations and governance, for organising and managing violence and for organising trade.[5]

All Pashtuns know their current particular place on their people's intricate genealogical chart, with its hundreds of "tribes," "subtribes," "clans," and *kor,* which derives from (assumed) common ancestors.[6] The same is true for the individual Taliban fighter. He is able to say exactly to which tribe and subtribe he belongs—unless he decides otherwise and sidesteps to the ideological level, often to make a political point. One Taliban interpreter in Kandahar in late 2000 replied with emphasis when asked to which tribe he belongs: "This doesn't matter to me. We are Muslims and do not know [i.e., recognize] tribes."[7]

The place a tribe or subtribe occupies on the Pashtun genealogical chart can change in time and space. A "tribe" might grow and split into "subtribes," and some "subtribe" might become a "tribe" in its own right. For example, the relationship between the Barakzai and the Atsakzai in southern Afghanistan has evolved: the latter was originally a "subtribe" of the former, but people in the region now often put both on the same level when asked which "tribes" live in their particular area. The Atsakzai have grown to become a tribe in their own right. In contrast, sometimes a whole tribe disappears.[8]

A lot of this has to do with the Pashtuns' nomadic origins, as the example of the Babozai tribe, again in southern Afghanistan, illustrates. In Zabul the Babozai are considered a subtribe of the Hotak in the Ghilzai "confederation," but in neighboring Oruzgan they are seen as a Nurzai subtribe in the Durrani "confederation."[9] This seemingly paradoxical situation arose because Babozai groups had migrated from Zabul westward, looking for greener pastures, and must have been accommodated by Nurzai. There are many reports in the literature about how, in past centuries when land was still available, larger tribal groups gave land and/or protection to incoming smaller ones. Such a move would make the newcomers either clients (*hamsaya,* literally "in the same shadow," that is, neighbors) of the host group (mainly when non-Pashtun) or, as in the case of the Pashtun Babozai, a new subtribe of their benefactors. This case demonstrates how unreliable tribal categories are and how tricky it can be if outsiders start treating them as if they were set in stone, such as the Durrani-Ghilzai divide, which is treated by some "tribal analysts" as dogma.

Today, some tribes—particularly in the southern region (Greater Kandahar)—cover such a large area that they are simply too big to have a single leader. The Nurzai, for example, stretch from Kandahar to Herat

Mongols, Protoss, Scots, Germans

Province. How difficult it is under such circumstances to come to a political decision became apparent before the 2005 parliamentary elections:
some Nurzai tribal leaders convened a series of all-Nurzai assemblies,
aiming to field joint candidates on which the whole tribe would concentrate its votes. But no candidate was acceptable to all Nurzai. As a result,
many local Nurzai candidates competed against each other and lost in
many places; the tribe subsequently felt underrepresented in the Wolesi
Jirga. Nurzai activists interviewed later described how it was impossible
to overcome subtribal rivalries and personal egos.[10]

There are, in reality, no permanently fixed places on the Pashtun
genealogical tree and no eternal, unchanging tribal institutions. Much of
what has been said about them are myths, idealized versions of a golden
past that probably never existed in a pure form and definitely not across
the Pashtun areas in the same way. Versions of Pashtunwali differ by
locale. They are locally called *nirkh,* which means "price" and refers to
the different prices used to settle blood feuds, that is, *badal,* which means
"exchange."[11] Some authors identify

> two [major] types of socio-economic organisational settings that are
> reflected in the Pashtuns' "code of honour," according to the predomi-
> nant form of land tenure: the *qalang* group amongst sedentary tribes
> where large, irrigated private landholdings exist and which, as a result,
> is socially stronger stratified (it is named after the tax share-cropper
> tenants must pay to the landlords) and the *nang* group amongst pas-
> toral hill Pashtuns which are socially more egalitarian (named after
> their central value, chivalry).[12]

Furthermore, it is highly doubtful whether there was always *one* undisputed leader at any given time on any given level of the tribal pyramid—
hence, the jirga as an (ideally) egalitarian body where decisions are taken
collectively and based on consensus. Rather, it was more likely that various aspirants fought each other in ongoing competition by exchanging
wealth and wisdom about the jirga for prestige and influence. Power
within a certain tribe or tribal segment likely had an ever-changing equi-
librium. The southern tribes (Durrani and Ghilzai, not the southeastern
tribes of Loya Paktia) know the institution of the *khankhel,* the subtribe
or "clan" from which "traditionally" the leaders of a particular segment of

a tribe, or the whole tribe, often come. But this does not prevent competition or a shift of power from "clan" to "clan."

Such changes are quicker in times of crisis. In the Popalzai tribe, for example, the former *khankhel* led by Muhammad Afzal Khan, who was killed in 1978 under the People's Democratic Party of Afghanistan (PDPA) regime, has been replaced by the Qaranagh, to which the Karzai family belongs (although not undisputedly). Other Popalzai "clans" around Kandahar—and possibly also Taliban deputy Mullah Baradar, who belongs to the same tribe—would dispute that the Karzais are *the* leaders of their tribe.[13] Among the Dzadran in Loya Paktia, the most influential (royalist) Babrakzai family has been effectively replaced by the Haqqani "clan"—the leaders of the Haqqani network, a semiautonomous part of the wider Taliban movement since the 1970s.[14] But even the Haqqanis lead only parts of the tribe, with other "clans"—such as the one of MP Pacha Khan Dzadran—leading other parts.

This lack of a "dynastic principle" among Pashtuns stands in the way of a coherent and continuous tribal leadership. This has been the case even at the very top of the pyramid in the Pashtun-dominated Afghan monarchy over the past centuries. Since 1747, not many rulers were replaced by an obvious heir; most of the time, succession was determined in protracted civil wars between brothers, half-brothers, "cousins," and other pretenders. Succession is also often less than straightforward on a lower level, as seen recently on the side of both the current government and the Taliban. When the leader of the Arghandab Alikozai in Kandahar Province, commander Mullah Naqibullah, died in October 2007, President Karzai "crowned" his son as the new leader of the tribe (putting an honorary turban on his head). Immediately, the Taliban attacked not only Naqibullah's house but also the district center in a fight that was one of the most violent that year, sensing that the president's perceived interference in the affairs of a tribe that is not his own had fueled internal support for them. In another case in neighboring Oruzgan, the 23-year-old Muhammad Daud succeeded his father, Rozi Khan, as governor of Chora district after the latter was killed accidentally in September 2008.[15] Initially welcomed and even elected by the local population (although in the presence of representatives of the provincial government, whom, it can be assumed, no one wanted to contradict at a funeral), Daud soon ran into difficulties and was undermined by a senior uncle who thought that he had more right to the position than the young man. This rival was immediately "adopted" and supported by a very influential local power broker who felt sidelined by the local International Security Assistance Force (ISAF) troops. On the Taliban side, Mullah Dadullah, a commander who had become notorious for his extensive use of suicide bombers and al-Qaida-style rhetoric, was replaced by his younger brother Mullah Mansur after he was killed by NATO forces in May 2005. Mansur then adopted the *takhallus* (surname) "Dadullah" to transfer his brother's image of a martyr to his own person. (He was later demoted by Mullah Omar for repeatedly ignoring instructions.) In other examples, the command over some Taliban fronts in Oruzgan changed to a brother or cousin after the original commander was killed. All three cases show that sons or brothers of tribal leaders often have difficulties filling the shoes of their fathers.

Starting with the 1973 coup, thirty years of conflict and gradual state collapse increasingly weakened and dissolved traditional social and political relations in Afghan society in general and in Pashtun society in particular. Mass migration enforced higher mobility and narrowed the urban–rural gap. This gradually undermined and transformed the traditional relationships of village, tribal, and ethnic communities. New elites challenged the elders and took their places. The younger generations questioned the authority of the "elders," whom they held responsible for these conflicts, or at least for their inability to solve them with the traditional means.

The impact on intratribal cohesion was negative. Many tribal leaders were eliminated by the PDPA regime; others lost their status to the social climbers of the jihad: the armed commanders and drug barons. The Taliban continued the killings. The elders' sons were not able to follow them directly because they lacked their authority. As a result, the jirga as the major conflict-resolving mechanism of the Pashtuns lost much of its authority. The powerful newcomers—on the national as well as on the local level—are able to ignore jirga decisions with impunity. This is illustrated by an almost twenty-year-old land conflict in Chora district (Oruzgan), where a commander dug an irrigation channel and distributed the new land among followers without giving the first right, as tradition and sharia demand, to the immediate neighbors. Challenged by government courts, tribal jirgas, and even mediation by ulama, he is still ignoring all decisions that went against him—thanks to superior firepower and protection from Kabul. Today, might often trumps Pashtunwali and even Islamic law. In an intact Pashtun tribal environment, ignoring jirga and ulama decisions would have been heavily punished.

In many Pashtun tribes, the temporary, egalitarian institution of the jirga has been replaced by a multitude of more-enduring tribal shuras, all of which previously claimed to represent the whole tribe. Some shuras still represent a form of "traditional" self-organization, but many are convened by new strongmen, on either the local or the central level, to demonstrate their own influence vis-à-vis foreigners. This makes them hierarchical in structure, a strong contrast to the egalitarian jirga where ideally all male members of a certain tribe or subtribe (in reality, all land-owning males in some areas, and the *mishran,* the elders of the families, in others) find a consensus about a certain conflict. Meanwhile, a shura deliberates and gives advice to a leader, who then decides whether to make use of it or not. Many Pashtuns now confuse these institutions and use both terms, jirga and shura, interchangeably.[16]

Rising levels of education have also changed the character of tribal representation. Beginning with the educational reforms during King Amanullah's reign (1919–1929), the tribal elites sent their sons to the cities to study. As a result, diaspora communities of certain provinces or tribes emerged in the big cities and grew in numbers. Their members absorbed modern skills and began to use modern means of communication but, at the same time, maintained links to their original *watan* and tribe. In this way influences of modernism penetrated rural communities. Today, many local tribal councils are still headed by the *spingiri* ("whitebeards," the traditional elders) while educated members (engineers or teachers) often deal with "foreign affairs," like contacts with visiting foreigners and the acquisition and implementation of projects. This diaspora–tribe relationship intensifies in times of crisis, such as regime change, when rural communities reintegrate their urbanized members linked with a fallen regime—be it communist or Taliban—smoothly and without too many ideological misgivings. However, in a significant number of cases, tribes were unable to protect the returnees against arrest and being killed after 2001. This forced many of the former Taliban and their original tribal groups back into the movement. Today some key support for the Taliban comes from communities who have prisoners in the Guantanamo system.[17]

The rising population and growing tribes make it physically impossible that, as tradition demands, all males gather in a jirga. This exacerbates the trend that participation in a jirga reflects growing social differentiation. While, on the one hand, the institution of the jirga is crumbling or changing its features under pressure from modernization and conflict, on the other hand, the use of traditional institutions of conflict regulation in times of crises is being revived as a fallback position. When the government is weak or absent, shuras and jirgas fill the local political and administrative vacuum as instruments to maintain links with the outside world. Today, "for the majority of Afghans, disputes are settled, if at all, at the local level by village elders [i.e., jirgas and shuras], district governors, clerics, and police chiefs," without any government role and often without it even noticing—estimates of up to 80 percent of all conflicts. In particular, jirgas and shuras are perceived as "more accessible, more efficient (in terms of time and money), perceived as less corrupt, and more trusted by Afghans compared to formal state courts."[18]

At the same time, the Kabul government and its international allies neglected and failed to support initiatives of key Pashtun tribes that aimed at reestablishing "(inner-)tribal solidarity" or "unity" in the post-2001 period. This left those (non-Islamist) tribal forces isolated, deprived them of funds, and weakened them vis-à-vis the resurging Taliban. As early as 2003 the Mangal Central Shura in the southeastern region implemented a decision that banned poppy growing on the tribe's territory, an area of the Mangal tribe that stretches over a number of districts in two neighboring provinces, Paktia and Khost. This was completely ignored by Kabul and external donors, including the UK, then the lead country for drug control. Donors failed to reward the Mangal tribe for this unilateral decision, even in the slightest way, concentrating on the eastern region exclusively. Later the Mangal committed themselves to defend their territory against the Taliban by a traditional Pashtun pact *(tarun)*. The Mangal also played a prominent part in the Tribal Solidarity Council that brought together Paktia's and Khost's major tribes in 2003–2004, an initiative that was met with the same ignorant response from Kabul.

The same neglect happened to the Dzadran Unity Meeting—the Dzadran being a particularly Taliban-influenced tribe—with two thousand participants in the spring of 2007 in Dwamanda, Khost Province.[19] Today, the Mangal Central Shura—left alone—barely exists anymore, a number of shuras compete for leadership, and the Dzadran remain deeply split, offering easy inroads for the Haqqani network.[20] The Mangal area, peaceful in 2003–2004, now is considered by the UN to be even more volatile than the Dzadran areas.

Kabul's fateful decision to pay self-defense groups (arbaki), which are nonpermanent, composed of volunteers, supplied by the tribe, and mandated by the jirga, through the provincial governors' discretionary funds considerably weakened another vital tribal institution that had stabilized Pashtun areas lacking government presence. This payment system started as early as 2001, followed by much closer cooperation in 2004 and 2005, during the first presidential and parliamentary elections when arbaki guarded polling stations, mainly in the southeastern region, in cooperation with the Afghan National Police. Subsequently it became more erratic again, depending on the availability of funds and the relationship of the particular governor with the central government. This left many arbaki unpaid for months at a time and lowered the enthusiasm of individual tribesmen to join this institution. When, for example, Paktia's new governor, Rahmatullah Rahmat—a former UN employee, who therefore was seen with suspicion in Kabul—took over, the government gave him a smaller amount of operational funds than his predecessor had received. Officially, the payment of these funds was stopped altogether. However, some governors with better contacts in Kabul still received them and were able to pay arbaki. At least in the southeast, another period of more permanent government funding of arbaki followed in 2007.[21] Even Afghan leaders apparently failed to understand (or purposely undermined) the character of the arbaki as an instrument controlled by the tribe, explained a tribal elder from the region to this author in April 2007: "In the King's time it was an honor to be member of an arbaki. Its members were provided with e'ana [rations, weapons, and ammunition] by the jirga." To pay the arbaki means to render it uncontrollable when payments stop. It seems that the Kabul government perceives tribal self-organization as a threat rather than a stabilizing factor and prefers a form of patronage that is not inclusive but serves only one side. This neglects the jirga's inherent principle of mitigating conflicting interests and instead tends to deepen conflicts.

Where Did the Taliban Come From?

Looking at the question of where the Taliban historically emerged from as a movement contributes to understanding how strong religious ideas and concepts shape their worldview and their political aims. Are those concepts the basis of their ideology or merely a reaction to political circumstances at a certain time? The Taliban—as a distinct movement—was not part of the first uprisings against the PDPA regime, which took place in June 1978 in the Pech Valley (now Nuristan) and Pasaband (Ghor) and in 1979 in Loya Paktia, Herat, Nangarhar, and elsewhere. Those were mainly spontaneous, community or tribe-based revolts against the new regime's revolutionary land and education reforms.[22] But from the beginning, these revolts incorporated religious motives and sometimes religious forms of organization. Before the Christmas 1979 Soviet invasion, the initial adversary, the pre-1980 PDPA regime, was fought because it was seen as communist and therefore godless by many Afghans. But the Soviet invasion added a strong nationalistic component: to fight a foreign occupation. This let resistance grow considerably.

The ideologically still-heterogeneous resistance was generally reinterpreted as a jihad, that is, as exclusively religiously motivated, while leveling other aspects of it, only after Pakistan officially and exclusively recognized seven Sunni Islamist resistance movements (the Peshawar Seven) and cut off all other resistance groups from incoming Western and Arab financial support.[23] The latter included secular leftists, who fought for ideological reasons and reflected the Moscow–Beijing split of the communist movement, and ethnonationalists. At their expense, the rise of the Islamist *tanzim* (literally, "organization," the Arabic term that Afghans used for the various political-military "parties" that fought in different periods of the civil war) was boosted; and the Taliban—madrasa and mosque students—were part of the various tanzim. The movement emerged from religious networks that were part of the 1978–1989 resistance, a broader movement that saw itself as religiously motivated. In the beginning, Taliban, led by their teachers, organized as madrasa- or mosque-centered networks ("fronts"), mainly linked to *Harakat-e Inqilab-e Islami* and *Hizb-e Islami (Khales)*. They did not constitute a movement of their own yet but were already known as "Taliban fronts."[24] Only when the mujahedin, in the eyes of the later Taliban, violated their own religious principles by not unifying to build the promised Islamic state after the collapse of the Najibullah regime in 1992 but fragmented (*shirk* is considered a major deviation in Islam) in a competition for power, did they establish their own, now ultra-orthodox movement.[25] Significantly, those mujahedin commanders that later became the major Taliban leaders stopped fighting after the collapse of the Najibullah regime and went back to their madrasas to study. As one early Taliban activist related, "Many of us . . . withdrew after Dr. Najib's defeat because we were not interested in the war booty. . . . When we saw that things became worse day by day and factional fighting increased, our central commander Mullah Muhammad Omar Akhund started from Quetta to bring together the Taliban in order to establish peace in Afghanistan."[26]

The primary motivation of the mujahedin, and therefore of the first-generation Taliban of the 1980s, can be described as political, based on a religious infrastructure. Religious motives—the fight of the Muslim true believers against the infidel invaders—were part of their political-military campaign but generally gained an upper hand only in the wake of the Pakistan-induced and Western-supported domination of the anti-Soviet resistance by militant Islamists. When the Taliban emerged as a movement after the Soviet withdrawal in 1992, it became more strongly shaped by religious motives. At its beginning stood a moral reaction against the atrocities and what it saw as a "betrayal of Islam" by the post-Najibullah mujahedin regime, the so-called Islamic State of Afghanistan. Only after its initial moves was the Taliban movement "adopted," supported, and instrumentalized by the Pakistani military establishment.

Although the madrasas or mosques at the center of those original Taliban networks were located on the territory of certain tribes, those tribes were not the primary reference of these fighting Taliban.[27] Mullahs in particular often did not "serve" in their own community or tribe and therefore were considered *pradai* (stranger, outsider) among the strongly in-group-oriented Pashtuns. Socially, as religious service-providers, mainly for births, weddings, and burials, and without land and status and therefore economically dependent on the local khans, mullahs and even higher-ranking ulama were of inferior status.[28] When rulers like Amanullah and later Muhammad Nadir and Zahir Shah, President Muhammad Daud, and even the PDPA regime started paying salaries to a substantial number of clergymen and gave them control over religious foundations (waqf), only the character of dependence changed.[29] They became state bureaucrats in the eyes of the society. Because of their role in the anti-Soviet resistance, the Islamic clergy—particularly the mullahs—rose from social inferiority to a position of political power. This position was strengthened further when the Taliban regime made them its "eyes and ears" in the villages and emphasized the collection of religious taxes (ushr and zakat), traditional income sources for the mullahs. This built on the unofficial power a mullah already had: he was often the only literate person in a village and had "the power of the sermon."[30] After the Taliban regime's fall, some ulama—those at the top of mujahedin tanzim—gained quasi-sacrosanct status as "jihadi leaders." Under the Karzai government, they serve as an unofficial "supreme advisory council" gathered by the president in crucial moments to obtain their support and "blessings" for key policy decisions. This is starting to resemble the functions of Iran's Council of Guardians, without being an official institution. The High Council of Ulama, headed by the late chief of the Supreme Court, Maulawi Fazl Hadi Shinwari, plays a second-tier role in this influential clerical lobby.[31]

Today many Taliban activities in Afghanistan's southeast and south are still centered around networks of ulama-led madrasas and mosques. In the southeast—where the Haqqani network, a semiautonomous entity within the broader Taliban movement, operates—the insurgent networks are largely based on "old or newly created" Deobandi networks. These are particularly strong in Pashtun areas of Ghazni and other Ghilzai areas to the east, like Katawaz in Paktika and Western Paktia as well as in areas of the Dzadran tribe (the border triangle of Paktia, Paktika, and Khost provinces).[32] Often these networks are linked to similar ones on the Pakistani side of the border. The Haqqani network's supply infrastructure in Pakistan was based on madrasas—at least until many of them were destroyed by drone attacks. Sébastien Trives's finding from southeastern

Afghanistan—that religious networks are stronger in flat areas, whereas the tribal "encapsulation" is stronger in mountainous areas—can possibly be applied to southern Afghanistan as well. Here, the role of clerical networks in reviving the Taliban after 2001 is reported, at least from northern Helmand and Zabul.[33]

Most of today's Taliban fighters—in particular the "forced" (majburi) and "discontented" (na-raz) ones in the south who are mainly motivated by local grievances rather than ideology and constitute the movement's bulk—are undoubtedly Pashtuns. This justifies a look at these questions: How rooted are the Taliban in Pashtun tribal society? And are they a "Pashtun" movement, or even *the* movement of the Pashtuns? Like the Pashtuns in general, the Taliban movement, both as a whole and in its constituent elements, is segmented.[34]

Organizationally, the Taliban are a network of networks. Its major networks are the "Kandahari" (or mainstream) Taliban and those of the Haqqani, Mansur, and Khales "clans" in the southeastern and eastern regions. The network of late commander Dadullah (although weakened after his death) in a much stronger way then others cuts across tribes and regions. All these networks, though, are associated with the Taliban mainstream, recognize Mullah Omar as their spiritual guide and its leaders (except possibly Khales junior), and are represented in the Taliban's Leadership Council (rahbari shura). This representation, however, seems to be rather symbolic.[35] The three southeastern and eastern networks are more regional than "tribal." Although their core leadership groups are relatively static and mainly recruited from one tribe, that of the network leader (the Haqqanis from the Dzadran, the Mansurs from the Andar and smaller "allied" tribes, and the Khales from the Khugiani), since 2006 the Haqqani network managed to expand beyond classical tribal boundaries to Wardak, Logar, and Kabul provinces. Also, the Dadullah network expanded into Ghazni Province and further north, beyond the Kandahari realm.[36]

On the local level, the Taliban fronts are strongly based in tribes or their smaller subgroups. Recruitment, operations, and succession patterns follow tribal lines in a majority of cases. These local networks have different levels, a hierarchy depending on how much area they cover, from a village or a cluster of villages (delgai) to a whole district (jabha). Only in exceptional cases—as in the southeast—are those boundaries crossed and the networks become regional. Today, it is estimated that some 80 to 90 percent of Taliban fighters operate in or close to their own communities, not least because most Taliban fighters are part-timers. (Besides, there are also "roving" units and a degree of mobility—often "Kandahari" Taliban are moved in when local groups behave too "softly" with the population—but those are exceptions.) The number of fighters one local commander is able to mobilize also defines his position and influence in the movement. During the Islamic Emirate of Afghanistan (IEA) period—when different networks competed for positions in the government—Taliban commanders tried to save their own fighters by not sending them to the frontlines. Local populations tend to see "external" fighters (those from other provinces and sometimes even districts) with suspicion and support their own. In 2009, for example, in Oruzgan Province, Tokhi groups on the so-called Westbank of Tirinkot decided not to allow "external" fighters to operate in these areas. One major reason is that local fighters tend to avoid exaggerated violence that could create cycles of revenge. Also, the Taliban rulebook for fighters (the *layha*) does not encourage "out of area" activity and regulates it heavily: front commanders on the provincial or district level who want to "carry out jihad" outside their area of origin must notify the commanders in the particular province or district and must "obey their orders."[37]

Significantly, the Taliban movement is plagued by one strong tribal fissure line, the Kandahari–Paktiawal rivalry. From the beginning, the Taliban rahbari shura was dominated by members of the Kandahari tribes, with a somewhat equal representation of the two major Pashtun confederations, the Durrani and Ghilzai, and smaller groups like the Kakar.[38] Meanwhile, southeastern, eastern, and northern Pashtuns are only marginally and symbolically present in the leadership. Former Taliban report a high level of mutual mistrust. Mainstream Taliban did and still do not allow anyone from the southeast or elsewhere to join their inner leadership circle. (Even the only Uzbek in the original leadership has not been replaced.) The two exceptions are Jalaluddin Haqqani and Abdul Latif Mansur, both from Paktia and leaders of their own semiautonomous networks. Haqqani, a southeastern Dzadran, had reportedly been appointed commander of all Taliban troops by Mullah Omar immediately after

9/11. Currently he is often counted among the rahbari shura members—but this is far from certain. Haqqani's commander role was extremely limited in time, and some interpret his appointment as one in which he was handed an impossible mission. Earlier, when he was an IEA minister, he did not have much influence on decision-making and was intentionally kept at the sidelines by the Kandahari Taliban leaders.[39] Mansur's appointment as head of the Taliban's political committee—the one theoretically responsible for "talks"—in early 2009 was inconsequential and does not seem to represent a change in attitude.[40] Mansur's name was not mentioned once in any report or Taliban statement linked to the reconciliation issue. Probably the committee has been downgraded at a time when there is not much chance for dialogue.

Even in their core southwestern region, despite relatively strong "tribal" integration, the leadership has been unable to prevent tribal conflicts from emerging on the local level. In Oruzgan, Durrani, and Ghilzai, commanders have already "traditionally" been competing for the post of provincial commander. Structurally this is underpinned by the existence of two larger separate Taliban networks active in the province: one mainly Durrani-based, operating from the Helmand and Kandahar to the southwest, and another mainly Ghilzai (Hotak, Tokhi) that operates from Zabul to the east. For the time being, the Durrani have the upper hand with the appointment of Rohullah Amin, a Helmand Khugiani. But the fact that he is from a minor tribe might be a sign of compromise. In the same province, a major blunder in 2008—the killing of a local Sufi leader, Pir Agha of Pattan, in Chinartu district—set a spiral of traditional revenge (badal) in motion and led to a deepening Durrani–Ghilzai enmity. This cost the Taliban access to a strategically important area after the local (Durrani) population strongly reacted against the atrocity committed by a Ghilzai commander. It even established a local anti-Taliban community force under a younger brother of the victim that was at that time completely unfunded by the government and managed to keep the Taliban out of this area for a while. This was a clear case where the parochial interests of a local commander overrode the nontribal attitude of the leadership.

At the core of the movement, in its Kandahari mainstream from which its leadership is recruited, the andiwali (comradeship) factor plays a decisive role in keeping the networks together. Among today's Taliban, there are three different types of *andiwal* networks: religious (their original madrasas and mosques), political (their original *tanzim*), and tribal (their ancestry and *watan*). Individual Taliban—leaders as well as fighters—can choose from these networks in any given situation, when mobilization, support, and solidarity are needed. But the common experience that unifies the Kandahari mainstream was gathered during the jihad against the Soviets.

Meanwhile, the tribal character of the Taliban becomes more visible at the periphery, distant from their strongholds in the south and their bases in Pakistan and wherever the leadership's influence is weaker. This was the case in Badghis prior to the elections in which three tribal groups competed for leadership and the Afghan government and the international forces temporarily made some inroads. The Taliban leadership, however, reacted more effectively and regained its influence there, mainly by appointing a strong figure, Abdul Mannan Niazi, as its Herat governor. He already held this position in the 1996–2001 period and wields strong influence all over the northwestern region.[41]

In 2008, a tendency to "retribalize" was observed in core Taliban areas like Helmand, Zabul, and Oruzgan: local Taliban retook control in their particular original areas from "out-of-area Taliban" who were accused of being heavy-handed toward the local population. This was possibly a response to Mullah Omar's earlier version of the layha, which emphasized keeping friendly relations with the local population: atrocities like killing "spies" and influential local leaders who worked with the government alienated the population. Significantly, this tendency occurred at the same time that some groups within the Taliban tried to reach out to the Afghan government or international actors, indicating that they did not believe in a military victory either and were concerned about indiscriminate slaughter of Afghan civilians.

The Taliban's Ideology

Recently some observers have described the Taliban propaganda as increasingly "nationalist": "The Taliban are becoming, or indeed have become, the standard bearers, the champions, of the Afghan-Pashtun vendetta against the Americans. It's a new development, a new political and historical force. It's not for nothing that the struggle against foreign occupation and humiliation is the one theme their propaganda hammers on and on."[42] A newspaper article confirms: "The latest refrain of Taliban commanders, their Internet magazine and from surrogates is that the insurgency represents Afghanistan's Pashtuns, who are portrayed as persecuted by the Afghan government. 'Pashtuns are suffering everywhere; if you go and check the prisons, you won't find any prisoners except Pashtuns; when you hear about bombings, it is Pashtuns' homes that have been bombed," said a Taliban commander from Kandahar Province who goes by the name Sangar[y]ar."[43] In addition, for many years some Pakistani authors have described the Taliban as a Pashtun movement. In particular this comes from a school close to the military establishment but anti-U.S. at the same time. It includes figures who had helped create the Afghan Taliban, like Pakistani chief of the army staff General Aslam Beg and former Inter-Services Intelligence (ISI) chief Hamid Gul, as well as Taliban apologists like columnist and former head of the Institute of Strategic Studies in Islamabad, Shireen Mazari. They argue that"the resurgence of the Taliban . . . now has become enmeshed with the resurgence of the Pashtoon type of nationalism against the occupying powers."[44] From there, it is a small step to labeling the Taliban *the* movement of the Pashtuns and ruling out any viable government in Afghanistan without their participation, in order to secure Pakistan's influence on any future government in Kabul.

Indeed, the argument that the U.S.-led intervention of late 2001 took away power "from Pashtuns" and that Pashtuns have been its main victims—originally expressed in Pashtun exile communities—can be heard in many Pashtun areas of Afghanistan. Following a series of U.S. Special Forces operations that claimed civilian casualties or, in one case, the lives of a family of an active Afghan National Army officer in Khost, even local former left-wingers stated that they would be bound to tribal solidarity if their tribe "decided to join the uprising against the Americans."[45] From Chak district in Wardak Province it is reported that the Taliban's "mobilization of foot soldiers . . . rests largely on an Islamic and nationalistic discourse against 'foreign occupiers'. . . . Thus, the decision of Taliban foot soldiers to support the Taliban insurgency in Chak is much more similar to the jihad against the Soviet occupiers, only now the US, the former supporter of the mujahideen, is seen as the enemy."[46] Another element often mentioned in conversations is the perception that the government in Kabul had been dominated by the Northern Alliance (NA), or "the Panjshiris," in the post-2001 years—and still is. This perception has been fueled not only by manipulations of intra-Pashtun tribal rivalries by local NA-affiliated government officeholders and commanders in the armed forces in an attempt to maintain their dominant position in the center but of late also by members of the Karzai government.[47]

It has been widely observed that Pashtun grievances indeed have translated into sympathy and even recruitment for the Taliban. But this is less due to Afghans' sympathies for the Taliban than to the lack of any significant political middle ground either in the current polarization between the Taliban and the deeply corrupt and therefore unattractive Kabul government or in the Kabul political landscape with its tainted mujahedin tanzim and marginalized new political parties. With more political space, Pashtuns could meaningfully identify with other existing political currents—from nationalism (Afghan Millat), leftism (PDPA successor groups), and Islamism (ex-mujahedin tanzim) to new pro-democratic parties.

Although its supratribal and supraethnic Islamist ideology refers to Afghanistan as a nation at times, and thus could be termed "nationalistic,"[48] the Taliban movement faces a few major hurdles that prevent it from becoming a "nationalist movement" of the Pashtun or all-Afghan variety. They lack appeal for non-Pashtun groups, despite some local inroads. This is bolstered by non-Pashtuns' negative experiences under the Taliban regime with its curbs on education, freedoms, and local traditions (also shared by many Pashtuns) and elements of ethnic cleansing. As for a Pashtun nationalist movement, the Afghan Taliban have never shown any inclination to identify with the irredentist demand for the creation of an independent Pashtunistan that existed on both sides of the Durand Line (the border not recognized by most Afghans and many Pashtuns inside Pakistan) between the late 1940s and the 1970s. This is clearly due to the fact that the Afghan Taliban still rely on Pakistani support to a significant extent and are not in a position to irritate this relationship. The Afghan Taliban would probably be better described as a "national-Islamist" movement that limits its activities to Afghanistan and is not involved in either irredentist campaigns or internationalist jihadism.[49]

The term *Taliban* hints at the movement's religious character and impetus. In its self-perception and self-presentation, the Taliban are an Islamic movement that does not recognize tribal, ethnic, or linguistic boundaries. This reflects the orthodox, conservative Islam of the Hanafi school *(mazhab)* to which most Sunni Afghans belong. Mullah Omar stated in 2008: "Our religion enjoins on us to avoid from indulging in any kind of activity involving prejudices based on ethnicity. The only bond, which binds us, is the bond of Islam."[50] This is repeated in the layha, the handbook with a code of conduct for the Talib in the field. Article 60 states that the "Mujahedin should refrain from tribal/ethnic *(qaumi)*, linguistic and local *(watani)* discrimination." A hadith of Abu Huraira is added to religiously bolster this instruction. An additional interesting aspect is provided by Wahid Muzhda, who had worked as a Taliban emirate official and is now a political commentator in Kabul: "Being an ethnic Tajik myself, I have been with the movement for half a decade. They listened to a Chechen national more raptly than the hearing they gave me or a Pashtun for that matter."[51]

In reality, the Taliban's ideology is much less clear-cut. A leading scholar described it as an "eclectic ad hoc" mixture full of "contradictions, breakouts, gaps, alterations and highly idiosyncratic interpretations."[52] It stresses "the importance of ritual and modes of behaviour," including outside appearance (clothes, haircut, shape of beard, and so on).[53] But in the day-to-day activities of the Taliban, theological intricacies do not matter much. It is unclear how much of a religious debate is really going on within the movement or the ulama close to it. If there is any, it remains invisible in its publications. Also, no such debate is occurring on the Internet as in the case of al-Qaida.[54] Some analyses claim that there is a Taliban Ulama Council, parallel to the leadership council (rahbari shura).[55] Indeed, ulama "shuras" gathered at various times in Kandahar while the Taliban were in power. For example, Mullah Omar was proclaimed the *amir al-mo'menin* in March 1996 by a gathering of twelve hundred religious scholars called a "shura."[56] After 9/11, another ulama shura met and "decided" to ask Mullah Omar to persuade Osama bin Laden to leave the country "voluntarily."[57] But already the numbers of participants in both events seem to indicate that this was not a standing body. Under the current circumstances, with expected drone attacks and ISI snatches, it is even more doubtful whether such a body could regularly meet. Inside Afghanistan, sharia courts—consisting of one judge and two ulama each—are part of the Taliban parallel administrative structures on the provincial and district levels. Their responsibilities are to solve disputes that "the district and village ulama have difficulty in solving," but apparently not to interpret sharia.[58] It is unclear how much authority the province or district sharia courts really wield vis-à-vis the military commanders on their level. Anecdotal reports confirm that instead the rahbari shura itself (or its members) occasionally involves itself in dispensing justice. If there really is an Ulama Shura, it has never published any document, fatwa, or statement. It rather can be assumed that individuals among the ulama are involved in advising Mullah Omar or the rahbari shura under Mullah Baradar (until his arrest in Pakistan in February 2010), but that both have made the final decisions. This relationship between the *amir al-mo'menin* and the ulama is "really" Islamic; it reflects the hierarchical shura principle—in contrast to the Pashtuns' jirga egalitarianism based on consensus.[59]

It has been stated repeatedly that the Taliban have—at least for a while—increasingly used internationalist jihadist rhetoric in their propaganda and even "became much more integrated in the international jihadist movement after 2001."[60] This, however, seems to have been a rather transitional period during which Mullah Dadullah, killed in 2007, copied al-Zarqawi's tactics from Iraq by training a large number of suicide bombers and, even more significantly, used this as an effective propaganda tool, given the West's terrorism fears. (The Haqqani network, which is known for its long-standing special Arab connections, follows the same line.[61]) Dadullah's course, though, triggered a rather extensive discussion within the Taliban in 2007 about whether it was "Islamic" to use suicide bombers—which, as a rule, cause more casualties among Afghan civilians than those seen by the Taliban as "legitimate" targets, namely, foreign troops and people linked to the Afghan government. Some Taliban cited the Quran that killing Muslims is *haram* (forbidden) and subsequently called "pious Taliban" by some Afghans—in contrast to "terrorists" like Dadullah. The anti-Dadullah line also seems to have support within the mainstream Kandahari Taliban: when Mansur Dadullah took over his elder brother's place and tried to follow the same line, he was reprimanded by Mullah Omar and even expelled from the movement for a period of time.[62] There were also rumors that the killing of Dadullah was enabled by information from within the Taliban ranks. In addition, the layha seems to be a reaction to this period, as it regulates the use of suicide bombers, warning against alienating the local population by causing "unnecessary" civilian casualties. In article 41(3) it stipulates: "During suicide attacks, the best attempts must be undertaken to avoid the killing of ordinary people and casualties." Mullah Omar reiterated this instruction in a message on the occasion of a religious holiday in October 2008:

> Be very careful when you face the general people and your innocent countrymen. Do not go for an attack which has a possibility of harming the general people. . . . Every act which is not in harmony with the teachings of Islam or is not according to the Islamic civilization or does not look good with the Muslim Ummah . . . like blasts in [mosques] and where there are gathering[s] of the general people, looting of the properties on the highways, cutting noses and ears in the name of [sectarian] differences which Islam forbids . . . or the burning of Islamic books must be strongly countered.[63]

Furthermore, internationalist jihadist rhetoric has not translated into action among the Afghan Taliban. There were no Afghans among the plane hijackers on 9/11. "There are no Afghans in al-Qaida's hierarchy and no Arabs in the Taliban command structure," nor has there been a single case in which an Afghan Talib had participated in a terrorist attack outside the movement's "area of operations" of Afghanistan and the tribal areas of Pakistan.[64] (This is different from the Pakistani Taliban, which, via allied Punjabi sectarian groups, are more closely linked to al-Qaida.) On October 7, 2009, Mullah Omar officially stated that the Taliban "did not have any agenda to harm other countries, including Europe, nor do we have such agenda today." In a statement on the occasion of the international Afghanistan conference in London in January 2010, the Taliban Leadership Council stated that "the Islamic Emirate want[s] to have good and positive relations with the neighboring countries in an atmosphere of mutual respect and take far-reaching steps for bilateral cooperation, economic development and prosperous future."[65]

Apart from some individuals, the Afghan Taliban have not bought into al-Qaida's jihadist agenda. When they use jihadist language, their primary target is fund-raising among their major donor group: private citizens or groups organizing mosque collections in Arab Gulf countries for them.

The Afghan Taliban's agenda is exclusively Afghan. They want to force the Western "occupation forces" to withdraw and to reestablish their Islamic emirate. For this, they need Arab money, sometimes channeled through al-Qaida connections, and—perhaps decreasingly—military know-how. As a result, the cooperation between these groups is a pragmatic symbiosis, but one in which al-Qaida needs the Taliban more than vice versa.[66] Therefore, Osama bin Laden gave an oath of allegiance *(bay'a)* to Mullah Omar, not the other way around. This must not be misinterpreted: al-Qaida did not become "subservient to the aims and methods of the Afghan Taliban. On the contrary, this purported subservience is a useful illusion that obscures al-Qaida's fundamental conflicts with the Afghan Taliban's aganda."[67] There is plenty of anecdotal evidence about mutual racist prejudices between al-Qaida's Arabs and the Pashtun Taliban that further limit the potential for cooperation.

The Taliban's lack of enthusiasm for global jihad is founded on their intention not to repeat their pre-2001 mistakes: to risk isolating themselves (or be isolated again) from the international community. Many in the Taliban blame al-Qaida—which planned the terrorist attacks of 9/11 most probably without the Taliban's knowledge—for the fall of their emirate and the loss of power in 2001. This latent conflict also might cause a break between the Taliban and al-Qaida under certain circumstances. However, the Taliban's Islamist ideology provides an instrument that creates cohesion among the fighters from segmented Pashtun tribes. One of the most important leadership instruments is the layha, published first in 2006 and updated in the spring of 2009. This code of conduct reflects the Islamic principles the Taliban's ideology is based upon and tries to rule out certain behavior that is linked to Pashtun customary law, like the right to make booty when fighting. As reality shows, the Taliban leadership is unable to implement it fully. This is determined by the network character of the movement, which allows local commanders a degree of autonomy.

The Taliban have gone through considerable changes in how they have presented themselves to Afghans and the world: from segmented networks within a larger guerrilla movement into a movement of their own, into a government, and back into an insurgent movement with elements of a shadow government. This development can be divided into four phases:[68]

1. 1979–1994: the proto-Taliban phase. "Taliban fronts" linked to different mujahedin tanzim emerged, but had not yet formed an integrated movement.
2. 1994–1996: the popular movement phase. This phase went from its emergence as an integrated movement to the capture of Kabul in 1996, when major parts of the Afghan population pinned their hopes on the movement's ability to end the factional war created by the mujahedin (before the capture of Kabul, the Taliban also dropped initial pro-monarchist tendencies).
3. 1996–2001: the state phase. During this phase, its Islamic Emirate of Afghanistan ruled over most of Afghanistan's territory. It consisted of two subphases, which cannot be dated because they cannot be clearly divided from each other by one event:
   - the early state phase, in which the IEA tried to accommodate the international community, engaging in pipeline diplomacy (some countries as well as the UN sent back positive signals) but the IEA was recognized diplomatically by only three countries (Pakistan, Saudi Arabia, and the UAE);[69] and
   - the isolated state phase, started by the first set of UN sanctions and the U.S. cruise missile strikes against al-Qaida camps after the terrorist attacks on two U.S. embassies in East Africa in 1998 and continued by the second set of UN sanctions, including a unilateral weapons embargo, spanning the time after al-Qaida's attack on the USS *Cole* in Aden in 2000 up to the events of 9/11 (during this phase, still, a UN mission existed that was mandated to bring together Afghan factions and groups in order to end the civil war).

4. From 2001: the resurgent guerrilla phase. This phase saw the return and consolidation of the Taliban as an organized armed movement. It also had three subphases:

- the post-9/11 reprieve, in 2002–2003, with the Taliban leadership in hiding, watching events in Afghanistan and contemplating political inclusion, rebuffed by the U.S. "no talks with terrorists" policy, followed by its first recruitments in Afghanistan;
- the resurgence phase, from 2003 to 2005–2006, with the gradual reemergence of the Taliban in most areas of Afghanistan; and
- the consolidation phase, from 2005–2006 onward, with a consolidated presence all over Afghanistan and parallel administrative structures.

For the fourth phase, a number of authors use the term "Neo-Taliban." Antonio Giustozzi, who makes the most developed argument for this, writes that the Neo-Taliban differ from "the old Movement on a number of issues. . . . They seem to have absorbed from their foreign jihadist allies a more flexible and less orthodox attitude towards imported technologies and techniques. . . . More important, the Neo-Taliban became much more integrated in the international jihadist movement after 2001 . . . and [undertook] first, shy attempts to court educated constituencies." He further notes that "old Taliban" were mainly represented in their top leadership while the Taliban footsoldiers represent a new generation.[70] It has already been shown above that the "integration" into the international jihadist movement—if it ever happened—was a very limited, temporary phenomenon. Only a very few, although prominent, Afghan Taliban commanders had played the global-jihadist card. It was virtually over with the killing of Mullah Dadullah. It also is doubtful whether it ever went beyond rhetoric and some techniques. With regard to the latter, one could equally argue that al-Qaida had "integrated" with the Tamil Tigers, who used suicide attacks first. Up to now, the Afghan Taliban have followed purely Afghanistan-oriented aims and have not subscribed to al-Qaida's internationalist jihadi agenda. This gap seems to have deepened over the past years. In 2007, in an interview with the Pakistani newspaper *Dawn*, Mullah Omar said: "We have never felt the need for a permanent relationship [with al-Qaida]." In May 2009, Taliban spokesman Zabihullah Mujahed stated in an interview that the Taliban are "one thing and al-Qaeda is another. They are global[,] we are just in the region."[71]

The more flexible Taliban attitude toward communication technologies as well as their highly effective and technically sophisticated propaganda machine (using the Internet, SMS, videos, DVDs, and so forth) seem insufficient to constitute a clear-cut difference between the "old" Taliban and the "Neo-Taliban." This merely signifies a change on the tactical level and has no visible implications for their strategy. It signals, however, that the movement is responsive to negative attitudes that some of the population—including Pashtuns—held against it during its regime, and that it is able to change positions. The ban on TV and videos (and on most forms of entertainment) and even of popular games at what the Taliban considered un-Islamic festivals (like the New Year festival, Nauruz) alienated many in its "natural" recruitment base.

The ability to change attitudes also shows in the case of the central issue of girls' education and, perhaps also, female employment. On entertainment, local Taliban groups still react differently to music at marriages or the use of audiocassettes; in some areas and at some times these are banned, at other times they are tolerated. Furthermore, communication technologies have significantly spread through Afghanistan only since 2001. Dropping its suspicions about TV, mobile phones, and the Internet in favor of utilizing them for propaganda purposes only shows the Taliban movement's adaptability toward technological progress.[72] Such an approach reflects positions held by earlier pan-Islamist modernizers like Sayyid Jamal al-Din Afghani (1838/1839–1897), who argued that Muslims should adapt "Western" technology while sticking (or returning) to the "original" values of Islam in order to withstand European colonial expansion.[73]

One of the main features of the Taliban is that it has shown more continuity than discontinuity between the pre- and post-2001 phases in its organizational structure, including the composition of its leadership, ideology, political aims, and program. Most importantly, the movement still adheres to its undisputed and single most important leader, Mullah Muhammad Omar, the *amir al-mo'menin*. Although the exact composition of the Taliban's second-highest body, the Leadership Council, still remains unclear, it can be assumed that it changed to an extent after 2001.[74] However, this was the result not of changes in the Taliban's political or ideological course but of physical losses, by killing or arrest. It seems clear that the shura's core still is mainly Kandahari and stems from the pre-2001 time. With Mullah Muhammad Hassan, Mullah Jalil, Qudratullah Jamal, Mullah Akhtar Muhammad Mansur, Amir Khan Muttaqi, Abdul Hai Mutma'en, and—until recently—Mullah Obaidullah, Mullah Baradar, Mawlawi Abdul Kabir, and Agha Jan Mo'tasem, the founder generation that occupied key positions in the pre-2001 Taliban emirate is still strongly represented. Most newcomers—like Hafiz Abdul Majid and Mullah Abdul Qayyum Zakir—are drawn from the southern provinces; non-Kandaharis still seem to have difficulties in getting into the core group.[75] Indeed, "relatively few of the 'old Taliban'" responded positively to Mullah Omar's early recruitment drives and "rushed to join the new jihad" in the initial phase, in 2002 and 2003.[76] But later their number rose, as a result of threats (by Afghan intelligence, Western troops in Afghanistan, and their minders in Pakistan) to be arrested and deported to the Guantanamo system.[77]

The Taliban footsoldiers are obviously mainly recruited from the younger generation. Their influence on strategic decision-making, however, can be assumed to be minimal. This generational change becomes significant only when representatives of the younger generation rise into leadership positions. This is becoming more likely now after the arrest of many "old generation" Taliban. The announcement that Mullah Omar has appointed two new deputies—Akhtar Muhammad Mansur and Abdul Qayyum Zakir—indicates that now both the old (Mansur) and the new generation (Zakir) are represented on this level.[78]

Information about whether the Taliban have really made inroads into "educated constituencies" remains too sketchy. It can be assumed that their massively increased media production must be run by members or sympathizers who are "Internet literate" and supposedly young. Anecdotal reports from Wardak Province indicate that university students or dropouts join insurgents there in significant numbers, to some extent as part-time fighters. However, it is unclear whether these are Taliban or Hizb-e Islami recruitments.[79] Even if recruitment among the educated is true, it remains an open question—and doubtful—whether this has impacted significantly on the movement's general political and ideological outlook.

The major physical change in the Taliban is that up to late 2001, they were a quasi-government with a statelike structure, ministries, subnational administration, and a security apparatus. After 2001 they were forced to reorganize as an insurgent or guerrilla movement without much of a "liberated zone" as a seat of a parallel government. More recently the Taliban have succeeded in gaining influence or control over large parts of Afghanistan's territory, operating in all 34 provinces. On parts of this territory, they have established a parallel administration, with provincial and district governors, judges, police, intelligence commanders, and even a system of taxation. According to NATO sources, Taliban governors exist in 33 of 34 provinces.[80] Even if much of this infrastructure does not exist permanently on the ground outside the southwestern region, and many functionaries are temporary absentees in their designated areas (and many have been killed of late), they constitute a "shadow" or parallel government. This "government" is embodied in the Leadership Council.[81] Its different committees and councils, for military, cultural, financial, and political affairs, resemble rump ministries and copy the pre-2001 Taliban government (and the current one in Kabul) but as a scaled-down version. Furthermore, the systematic use of the name and insignia of the Islamic Emirate of Afghanistan on official correspondence, "nightletters," and online publications shows that the Taliban consider themselves a statelike entity and the legitimate ruler of Afghanistan—even more so after the self-delegitimization of the Karzai government by the faulty 2009 presidential poll. They demand that journalists and aid organizations obtain permits to enter areas controlled by them, issue statements and correspond with foreign states and international organizations, pledging "good and positive relations with all neighbours based on mutual respect" and "constructive interactions . . . for a permanent stability and economic development in the region."[82] By this, the Taliban claim the continuity of their emirate that, in their eyes, has been unlawfully removed by a foreign intervention and replaced by a "puppet administration."

Neither during their regime nor currently have the Taliban developed a sophisticated political program. Their main aims can be distilled into two points: independence (through withdrawal of all foreign troops) and establishment of an Islamic system. In their own words: "We want to gain independence of our country which is our natural right and establish an

Islamic system as a panacea for all our economic and social problems."[83] This echoes the approach of Islamist movements elsewhere who simply claim that "Islam is the way" and Quran and sharia make further programmatic explanations superfluous. The Taliban's currently stated precondition for any negotiations is a complete withdrawal of Western troops. During their pre-2001 reign, the Taliban showed that, inspired by their urge for political recognition, they are capable of political compromise on issues of importance for the international community, such as terrorism and drugs. Indications are that this is still the case on issues of terrorism (for example, they are distancing themselves from international jihadi terrorism, although an open declaration of such would be difficult to obtain). They accept some degree of political pluralism, and are open-minded on girls' education issues, and on some human and women's rights. With their frequent positive responses to vaccination campaigns, the UN Peace Day, and even access to "prisoners"—that is, victims of kidnappings—the Taliban already are responding to aspects of international humanitarian law.[84]

Conclusions

The dualistic nature of today's Taliban movement makes it extremely resilient. Its vertical organizational structure, in the form of a centralized "shadow state" and its supratribal, supraethnic Islamist ideology, and its horizontal, network-like structures that reflect its strong roots in the segmented Pashtun tribal society give it an elasticity that has allowed it to survive (as an organization) the escalated US military onslaught, including a kill-or-capture campaign against its mid-level cadres, started with the so-called troop "surge" in early 2009. It has not only survived but keeps up a high intensity of its own operations, including an assassination campaign against officials and sympathizers of the Kabul government. The elasticity in its horizontal dimension—based on Pashtun individualism—allows discussion, dissent, and sometimes a cacophony of different voices within the Taliban, a sufficient degree of autonomy of decision-making and action on the part of local commanders, and prevents them from feeling overcontrolled. Subsequently, none of the temporary and relatively minor splits within the movement have seriously weakened the organization.[85]

A counter-insurgency strategy, with "reintegration" of "reconciled" fighters as one of its main components which effectively treats the Taliban as outsiders to Afghan society ignores facts that root the Taliban deeply into the Pashtun tribal society: that recruitment of fighters in the local "front" commanders' own tribes seems to be the general rule; that madrasas and mosques—crucial institutions in a deeply religious society—often are focal points for mobilization and ideological support; that common tribal links are further stabilized by *andiwali*, based on joint participation in the jihad against Soviet occupation and what is perceived as yet another occupation.

Moreover, despite their supratribal Islamic ideology individual Taliban can simply not disconnect fully from their tribal roots. It would mean loss of status, identity, and protection, as tribal backgrounds serve as a fallback in times of crises, and would deprive them of a central element of their success as a movement. According to the colonial and pre-1978 literature, Pashtuns generally have identified as Pashtuns first and Muslims second. While this balance between identifying with a certain ethnic groups and being Muslim in their self-identification has changed with many Afghans, primarily as a result of the jihad, with Muslimness having come to the foreground, Islam and Pashtunwali have never been seen as contradictory by Pashtuns. For them, the two concepts perfectly integrate, despite certain objective contradictions, such as their judicial aspects.

Politically the Taliban—as a movement—aspire to aims larger than its individual members' tribal realms: to regaining political power on the "national" Afghan level and the reestablishment of its emirate. (This does not rule out, though, any ability to compromise, temporarily or for good.) At the same time, they have not raised the banner of Pashtun irredentism—that is, a "reunification" of all Pashtun areas in a "Pashtunistan." This would not go down well with Pakistan, their main ally.

The Taliban's supratribal ideology, Islamism, also keeps the door open for non-Pashtun elements to join the movement. This has allowed them to systematically expand into non-Pashtun areas of the north and west. The reference to "Islam" provides an umbrella that creates cohesion in an otherwise—ethnically and politically—heterogeneous movement. As a result of the political upward mobility of the Afghan clergy in the wake of the post-1978 conflicts, mullahs and, to a lesser degree, ulama play a key role in the movement's organizational structures in general and in its increasingly successful forays into the non-Pashtun north more specifically. The system of reference individual Taliban or their leaders allude to—tribal, nationalist, or Islamist—depends on the circumstances under which certain decisions are taken and on the particular tactical or strategic aim at stake.

The fact that the Taliban have shown more continuity than discontinuity between the pre- and post-2001 phases in the major aspects - the organizational structure including the composition of its leadership, ideology, political aims, and program as well as, most significantly, the undisputed leadership of Mullah Muhammad Omar—argues for a centralistic approach to a political solution that includes the Taliban. This also explains why there is no organized or clearly recognizable "moderate" (or any other "political") "faction" within the Taliban – no single group can politically afford to visibly challenge Mullah Omar's leadership. This does not preclude the existence of different positions in the movement, including that of pragmatic, politically thinking, pro-talks Taliban who understand that a political solution is desirable but who are still conservative Islamists, includingthe so-called "pious Muslims" who think it against Islam to indiscriminately kill scores of fellow Muslims. An emphasis, by international actors, on a political solution can weaken the elements that favor a purely military approach, often combined with a hypertrophic recourse to terrorist means. This is even more important as both tendencies compete for the allegiance of the non- or less-political, locally-based *majburi* and *na-raz* footsoldiers.

For the sake of a political solution, it is important to notice that although a large majority of the Taliban leaders and fighters are Pashtuns this does not make their movement *the* (only) "representative" of *all* Pashtuns. Since the late 1940s, with the emergence of the reformist movement of the Wesh Zalmian that originated in Kandahar, there was always a pluralist political choice in Pashtun society.[86] The armed conflicts of the past thirty years, however, have narrowed the political space. Poor post-2001 decisions that marginalized political parties have further aggravated the problem. In today's violent atmosphere, between the anvil of the Karzai government that often signals its "Pashtunness" (and its international allies) and the hammer of the Taliban, it is necessary to generate viable political alternatives for Pashtuns. A political middle ground needs to be opened that can attract those Pashtuns (and other Afghans) who both oppose the Taliban and the corrupt Kabul government.

Tribes cannot assume the role of independent actors because they rather are an "arena in which political competition takes place," as Bernt Glatzer had remarked.[87] This insight should discourage attempts to make "tribes" instruments for stabilization, as has been done with different forms of "local defence initiatives", like their latest incarnation, the so-called Afghan Local Police.[88] At the same time, it is not too late to strengthen the internal cohesion of certain tribes and their particular institutions by supporting their ability to reestablish functioning, legitimate decision-making bodies (jirgas, shuras) that can allow other political forces than the Taliban to play a stronger role again.[89] Forcing the Taliban into competition with forces of a different political character in the arena of their own major recruitment base might break their spell. External actors should simply provide a relatively even playing field, a framework of security and—where requested—a role as a neutral arbiter. However, they should refrain from being seen as taking decisions on Afghans' behalf and be aware that interference often deepens, instead of remedies, existing rifts.

The Afghan government's draft "Afghanistan Peace and Reintegration Program"—as well as the Western-dominated creation of an artificial division between "reconciliation" and "reintegration"—still treats the problem mainly as a technical one. Based on the hypothesis that most Taliban fighters are motivated by poverty and economic exclusion, it supposes that the Taliban problem can be solved by economic and social incentives. This underestimates the political motives that drive the Taliban insurgency. Furthermore, the U.S. approach (using the "surge" to weaken the Taliban before any talks) and President Karzai's approach (favoring immediate direct contacts) are not congruent. Part of the question is whether there will be a genuine Afghan lead—but based on a genuine national consensus—or a continuation of the de facto U.S. lead. Only when these hurdles are removed can a mechanism and process be designed to address the different layers and currents within the Taliban. The June 2010 peace jirga and the November 2011 "Traditional Loya Jirga" in Kabul have not brought this clarification process forward. Only an approach to reconciliation that is based on genuine broad participation and buy-in of Afghans can lead to an outcome in which the Taliban can be absorbed into the political mainstream and Afghan society. An approach imposed from the top down, even if covered with rituals of surrogate participation, will always be vulnerable to spoilers.

7 / Ethnic Minorities in Search of Political Consolidation

Lutz Rzehak

The new political order that was to be introduced in Afghanistan after 2001 brought new hope to linguistic and ethnic minorities. In the so-called republican era under Muhammad Daud between 1973 and 1978, Afghanistan was meant to follow a Jacobin way to national unity, which meant the unification of all Afghans based upon the rejection of ethnic differences. During this period the inhabitants of Afghanistan were forbidden to choose a *laqab* (a kind of surname), which was an ethnic epithet like Ahmadzay, Baloch, Popalzay, Badakhshi, or Pamiri. With the Saur revolution of 1978 this situation started to change rapidly. The communist rulers understood very quickly that for the spread of their political ideas among the population of Afghanistan it would be very useful to recognize everybody's identity from the outset. National policy followed the Soviet example, and first priority was thus given to language. In 1980 five languages were officially promoted to the rank of "national languages" of Afghanistan, to be distinguished from the official languages Persian (Dari) and Pashto, on the one hand, and from the languages of smaller minorities, on the other hand. The 1990s were dominated by civil war and political chaos. The front lines often ran along borders that could be described as essentially ethnic boundaries, and the civil war took the shape of numerous ethnic wars all over the country. During the reign of the Taliban, ethnic differences were to be rejected again by a very specific interpretation of Islamic order, but the linguistic concept of that time was preferential treatment of Pashto.[1]

As a result of all of this confusion, the ethnic factor gained in importance to such an extent that after the fall of the Taliban it was regarded necessary to mention the ethnic composition of the country in the constitution that was approved in 2004. Chapter 1, Article 4, Paragraph 3, of the new Constitution of Afghanistan says: "The nation of Afghanistan is comprised of the following ethnic groups: Pashtun, Tajik, Hazara, Uzbek, Turkman, Baloch, Pashai, Nuristani, Aymaq, Arab, Qirghiz, Qizilbash, Gujur, Brahwui and others."[2] This article declares unmistakably that national unity is not to be based upon the rejection of ethnic differences. Smaller groups, in particular, pinned their hopes on the new legal order. Language planning activities started for Turkmen, Uzbek, Balochi, and other languages. Numerous cultural associations were founded to defend the languages or cultural heritage of various minority groups. It seems that the idea of a civil society with its voluntary civic and social organizations and institutions was realized in no field as successfully as in the field of culture and languages. Besides, Afghanistan has undergone remarkable changes in its infrastructure and in its communications systems. This could not remain without consequences, especially for the self-understanding of those minority groups that are not settled in just one region but are spread all over the country. This chapter analyzes the diversity and dynamics of the ethnic identities of minority groups and their attempts to appear as players in national politics. As a case study, I will focus on groups known under the ethnic name *Baloch* in Afghanistan. I take my material from numerous field studies in different parts of Afghanistan carried out between 1988 and 2010.[3]

The Concept of *Qaum*

The enumeration of ethnic groups in the new constitution established a nomenclature of legal relevance. Such enumerations create the impression of clearly distinguishable units that are based upon comparable criteria.

But things are less clear in everyday life. One may ask why the speakers of five quite different languages (Ashkun, Bashgali, Prasun, Gambiri, and Waigali) were consolidated under the common name "Nuristani" in the nomenclature of the constitution, whereas the so-called Brahwui (Brahui), who have always been considered a Baloch tribe but who have a different first language, were listed separately. Baloch political activists in and outside of Afghanistan never tire of underlining the tribal unity of Baloch and Brahui.[4] One may also ask why the speakers of Pamiri languages remained unmentioned, even though, in addition to this linguistic distinction, they follow Ismailism and thus belong to a religious minority. Or should they be assigned to the group of Tajiks, notwithstanding linguistic and religious differences?

Many, but not all, of these questions can be explained by the fact that this nomenclature undoubtedly reflects the balance of political and military power as it existed in 2004 when the new constitution was approved. Other questions are related to the ambiguity of these group names. Some of them are less mutually exclusive than others, and the borderlines between groups can be defined more easily in some cases. Some designations are more expandable than others, making it a question of interpretation who can be assigned to a certain group, whereas no interpretation is imaginable with regard to other groups. Some designations describe groups in status quo; other designations describe groups in a nascent state. The ethnic nomenclature is based upon a variety of mixtures of very different criteria. Language is a possible distinctive feature, but it must not be applied necessarily in all cases. The same can be said about other criteria, such as origin, religion, tribal belonging, way of life, and region of settlement. What all of these designations have in common is that in most local languages of Afghanistan they can be consolidated under the generic term *qaum,* which, however, can be applied to other groups as well and which is no less ambiguous than every single category.

In this respect the nomenclature of the constitution indeed reflects the ethnic reality. Hence, the ambiguity of the term *qaum* caused evident difficulties when the text of the Constitution of Afghanistan was translated from Dari or Pashto into English. Some translators chose "ethnic group" as the English equivalent; others preferred "tribe."[5] Due to the polysemy of this word, no equivalent can be the only right translation. In some cases the word *qaum* can be used more or less synonymously with terms like *qabila, tayifa,* and others describing tribal units of different size and different genealogical depth. In other cases this word approaches the meaning of terms like *melliyat,* "ethnic/national group," or even *mellat,* "nation." Usages with other meanings that are more or less related to the ones mentioned here are also imaginable.

The concept of qaum is that of a continuum in which social groups, including or excluding other groups, define their position in a certain space and in a certain time.[6] It expresses identity as a rather cumulative or polymorphous feature that can be imagined as a pool of fragmentary characteristics like common descent, language, culture, shared history, customs, way of life, religion, neighborhood, and so on. Depending on the situation, selected features of that pool can be called up or be disregarded in order to qualify someone as belonging to a certain group of individuals or as being different from others. The situation-dependent character of identity entails a wide range of possible constellations. The same criteria by which certain groups are excluded from a particular qaum can be regarded as less important when other groups shall be qualified as belonging to the same qaum. Choices of that kind are not subject to individual will, judgment, or preference but follow social rules. This becomes evident when analyzing how the concept of qaum works with regard to groups known under the ethnic name *Baloch* in Afghanistan.

The majority of the Baloch live in more or less compact settlements in the southwestern provinces of Nimroz, Farah, and Helmand (see Figure 7.1). Sometimes these provinces are, at least partially, imagined as the Afghan part of a greater Balochistan, which includes the southwestern parts of Iran and Balochistan Province of Pakistan as well. For the Baloch in southwestern Afghanistan, the geophysical constellation is more conducive to closer relations with the Iranian part of that greater Balochistan than to Pakistani Balochistan. Zaranj, the center of Nimroz Province, is situated only seven kilometers from the border between Afghanistan and Iran. From here one can get within less than one hour to Zabol, the closest town in the Iranian province of Sistan and Balochistan, without leaving Baloch territories. The usual way to Quetta in Pakistani Balochistan goes via Helmand, Kandahar, and Spin Boldak— that is, through regions that are dominated by Pashtuns and that have

	Province	Language	Tribal belonging (kaumi)	Belief
West and South	Nimroz, Farah, Badghis, Herat, Helmand	Balochi	Known	Sunni
	Kandahar	Pashto	Unknown ("Only" Baloch)	Sunni
	Zabol, Wardak			
Central Regions	Oruzgan	Persian	No information	Sunni, Shiite
	Daykundi			
	Kabul, Ghor			Sunni
North	Sar-e Pol, Balkh	Uzbek, Persian or Pashto	Unknown ("Only" Baloch)	Sunni, Shiite
	Kondoz, Takhar, Badakhshan	Persian		

Figure 7.1. Baloch settlements in Afghanistan.

lacked security in recent years. Less-compact Baloch settlements in the provinces of Herat and Kandahar can be regarded as sporadic extensions of these compact settlements in southwestern Afghanistan. Zaranj plays the role of an unofficial capital for all Baloch of southwestern Afghanistan. Although non-Baloch groups hold official political power in Zaranj today, these groups usually have to come to terms with the Baloch population of the province. Hence, refugees from Pakistani Balochistan are given land in the province on a regular basis.

In southwestern Afghanistan the Baloch have traditionally been nomads, and some of them continue to lead a nomadic way of life today. Over the course of the twentieth century most Baloch settled down in the southwest and started a sedentary way of life based on pastoralism and irrigated agriculture.[7] Repeated droughts during the last two decades caused many Baloch to give up livestock farming and agriculture, however. Cross-border trafficking and drug smuggling began to play a greater role in their life. During the civil war, many Baloch fled southwestern Afghanistan and became refugees in Iran.

Besides these angular-shaped settlements in the western and southern provinces of Afghanistan, there are numerous splinter groups all over the country that are also referred to as Baloch. Very little information is available about these splinter groups in the anthropological and historical literature.[8] According to information presented by Baloch members of the Afghan Parliament, such splinter groups can be found in the provinces of Zabol, Wardak, Oruzgan, Daykondi (Kejran district), Kabul, Ghor, Sar-e Pol (Sozmaqala district), Balkh (Sholgar district), Samangan (Dara-ye Suf district), Kondoz (Chardara district), Takhar (Rostaq district), and Badakhshan (Keshm district). Most of them are said to lead a seminomadic or settled way of life today, meaning they have built up solid dwellings where all members of a family live at least during wintertime.

This was the case among the Baloch in the region of Kaiwan in the Rostaq district of Takhar Province and in the Sholgar district of Balkh Province, which I visited in 2008 and 2010. In both places the Baloch live in solid buildings made of clay and are engaged in pastoralism mainly. During summertime the herds of sheep and goats are pastured by professional herdsmen while most of the families remain in the villages. Agriculture is less important. The Baloch of Takhar explain this by the fact that they own only unwatered land *(lalmi).* Irrigated land *(abi)* is held by other groups, mostly by Uzbeks, in this region. Wheat is the most important crop. The Baloch of Takhar produce almost no vegetables or fruit. Representatives of the Baloch of Sholgar explained that the Baloch are pastoralists "by nature" and are therefore less interested in agriculture, although they keep quite fertile lands on the banks of the Sholgar River. In recent years continuous drought and the death of animals have caused a notable labor migration among younger males, mostly to Iran.

Ways of Being Baloch

In Kabul in 2008, a 20-year-old male from Rostaq, Takhar Province, said to me during an interview, "My classmates at Kabul University often laugh at me and ask me how I can be Baloch if I don't know Balochi.

Besides that, my classmates say that Baloch men are usually tall in stature and they reproach me for being so small." This statement shows that many features that are usually taken as criteria to qualify a specific person or group as belonging to the qaum of Baloch are stereotypes. Commonly held public beliefs about specific social groups are part of the social reality, and often they are essential elements in the concept of qaum. The selection of elements presented here is based upon observations about what was identified as important by the Baloch themselves and by others. Moreover, I draw on some publications made by Baloch intellectuals.[9] I have also chosen some features that were not mentioned directly during the interviews or in these publications, because they proved to be of importance in social interaction.

In the southern and western parts of Afghanistan almost all Baloch speak Balochi as their first language. Only the members of the Brahui (Brahwui) tribe kept their own language (also called Brahui) as a first language, but all of them speak Balochi as a second language. In the southwest the Balochi language is an important but not a sufficient feature for being qualified as Baloch. In Zaranj, Balochi is used as a lingua franca, and even in neighboring provinces like Farah and Helmand I met many persons who belonged to groups other than the Baloch but who spoke Balochi fluently as a second language. Some of them even proved to be Balochi language activists.[10] However, the situation is fundamentally different among the Baloch splinter groups in other provinces of Afghanistan. None of them speak Balochi, and other languages (Persian, Pashto, and Uzbek) are used as their first language. If they are bilingual, the other language they know might be almost any language that is spread in the region of their settlement, but not Balochi.

As far as the Baloch of Takhar are concerned, they speak Dari Persian, or Farsi, as they call it. Their language shows many features that are characteristic of the dialects of northeastern Afghanistan and can be classified as one of the local dialects. There is one village with Uzbek-speaking Baloch. Without being asked about their language, many Baloch in Takhar declared that already their ancestors had given up Balochi and switched to Persian because this was the dominant language of that region. This shows that the missing knowledge of Balochi is assessed as an ethnic deficit. Otherwise they would hardly have tried to justify themselves in advance. However, nobody remembers how many generations ago the Balochi language was given up. If they really switched from Balochi to Persian—whenever this might have happened—some Balochi substratum might be found in their language, be it in the lexicon or some morphological or syntactical features. I checked numerous lexical items where such a substratum might be expected: terms of kinship and social structure, agricultural terms, terms related to stock keeping and dairy, handcrafts, and many others. I found no Balochi substratum.[11] Except for their claim and their evident feeling of an ethnic deficit, there is not a scrap of evidence that the Baloch of Takhar ever spoke Balochi before.

The situation is quite similar among the Baloch groups in Balkh. In Sholgar district there is a Pashto-speaking group named Baloch embedded in a group of Pashto-speaking Pashtuns, and a Persian-speaking group, which is also named Baloch and embedded in a group named Kandahari ("from Kandahar"). All of these Kandaharis speak Persian, and with the exception of the Baloch branch, they also claim to be of Pashtun origin. The Pashto spoken by the Baloch of Sholgar is a variety of southern Pashto found in the region of Kandahar, and the Persian of the other Baloch group of Sholgar hardly differs from the Persian dialect of the Kandahari, which, by the way, shows many similarities with the dialect of the Hazara. No Balochi substratum has been found so far in the language varieties of these Baloch groups either, but unlike the Baloch of Takhar the language question was not discussed as an ethnic deficit.[12]

In southwestern Afghanistan the Baloch share a common cultural and historical memory with the Baloch in other places of greater Balochistan. They believe that all Baloch are descendants of a mythological ancestor named Mir Hamza who lived in Aleppo at the time of the prophet Muhammad. According to this tradition the Baloch were divided into forty-four tribes called *bolak* when they migrated to Balochistan. The tradition says that at that time their leader was a person called Mir Jalal Khan, son of Jiyand, and that Mir Jalal Khan had four sons who became the founders of famous Baloch tribes.

This genealogical tradition is kept in memory in epic songs, which are always performed with a stringed instrument called *suroz* and which remain popular today.[13] A very famous hero of these songs is Mir Chakar, who was the leader of the Rind tribe during a long-lasting war with the Lashar tribe. Even today, when modern mass media have made other musical genres increasingly popular, every Baloch in southwestern Afghanistan has some basic knowledge of Mir Chakar and his adventures. Furthermore, these epic songs are also spread through modern mass media. There are many audiocassettes, CDs, and DVDs with Baloch singers who perform these epic songs along with others.

The Baloch in Takhar and Balkh provinces have almost no knowledge of this genealogical and epic tradition. The few things that some of the Baloch of Takhar mentioned about the origins and the history of the Baloch had been found on the Internet by a local intellectual who works as a physician in the district center. And this had happened only a few weeks before my visit. The Baloch of Takhar and Balkh don't know a stringed instrument called *suroz*, either. Historical knowledge is mainly transmitted in the form of free narrations. Moreover, they have very poor knowledge of their history in general. The Baloch of Takhar do not remember when they came to northeastern Afghanistan and where they come from originally. They guess that they migrated there three hundred years ago, but this could have been two hundred or five hundred years ago as well. They claim that they must have come from somewhere in Balochistan, but the only reason for this is the belief that Baloch must originate from Balochistan. The only fact they have no doubt about is that when the Baloch migrated to northeastern Afghanistan, they first arrived to a place in Badakhshan called Keshm, and later on some of them moved from Keshm to Takhar. Thus the Baloch of Takhar and the Baloch of Badakhshan are said to be of the same origin. They don't know the time of these latest migrations either. Remembered names and events never go back in history beyond these migrations from Badakhshan to Takhar.

The Pashto- and Persian-speaking Baloch of Sholgar in Balkh Province have no narratives or other traditions that would establish any connection with the Baloch of greater Balochistan either. They claim that they came from Loy Kandahar ("Greater Kandahar"), which included today's provinces of Kandahar, Oruzgan, and Daykundi. Some of them remember that their ancestors had lived in the Kejran district of today's Daykundi Province, and they still maintain ties to Kejran. According to their tradition, they moved to Balkh in the time of Amir Abdul Rahman Khan at the end of the nineteenth century.

In southwestern Afghanistan as well as in Iran and Pakistan the Baloch have a tribal organization or *kaumi,* as they call it, which can be seen as the main framework of their social structure. On a higher level, different tribes *(kaum)* can be distinguished. In Balochi the word *kaum (qaum)* can be used to describe all Baloch in the sense of "the Baloch nation," but the tribes are also named kaum.[14] Every Baloch knows exactly which tribe he belongs to, although, unlike most Pashtuns, they may not know every linking element between themselves and the founder of the tribe. Due to numerous migrations in the course of history, Baloch tribes of that level are plurilocal to a high degree. Hence, members of a particular tribe can be found not only in southwestern Afghanistan but also in Iran, Pakistan, and even among the Baloch of Turkmenistan. Tribal ties on that level are maintained by tribal elders.

In everyday life, belonging to a certain clan *(pisrand, tayifa)* is much more important. The common ancestor of a clan usually lived six or seven generations ago, and most Baloch know the complete genealogy up to the common ancestor of the clan. This is the level where marriages are arranged and where most economic questions, politics of the day, and other current affairs are discussed and solved. Clans create the most important solidarity groups in everyday life. In southwestern Afghanistan, some groups are referred to as *augan-baloch,* or Pashtun-Baloch. These are splinter groups of Pashtun origin that were incorporated into the tribal organization of the Baloch. Most of them completely switched over to Balochi as their first language, whereas some elder persons may know Pashto as well. It is worth mentioning that notwithstanding their incorporation into the tribal organization of the Baloch, these groups often maintain relations with their Pashtun "father" tribes as well. Many *augan-baloch* have an idea about the circumstances surrounding how they became Baloch.

The Baloch of Takhar, by contrast, have no idea at all which tribe they belong to and have no clan system either. In Takhar most Baloch remember only their father, their grandfather, and their great-grandfather. Actually there are some group names like *Sher-e paylich* ("barefooted tiger"), *Shamari, Ewazi, Telajat, Gadayi, Isabayi, Tablak, Temuri;* but these are rather loose groups of distant relatives and not solidarity groups. No linking genealogy is known, and, far more important, these groups have no elders who would represent group interests. If there is any integrating unit, this would most likely be the village on a higher level and the extended family on a lower level.

As far as I could find out, the situation is quite similar among the Baloch of Sar-e Pol, Kondoz, and some central regions like Zabol and Wardak. In Balkh the Persian-speaking Baloch are a subtribe of the Kandahari, and the Pashto-speaking Baloch are a subtribe of the local Pashtuns. There are neither genealogical traditions nor other indications that would allow establishing links to the tribal system of the Baloch in Nimroz and greater Balochistan. Obviously these Baloch groups had been incorporated into the tribal system of the Pashtuns long before they migrated to northern Afghanistan. The Pashto-speaking Baloch of Kandahar seem to be the only non-Balochi speaking Baloch in Afghanistan who are integrated into the common tribal system of the Baloch.

For the Baloch of southwestern Afghanistan, being Baloch means to "make Balochi." They have a very lively code of honor, named *nang-u mayar,* with a highly sophisticated system of moral values and rules of behavior. Many of these values and rules of behavior are transmitted in the epic tradition and in other genres of folk literature. Public authorities are seldom contacted in case of material or physical damage; in southwestern Afghanistan the Baloch prefer to solve such problems "in the way of the Baloch," as they say, using the influence of elders or tribal councils or seeking bloody revenge when unavoidable. From a structural point of view this code of honor is quite similar to the Pashtunwali of the Pashtuns. Hence, it is no surprise that similar moral values and rules of behavior are shared by the Persian- and Pashto-speaking Baloch of Sholgar, which have been incorporated into groups of Pashtun origin.

In all the stories that I have heard among the Baloch of Takhar, the word for "honor" *(ghairat)* was used exclusively when they talked about the past. The Baloch of Takhar love to remember the "good old times" before the Saur revolution of 1978 when they had a strong leader named Wakil Mosa who was a deputy of the Parliament and to whom they could apply in case of difficulties. Today they would like to refer to public authorities in case of physical or material damage, but usually they have to bear the interference of local mujahedin who are not Baloch. The Baloch of Takhar don't remember any cases of blood revenge.

As far as the way of life is concerned, the Baloch of southwestern Afghanistan and the Baloch splinter groups in northern Afghanistan have undergone many changes during the last decades. But even with regard to the nomadic past there is a remarkable difference between the Baloch all over western and southern Afghanistan, on the one hand, and the Baloch of Takhar, on the other hand. In southern and western Afghanistan, as well as in other parts of greater Balochistan, the Baloch lived in black tents called *gidan* and made of goat hair. Similar tents are still used by Pashtun nomads all over Afghanistan and by the Baloch groups in Sholgar as well. The Baloch of Takhar know these black tents only from Pashtun neighbors. They themselves lived in tents of a completely different type, which they called *kappa* and which can be described as small yurts of a rather simple construction type. Dwellings of this type called *kappa* are known in greater Balochistan as well, but they are not used by Baloch there. Furthermore, the owners of these dwellings are regarded as being of low prestige in the social hierarchy of the Baloch.

When I asked some Baloch in Takhar what was typical for the Baloch and by which features of culture or way of life they could be distinguished from other groups in the region, I got a similar answer several times: it was always mentioned that in former times the Baloch were famous for their fighting with wooden sticks *(chobzani).* They described these sticks as being about 3 meters long and as thick as a cigarette packet. As soon as the fighting with sticks came up, they started to tell unimaginable stories about how one single Baloch fought with a stick against seven wolves or how one single Baloch who was armed only with a wooden stick put the whole population of an Uzbek village to flight. This indeed might be a shared feature with the Baloch of southwestern Afghanistan, because they have a traditional dance called *lattgwazi* that is performed with wooden sticks and is well known among the Baloch of Iran, Pakistan, and Turkmenistan as well. But when I described this dance, the Baloch in Takhar dismissed this, saying that this was a dance in the Kandahar style, meaning this was not their way to dance. The Baloch of Sholgar didn't know this dance either.

All Baloch in southwestern Afghanistan and most Baloch splinter groups all over the country are Sunni Muslims. Sunni Islam is a very important feature of their identity. If this needs any proof, the following incident might suffice. In 2008 a Baloch intellectual published a book about the culture of the Baloch where the text was presented both in Balochi and in Persian. The Balochi text correctly observed that the Baloch despise the *sigha*, a fixed-term marriage allowed in Shiite Islam. Due to an obvious misprint, the Persian text said that the *sigha* is accepted by the Baloch.[15] Seldom has a misprint caused as much political trouble as this one. The author of this book was called a traitor publicly, and it is reported that he can hardly go back to his original home place in Nimroz even for a short visit from Kabul, where he now lives.

However, there are some Baloch groups in northern and central Afghanistan who follow Shiite Islam. The Persian-speaking Baloch in Sholgar are Shiites like all other Kandahari, and they reported that Shiite Baloch could also be found in the provinces of Daykondi, Sar-e Pol, Samangan, and Kondoz. Amazingly enough, the Shiite Baloch of Sholgar live in close proximity to Pashto-speaking Baloch who are Sunni. Notwithstanding the fact that both groups claim to be Baloch, they would never intermarry. In Afghanistan, marriage relations are usually a quite trustworthy indicator of social proximity or distance.

With the exception of the name, the Baloch splinter groups of northern Afghanistan do not have much in common with the Baloch of southwestern Afghanistan. They do not speak Balochi, and they have no tribal system, which is the basic framework for social interaction among the Baloch in southwestern Afghanistan. The Baloch of Takhar have no code of honor comparable with that of the Baloch in southwestern Afghanistan. They do not know the epic tradition of most other Baloch, and they do not share a common knowledge about Baloch history. Remarkable differences exist with regard to other features, like dwellings, oral folklore, folk dances, and religion in some cases.

In southwestern Afghanistan and in neighboring areas of Iran, Baloch who have given up their mother tongue and do not accept the code of honor and other traditional values of behavior—persons who have given up the "good way" taught to them by the fathers and grandfathers—are sometimes called *kafer baloch*, "ingrate or rejecter Baloch." This is by no means a compliment. So how do the Baloch from southwestern Afghanistan relate to Baloch splinter groups in other parts of the country today? Are they accepted as Baloch, notwithstanding the fact that they do not know the "good way" of the Baloch? In a society where ethnic belonging gained in importance so much that it was regarded necessary to fix the ethnic composition in the constitution, this question is far from being only theoretical or rhetorical.

Political Challenges and the Dynamics of Ethnic Identity

In the modern society of Afghanistan, with growing mobility, striking economic difficulties, and an increase in the importance of ethnicity, the Baloch of the southwestern parts and Baloch splinter groups in other parts of the country have been able to establish ties with each other that had never existed before. As far as I know, representatives of Baloch from southwestern Afghanistan and of Baloch splinter groups in northern Afghanistan made noteworthy contact with each other for the first time in the 1970s, when a Baloch member of the Afghan parliament who came from Nimroz originally met some Baloch from Takhar in Kabul. It is reported that he was surprised when he heard that in Takhar the Baloch didn't know which tribe they belonged to. He told them that they belonged to the tribe of the Gurgej because this was his own tribe. It is also reported that later on in the 1980s a Baloch politician who was the chief of the Afghan trade union and who also came from Nimroz originally met some Baloch from northern Afghanistan. He told them that they must be Rakhshani.[16] One can easily guess which tribe he belonged to: Rakhshani, of course. The common name *Baloch* was, obviously, a sufficient criterion for Baloch political leaders to accept the Baloch splinter groups of northern Afghanistan as members of the same kaum; but at that time the concept of qaum was dominated by the interests of particular tribes. The language difference was ignored, and missing tribal links could be created easily, if necessary, in order to strengthen the position of one's own tribe within the Baloch community.

When a new wave of language planning for Balochi started after 2002 and a Balochi dictionary was prepared in order to provide a lexicographical basis for the process of making Balochi suitable for the communicative purposes arising from the new status of this language in Afghanistan, this evoked a supratribal movement of the Baloch in Afghanistan, with Zaranj as the main base. In 2005 a cultural center for the Baloch was founded in Zaranj, and in 2008 it was transformed into a Balochi academy. The formation of this cultural center, which, according to its program, wanted to protect not only Balochi language and culture, but the social and political interests of the Baloch as well, was a direct result of the language planning activities. Originally this organization was named in Balochi in a rather romantic way, "Caravan of the Balochi language."[17] Later on this organization appeared under another name, which is very long, and less romantic, in Dari: "The Cultural Organization for the Stability and Defense of the Rights of the Baloch of Afghanistan."[18] The Dari word used here for "stability" is *ensejam*, which also means "harmony" or "concinnity." The derivate adjective *monsajam* means "stable" and "harmonized." During the last years I heard these words many times when Baloch were talking about politics. It expresses the demand for being recognized not only as a minority that is commonly identified with some frontier tribes in the southwest, but as a minority with settlements all over Afghanistan and with the justified claim to play a role in national politics. The Balochi language was important to bring the first cultural organization into being, but for its activists it is not an exclusive criterion with regard to non-Balochi-speaking groups in other parts of Afghanistan. Yet other criteria, like tribal structure, code of honor, or way of life, are not exclusive criteria either. Today most activities are oriented toward the unity of almost all Baloch of Afghanistan. In southwestern Afghanistan there is even some tendency to suppress tribe and clan differences, at least on the political level. At any rate, Baloch politicians from southwestern Afghanistan do not try anymore to recruit Baloch splinter groups from other places for their own tribes.

In August 2008 a meeting of Baloch leaders from all over Afghanistan was held in Kabul where they met president Karzai and discussed their political aims as Baloch in the multiethnic society of modern Afghanistan. One of the most remarkable ideas proposed at this gathering was the relocation of Baloch splinter groups from northern Afghanistan to Nimroz, where they would be given land for farming and building free of charge.[19] This seems to be a rather utopian plan of highly motivated and committed political activists, and no measures have yet been taken to implement this plan. It is said that it will be put into action only after the reconstruction of the Kamal Khan dam, which will supply fertile lands at the banks of the Helmand River with irrigation water. Then Baloch from other regions can acquire irrigated land. This could be attractive in particular for the Baloch of Takhar, who own no irrigated land there, but more important is that the Baloch of Nimroz hope that such ethnically oriented relocations of population can avert the actual danger of becoming a minority in their homeland.

It is worthy of mention that the Shiite Baloch of Sholgar in Balkh were not invited to this country-wide gathering of Baloch representatives. Although many elements of the concept of being Baloch might be ignored in order to create a more numerous minority group, differences in religious belief seem to remain an insurmountable barrier on the way to unity. And there are other barriers as well. Today there are at least four organizations that claim to protect the cultural and political interests of the Baloch of Afghanistan. Beyond the above-mentioned organization with its local base in Nimroz, there are three other organizations led by well-known politicians. One organization can be assigned mainly to the Brahui tribe, which gained much power during the civil war. Another organization is accepted by the Pashto-speaking Baloch of Balkh as representative, but they do not want to be associated with this group only. The fourth organization, based in Kabul, can be seen as a spin-off of the first organization that originally had been founded in Nimroz. To a certain extent this range of organizations reflects the ethnic plurality within the greater qaum of Baloch, but beyond that, for an ambitious person, the foundation of a cultural association is always a good opportunity to make a political career. Hence, the typical mutual reproach toward the political activists who lead these organizations is that the organization was founded for reasons of individual influence and enrichment only.

Conclusions

Ethnic groups are often seen as naturally grown units that can be defined by themselves. This makes claims that are raised as ethnic demands appear to be justified to a great extent, and in modern Afghanistan ethnic interests have a legal basis according to the new constitution. The case of the Baloch shows that a common name can stand for a wide variety of different groups with differing concepts of being Baloch. These concepts in fact can be understood only in and of themselves but not by being reduced to the name *Baloch*. Furthermore, the case of the Baloch shows that a common ethnic name can nonetheless be a sufficient criterion for qualifying a specific group as belonging to the same qaum, if these groups have joint interests in political or economic resources. This could have been a particular tribe in previous times, but due to the new legal framework it is usually the bigger group of all Baloch that is to be strengthened this way. The case of the Baloch also demonstrates that ethnic claims can overlap with the individual interests of political activists and can be exploited for a political career. The case of the Baloch shows that ethnic alliances are far from being naturally grown units. Ethnic alliances are matters of interest.

8 / Red Mosque

Faisal Devji

On July 10, 2007, Pakistani soldiers stormed the Red Mosque complex of Islamabad in an assault that killed some two hundred people, thus ending months of aggressive and well-publicized provocations by the students and teachers of its men's and women's seminaries. Instead of posing a challenge to the Pakistani state, however, the assorted kidnappings and armed incursions carried out by residents of the Red Mosque, not to mention the threat of suicide bombings, had presented it with a symbolic confrontation in the media. Indeed, the mosque's religious radicalism in the carefully controlled environment of the capital compromised Pakistan's security far less than the secular struggle for autonomy in its restive province of Balochistan did. The entire incident, therefore, had more the character of a warning than a problem of national security, such that Pakistani opinion both for and against the army's action continues even now to be dominated by rumors that the whole crisis had been staged, whether by the government or by the militants themselves.

But if it was the mosque's performance of impunity in the glare of media attention that had challenged Pakistan's government (or rather the law-and-order image that gave its military rulers their legitimacy), the violent resolution of this confrontation by its army was equally theatrical in nature. It was no accident that this military resolution had the code name Operation Silence, implying thereby its aim to muzzle rather than merely control dissent. So the army's siege of the Red Mosque, and the negotiated settlement that Pakistani mediators had nearly reached with its leaders, the brothers Maulana 'Abd al-'Aziz and 'Abd al-Rashid Ghazi, were also broken off for demonstrative reasons. Possibly encouraged by the United States, General Musharraf seems to have decided that these men and women needed to be taught a lesson, not for the sake of a principle but in order to secure his own reputation as someone who did not cut deals with terrorists. In seeming to break with the long-established policy of tightening and loosening the government's control of militant outfits for reasons of state, Musharraf might have been capitulating to the American policy of refusing to deal with these groups, a move that was backed by many in Pakistan's liberal establishment, who have a long history of supporting military rule to safeguard their social privileges against the demands of Muslims and Marxists alike.

Searching for a regional precedent to Operation Silence, the Indian press immediately drew comparisons between the Red Mosque and the Golden Temple, which was attacked on Indira Gandhi's orders during Operation Bluestar in 1984. Occupied by armed divines and their students demanding Sikh autonomy, this shrine was besieged by Indian troops and eventually stormed, with the loss of over four hundred lives. Shortly thereafter Mrs. Gandhi was assassinated by her Sikh bodyguards, some four thousand Sikhs were massacred in Delhi, and the Sikh-dominated province of Punjab was given over to an insurgency that lasted a decade and sent many thousands to their deaths. While Operation Silence certainly follows the precedent of Operation Bluestar, it also suffers in the comparison. Similarly, the Red Mosque episode suffers in comparison with the storming of Mecca's Great Mosque by French-backed Saudi troops in 1979, which evicted the armed supporters of a self-proclaimed messiah and killed hundreds. In a video released on September 20, 2007, Osama bin Laden added another precedent to Pakistan's attack on the

Red Mosque, which he compared to the destruction of the Babri Masjid by Hindu militants in 1992, an event that was preceded and followed by riots and massacres in many parts of India. Unlike its more illustrious predecessors, including Srinagar's Charar-e Sharif shrine and Hazratbal mosque, both of which were besieged by Indian troops after being occupied by militants in 1995 and 1996, respectively, the Red Mosque was not a particularly sacred or even well-known site, and rather than demanding a separate state or proclaiming a messiah, its defenders wanted only to "clean up" society in the manner of NGOs, citizens' groups, and other do-gooders.

Comparing those holed up in the Red Mosque to the Taliban or al-Qaida is also misplaced. For one thing, their kidnappings and forcible closing of immoral businesses were attempts to court publicity that resulted not in the meting out of any Islamic punishments so much as in the almost Maoist "reeducation" and subsequent release of alleged prostitutes. And for another, the presence of large numbers of armed and veiled women at the Red Mosque harked back to the images and participation of women in the revolutionary Shiism of Iran or Lebanon rather than to the masculine character of Sunni militancy, especially of the anti-Shiite kind that we are told dominated the Red Mosque. Neither of the institution's leaders, for example, made any anti-Shia statements in the numerous interviews they gave to the press throughout its crisis. So in an interview with Al Jazeera, the last filmed on the mosque's premises before Operation Silence began, 'Abd al-Rashid Ghazi went so far as to discount the received wisdom about his father having been killed in either a sectarian or a domestic quarrel, blaming his assassination on the government instead. Moreover, he immediately contradicted Al Jazeera reporter Rageh Omaar's description of the Lal Masjid as a "conservative" institution. Ghazi rejected this appellation by pointing to the institution's women's madrasa, which he claimed not only was the world's largest, but also included English and science as part of its curriculum. And even though the mobilization of women in Pakistan is characteristic of national movements, whether represented by secular organizations like the Pakistan People's Party or religious ones like the Jama'at-e Islami, their participation in both movements has always been minor and even cosmetic. For whether they are mobilized for religious or secular purposes, in moderate or militant organizations, women's groups in South Asia tend to be Hindu instead of Muslim.

So the militarization of women and their deployment shoulder to shoulder with men in the Red Mosque was most unusual and probably derived from Iranian examples. This is also true of the only other militant women's organization among South Asian Muslims, the Dukhtaran-e Millat, or Daughters of the Community, in the Indian portion of Kashmir, whose members are similarly occupied with doing things like shutting down video shops. Interesting in this respect is the fact that the Pakistani government chose to demolish the women's seminary once they had occupied the Red Mosque, as if trying in this way to reassert the masculine character of Muslim religiosity against the militants, who in turn protested vociferously against this effort to exclude women from their society. Indeed, as part of their reaction to the Red Mosque's storming, these militants embarked upon a remarkable program of building identically named mosques and women's seminaries in other parts of the country, thus championing the participation of women in education and public life for the first time. And this great transformation has been achieved at a single stroke, as it were, because it proceeds not from any ideological imperative but rather from a media event.

This mixing of genders and genealogies, in which nationalist and Shiite forms are grafted onto the traditionally masculine organization of Sunni militancy, seems to indicate the latter's breakdown into more generalized social groupings within the Red Mosque, suggesting that their militancy was individual rather than collective and amateur rather than professional. Instead of representing an ideological movement or constituting a militant group, these aggressive but disparate men and women would more correctly be described as forming a civil-society organization. Indeed, in statements and interviews before its storming, residents of the Red Mosque complex more often than not spoke about such civil-society issues as the lack of security, transparency, and equal opportunity in Pakistan rather than about any specifically religious subject, suggesting thereby the mutation of Sunni militancy into the kind of mobilization that is neither nationalist nor in fact militant in any professional way but perhaps nongovernmental. So in an interview given to Tom Lasseter of McClatchy Newspapers on June 17, 2007, in the run-up to the battle over the Red Mosque, the soon-to-be-martyred Maulana 'Abd al-Rashid Ghazi voiced sentiments about the United States, a country he thought of as being inimical to Islam, that would not be out of place on the lips of anyone advocating international development: "How much money has been spent on the war on terror? If these billions had been spent on us, on basic education, on food, then we would love the Americans. The Americans are not getting benefit from Iraq or Afghanistan. Hatred will not bring you any positive results—hatred from Afghans, hatred from Iraqis, hatred from Pakistanis."[1] 'Abd al-Rashid Ghazi, in the frequent interviews he gave to the press by way of his mobile phone, even as Pakistani soldiers stormed the Lal Masjid and killed his mother, spoke in an Urdu that was heavily laced with English words about the need for "transparency," itself a key term among NGOs. His similarly revealing and self-consciously "final" statements were dedicated to such issues as urging abstention upon one of his companions at the mosque who had confessed to drinking alcohol. Typically these quotidian revelations, lacking any programmatic content and indicating the far-from-pious nature of some of the militants, were interrupted by unimaginative interviewers looking for newsworthy information like the numbers of dead and wounded. In all this the call for an Islamic order, whose Taliban-like character the global media had repeatedly emphasized, was invariably subordinated to civil-society concerns and voiced in the most nominal fashion. Here, for example, is what Ghazi had to say about such an Islamic order in the interview given to Tom Lasseter: "We don't care if Musharraf remains or not—we don't want to change the face, we want to change the system. . . . The system has failed; it is not working. The same people keep coming from the same families to rule the country, and they exploit everyone in Pakistan. We want to abolish this system; an Islamic system should be enforced. There comes a point when people stand up, when they rise up against the system."[2] Of course the nature of an Islamic order as defined by the Red Mosque's authorities was illustrated by the attacks led by burqa-clad women against video shops and alleged prostitutes, but these incidents were, after all, attempts to court publicity by offering the media completely stereotyped images of Muslim extremism drawn from around the world and put together randomly with no attempt at ideological uniformity. A closer look at the Red Mosque brings something quite different into focus. For instance, the "co-ed" character of the mosque's seminary, which not only included large numbers of women but also sometimes put them in close proximity to men, was scandalous for a supposedly conservative Sunni institution. This scandal was made evident with the arrest of the Red Mosque's leader, Maulana 'Abd al-'Aziz, while trying to escape the premises disguised in a burqa, clutching a handbag, and according to some reports, wearing high-heeled shoes. What were high heels doing at the mosque anyway, and how had the divine learned to wear them? According to Pakistani officials, 'Abd al-'Aziz was spotted because of his height and paunch, though one of the women among whom he was hiding tried desperately to convince the soldiers who would search him that the divine was her "aunty."

Although masquerade and cross-dressing are forbidden in Muslim scripture, the burqa has become a secular garment widely adopted as a male and female disguise all over South Asia. Celebrities wear burqas to remain anonymous or gain publicity by being discovered under them, as an Indian pop singer who happens to be neither female nor Muslim did when visiting the Sufi shrine of Ajmer not long before the Red Mosque events. Suspected criminals also wear them to avoid media exposure when being presented in court. And so it was bizarre but not unprecedented that Maulana 'Abd al-'Aziz should have appeared in a television interview following his arrest still in a burqa, even going so far as to veil and then unveil his face as if to demonstrate his disguise or discovery. The attempt to humiliate and disgrace 'Abd al-'Aziz by this display, however, was undercut by his apparent willingness to be filmed in women's clothes as well as his smiling countenance throughout the interview. Rather than marking women with the sign of Muslim patriarchy, in other words, the burqa actually does the opposite and unmarks both men and women in such cases, thus proving that no sartorial practice is univocal in character.

All of this suggests that the Red Mosque was linked more to the everyday and even secular practices of modern life in the region than to any religious or cult behavior. This is made clear by the fact that it was the supposedly traditional Maulana 'Abd al-'Aziz who tried to escape the besieged institution, not his more modern brother Maulana 'Abd al-Rashid Ghazi, who had studied history at Pakistan's most prestigious university and had also worked both for UNESCO and for his country's ministry of education. It was this Westernized man who announced his impending martyrdom to the world by sending a text message from his mobile phone. What we see here is an example of the gradual transformation, or at least flattening out, of Islamic militancy, which has in many parts of the world been weaned off its dependence on highly organized or institutional forms to become yet another kind of voluntary association that individuals join for their own reasons, often as part-time members rather than full-time radicals. What is interesting about this flattening out of militancy as it spreads through society, in other words, is the fact that it changes not so much into a popular or national movement as into a relatively open and undisciplined sort of activism within civil society.

This curious transformation was made evident by the failed suicide attack in Glasgow and the equally fruitless car bombings in London that occurred at the end of June 2007, coinciding with the Red Mosque crisis and separated from its assault by just over a week. Though they were highly educated professionals by occupation, the Indian, Jordanian, and Iraqi doctors involved in these incompetent actions betrayed a complete lack of professionalism in their militancy, which seems to have become some kind of extracurricular activity for them—though of course one of a rather conclusive sort. Indeed, Muhammad Haneef, an Indian doctor detained and then released in Brisbane for alleged links to his cousins and fellow doctors among the would-be terrorists in the UK, proclaimed his innocence to Australian police in a statement leaked to the press precisely by stressing his "professionalist" lifestyle and denying any association with militancy, which he tellingly described as an "extracurricular activity." In this sense these men's medical occupations had nothing to do with the terrorist attacks they had planned: the attacks simply represented an aspect of their social lives.

Naturally some kind of relationship must have existed between the public and private lives of these doctors, perhaps based on the notions of altruism and self-sacrifice that are meant to inform medical as much as terrorist practices, but my point is that the latter remained distinctly amateurish in character. And if such an attitude is understandable among individuals and small groups whose terrorism is essentially a do-it-yourself phenomenon, its novelty becomes apparent within a radical institution like the Red Mosque, whose leaders betrayed a notable lack of professional certainty or ideological conviction. In his interview with Tom Lasseter, 'Abd al-Rashid Ghazi, when asked if the 9/11 attacks had altered his admiration for Osama bin Laden, responded with a remarkably provisional but entirely typical statement that recognized the plurality of militant behavior within a kind of terrorist civil society, while deferring any judgment about it:

> It is a difference of opinion, but I am not saying he is wrong. I do not think innocent people should be targeted. He has his own argument. I'm not saying he's totally wrong. I am not convinced on this issue, but otherwise, yes, I am convinced by him. For example, there is an American enemy in Afghanistan and Iraq. I am convinced that American soldiers should be targeted and killed in whatever way possible. And in doing that, if some civilians are killed, but the main target is the enemy, its OK. But if the main target is a market, is innocent people, then I do not agree. But both sides have their argument, both sides have their logic—there is no conclusion.[3]

Analysis of the Red Mosque events was dominated by the institution's apparently close relationship to the Pakistani state. Attention also focused on the government's supposed encouragement of the crisis in its initial phase, so as to divert attention from the popular movement building up around the refusal of the country's chief justice to accept his dismissal at General Musharraf's hands. There is no doubt some truth to both these allegations, with the breakdown of relations between government and militants only illustrating the impending breakdown of the regime as a whole. Like all military dictatorships, this regime compensated for its lack of popular support by relying upon a limited number of institutions and organizations in civil society. But if the movement of lawyers and other professional groups coalescing around the dismissed chief justice signaled the detachment of these former clients from Musharraf's regime, that of the Red Mosque's students and teachers signaled the corresponding detachment of the general's religious clients from his government. In this sense both secular and religious protesters belonged to the same movement, however opposed they might be to one another.

The provocative activities of the Red Mosque's students and teachers can be seen as attempts to occupy the arena of antigovernment struggle in Pakistan's civil society, not least by frightening General Musharraf's secular opponents into supporting his military regime once again. After the storming of the Lal Masjid, these attempts were followed up in suicide attacks across the country, especially by militants targeting soldiers, policemen, and the ubiquitous Chinese technicians in the country to work on infrastructure projects. Importantly, these retaliatory attacks by militants both associated with and unconnected to the Red Mosque sought to share the limelight with this media event that had a global impact only because it happened to occur in Pakistan's capital within easy reach of the world's cameras. After all, no such reaction had been forthcoming following the army's far more destructive operations in Balochistan or the North West Frontier Province (as the province of Khyber Pakhtunkhwa was then known). Militant retaliation for the Red Mosque assault, therefore, marked not the escalation of radicalism in Pakistan but, rather, its dispersal and splintering—for the coming together of such disparate ideas and practices indicates the fragmentation of Islamic militancy into a violent but pluralistic kind of civil-society activism.

9 / Madrasa Statistics Don't Support the Myth

Tahir Andrabi, Jishnu Das, and Asim Ijaz Khwaja

O ver the past few years, U.S. and international foreign policy concerns have focused on the rise of extremism in the Islamic world. Pakistan, considered pivotal in the war on terror, is mentioned as a prominent case. There is by now a widespread conventional narrative surrounding the role of the Pakistani educational system in the rise of religious extremism in the country. The general claim is that the public schooling system in Pakistan is failing, especially for the poor. As a result, large numbers are either not enrolling in the state system to begin with or exiting through attrition. Madrasas have proliferated to fill the vacuum as a result of the failure of the Pakistani state and society to provide mainstream schooling opportunities for its children, especially for the poorest segments of the population. This narrative has been presented in the international media and also in policy circles in the United States in many studies. The Af-Pak policy framework developed under the Obama administration has also put particular emphasis on this point.

This narrative is meant to hold true especially in the northwestern province of Pakistan bordering Afghanistan. The public imagination has focused on the madrasas as the incubators of the Taliban. In fact, it is often stated that the leader of the Afghan Taliban, Mullah Omar, studied in a madrasa in the North West Frontier Province, now named Khyber Pakhtunkhwa (KPK). The fact that the tribal areas of Pakistan bordering Afghanistan are embedded in an integral way in the geography and culture of KPK and are deemed to be the sanctuary of Taliban-led attacks on NATO and U.S. troops in Afghanistan has meant that the madrasa consistently remains a focus of world attention.

The last population census in Pakistan was conducted in 1998. Pakistan has four provinces—Khyber Pakhtunkhwa (KPK), Punjab, Sindh, and Balochistan—and four territories with special status: Azad Jammu Kashmir (AJK), Federally Administered Northern Areas (FANA), Federally Administered Tribal Areas (FATA), and Islamabad, the capital territory.[1] We have complete data on village characteristics for the four provinces, about 93 percent of the country's population. Urban areas represent 33 percent of the population. Directly contrary to this general understanding, published and verifiable data sources demonstrate that madrasa enrollment has been quite low across Pakistan.[2] Household-level data collected by us in the Learning and Educational Achievement in Punjab Schools project reveal that madrasa enrollment not only was small but also did not follow any consistent pattern across households.[3] In fact, there was considerable variation within households in schooling choices and madrasa enrollment. Districts in KPK and Balochistan that border Afghanistan have had slightly higher madrasa prevalence than in the rest of the country. There has been dramatic change in the Pakistani education landscape, but this change is best characterized by a rise in private schooling and not madrasa proliferation.[4] These private schools are a grassroots, decentralized phenomenon in large part driven by mom-and-pop entrepreneurs largely unaffiliated with any chains or organizations, religious or otherwise. Both in terms of levels and trends, private schools were a considerably more significant phenomenon in Pakistan at both the urban and the rural level.

However, because of lack of data on establishments, we could not address the important question on whether the rise of private schooling had created meaningful school choice at the village level. This question is relevant given the considerable heterogeneity existing in the rural areas at the country level, particularly in the poorest segments of the population. If the answer to the question is in the affirmative, then the impact of the madrasa at the village level would be muted. We could also not examine if there was a socioeconomic pattern that pertained to the schooling location decision of public schools, private schools, and madrasas at the village level for Pakistan as a whole and KPK in particular.

A new data source, the National Education Census (NEC), conducted by the Pakistan Federal Bureau of Statistics (FBS) in 2005, allows us to fill in the gaps in this debate. The NEC has several features that make it especially suitable to analyze this question. First, it is the only national-level data source that provides a full enumeration of all the schooling types—public schools, madrasas, and private schools—in Pakistan. Secondly, and importantly, the data collected by the FBS has a coding scheme that allows us to merge it with the 1998 Pakistan Population Census at the village level. Given that we have data in the census on over 46,000 villages in Pakistan, combining the two data sources provides a comprehensive look at education in rural Pakistan at the most disaggregated geographical level possible. Moreover, the census provides us a rich array of socioeconomic indicators at the village level: village housing construction type, electricity and water availability, numbers on adult education levels, TV, radio, and newspaper penetration, as well as number of people registered in government national identity card databases. These data allow us to construct a village-level socioeconomic status index using principal-component analysis. Going to a disaggregated level within rural areas and classifying villages in terms of size, physical infrastructure, and other socioeconomic characteristics, one can examine the important questions of madrasa location vis-à-vis indicators of poverty. The census allows us to construct measures of population at the village level as well as of population density. Village wealth (we use the term *wealth* broadly as encompassing the other socioeconomic status dimensions as well), together with village size in terms of population and population density, allow us to characterize the location decision of all three school types—public, private, and madrasa.

Having done this, we find that public schooling is the dominant option for the rural population, with virtually every village having a public school.

Private schools have a large rural presence, with 23 percent of villages having a private school. By contrast, only 7 percent of the villages in the country have a madrasa. The establishment data thus confirms our earlier household analysis. Unlike public schools, both madrasas and private schools are largely absent from the poorest villages. The key difference is that private school prevalence increases dramatically as villages become larger, more densely populated, and better off in socioeconomic terms. Madrasa prevalence, on the other hand, does go up with density and population but remains flat relative to the village socioeconomic status.

Based on the above findings, one can reasonably conclude that public school location is largely based on equity concerns based on providing access to poorer segments of the population. The evidence also supports the point that private schools, being a market-based phenomenon, are going where the demand is and where they can find locally educated women to serve as teachers. The flat madrasa location pattern as villages become better off belies any simple explanation. The data depict a relatively stable but low per capita demand for this type of education, independent of village social and economic conditions. One striking fact is hard to explain. Of the meager 7 percent of the villages that have madrasas, more than half of those (4 percent) also have private schools. Madrasas locate, albeit in a much smaller number, precisely where private schools are locating. A robust predictor for whether a village has a madrasa is whether it has a private school. At least at the national level, the conventional story does not fit the facts!

Khyber Pakhtunkhwa does provide some support to an enhanced Afghan border effect as far as madrasas are concerned, but the data here too do not support a simple story. It is true that madrasa prevalence is higher in KPK, with 13 percent of the villages having a madrasa, but the private schooling numbers there are close to the national average, with 22 percent of the villages having a private school. But as in the national numbers, of the 13 percent of villages that have a madrasa, more than half (8 percent) also have a private school. Public school location in KPK is if anything more equity-minded, as public school provision is relatively higher in the poorer villages.

Going further down and looking at a regional breakdown of KPK, we find that the seven districts surrounding the tribal region Waziristan do have a higher prevalence of madrasas within KPK—actually, the highest prevalence in any region of Pakistan—with 33 percent of villages having a madrasa. But the same pattern of private school provision is visible here as well. Roughly half of these villages have a private school as well, and the number of villages having a private school is almost the same (31 percent). Madrasas do locate more in larger and densely populated villages, but as in the rest of the country there is no change in their presence as villages become more prosperous. Interestingly, growth in private schools far outstrips that of the madrasas, and the number of private schools formed in the half decade since 2000 is 70 percent greater than the number of madrasas formed in the same period.

We next present a more detailed analysis of rural areas of the four provinces of Pakistan where a majority of the population and the poor reside. Importantly, households residing in the larger and better-off villages of Pakistan are the single largest and a fast-growing demographic group in Pakistan and can thus give a better idea of the educational trends in the country. A point often forgotten in discussions of education in Pakistan is the ubiquity of public schools in the rural landscape. Virtually every village in Pakistan in our data has at least one public school present and a considerable number have more. Private schooling is the next most prevalent option, with about 22 percent of villages now having at least one private school. Madrasa is the least prevalent option at the village level, with only 7 percent of the villages with a madrasa presence.

Village sizes vary considerably in Pakistan in the 46,000-plus villages in our sample of the four provinces of Pakistan. The median population is 1,169, with the 99th percentile being 12,176 and the 1st percentile a village of only 15 people. Thus if schools locate in larger villages, looking simply at village numbers without weighting them for population could be misleading. The numbers show that it is indeed true: the prevalence of schooling opportunities in larger villages is greater. The numbers for madrasas, private schools, and girls' public schools jump up, but the relative rankings remain similar: 17 percent of people live in villages with a madrasa, and 45 percent of people live in a village with a private school. Almost 20 percent of the Pakistan rural population is living in villages with three or more private schools, as compared to only 5 percent for madrasas—private schools and madrasas are both more prevalent in larger villages both across and within villages. School choice in the larger village is very much a fact of life in present-day Pakistan.

We now take a slightly different look at the data to examine further the range of schooling options at the village level. We classify every village in the four provinces as of one of the following types: (1) there are no schooling options in the village, (2) both madrasa and private school exist in the village, (3) a private school exists but not a madrasa, or (4) madrasas are the only schooling option. Figure 9.1 provides this detail for Pakistan as a whole and for each of the four provinces. As said earlier, because villages with school presence tend to be larger than the average, we use percentage of population living in a village with a particular school as the measure of prevalence.

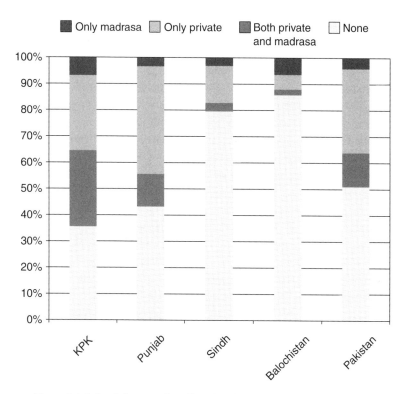

Figure 9.1. School choice at the village level: Pakistan and the provinces.

At the national level, only 4 percent of the rural population lives in villages where a madrasa exists and there is no private school. In contrast, 32 percent of the rural population lives in villages where there is a private school but not a madrasa. Thirteen percent of the population lives in a village where there is a madrasa but additional school choice exists in that a private school is present and importantly over half the rural population of Pakistan lives in villages where there is neither a madrasa nor a private school.

In terms of provincial variation, population living in madrasa-only villages ranges from 3 percent to 7 percent. KPK has the largest madrasa prevalence, but the absolute differences are very small. Its pattern is remarkably similar to that of the country as a whole. Only 7 percent of the rural population of KPK lives in a village where there is a madrasa but not a private school, while 13 percent of the population lives in a village where there are both private schools and a madrasa. A significantly larger 29 percent of the population lives in a village with a private school but not a madrasa. The ground reality is that for the majority of the rural population, private schools are a more available option, but apart from Punjab—the most populated province by far—the majority of the rural poor in the other three provinces have access to neither.

The data reveal somewhat surprising similarities and differences among the provinces, given the conventional wisdom. Rural KPK is more similar to Punjab in terms of madrasa and private school distribution. Rural Sindh, which has low numbers for both madrasas and private schools, is more akin to Balochistan in terms of extremely low prevalence of private schools and the large number of villages where neither are present. Given the sparseness of population in Balochistan and its remoteness, it is best to treat its educational pattern as sui generis (no pun intended!).

Thus the basis of the madrasa mythology cannot be found at the level of the province. KPK is surprisingly "normal." Any search for madrasa proliferation will have to be seen in pockets of population within the provinces. Two distinct subregions—Swat in KPK and Waziristan in FATA—have been known in recent years for Taliban-style violence. Although we don't have data on the tribal territories, we break the settled districts of KPK down into four regions: (1) three districts in the Hazara region largely composed of non-Pashto speakers; (2) eight districts in the larger Swat region; (3) seven districts bordering Waziristan; and (4) six districts in the region surrounding Peshawar. Figure 9.2 follows the same definitions of prevalence as in Figure 9.1. Only Waziristan stands out from rest of the provinces. Districts bordering Waziristan do have a higher prevalence of madrasas within KPK—actually, the highest prevalence in any region of Pakistan—with 57 percent of the population living in a village with a madrasa. But the same pattern of private school provision is visible here as well. More than two-thirds of this population live in villages that have a private school as well, and the percentage of people living in a private-school-only village (21 percent) is a little greater than the percentage of those living in madrasa-only villages (17 percent).

We now come to our final question: Can we trace out from the data the economic, social, and demographic determinants of school location? Private schools in Pakistan are mostly for profit, and we should expect them

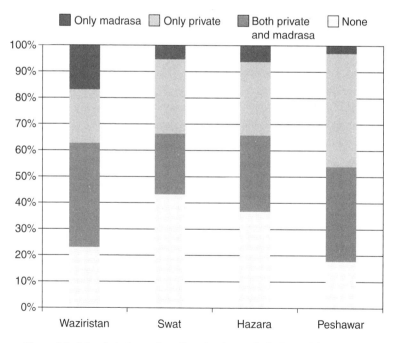

Figure 9.2. School choice at the village level: Rural Khyber Pakhtunkhwa.

to locate where demand is the greatest. We should see large numbers in urban areas and then in richer, larger, and more densely populated villages. Private schools are also resource-constrained in terms of finding low-cost teachers, so that again pushes them toward larger villages where there is an available pool of low-wage teachers.

Governments could be driven by equity and providing access to the poor, so one should expect to see government schools by such considerations to locate disproportionately in smaller and poorer locations. Governments hire typically at the provincial level and have the mechanism of teacher postings and transfers, so the resource constraint at the local level is not binding for them and they should be able to bring in teachers to the smaller and poorer villages. Both these factors would make government schools less sensitive to village size, density, and wealth. Alternatively, given the commonly held perceptions of inefficiency and corruption of the government, one might think government schooling patterns would not be sensitive to the plight of the poor.

Of these three types, it is the hardest to speculate *a priori* about the location decision rule of a madrasa. We do not know whether the madrasa "market" or target population lies among the poor or whether they are resource-constrained at the local level and thus subject to variation in availability of teachers at the local level. This is because the sources of funding for the madrasas are not fully known—whether their funding comes from local or outside sources, such as government subsidies or foreign financing, remains largely unexamined at this scale and level of disaggregation. The number of madrasa students in nationally representative household surveys is so small that we do not have enough samples to meaningfully say anything about this population. Getting a definitive answer to the madrasa question would require large-scale and detailed data on school financing, teacher recruitment, and potential student socioeconomic data that has to be generated through specially designed surveys. Without looking at such data, we can only conjecture about madrasa demand-and-supply constraints. A neutral hypothesis could be that there is an underlying uniform demand for religious education, independent of the socioeconomic conditions at the local level. Our location analysis is a necessary first step in moving forward on the question of what determines the spread of madrasas at the local level.

The establishment data reveal an interesting picture. In economic language, the elasticity of private school prevalence vis-à-vis village socioeconomic status is much greater than that of the madrasa. Perhaps the most striking finding is that madrasas also do not locate in areas where there are fewer schooling options. In fact, they locate, albeit at a much smaller level, precisely in areas where private schools and girls' public schools locate. KPK does not stand apart from the national picture. Although the prevalence of madrasas is marginally greater there than in the country as a whole, KPK follows the same pattern as the rest of the country with private schools increasing their presence as villages become better off and madrasa prevalence being relatively flat across the socioeconomic spectrum of villages. In KPK, public schooling is marginally more responsive to poorer villages and its presence there is larger than the national average. Waziristan follows a similar pattern.

Our analysis points out a clear decision rule for private and public school location. Private schools are locating where demand is high and resource constraints are low. They are locating in urban areas and seem to be clearly catering to the newly emerging rural "middle class." However, as soon as villages start getting even a little better in terms of their socioeconomic status, the private school numbers take off. In fact, their largest growth has been in the larger, better-off villages. Public school location is clearly following an equity consideration. Their location pattern is skewed toward the poorer villages of the country. The madrasas, on the other hand, do not show a clear pattern at all. If anything, the best that can be said is that there is a very small demand for the madrasa that is fixed in per capita terms and does not vary very much with any observable economic or demographic characteristics of the country. From the point of view of a poor Pakistani or a poor resident of KPK, the madrasa is largely an irrelevant alternative.

Conclusions

The above findings have important implications for policy reform. The claim that madrasas are the schooling option of choice for the poorest segments of the population is incorrect. The data show that people living in rural areas to some extent and in poorest villages to a large extent have access only to public schools. If one is concerned about alleviating the problem of access to education for the rural poor, then the discussion should not focus on madrasas (or private schools, for that matter), as both private schools and madrasas are not locating there. The discussion has largely got to be about the public sector. Policy should focus on improving quality and learning outcomes in public schools, which, as we show in other research, is really low. The government should concentrate on expanding its role mainly in these areas that are not covered by other schooling choices.

We have discussed elsewhere in detail that the existence of a pool of moderately educated women at the village level has provided the impetus behind the rise of private schooling in the rural areas. As the number of educated women in rural areas is increasing with time, it will create a further expansion of private schools in the moderate- to high-socioeconomic status-index villages, thus creating a positive feedback loop. The key policy implication in these villages is for the government to ensure that such local pockets of educated women expand (through spread of girls' secondary education) and that steps are taken to ensure that the education market performs competitively and efficiently. The issue of public girls' schooling in the poorest areas needs to be reemphasized.

According to the census, approximately one million youth are turning 18 and potentially entering the labor market every year. One of the most pressing problems of the day is training them to participate effectively in the society around them and be productive economically. School reform to achieve credible learning and academic outcomes is critical in this regard. Policy debate on education in Pakistan is rightfully turning its focus toward issues such as teacher absenteeism, merit pay, decentralized school management, and learning outcomes, to name a few. Our other work has pointed out that private school governance, management, and functioning provide significant lessons for the much-needed process of public school reform.[5] Given the madrasa's peripheral status in the Pakistan education landscape, focus on the madrasa does not add any insight into the crucial issue of improving the vast majority of public schools. We recognize that fighting terrorism, militancy, extremism, and violence is perhaps the most pressing problem confronting the Pakistani state and society, but there is limited overlap between the issue of education and that of extremism. Viewing the debate on Pakistan education solely from the lens of violence and extremism takes much-needed attention away from real measures desperately needed at this time in schooling that people are actually using.

Our study raises some deeper conceptual questions as well, regarding how to infer preferences of people in that part of the world. As one moves up the prosperity ladder in the rural areas, schooling options increase. Although the madrasa prevalence does go up, the marginal increase in private school prevalence is much greater. In the context of school choice and parental decision-making, private schools have emerged as the more desirable alternative to government schooling for the bulk of the Pakistani rural population. The data imply that Pakistani parents beyond the poorest of the poor are actively making educational choices regarding their children's future. One expects this trend to continue, as a comparison of the data from 1999 and 2005 shows that the growth in private schools remains strong. Although there is much discussion of the average Pakistani having "extreme" preferences, these data show remarkably "normal" behavior on the part of Pakistani parents. Our related work shows that children in private schools show more civic skills, habits, and dispositions, exhibit less gender bias, and have greater trust in institutions.

The direction of causality running from madrasas to extremism is extremely difficult, if not impossible, to disentangle. The statistical analysis in this paper has little to say on this issue. Violence and militancy or suicide bombing coming from young men affiliated with some madrasas is more of a security than an educational issue. We would argue that even if one were concerned about issues of extremism, the more important target for policy study is not the madrasas but instead the ideological bent of the majority of the population. An approach focusing on more representative data with their richer choice patterns and an unmistakable trend toward private schools would give us a better idea of where the youth of the country are heading and where their families' deeper preferences lie. A majority of KPK regions show patterns of schooling much like those of Punjab and average Pakistan. Districts around Waziristan do stand out in terms of madrasa prevalence. But it is remarkable that even after the traumatic aftermath of 9/11 and violence in the area, private-school growth outstrips madrasa growth in that area. The glass is certainly more than half full even around Waziristan.

10 / Will Sufi Islam Save Pakistan?

Farzana Shaikh

I n a briefing paper published in 2009, the Heritage Foundation, a conservative U.S. think tank, called on Pakistan to restore "its deep culture of pluralist traditions" and challenge the wave of Islamic extremism that threatened its survival.[1] Among the traditions singled out for attention was Sufism. Mediated in Pakistan by the dominant Sunni Barelvi tradition, which is known for its veneration of Muslim saints and their shrines, it was judged by the Heritage Foundation to hold the promise for Pakistan to evolve as a "moderate" and "modern" Muslim state. Its recommendations have been echoed by other U.S.-backed initiatives, including the Washington-based World Organization for Resource Development and Education (WORDE). In its report published in April 2010, WORDE advocated strengthening Pakistan's main Islamic network, the mainstream Barelvi Ahl-e Sunnat al-Jama'at (lit. the Followers of the Traditions of the Prophet Muhammad),[2] which favors the authority of Sufi *pirs* (spiritual masters), in order to defeat radical Islam and promote U.S. foreign policy goals.[3]

These concerns have an established pedigree, though, with roots that in the past had little in common.[4] In 2003 the Rand Corporation, a right-wing U.S. policy group, in a broader report on the Muslim world had also highlighted the role of Sufis as valuable partners for America to help forge a "modern, democratic Islam."[5] Rand revisited the issue in 2007 when it cast Sufis as the West's "natural allies" in the war against radical Islam. While recognizing that Sufism was largely a "traditional" phenomenon that sometimes made room for radical and militant tendencies, Rand argued that the majority of Sufis fell "on the moderate side of the divide" and that some even favored "modern" Islam.[6]

Nowhere did these recommendations receive a closer hearing than in Pakistan. In 2002 the country had embarked on a fresh engagement with Islam driven by the exigencies of the post-9/11 world. It involved a radical reorientation that forced Pakistan to sever its links with its erstwhile protégés, the Afghan Taliban, and to revive its long-held claim to act as the chief interlocutor of moderate and modern Islam. Galvanized by his idea of "enlightened moderation," the country's then military leader, General Parvez Musharraf, urged Muslims in Pakistan "to shun militancy and extremism" and "promote Islam . . . as the flag-bearer of a just, lawful, tolerant and value-oriented society."[7]

A core objective of this program was the appropriation of Sufism. Pitted against the harsh and often retrograde versions of Islam favored by more orthodox Sunni Muslim movements, notably those informed by the Deobandi and Ahl-e Hadith traditions,[8] Sufism was projected as the gentler face of Islam. More importantly, in contrast to imported varieties of Arabian and Wahhabi Islam, Sufism was vigorously promoted as indigenous and natural to Pakistan. Musharraf's barely concealed objectives were not only to strengthen Sufism as a key signifier of Pakistan, but to burnish his country's moderate image and, in doing so, stake its claim to be modern.[9]

The terms of this agenda were spelled out by him in 2006 following his appointment of a National Council for the Promotion of Sufism, which aimed to encourage values commonly associated with Sufism, notably an appreciation of tolerance and pluralism, and to project Pakistan's "soft power" abroad.[10] But the National Council was widely perceived as a gimmick conceived by a military regime anxious to bolster its legitimacy by playing to a liberal lobby at home and abroad. These perceptions were not unfounded: the National Council achieved little beyond the sponsorship of a few musical events. Nevertheless, it is worth noting that since then, this much-mocked measure has received the endorsement of an elected government led by the Pakistan People's Party (PPP). In June 2009 it announced plans to establish a new seven-member Sufi Advisory Council, headed by a leading cleric from the Barelvi-dominated party, the Jam'iyat-e 'Ulama-e Pakistan (JUP). Known for its strong endorsement of intercessionary ritual practices associated with popular Sufism, the JUP's involvement in the Advisory Council was an astute choice by a government that is intent on surpassing its predecessor's efforts to use Sufism to "combat extremism and fanaticism."[11] Although this latest venture has also met with some skepticism, its prospects appear to have been enhanced by a noticeable shift in public opinion. It points to a deepening interest in the potential of Sufi Islam as a counter-narrative challenge to the more extreme versions of Islam that now hold sway over many parts of Pakistan.

This interest is not, as some have insisted, entirely driven by an external neoconservative agenda.[12] The question of empowering some versions of Islam over others as right for Pakistan goes back to the inception of the state, when rival versions of Islam jockeyed for official patronage. It set in motion a debate, which resonates to the present day, suggesting that, ultimately, the survival of Pakistan depends upon empowering the right kind of Islam. Until now much of the debate has centered on the conflicting visions of Islam favored by Muslim modernists and their adversaries among Islamists with the respective merits of each side yet to be settled. What is not in dispute, however, is that since independence the modernist agenda has been dominant, even if its political control over the Pakistani state is now vigorously being challenged. This ensured that, notwithstanding strong challenges, the modernist vision remained decisive in influencing which Islam would be embodied by Pakistan and whether, as in the case of Sufism, it qualified as the right kind of Islam.

This raises three questions: Has the wider empowerment of Sufism in Pakistan been inherently constrained by the terms of a dominant modernist discourse that has been ambivalent about (if not hostile to) popular Sufism? Is the current state appropriation of Sufism exceptional, inasmuch as it is driven by both domestic and foreign imperatives? In the current climate of worldwide Muslim anger against a U.S.-led war that is perceived to be against Islam, does the polemical use of Sufism as the right kind of Islam risk conflating the war for Pakistan's survival with the defense of Islam?

Popular Sufism and the Making of Pakistan

It is now commonplace to suggest that the idea of the modern state in Pakistan rests largely on the legacy of its three patron saints—the educational reformer, Sayyid Ahmed Khan (1817–1898); the poet and ideologue, Muhammad Iqbal (1877–1938); and the country's founder, Muhammad Ali Jinnah (1876–1948). All three have left a lasting imprint on the contours of Muslim modernist discourse in Pakistan and its relation to Islam. At its heart lay the construction of the rational Muslim individual with the power directly to apprehend God's law (sharia) and a concomitant desire to be free of "ideologies of mediation" associated with popular Sufism.[13]

None was singled out for greater attention (and reprobation) than the ideology of dependence that was seen to define the relation of the Sufi pir and his follower *(murid)*. Judged to be a corruption of classical Sufism, the reform of so-called *piri-muridi* was a key concern for Sayyid Ahmed. Although he was conscious that devotional practices such as *dhikr* (divine remembrance) associated with *piri-muridi* were an integral part of Sufi piety, Sayyid Ahmed's rationalist temperament failed to accommodate the idea of divine mediation attributed to local saints and their descendants *(sajjada nishin)*. His solution was to bring Sufism more in line with his modernist understanding of Islam. He did so by calling for a *sunna*-centric and sharia-minded Sufism that would situate the pir squarely within the boundaries of what Sayyid Ahmed judged to be proper Islam.[14]

These ideas were vigorously pursued by Muhammad Iqbal, who tackled the problem of Indian Sufism as part of his larger project to reclaim Quranic truth. Although he was more categorical than Sayyid Ahmed in calling for an end to *piri-muridi*, Iqbal also stopped short of advocating the abolition of Sufism. Instead, he favored a return to classical Sufism but reinterpreted it as a "project of resistance" with the power to mold the modern Muslim.[15] As such, it stood in opposition to Indian Sufism, which Iqbal believed had fundamentally vitiated the Muslims' capacity for autonomy. He claimed the blame lay with Hinduism, which had corrupted Sufi Islam by promoting quietist tendencies that had left Muslims passive and dangerously vulnerable to political domination.

In the context of late colonial India, when questions of Muslim identity and self-government were being fiercely debated, Iqbal's emphasis on the need to purge Islam of Hindu influences in order to promote Muslim autonomy was enthusiastically received by leaders of a burgeoning Muslim separatist movement.[16] They included Muhammad Ali Jinnah, who made no secret of his impatience with most forms of popular religion (although he reserved almost as much scorn for the established religion of the *ulama*). Unlike Iqbal, however, Jinnah's objections to ideologies of religious mediation were not grounded in a theological position. Rather they stemmed from more explicitly political concerns.

They centered on the challenge posed by such ideologies to Jinnah's efforts to establish his claim to be the "sole spokesman" for an Indian Muslim "nation." It was defined by the direct commitment of individual Muslims to the symbols of Islam and sought to transcend the boundaries of control exercised by local tribal and spiritual leaders. But the task of delegitimizing these intermediary structures of power proved to be a daunting challenge for Jinnah, and one that he would never fully confront. In vast swaths of rural Punjab and Sind, where powerful pirs and their descendants *(sajjada nishin)* controlled the local population, Jinnah was compelled to co-opt their support. Their role was no less significant in the North West Frontier Province (present day Khyber Pakhtunkhwa). Here too Sufi leaders lent Jinnah vital support and helped mobilize their followers in his favor.[17] But here, as in Punjab and Sind, the co-operation of these holy men came only in exchange for assurances that Jinnah would protect their social and economic interests.[18] Although left with no choice but to accede to these demands, Jinnah did so equivocally and in the uncomfortable knowledge that loyalties sustained by saintly power gravely compromised his vision of Muslim nationalism as a credible force.

These unresolved tensions between local Sufism and Muslim nationalism with its appeal to the universal symbols of Islam persisted after the independence of Pakistan in 1947. But they also provided fresh opportunities for Pakistan's postcolonial leadership to resort to new strategies aimed at appropriating the power of Sufi pirs in the service of the modern state. In this regard Pakistan stood in contrast to other Muslim states—whether unambiguously secular like Turkey, or sternly reformist like Saudi Arabia. For unlike their brutal suppression of Sufism, Pakistan's governing modernist elite chose to accommodate local Sufism. The reasons had much to do with the uncertain ideological foundations of the new state, which encouraged governing elites to harness innumerable versions of Islam, including Sufi Islam, as agents of political and ideological legitimization.[19]

However, for much of the 1950s, Pakistan's leadership showed little sign of wanting to engage with local Sufism. Although the power of local pirs was widely acknowledged, their support was rarely sought by a leadership confronted by a religious establishment that challenged its right to interpret the meaning of Pakistan's Islamic identity. One reason for the ambivalence of the political classes toward the Islam of local Sufism lay in their indebtedness to the terms of the modernist discourse favored by Pakistan's ideological precursors. Their condemnation of popular Sufism as a corrupt and backward expression of Islam is likely to have led many among their political heirs to assume that turning to pirs would be judged unworthy of modern Muslims and in breach of the standards of proper Islam.

The issue was particularly sensitive for a political leadership that lacked formal knowledge of Islamic law and was unsure of its Islamic credentials. Nowhere was this vulnerability more tangibly displayed than in the leadership's decision to endorse the preamble to Pakistan's constitution. The Objectives Resolution, approved in 1949 (and incorporated in all three of the country's constitutions), formally recognized Pakistan's identity as Islamic. In what has since been regarded as a major concession to religious orthodoxy, the leadership also agreed to commit the state to "enable" its Muslim citizens to "order their lives . . . in accord with the teaching and requirements of Islam as set out in the Holy Quran and the Sunna."[20]

But this bitter compromise with their Islamist foes over Pakistan's constitutional identity took its toll on state leaders. Beleaguered, they turned to their old allies among local pirs in order to harness the rhetoric of Sufi Islam in the service of the state and fend off further challenges from the formidable alliance between the ulama and Islamist parties. It set in motion a process that involved the creative appropriation of Sufism by a postcolonial leadership still wrestling with the legacies of Muslim modernism. This entailed moving Sufism along the tradition–modernity axis and recasting it as modern. Henceforth local saints and their activities would be regarded as forces of development, rather than as agents of backwardness—the condition to which they had been unequivocally relegated by Pakistan's modernist forbears.

It marked the onset of a new relationship between Pakistan's modernist elites and popular Sufism.[21] The transformation was not, however, intended to project Pakistan as a "modern" Sufi state; instead the aim was to mold local Sufism and bring it in line with a state whose modernity would continue to be informed by a broadly Islamic reformist agenda. The trend was set by Pakistan's first military ruler, General Ayub Khan (1958–1969), whose attempts to bring Sufi shrines under bureaucratic management were equated squarely with a program of development. These attempts were ideologically reinforced by the promotion of local spiritual leaders as moral exemplars, whose gifts were seen to lie in the power to instruct Muslims to gain direct access to the divine rather than to engage in practices of intercession that were perceived as superstitious.

But Ayub was also concerned to mobilize local Sufi pirs as bulwarks against his critics in the religious opposition. Faced with their routine denunciation of his policies as un-Islamic, he sought the backing of rural pirs to promote an alternative interpretation of Islam based on a reformed and modernized Sufi Islam to shore up the fragile legitimacy of his regime.[22] In doing so, Ayub widened the arena for competing versions of Islam, which in time would accentuate the chronic uncertainties over Pakistan's identity in relation to Islam.

Pakistan's first democratically elected leader, Zulfiqar Ali Bhutto (1971–1977) was rather less of a modernist than Ayub; indeed, he has been seen to represent a break with "Iqbalian modernism."[23] It is certainly true that Bhutto's populist style put him more closely in touch with the values of rural Pakistan, and especially of his native Sind. But he also drew more heavily on an egalitarian culture associated with popular Sufi saints to project his own modern vision of Pakistan. Grounded in the rhetoric of

"Islamic socialism," his vision came to be widely regarded as standing in opposition to the hierarchies of traditional society.

Bhutto's understanding of Pakistan as a nation with a pronounced territorial dimension rooted in regional identities (rather than merely an ideological construct based on Islam) also helped tighten the bonds between local Sufism and his modern nation-building project. It is perhaps no coincidence that under Bhutto one of the most potent manifestations of this relationship came to rest with the iconic Sindhi Sufi saint, Lal Shahbaz Qalandar of Sehwan Sharif, whose shrine *(dargah)* has been described as the "geographical centre of Bhutto's political spirituality."[24] Ultimately, however, for Bhutto, as for Ayub, the value of local Sufi Islam lay in its power to serve as a prop against the Islam peddled by his religious opponents. But it is worth noting that Bhutto's fiercest critics also included urban-based modernists, who held that his championing of rural popular Sufi "folk" Islam was an affront to the modern religious mentality they believed Pakistan had been created to embody.

Their concerns received a sympathetic hearing from General Zia ul-Haq (1977–1988), who ousted Bhutto before presiding over his execution. Strongly influenced by Deobandi traditions, he favored a strictly doctrinaire approach to Islam. This strengthened the hold of the ulama, but also of a Sunni bourgeoisie that claimed to speak on behalf of the common man against corrupt bastions of rural power—Sufi pirs and landed magnates—who were seen to be symbiotically related.[25] Nevertheless, Zia, like his predecessors, was also tempted to mold Sufism to fit the ends of his modern program of Islamization. Although he tended to rely more on the "language of the ulama" than on "the symbolism of the sufi" to drive home his message, he remained mindful of the immense popular appeal of local saints.[26] This was especially true of rural areas where support for his military regime was more tenuous.[27] Here Zia continued with earlier policies, which ensured the preservation of holy shrines. But he also promoted a subtle ideological shift, aimed at minimizing the gap between Muslim saint and Islamic scholar and easing the tension between the worship of saints and obedience to the sharia.[28] By doing so, Zia also paid his dues to the modernist state.

The democratic interregnum of the 1990s, dominated by Benazir Bhutto and Nawaz Sharif, revived the state's pronounced engagement with local Sufism. As before, it was aimed at preempting moves by the ulama and religious parties to challenge the politicians' right to interpret "true" Islam. But unlike their predecessors, Bhutto and Sharif confronted a more complex political landscape. The expansion of Deobandi reformism encouraged by Zia had not only strengthened ulama parties but also empowered a network of violent, Sunni sectarian, religio-political groups inspired by Wahhabi or Arabian Islam. They now represented as much of a threat to the governing classes as to the pillars of the formal religious establishment. These new circumstances presented fresh dilemmas to a leadership accustomed mainly to shoring up its position vis-à-vis the ulama and Islamist parties like the Jama'at-e Islami. Thus, even while both Bhutto and Sharif sought, much as in the past, to appropriate Sufi Islam as a political resource, both had to consider new alignments in a context where the contestation over the terms of Islam in Pakistan had become more acute and where Sufi Islam itself was drawn ever deeper into the arena of these competing interpretations.

Bhutto appeared to be better placed than Sharif to withstand the test of these new challenges. With strong roots in rural Sind and across Punjab—both bastions of Sufi Islam—she deftly combined the secular politics of her Pakistan People's Party with an enthusiasm for Sufism.[29] The cult of the charismatic Sindhi Sufi saint Lal Shahbaz Qalandar, robustly cultivated by her father, was rejuvenated, and in a clear riposte to the austere Islamization of the Zia years, she warmly endorsed public celebrations at holy shrines across the country. Like her father, Bhutto also had a modern project of her own for Pakistan. This was based not on Islamic socialism, but on democracy, which she equated with pluralism. Reminiscent of Jinnah's secular vision, Bhutto projected Pakistan as a modern, progressive society where Muslims and non-Muslims enjoyed equal rights. Popular Sufism in Pakistan, with its inclusive culture of tolerance and its appeal across caste, class, and religion, served as a powerful motif to enhance this picture of a democratic Pakistan.

By the time Bhutto was returned to power for the second time in the mid 1990s, however, her engagement with popular Sufism was more muted. This stemmed in part from changes precipitated by the onset of intense Sunni religio-political activism that targeted the country's Shia minority.[30] Bhutto's Shia background with its attendant Sunni sectarian suggestions of heterodoxy now emerged as a political liability—a liability she could not afford to amplify by openly appealing to Sufi pirs, long accused of degrading Islam. According to some observers, it was Bhutto's sensitivity to this issue that led her to explore an alliance with the established Sunni ulama party, the Jam'iyat-e 'Ulama-e Islam (JUI). The party had emerged as a potent power broker under General Zia and would eventually become instrumental in persuading Bhutto to back its protégés, the Afghan Taliban.[31]

The political landscape that confronted Sharif was arguably more complex than that negotiated by Bhutto. Sunni sectarian discourse had intensified, and the spread of Saudi-inspired Wahhabi Islam had grown more pronounced. Both encouraged the promotion of markedly austere versions of Sunni Islam, which now sought expression in forms of religiopolitical activism that came to be associated mainly with Sunni militant groups. These groups proliferated in the 1990s and had a strong presence in urban, especially southern, Punjab, where they drew on solid constituencies bound together by common business interests, kinship ties, and, often, a shared experience of working in the Middle East. But the sharpening of these sectarian identities also deepened the awareness of sectarian differences—differences that hinged very largely on questions of setting the standards of "true" Islam. They helped galvanize a fresh campaign against the scourge of "ignorant" Islam that was judged to hold sway in Sufi shrines and sanatoriums *(khanqahs)*.

These circumstances placed significant constraints on Sharif's engagement with popular Sufism. Indeed, his appeal to the language of popular Sufism, especially during his second term in office (which ended following a military coup in 1999), showed every sign of shrinking. Conscious of the hostility among his predominantly urban supporters to the influence of local pirs (who were, more often than not, rural magnates and Shia), Sharif moved to strengthen his Muslim reformist credentials. The Tablighi Jama'at, a proselytizing movement founded in central India in the 1920s, served as the perfect vehicle. While known for its emphasis on correct Islamic practice and its rejection of the rituals of popular Sufism, its grassroots approach to Islam allowed Sharif to articulate a new modernist discourse that was more devout than doctrinaire in spirit.[32] The Tablighi Jama'at's deceptively unpretentious approach to Islam, with piety at its center, was seized on by Sharif to project his own vision of modern Pakistan—a vision that also suited the predominantly Punjabi urban classes of the new Pakistan that Sharif had come to represent. Economically liberal but socially conservative, piety served them as a perfect substitute for the spirituality they equated with the degraded Islam of popular Sufism.

In recent years (and in a somewhat curious twist) the language of piety has also found its way into the discourse of some Sufi masters engaged in shaping the politics of Sufism in Pakistan. They include Shaikh Wahid Bakhsh Rabbani (1910–1995), who rose to prominence in the 1990s as a fierce nationalist committed to the idea of a socially active Sufism as the basis of Pakistan. He urged a return to piety as the "backbone of power"—military, economic, and political—in Pakistan.[33] But Rabbani also warned that the vision of Pakistan as a "moral community grounded on knowledge and piety" was in danger from "Sunni-centric" religious sectarianism advanced by Wahhabi and Salafi doctrines and by modern-day Deobandis.[34]

His ideas anticipated many that have since come to be associated with the more recent campaign of the Pakistani Sufi scholar Muhammad Tahir ul Qadri (b. 1951).[35] A key figure in the firmament of Barelvi Islam and a strong defender of Sufi saints, Qadri has recently attracted attention in the West for his outspoken condemnation of the violent rhetoric espoused by al-Qaida and the Taliban. Qadri, like Bakhsh, is a native of southern Punjab who combines Sufi scholarship with active engagement in the social and political affairs of Pakistan. In the 1980s he formed his own political party, the Pakistan Awami Tehrik (now virtually defunct), and is regularly featured on the broadcast media in Pakistan as a leading commentator on Islam. But it is through his global educational organization, Minhaj ul Quran International, with branches in more than a hundred countries and head offices in London, New York, and Toronto, that Qadri has gained a wider audience for his message.

Its dominant theme, informed by an appeal to Sufi devotionalism, is the unequivocal rejection of violence committed by Muslim militants acting in the name of Islam. Qadri blames their activities on the influence of rising numbers of Wahhabis and their Salafi partners, in Pakistan and elsewhere, whom he compares to the Khawarij (or "exiters")—a seventh-century Muslim sect that broke with mainstream Islam to develop a fanatical attachment to righteous violence. In October 2001 Qadri was one of the first senior Muslim clerics to denounce the September 11 attacks and to call on Muslims to reject Osama bin Laden and "see the difference between jihad and acts of terrorism."[36] Although he is also a vocal critic of current Western policies in Afghanistan and Iraq, Qadri remains implacably opposed to al-Qaida and its allies, who use violence to further their religious and political objectives.[37]

But it was not until March 2010, after he issued a 600-page fatwa (ruling) that warned suicide bombers they risked "going to hell," that Qadri was brought to international attention.[38] He owed his success not only to his decision to publish the fatwa in English and to launch it in London rather than in Islamabad, but to the substance of his ruling, which appeared to go much further than any other in its condemnation of suicide attacks. For while earlier rulings against suicide bombings had, at best, questioned their permissibility under Islam and, at worst, condemned them as a sin *(haram)*, Qadri branded them as the acts of infidels *(kufr)*.[39] The purpose was to convey more than mere passive unbelief: what was intended was clearly to shock his militant interlocutors by casting their deeds as tantamount to *actively striving* to deny God.

In the ultimate analysis, however, what was significant about Qadri's message was not so much the power of its theological nuances. Rather, its value lay in the possibilities it offered to an internationally sanctioned discourse to draw on a counter-narrative *within Islam* that rejected terrorism *and* to a fragile civilian government in Pakistan, whose Islamic credentials had been sorely tested by its involvement in a war widely perceived to be a war against Islam. By drawing upon Sufism (albeit as interpreted by his own Barelvi school of Sunni Islam), Qadri was able skillfully to employ a discourse that could now be projected as both intrinsic to Islam and indigenous to Pakistan.

Its implications have not been lost on the ruling PPP, which has struggled to justify its controversial military alliance with the United States by attempting to project its government as a standard bearer against the "anti-Islamic forces" represented by al-Qaida and the Taliban. A key part of this exercise has been the PPP's appropriation of Sufism as the real face of Islam and the party's natural ally. It is well placed to do so, for in comparison to other parties the PPP has been far less ambiguous about the place of popular Sufism in Pakistan. For this too there are good reasons. The PPP is strongly rooted in rural Sind and rural southern Punjab, where Sufism is deeply entrenched and still powerfully attached to a populist ethos that has, in contrast to earlier modernist thinking, been wary of the excessive rationalization of Islam.[40]

However, what explains the PPP's current enthusiasm for Sufism (and which may well be invisible to U.S. think tanks charmed by the apparent convergence of views) is the party's social composition. Although widely associated with a pronounced secular agenda, the PPP's strong rural roots require it to function, in ideological terms, as an awkward coalition that includes the "horizontal relations" typical of the PPP's modern urban constituencies as well as the "vertical relations" associated with more traditional forms of authority in the countryside, such as the nexus between pirs and their followers.[41] This dichotomy has been carried by the PPP to the heart of a self-styled secular government, where the incumbents of two of its most senior posts are the descendants of prominent Sufi pirs, who also act as the guardians *(sajjada nishin)* of their holy shrines.

They include the current prime minister, Sayyid Yusuf Reza Gilani, and the former foreign minister, Shah Mehmood Qureshi, who held office until February 2011. Both hail from influential religious families in southern Punjab, where British colonial officials assiduously cultivated hereditary pirs as leaders, Westernized them, and secured their fortunes through gifts of land in exchange for political support. Gilani's family traces its roots to the sixteenth-century Sufi pir Sayyid Musa Pak, whose shrine in Multan still serves as a focal point for the Qadiri Sufi order to which Gilani belongs. Since taking office, Gilani has strengthened these Sufi roots by marrying his son to the granddaughter of Sind's leading spiritual leader, the pir of Pagaro.[42] Like Gilani, the former foreign minister, Shah Mehmood Qureshi, belongs to Multan, where he is the custodian of the shrine of the twelfth-century saint Shaikh Bahauddin Zakariya of the Suhrawardi Sufi order. As a descendant of Bahauddin, Qureshi not only partakes in a strong tradition of hereditary leadership over the Suhrawardia order in southern Punjab, but also continues his family's reputation as rulers and kingmakers.[43]

Notwithstanding these Sufi connections, it is important to recognize that the government has also been well served by a climate of public opinion in Pakistan that appears to be increasingly responsive to the idea of Sufism as a counter-narrative against the extreme versions of Islam favored by al-Qaida and the Taliban.[44] This shift owes much to the popular revulsion against the escalation of violence perpetrated by militant groups, which has led to the deaths of thousands of civilians. Public opinion has also been inflamed by militant attacks against Sufi shrines and local spiritual leaders. The most devastating such attack occurred in June 2010 when suicide bombers killed more than fifty people at the shrine of the Sufi saint Hazrat Data Ganj Bakhsh Hujwiri in Lahore.

But it is especially the Federally Administered Tribal Areas (FATA) and others parts of the newly named province of Khyber Pakhtunkhwa (formerly the North West Frontier Province—NWFP), long known for their attachment to popular Sufism, that have borne the brunt of such attacks.[45] Some of the worst strikes occurred in 2009. In March the shrine of the famous seventeenth-century Pashtun Sufi mystic and poet Abdul Rahman Mohmand, or Rahman Baba, in Hazarkhwani near Peshawar, was reduced to rubble. Other high-profile acts of violence included the destruction of the shrine of Bahadur Baba in Nowshera; the forced occupation and closure of the shrine of Pir Baba in Buner district; and the destruction of the shrine of Shaikh Baba in Bara Sheikhaan in Landi Kotal in the Khyber Agency of the FATA.

The struggle to secure a space for Sufism has also widened the scope of religious conflict, as in Bara in the Khyber Agency of the FATA. Here one of the region's most important spiritual leaders, Pir Saifur Rahman, who also enjoys a following elsewhere in Pakistan, was forced to leave the area in 2006 and settle in Punjab. The move followed clashes between the pir's supporters and those loyal to a local pro-Taliban Deobandi leader, Mufti Munir Shakir.[46] Although the federal government has sought to extend its Sufi campaign into northwestern regions, its progress has been brutally thwarted: Pir Noor ul Haq Qadri, an independent parliamentarian and federal minister from the Khyber Agency, has been repeatedly targeted by militants and a number of his family members have been assassinated.[47] Nor has the government been able to call on the resources of the provincial Khyber Pakhtunkhwa government, headed by the Awami National Party (ANP). Although the party subscribes to a tradition of nonviolence that many believe could yet be tailored to accommodate Sufi values of tolerance, the party has resolutely eschewed appeals to religion, prefer-ring instead to accentuate Pashtun ethnic identity as a more potent alter-native to Islamism.[48]

The federal government's attempts to harness Sufism as an ideological weapon in the war against "terror" have also been undermined by the historical association of popular Sufism as an ally of power bent on main-taining the status quo. Under British rule, pirs had emerged as vital medi-ators between the colonial administration and the local population. This was especially true in rural Sind and Punjab, where they served as indis-pensable power brokers in command of both ample economic resources and religious authority. Since then, the readiness of pirs to be co-opted by successive governments to maintain peace in the countryside has led to claims that their promotion of "docile" Sufism is intended to rationalize existing hierarchies of power.

This historical legacy has shaped perceptions of popular Sufism in Pakistan, where it still haunts public debates. Indeed, the adoption of Sufism by the government as an instrument of policy is regarded with suspicion, amid suggestions that the real purpose is to serve the interests of the United States, upon which the government depends for its survival and to justify inequalities of wealth. Indeed, both Gilani and Qureshi have been singled out as having a particular stake in maintaining a sys-tem that allows them to augment their political standing and justify their wealth by invoking their sacerdotal authority.[49] The fact that the U.S. gov-ernment chose, in its allocation of funds for the protection of Pakistan's Sufi shrines in 2010, to give priority to the mausoleum of Gilani's patron saint, Sayyid Musa Pak in Multan,[50] has deepened these suspicions.[51] This may explain why, especially at a time of intense anti-U.S. sentiment in Pakistan, those in favor of Sufism have called for greater discretion on the part of Western powers supporting their campaign. They fear that Sufism in Pakistan could be irreparably damaged if it is perceived to be no more than a part of Washington's agenda to soften Muslim resistance against the United States and its policies abroad.[52]

Ultimately, however, it is the contested nature of Sufism that is likely to pose the greatest challenge to the goals of a purported Washington–Islam-abad axis. For Sufism, like Islam, finds many expressions in Pakistan. These range from the broadly reformist concerns of mainstream Barelvi

Sufism to the mystic reflections of the ubiquitous *qalandars* (religious mendicants), who frequent holy shrines in search of the call of long-dead Sufi saints.[53] Wide differences also separate the political manifestations of Sufism. The main "party of the pirs," the Jam'iyat-e 'Ulama-e Pakistan, representing Barelvi Islam, shares little with Sufi pirs such as Maulana Muhammad Ajmal Qadri, who heads his own branch of the Qadiri order and is leader of his own faction of the main ulama party, the Jam'iyat-e 'Ulama-e Islam, which maintains close links with Taliban factions. Nor have Sufis in Pakistan been averse to the appeal of violence. The Hurs, warrior Sufis of Sind, owe allegiance to the Pir Pagaro, who leads his own faction of the nominally secular Muslim League. As recently as 2002 the much-revered Sufi leader of the JUP and head of the Ahl-e Sunnat, Shaikh Ahmed Noorani (d. 2003), urged his supporters to take up arms on the side of the Taliban against Western forces in Afghanistan.

This contested Sufi landscape suggests that any attempt to gain a monopoly over the expression of Sufism in Pakistan is likely to elude the country's leaders as much as their foreign sponsors. For it is far from clear which of the many contested versions of Sufism would form the central narrative of any program of action against the militants' campaign and whether, once established, it would enjoy a consensus durable enough to tackle the militants' formidable challenge. What is also certain, if Pakistan's history is anything to go by, is that the state's claim to act as the sole arbiter of Islam, including Sufi Islam, will be met with resistance not just from its militant foes but from a broader spectrum of society wary of a state that is deeply implicated in using Islam to legitimize political control.

Reflections: The Struggle for Pakistan or the Defense of Islam?

The most immediate danger facing Pakistan from these currents of contestation is the onset of what has recently been described as "faith wars," pitting followers of different Muslim traditions against each other.[54] As in the past, much of it is likely to be fueled by questions that hinge on "right" and "wrong" Islam—questions that Pakistan's modernist governing elite have long regarded as its prerogative to determine. Today that prerogative is being challenged as never before by groups set on a course of lethal confrontation with the state. While the resort to arms by both sides has undoubtedly raised the stakes of the current conflict, the state has found it harder to maintain its authority. Its struggle has been compounded by the terms of a modernist discourse to which it has long subscribed, but whose guidelines for standards of "right" Islam appear to be losing their force, especially with regard to the popular Sufism in which resources are now invested.

There can be no doubt that the challenges facing Pakistan's ruling elites today are far more formidable than any confronted by their predecessors. In the past, state leaders were preoccupied chiefly to contain the ambitions of a religious establishment that demanded the equal (if not the sole) right to interpret Islam—a right the politicians could not afford to concede for fear of losing their legitimacy. Today that pressure has intensified as the state endeavors not only to define Islam but to define the right kind of Islam for Pakistan. The assumptions of modernist thinking upon which the state had long relied no longer apply. Indeed, many modernist assumptions regarding the standards of proper Islam appear to be totally at odds with the discourse on Sufism favored by the Pakistani state today. Where Pakistan's presiding figures—Sayyid Ahmed Khan, Iqbal, and Jinnah—accorded little (if any) legitimacy to popular Sufism as the benchmark of right Islam, today's leaders seek to equate the two. And where once modernists like Iqbal hailed the purity of "Arabian Islam" as the best antidote to the corrupt "pantheism" of local Sufism, today's leaders reject its by-products (Wahhabism and Salafism) as undesirable foreign imports whose strict emphasis on doctrine is judged to run against the spirit of inclusiveness as expressed by the "right" Islam of Sufism.

It is still too early to tell whether these developments signal a radical reversal in the fortunes of modernist thinking and its role in shaping the contours of the Pakistani state. Yet Pakistan is no stranger to the discursive storms of the right and wrong kinds of Islam. In the 1970s the state's decision to designate the Ahmedi minority in Pakistan as non-Muslims for subscribing to what was deemed (at the time and since) to be the wrong kind of Islam, led to the group's blanket disenfranchisement and to its subjection to violent state-sanctioned discrimination. These storms resurfaced in the 1980s when the state avidly empowered Sunni Islam as the right kind of Islam against the false Islam that was seen to attach to

Shiism. Since then controversies of right and wrong Islam have routinely unleashed orgies of sectarian violence, which have scarred Pakistan. Today they could be set to take a further toll as the state moves again, aided and abetted by its foreign sponsors, to tie popular Sufism with its current perceptions of the right Islam for Pakistan.

Given the damage inflicted on Pakistan by the politicization of Islam at the behest of successive regimes, the latest attempt to empower Sufism could prove to be a dangerous gamble that spells the polarization of an already deeply divided society. Far from healing religious conflict, it could embolden groups like the Barelvis, marginalized by the state since the 1980s, to use the opportunity to promote Sufism as a way of settling scores with their Deobandi rivals. Indeed, the formation of the Sufi Advisory Council (SAC) and the key role reserved for Barelvi parties in promoting Sufism has reinforced expectations that the state will act to strengthen one version of Islam over others. These expectations were vividly demonstrated in July 2010 when senior Barelvi clerics led demonstrations across Pakistan calling on the state to sanction "armed retaliation" against Deobandi groups, which they held responsible for masterminding the attack on the shrine of the Sufi saint Data Ganj Bakhsh Hujwiri in June.[55]

This has raised the specter of Pakistan's fight against terrorism turning into a religious war in defense of competing ideologies of Islam that now must surely include popular Sufism. This risks further obscuring the question of the real objectives of the war being waged by Pakistan and its allies abroad. For most Pakistanis, however, the answer is clear: the fight against terrorism is not a struggle for the defense of Islam (or any version of it), nor a war to pit "good" Muslims supported by the state against "bad" Muslims associated with the Taliban: it stands above all, as it must, as a fight for the survival of Pakistan against those who would seek to subvert it and to operate in defiance of its laws.

11 / The Politics of Pashtun and Punjabi Truck Decoration

Jamal J. Elias

T his chapter is an attempt to understand the nature of sociopolitical change in Pakistan through an examination of patterns of decoration on Pakistani trucks, with an emphasis on examples of painting as a part of the decorative program. Underlying this analysis is the recognition of vehicular art as a legitimate form of cultural expression and its status as a visual regime unto itself in addition to being an expression of the wider such regime of Pakistani society at large.

Ninety-six percent of the freight in Pakistan is carried by trucks, which ply approximately 250,000 kilometers of roads and account for approximately 37 percent of registered vehicles. Truck transport has been gaining in importance (especially relative to railroads), and over the 1990s, truck freight volume grew at an average rate of 12 percent per year.[1] Virtually all privately owned Pakistani trucks are decorated with a combination of designs, representational art, epigraphy, and applied forms of ornamentation. Wear and tear necessitates an overhaul of an individual truck's decorative program approximately every five years. This is an expensive undertaking: in 2007, it cost up to Rs.400,000 (US$7,000 at the time) to have the coachwork completed on a Bedford truck, the iconic vehicle of Pakistani truck arts. In contrast, the cost of decorating a triple-axle unibody vehicle such as a Hino or Nissan in the Balochistan style was between US$12,000 and US$16,000. These figures are several times Pakistan's annual per capita income, making it clear that not only does the decoration of trucks carry substantial significance for a broad section of Pakistani society, but it also represents the largest art industry in the country.

Pakistani trucks, despite the expense lavished on them by their owners and drivers and their function as a visual spectacle, are first and foremost *working* vehicles, defined by their economic function as haulers of goods and makers of money. Decoration never assumes the status as the primary function of the truck, yet truck decoration is pervasive in Pakistan and does not represent the preoccupation or expression of an art subculture. The Pakistani truck is a cultural vehicle in the sense that it carries in it and on it an array of cultural messages and expectations.[2] It is also the most widespread expression of visual material culture in the country, saying more about the visual regime of Pakistan than other forms of art and visual expression that are traditionally treated as legitimate windows into the beliefs, practices, and dispositions of members of Pakistani society at an individual and a collective level. At the same time, the evolution of truck decoration reflects social processes of hybridization that are often the result of collective creativity in everyday life and in all forms of development, not just in the arts.[3] It is therefore legitimate and fruitful to examine the visual world of the truck in order to gain an understanding of the political and socioreligious dispositions of broad sections of Pakistani society.

Truck Decoration

As I have discussed elsewhere, from a decorative perspective, a truck has three separate aspects, these being the front, the back, and the (two) sides.[4] These aspects are used to signify distinct things: typically the sides are used to situate the vehicle and the individuals associated with it within a wider physical, attitudinal, and societal geography. They display the name of the transportation company as well as credits of the painter and others involved in the building and decoration of the truck. The sides are never used for mural or panoramic art (despite their width) but rather for small tableaus, most commonly of landscapes and famous buildings, imagined individuals (such as beautiful women), animals, or animals and people in idealized landscapes. All of these constitute themes of implacement, either in the literal sense (as in the name of the transportation company) or in a signified sense (as in images of idealized inhabited or uninhabited spaces).

The front and back of the truck are each divided into two sections. On the front, the upper section extends from the top of the vehicle to the bottom of the windshield; on the back, it goes as far as the tailgate, which may or may not be included in the upper section. The upper section of the back is the only part of the vehicle where there are large paintings, often portraits, located on the four or five wooden slats that slide in above the tailgate of most trucks in order to secure tall loads. Paintings on the back are only rarely religious; more frequently they are of celebrities from the world of entertainment or else heroes from national or subnational culture (tribal leaders, politicians, war heroes, and so forth). The lower section of the back typically displays writing, particularly humorous verses, pithy sayings, and popular moral and ethical exhortations.

In contrast to the back of the truck, where the bottom section is humorous or whimsical and the top is either panoramic or represents icons of popular culture, the front of the truck is far more formal in its layout. The bottom half of the front of a truck parallels the back in its use of poetry and aphorisms. However, in contrast to the whimsical character of the writing on the back, the epigraphy displayed on the front lower section, though almost never religious, represents what the owner or driver would consider to be high literature.

It is the back of the truck, and particularly the subjects and techniques of portraiture there, that provides some of the best indicators of sociopolitical and religious attitudes. The images appearing on the back often possess multivalent significations. For example, most writings on Pakistani and Afghan truck decoration emphasize the importance of a winged horse with a human head on the backs of trucks, identifying it unproblematically with the figure of Buraq as it appears in premodern Islamic album painting. This is, however, overly simplistic and fails to recognize the complexity of culture and representation in Pakistani and Afghan society. The tradition of Islamic representational miniature painting does not occupy a visible place in public life in these countries, and there is no indication that the majority of truck owners, drivers, and painters are aware that the image instantly recognizable as that of Buraq by scholars and others familiar with such subjects in premodern Islamic painting is a religious image in a strict sense. In my interviews with them, drivers, owners, and artists referred to the mythical winged horse as a "fairy" (*pari* or *khaparey*).[5] Some truckers believe that it was a fairy that carried the Prophet on the *mi'raj,* but others do not make the connection between Muhammad's vehicle and *paris,* which remain an important part of popular belief in Afghan and Pakistan society, especially in alpine areas, where they are said to bewitch people and carry off children.

The fact that the winged horse frequently appears on parts of the vehicle that are not otherwise loci for religious representation indicates that this image is seen as a feminine rather than an explicitly or exclusively religious figure. The image is never captioned in a way that would suggest a connection to Islam; it appears infrequently on the back of the truck, and seems to be less common in that location today than it was in the 1970s and 1980s. It is probable that the winged horse, as "fairy" *(pari),* has lost all Islamic significance for many truckers (if it ever possessed any in the first place) and has become part of the general palette of pictorial themes from which owners and painters choose what to represent on the truck, and more narrowly from signifiers associated with femininity or with flight and speed. But the religious association is not entirely lost: it is clearly there among the more educated members of trucking society, even if the association of the *pari* with Buraq is imposed upon their understanding during the formal moment when they discuss the image with an interviewer who is perceived to be needful of a more Muslim sensibility from the trucker. Even tangential associations of the winged horse with explicitly religious signifiers are few and far between, and when they do exist, they are in forms that do not fit traditional patterns of religious representation.

Images on trucks therefore possess ambivalent or multivalent significations, their messages shifting with different audiences and also across time. The latter point is not clear in the case of the winged horse because this particular image has not made any significant shifts of signification in the years of my study, although in the mid-1970s Dutreux had already noticed that Buraq did not fit comfortably into the easy categories of religious imagery on Afghan trucks.[6] The pattern of shifting signification as well as loss of vitality as a signifier is readily apparent in other images, most significantly Shia iconic images of Husayn's horse and Ali's familiar symbol, the lion, and in the traditionally talismanic chukor partridge.

The front of the truck in Figure 11.1 provides an excellent example of a truck displaying talismanic and prophylactic signs. It combines explicit textual messages to complement the iconic ones meant to defend against the evil eye. The formula *Ma'shallah* repeats itself six times in this image: on red spade-shaped plaques on either side of the second panel (to the outside of representations of the Ka'ba and the Prophet's Mosque); once on a rectangular panel to the left beneath the white boomerangs (the other side says "ya Allah khayr!" (O God! Good Fortune!); once on a violet panel between these yellow rectangular pieces; and twice on the chukor partridges immediately below this. In addition, the narrow panel directly above the boomerangs states "Cursed be the evil eye!" (bad chashm par la'nat), "May [my] life end, but not faith!" (jan jay par iman na jay), and "May you be well!" (khayr ho ap ki).

In light of these explicit messages guarding against misfortune—and appealing to God directly in that respect—it is not inconceivable that the images of the winged horse, which appear in the same row as the boomerangs, fulfill a prophylactic or apotropaic function in this context, since other images in its immediate vicinity do just that, either explicitly or implicitly. Stars and crescents are multivalent nationalistic and religious symbols for Muslim Pakistanis, signifying the related positive characteristics of religious pride and patriotism. The boomerang is almost certainly a cheaper substitute for ram or ibex horns, believed to bring good fortune by many people in Pakistan.

Most important of all are the two images of partridges on the tiara *(taj)* directly above the windshield. Partridges are kept as pets in Pakistan and Afghanistan because of a belief that they help guard against the evil eye and spells. Visual representations of the partridge, therefore, possess a clear prophylactic purpose, guarding the truck, its cargo, and those associated with it. That message is made explicit in this instance by inscribing the partridges with the word *Ma'shallah,* the commonest formula deployed

Figure 11.1. Detail of the front of a Bedford in the Peshawari style showing a variety of talismanic and other objects, Rawalpindi, 2003. © Jamal Elias.

to seek protection from the evil eye in Afghanistan and Pakistan. Images of partridges appear very commonly on the front of trucks, especially on vehicles that display a belief in intercessory forms of Islam. Such vehicles are more likely to incorporate belief in the evil eye and the necessity of guarding against it than are trucks advertising other ways of being Muslim, though these symbols are by no means entirely absent from such vehicles.

By the mid-2000s, the image of the partridge had migrated from the front of the truck—where it occupied a space within the established array of talismanic symbols, objects, and phrases—to the back of the vehicle.

The vehicle in Figure 11.2 is an example of just such a dump truck from near Rawalpindi. In this instance, the partridges have migrated from the front of the truck to the back with their sign value almost completely intact: they appear as a pair facing each other as they normally do on the front of a vehicle, and directly above them is a reference to God: "Glory be to Your creation!" (subhan teri qudrat). The call of a partridge is believed by many Pakistanis to sound out these words—one of many examples of how all of nature bears witness to the glory of God. Although not specifically a reference to the evil eye as in the case where partridges appear together with the *Ma'shallah,* the references to God and the piety of partridges retain their religious significance and keep alive the connection to their prophylactic function in society.

Figure 11.2. Partridges on the back of a dump truck,
Rawalpindi, 2003. © Jamal Elias.

Other trucks bear an almost identical painting from the same workshop; the partridges appear in exactly the same pose against backgrounds of autumnal alpine landscapes, but despite the identical visual representation, they bear no reference to the partridge's call as an invocation of God, nor any other reference that would suggest an awareness of the religious significance of partridges in Pakistani culture. To anyone unfamiliar with this significance, the partridges appear as nothing other than colorful birds in a sentimental landscape.[7] Still other trucks display a single partridge on the back of a truck. In such instances, the partridge appears alone against an alpine landscape, standing in a pose substantially more naturalistic than those in the paintings I have just mentioned. There are no indications of any religious significance to the bird, nor any talismanic or prophylactic signifiers that would suggest such a function. Detached from any such signifiers, the partridge arguably has shed its sign value and now is just one of many pleasing images that appear on the backs of trucks.

The same process of shifting signification is encountered in the case of an image that possesses iconic status within Shia circles around the Islamic world. A white stallion is instantly recognizable by many Shias as Zu'ljanah, the horse of Imam Husayn that, according to myth, was given to him by the prophet Muhammad and served as his mount during the siege at Karbala when Husayn was martyred. To this day, a riderless white stallion occupies the central place in annual processions commemorating the martyrdom of Husayn on the 10th of Muharram, the first month of the Islamic calendar.[8]

The truck in Figure 11.3 is unambiguous in its Shia identification. The white horse's flank is emblazoned in blood red with the name "Mashhadi Flyer" (tayyara)—Mashhad, in northeastern Iran, is one of the holiest Shia cities and a center of pilgrimage. Furthermore, the horse is peppered with silver rivets signifying wounds suffered while carrying Husayn on the battlefield. On either side of the horse are the names of the Shia heroes, Hamza and Ali.

Similar to the case of the partridge above, Figure 11.4 shows a truck with a white horse painted by the same artist as the previous one. The two paintings are virtually identical, with the white stallion in the same

Figure 11.3. Image of the horse of Imam Husayn on the back of a dump truck, Rawalpindi, 2003. © Jamal Elias.

pose against a background of green foliage. In this instance, there are no indicators that this truck has any formal Shia affiliation. Other than the advertisements for the painters, the remaining epigraphy comprises generic statements, an Urdu prayer wishing "May you always be happy, that is my prayer" (sada khush raho, ye du'a he meri), and a rhetorical Punjabi aphorism with ambiguous, possibly religious, significance of a very generic sort: "Why have you given me a cheating, thoughtless lover?" (kyun ditta ay asakun rol beparvah dola).

By popular consensus, Husayn's horse is believed to have been white, but this has not prevented an image of a black-and-white stallion from gaining popularity in the truck art of the Potohar Plateau. Some such paintings include the names of the Shia heroes such as Hamza and Ali, and the horse itself bears rivets representing wounds as in Figure 11.3, but others have no signifiers indicating any religious importance to the image. The riderless horse leaves the confines of Shia iconography and enters a wider world of images popular among truck owners and artists, with works by well-known painters being copied and circulating widely in the world of trucker decoration.

Figure 11.4. Painting of a white horse on the back of a dump truck,
Rawalpindi, 2003. © Jamal Elias.

Portraiture and the Modern

As the shifting signification of the images discussed above makes apparent, the back of the truck remains the most semiologically undetermined aspect of the vehicle, and the one on which personal expressions have always played a greater role. The location of pithy statements and jokes, it is also the part of the truck to display some of the most specific sociopolitical statements in truck decoration.

The back remains the only part of the truck utilized as a canvas for large paintings, and there are few rules concerning what can be displayed there, the only apparent one being that there are no representations of sacred individuals and places, or ones subject to religious veneration, with the notable exception of the Shia images discussed above. But even this rule is not observed equally, and in recent years there are many examples of trucks with religious themes on the back, as subjects of portraiture, landscape, and architecture, as well as sloganeering.

Portraits on the backs of trucks can be of religious figures in a broader sense, though they are more famous as celebrities of popular culture, such as the late Nusrat Fateh Ali Khan. Khan was a formally trained performer of *qawwali*, the musical meditational ritual of the Chishti Sufi order, and therefore can be seen as a religious figure. However, *qawwali* is so pervasive in popular Pakistani culture that few people beyond Chishti Sufis and the very well-informed actually think of it as formally religious rather than just part of the wide range of love poems and songs that play on their ambiguous messages of the human versus divine nature of the beloved. On very rare occasions one encounters images of prominent Sufi figures such as Khwaja Muinnuddin Chishti, the eponymous founder of the Chishti order, although even he is more likely to appear iconically represented by his mausoleum in Ajmer.

The use of the back for religious slogans is much more common, particularly by politicized religious groups. Figure 11.5 shows the back of a dump truck that provides an excellent example of the blurring of boundaries between Sunni religious groups in modern Pakistan, with explicit references to the Tablighi Jamaʻat existing side by side with a clear exhortation to armed jihad, anathema in a strict reading of the movement's teachings.[9] The top of the truck declares "O God, aid us!" (ya Allah, madad), flanked on either side by affirmations of the legitimacy of the first four Sunni caliphs (khilafat-e rashida and haqq char yar). The beseeching of divine help occurs here in a formula that is normally used to ask for Ali's aid (ya Ali, madad); together with the references to the "Rightly-guided" Sunni caliphs, the top of the truck could be seen as an attempt to assert a Sunni identity against a Shia one.

Below this is a couplet:

Your servant is a sinner, but You are merciful, O Lord!
Showing grace to Your servant is Your glory, O Lord!

banda to gunahgar he tu rehman he Mawla
bande pe karam karne teri shan he Mawla

The green flag behind the crossed swords says "Al-Jihad"; the two medallions on either side of it declare "Long live the call of Tabligh!" (daʻvat-e tabligh zinda bad).

Religious imagery on the back of trucks takes such different forms that categorizing it as religious in its primary significance is to misconstrue the place of the individual subjects represented on the truck as well as that of

Figure 11.5. Back of dump truck displaying Islamist slogans,
Turnol, 1997. © Jamal Elias.

religion and the religious in Pakistani society. The placement of religious
slogans on the back represents a migration of signifiers to a place where
they previously did not reside, and therefore a shift in the syntax through
which trucks communicate their messages. For contemporary religious
groups such as the Tablighi Jama'at to advertise themselves and their ideology on the back of a truck probably relates to the need of politicized
religious groups to shift the visual syntax in order to have their messages
(and perhaps even their identities) noticed by the intended audience. The
modest increase in the frequency with which Sufi-themed images are seen
on the backs of trucks in recent years might represent a response to the
practices of more politicized groups and the consequent growing acceptance of new rules of syntax among a wider population of truckers.

The most frequent religious images on the backs of trucks remain
those of politicized Islamist groups, a phenomenon that should be seen,

not as part of some formalistic thematic classification of religious images as part of the decorative program of Pakistani trucks, but as one of the notable ways in which the back of the truck is used to convey sociopolitical attitudes as well as concern with contemporary issues. In this regard, such images belong more appropriately to the wider category of portraits that appear on the backs of trucks. Portraiture on trucks has many functions and is used differently among individuals from different parts of Pakistan. It is most frequent among Pashtuns and truckers from Hazara, although it is not entirely uncommon in the Punjab, particularly on the Potohar Plateau. Portraits can be of celebrities in popular culture or else of male members of one's family. Most commonly, however, truck portraiture evokes the heroic or the exemplary. It is seldom entirely personal, reflecting as it does a desire to advertise individual attitudes and to communicate with a wider (though specific) cross section of society.

A substantial proportion of the heroic portraiture on trucks is of figures of national significance. Of the individuals associated with the formation of Pakistan, I have never seen a portrait of Muhammad Ali Jinnah (referred to by Pakistanis as Quaid-e-Azam, or "The Great Leader") on the back of a truck, although smaller images of him appear on the sides of trucks and also in the hammered metalwork applied to the body. Iqbal, the ideological rather than political founder, is encountered on the back occasionally, represented in a famous pensive pose that appears in official publications and on posters throughout the country. The preference for Iqbal over Jinnah is most likely because the majority of truckers either do not identify at a personal level with Jinnah, a very Westernized citizen of Bombay, or belong to the section of religiously politicized modern Pakistanis that sees Jinnah as possessing values at odds with their own and their vision of Pakistan. In contrast, Iqbal is widely believed to have been an advocate of greater Islamization, giving an avowedly Islamic character to Pakistan, and of a broader awakening of pan-Islamic pride and mobilization.

Iqbal and Jinnah do not only differ in their ideologies as imagined by sections of modern Pakistani society, but also in their relevance to Pakistani modernity. Despite his centrality to nationalistic discourse and in the "Pakistan Studies" curriculum in schools, for many Pakistanis Jinnah has receded into the mists of history, belonging to a time that is irrelevant to the realities of modern Pakistan. Iqbal, on the other hand, as a religious and nationalistic poet as well as an ardent advocate of pan-Islamism, is as relevant today as ever. Truck portraiture is an arena for the socially relevant, and in this Iqbal shares space with national heroes of more recent vintage.

There is a regional and ethnocommunal dimension to who is recognized as heroic. Thus Zulfiqar Ali Bhutto and his daughter, Benazir Bhutto, are popular subjects of truck portraiture in Sindh, understandably so because they belonged to the feudal aristocracy of that province, which also constitutes the heartland of their political party, the PPP (Pakistan People's Party). General Ayub Khan, the first military ruler of Pakistan, who was forced out of office in the period preceding Bangladesh's war of liberation from its status as East Pakistan, is still relatively common on trucks from his home region of Hazara.

There are other examples of heroic figures from the past that appear in truck portraiture; the majority of these are military figures. The most common among these is Major Aziz Bhatti, killed in the 1965 war with India and awarded the Nishan-e Haidar, Pakistan's highest medal for bravery, which is, by tradition, awarded only posthumously. The majority of heroes and exemplars appearing in truck portraiture are contemporary figures rather than those from the past, although Major Aziz Bhatti arguably has greater contemporary relevance than his death half a century ago might suggest. He plays a prominent role as a hero in Pakistan's annual Defense Day celebrations *(yawm-e difa'-e Pakistan),* is studied by all schoolchildren as part of their mandatory "Pakistan Studies" curriculum, and is the subject of poetry and song. As such, Bhatti is very much alive in the imaginations of contemporary Pakistanis.

Military heroes like Major Bhatti remain popular subjects in truck portraiture and, in a wider sense, reflect the prestige the armed forces have historically held among the Pakistani populace. Homages to fallen military heroes are an important means of advertising one's participation in a collective consciousness and of publicly positioning oneself in the spectrum of Pakistani sociopolitical ideologies. Truck portraits commemorate Captain Karnal Sher Khan, the first and (to date) only recipient of the Nishan-e Haidar to hail from Khyber Pakhtunkhwa, whose birthplace of Nawan Kiley in Swabi district has been renamed Karnal Sher Khan Kiley in his honor. Captain Karnal Sher Khan died in the Kargil conflict of 1999, a largely unacknowledged war that was begun by the Pakistani military ostensibly without the knowledge of the elected prime minister of the country. During and after the conflict the military categorically denied the involvement of Pakistani regulars in the hostilities, maintaining that the incursion had been conducted by Kashmiri separatists with Pakistani logistical and moral support.

From the perspective of political analysts as well as the liberal educated elite of Pakistan, Kargil was an absolute disaster for Pakistan. Following the conflict, India made a dramatic increase to its annual military budget, which was already beyond anything with which Pakistan could hope to maintain parity. The incident undermined Pakistan's credibility internationally as well as with those Kashmiris in Indian-administered Kashmir who supported a political solution to the long-running conflict. And finally, the violation of the chain of command in Pakistan represented by this action undermined the democratic government of Nawaz Sharif, who tried to remove General Pervez Musharraf—widely believed to have been the architect of the Kargil misadventure—from his post as head of the army, precipitating the coup d'état that brought about the nine-year military rule of General Musharraf.

Seen through the lens of truck decoration, questions of democratic legitimacy and international treaties do not carry the same significance in Pakistan's visual regime as they do in scholarly and journalistic analyses of Pakistani politics. In the mirror of the truck, the righteousness of Pakistan's cause in Kashmir is an implicit assumption, and the heroism of Pakistan's soldiers and military is independent of the culpability, competence, and legitimacy of the rulers, including the generals. Indeed, Musharraf was not to be seen on the backs of trucks even before his popularity ratings plummeted in 2007. Musharraf's lack of popularity was a constant in interviews I conducted with truckers from different parts of the country, the majority of whom disagreed with the governmental policy of supporting the United States–led coalition in Afghanistan. This policy is viewed as a misrepresentation of national interests, as was the pursuit of Osama bin Laden. He was referred to with open admiration and affection by many truckers, but is not represented on the backs of trucks because of the conviction among owners, drivers, and painters that they will face retaliation from the police and intelligence community if they do this.

The choice of subjects used in political portraiture conveys the explicit message that contemporary rulers and generals are not suitable subjects for representation, in all likelihood because the leadership of modern Pakistan is not viewed by truckers as representing themselves either politically or ideologically. This fact was made clear by a Pashtun driver from Quetta (who wished to remain anonymous) when discussing the image from the back of his truck which appears in Figure 11.6. When questioned as to the identity of the subject of this painting, he said: "He's our president." When I remarked that the portrait did not resemble Musharraf very much, he replied: "Not Musharraf! Our president Saddam!"

Recognizing Saddam Hussein, who had been captured by U.S. troops only a few days before this interview, as "our president" *(zamunzh sadar)*

Figure 11.6. Back of a truck with the image of Saddam Hussein, Rawalpindi, 2003. © Jamal Elias.

reflects a pan-Islamic notion of Pakistani citizenship in which the U.S. occupation of Iraq is part of a wider attack on Muslims that includes Pakistan, Afghanistan, and other conflicts of the day. Figure 11.6 visually affirms this attitude: Saddam Hussein's epaulets and the microphones display the Iraqi flag (albeit drawn incorrectly), while the two missiles behind his head are clearly Pakistani: they bear the Pakistani flag and the names "Ghauri" and "Shaheen," two types of missiles developed by Pakistan and sources of great pride in many sections of Pakistani society.

Identification with and admiration of Saddam Hussein is not based in an established historical relationship between Iraq and Pakistan. If anything, through much of their histories the two countries have fallen on opposite sides of Cold War alliances. Identification with Saddam stems from pan-Islamic sympathies held by the majority of truckers as well as by wider sections of Pakistani society. Such attitudes are deliberately engendered in the citizenry by the state, both through the formal educational system as well as all other propagandist tools aimed at strengthening national ethos. They are also very much part of Pakistan's self-vision as a state. But popular feelings of pan-Islamism do not reflect those of the government, the high-ranking ulama, or the shapers of educational policy. Instead, it is a direct consequence of Pakistan's involvement in Afghanistan following the Soviet invasion in 1979 and of its Kashmir policy. In both instances, pan-Islamic feelings have been consciously employed for the express purpose of encouraging the populace to support and participate in the Pakistani government's regional policies. However, as is clear from the lionization of Saddam Hussein at the very moment when Pakistan had taken a strong official stance in sympathy with the coalition *opposed* to the regime in Iraq, popular opinion in Pakistan runs counter to national policy and finds expression in the visual regime through the truck and other venues.

Saddam Hussein was not personally religious, and the Ba'ath party, which ruled Iraq from 1968 to 2003, was socialist and secular, allied with the Soviet Union, which was viewed with suspicion and hostility by the majority of Pakistan's public. However, when Saddam Hussein's regime came under serious threat from a U.S.-led international coalition, he consciously courted the sympathies of Muslims around the world by representing himself in a pious fashion. Images of Saddam praying were a staple of Iraqi propaganda in the years between the first and second U.S.-led wars in Iraq, and versions of these made their way into Pakistani popular art as early as the first war, when posters, calendars, and postcards depicted Saddam as personally pious and with the signifiers of nationalistic and pan-Islamic defense that are normally associated with national military heroes.

In the majority of posters of Saddam Hussein circulating in Pakistan through this period, his religious credentials related directly to his promise to "liberate" Jerusalem. However, in Pakistan, visual and textual signifiers recast Saddam, the potential "liberator" of Jerusalem, as a Muslim hero on the backs of trucks as early as the first war in Iraq, when portraits celebrated him with statements such as "Long Live President Saddam Hussein, Warrior of Islam!" (mujahid-e islam sadr Saddam Husayn zinda bad).[10]

The lionization of Saddam Hussein continued in truck decoration during the early years following the U.S.-led invasion of Iraq in March 2003, with many portraits clearly influenced by the widely distributed posters. He was shown kneeling in the same position and dressed identically, with the significant addition of a string of prayer beads that helped make his religiosity appear more contemplative. Military hardware and troops continued to be important elements of the background. However, the Dome of the Rock was replaced by the Ka'ba, which is a much more vibrant Islamic icon in Pakistan than the former. Awareness of the Dome of the Rock and the symbolic value of Jerusalem is dependent upon a degree of familiarity with Islamo-Arab politics concerning Zionism and the legacy of imperialism that is not widespread among Pakistani truckers, such that being "liberator" of Jerusalem has limited iconic value. Instead, the evocation of the Ka'ba elevates Saddam Hussein to the defender of the faith itself, because the image clearly suggests that it is the holy heart of Islam in Mecca that is at threat, and for the defense of which Muslims must rally behind this sacred warrior-president.

A related visual idiom is portraits on the backs of trucks celebrating Abdul Qadeer Khan, the "father" of Pakistan's nuclear weapons program. In January 2004, Khan confessed to involvement in an international smuggling operation that transferred restricted uranium-refining technology to Iran, Libya, and North Korea in violation of international as well as of Pakistani law. Despite the political embarrassment caused by this revelation, General Musharraf pardoned Khan and placed him under informal house arrest. Subsequently Khan alleged that he had been scapegoated by the government, which had itself been involved in and informed of the network's dealings, and that his televised confession and apology to the nation were made under duress and through appeals to his patriotism.

Despite international pressure, General Musharraf could not take any substantive actions to censor Abdul Qadeer Khan. Perhaps the fear that Khan might reveal secrets harmful to the Pakistani government played a part in the decision to pardon him. But critically important to Musharraf's decision in this regard was Khan's enormous popularity in Pakistani society. Colleges, schools, and laboratories are named after him, as are streets and wings of hospitals, making him the single most celebrated national hero of the last two decades. That his prestige was untarnished by his ambivalent confession and subsequent pardon and house arrest is readily apparent from the image in Figure 11.7. He is referred to as "the honorable" *(muhtaram)* Doctor Abdul Qadeer Khan, with a flag of Pakistan displayed prominently on his lapel. Around his head are representations of the missile that embodies nationalistic pride in Pakistan, and the titles "The Pride of Islam" *(fakhr-e islam)* and "Benefactor of the Nation" *(muhsin-e qawm)*, which rhetorically emphasize his stature as a true national hero.

The example of Abdul Qadeer Khan, like that of Saddam Hussein, emphasizes the lack of legitimacy of the Pakistani government but not of the concept of the state or nation. Symbols of modernity and statehood constitute important features in the visual language through which national (and transnational) heroes are represented in truck portraiture. Advanced weaponry—rather than the swords and horses of a romanticized past—are central elements in reinforcing the legitimacy of such heroes, as are nationalistic symbols, in particular flags. Figure 11.8 shows a truck from Quetta, Balochistan, with a portrait of Nawab Taimur Shah Jogezai, the leader of the Kakar Pashtun tribal federation toward the end of the period of British rule, revered by many Pashtuns as a wise and upstanding statesman who negotiated for the collective interests of the Pashtun people. Here he is depicted with Pakistani flags in the

Figure 11.7. Portrait of Abdul Qadeer Khan, founder of Pakistan's nuclear weapons program, Turnol, 2007. © Jamal Elias.

background, wearing formal Western dress of a sort no longer seen in Pakistan, nor ever publicly sported by Pashtun politicians, who, like the majority of Pakistan's political class, take great care in their manner of dress to appear as populists and "authentically" Pakistani.

In contrast to the representation of Jogezai, Figure 11.9 depicts a contemporary Pashtun politician, Mahmud Khan Achakzai, president of the Pakhtunkhwa Milli Awami Party, the major Pashtun nationalist party in Pakistan. In contemporary Pakistan, Achakzai is one of the most important political figures agitating for minority ethnic rights as well as for secular subnationalist interests against Islamist forces such as the Jam'iyat-e 'Ulama-e Islam (JUI) and various militant groups (such as the Tehrik-e Taliban-e Pakistan or the Tehrik-e Nifaz-e Shari'at-e Muhammadi) with whom the JUI is affiliated. In this image, Mahmud Achakzai is depicted with the same set of symbols seen in images of other national and transnational heroes: a flag (of the Pakhtunkhwa Milli Awami Party in this case) and microphones, which are also seen in Figure 11.6.

Figure 11.8. Portrait of Nawab Taimur Jogezai on a truck from
Quetta, Turnol, 2007. © Jamal Elias.

In all cases, the leader is depicted with visual symbols that signify
authority and access. High-tech weaponry, flags, microphones, and
(with the exception of Achakzai, a populist politician) Western dress all
signify goods and status that lie beyond the reach of truckers, who as a
class constitute a politically marginal group regardless of their regional
or ethnic background, although they are economically and attitudinally
more representative of the wider population. The heroic, in this imagining, is of two types, both of which constitute the modern leader. The first,
represented by the military hero, evokes religio-social values held by the
truckers in their understandings of their place in the world as Muslims as
well as citizens of Pakistan. The second, represented by local political and
tribal heroes, evokes their acute sense of personal marginality and lack of
empowerment within the national structures of power and allocation of

Figure 11.9. Truck with image of Mahmud Khan Achakzai, head of the
Pakhtunkhwa Milli Awami Party, Turnol, 2007. © Jamal Elias

resources. Through his stereotypically colonial-statesman-like dress and
appearance, the late Nawab Taimur Jogezai symbolizes a tribal ethnic
leader who is comfortable in the halls of power of the late colonial and
early Pakistani states, where he can represent the interests of his marginal
and disenfranchised tribal followers. Similarly, the microphones in Figure 11.9 make Achakzai, quite literally, *the spokesman* of Pashtun nationalist interests, which are visually represented by the flag behind him.

Conclusions

Images on the backs of trucks—and on the trucks in general—become
what have been called the "bearer[s] of a multitude of possible meanings,
both potential and actual, that vary over time and in different contexts.
Potential meanings are actualized or operationalized in many ways,
making a connection to the world (that is, to other bodies) through their

psychocorporeal impacts on practices as well as through consciously articulated interpretations, whether oral or written, whether denigratory or celebratory."[11] Neither the reflection of an unchanging religious ideology, nor a static sociopolitical view, nor a stagnant aesthetic, the back of the truck becomes the most easily deciphered aspect of the corporate artistic enterprise that is Pakistani truck decoration, a window into the visual regime of popular culture in Pakistan.

12 / The Afghan Mediascape

Nushin Arbabzadah

This chapter provides a historical overview of the media in Afghanistan since its inception in the late nineteenth and early twentieth centuries. Comparing newspapers and audiovisual media in times of censorship that were interspersed with periods of liberalization, it explores how Afghan news editors responded to the political and economic conditions of the country, trying to shape public opinion in a largely illiterate society where oral, informal sources of information transmission offered an alternative, rival model of public information. Some of the key characteristics of the Afghan media—a striking reliance on translated materials, a limited geographic coverage of the country, and the dominance of Persian as the language of the media—were present from the publication of the first newspapers. Providing a chronological overview of key developments from 1873 to 2010, this chapter identifies thematic continuity and structural change, exploring the ways producers of media tried to shape Afghan identities in response to wider, transnational global trends. It then shows how the contemporary Afghan mediascape is being shaped by a new set of media owners, which includes businessmen and former warlords alike. The result is a highly dispersed and incoherent mediascape characterized by geographic, political, and social divisions, separating Kabul from the provinces, literate Afghans from the illiterate majority, and finally, rural regions from urban centers.

The Early History of the Afghan Media

The first Afghan newspaper, *Shams al-Nahar*, was published in March 1873. Its editor put forward the newspaper's raison d'être as follows: "The peoples of the dominions of Afghanistan and Turkestan live in extraordinary comfort and safety under the rule of Amir Shir Ali (r. 1863–1869) and the subjects and exalted peoples of these realms have taken notice of useful advancements and desire to see news *(akhbarat)* and draw benefits from it."[1] It is also in this first newspaper issue that we find reference to the informal channel of communication from whence the public usually drew news and information: the first editorial ever printed in Afghanistan promised to "try to never publish nonsensical bazaar news."[2] The paper's purpose, then, was to offer an alternative to "bazaar news," the traditional informal source of public information, by printing timely and accurate reports. But despite *Shams al-Nahar*'s own reassurances, timely and accurate Afghan news is not found in any of the sixteen pages of its first issue. Instead it translated reports from faraway places such as London and New York, China and Prussia, while the content of these reports reveals a taste for the Islamic genre of the strange and wondrous rather than hard and factual news. Even more striking is the absence of factual reports from the dominions of Turkestan and Afghanistan, whose people, as the editorial explained, desired to receive news. Reports from these realms were chiefly about the weather, a politically harmless subject and perhaps the only matter that could escape state censorship. For such early editors, geographical proximity to various parts of Afghanistan was rendered meaningless in the absence of roads, a functioning communications infrastructure, and perhaps more importantly, freedom of speech. Even from the northern province of Badakhshan, a place where the paper had one of its few correspondents, the only news was about the weather, followed by an account of non-Muslim Kafir religious traditions narrated by a new Muslim convert from the region of Kafirstan. It appears, then, that for nineteenth-century Afghan editors, American and European news was much more easily accessible than Afghan news, not only because of state censorship, but also because of a lack of communications infrastructure further exacerbated by the precariousness of traveling on roads controlled by highway robbers. This paradox has shaped the development of media in Afghanistan to this date.

From the first issue of *Shams al-Nahar* until today, the coverage of Afghanistan has been the least-developed aspect of the Afghan media, with translated content dominating much of the news output. In contrast to the sheer political and logistic difficulties of gathering Afghan news, international news was more easily accessible to early Afghan editors, even in the 1870s, via the Urdu newspapers of neighboring British India. Here we see the figure of the translator emerge as a key shaper of the Afghan media. Such translators' careers often culminated in diplomatic missions, cementing the link early on between media and politics. These, then, were the conditions that resulted in the striking dominance of foreign news over local reports. Thus, from their inception Afghan media have been shaped by the paradox of being run from inside Afghanistan yet lacking the capacity to reflect the country's on-the-ground realities. As such, the first newspaper contained the seeds of the key future challenges of the Afghan media.

The next newspaper, *Seraj al-Akhbar Afghaniya,* appeared in October 1911. Here too we learn of the editors' goals on its first page: "It is obvious that in our times, news amounts to a language *(zaban)* of peoples and countries. Nowadays, apart from primitive and Beduin tribes *(wahshi wa badwin)* there is no government or people that does not own a newspaper."[3] Establishing a newspaper, then, allowed Afghanistan to join the rest of the "civilized" world. Mahmud Tarzi (1865–1933), the paper's editor-in-chief, is credited with being the founding father of the Afghan media. Between 1911 and 1919, *Seraj al-Akhbar* was published regularly, twice a month, its layout and content serving as a model emulated by future generations of Afghan newspapers. The sheer number and thematic scope of its articles are impossible to summarize briefly, and so I will focus on the key aspects of the newspaper that are of relevance to this chapter's overall argument.

Looking at the content of *Seraj al-Akhbar* during its eight years of publication in comparison to its predecessor, we find both continuity and change. Like *Shams al-Nahar,* this paper owed its emergence not so much to internal dynamics as to an engagement with the media outside of Afghanistan, chiefly of British India. Tarzi regarded it as a means of not only Afghan self-expression but also national defense. Hence, in the issue celebrating the launch of the paper's second year of publication, Tarzi wrote, "A nation that has no newspaper is rendered incapable of defending itself against lies and misconceptions."[4] True to this mission, the bulk of the paper's content served exactly this purpose, representing one man's mission to project a specific image of Afghanistan to the outside world. Here we encounter a set of contradictions that merit further scrutiny. To begin with, elsewhere, at the time, newspapers served to create an imagined community of readers who came to understand themselves as nations, but in Afghanistan *Seraj al-Akhbar* was rendered incapable of achieving this goal because of mass illiteracy. Judging by accounts of foreign visitors, such as the American engineer A. C. Jewett, the number of literate Afghans in the 1910s was exceedingly limited, even among the elite circle of courtiers.[5] Even this small community was partly composed of returnee Afghan political exiles, including Tarzi himself. The lack of literacy, then, was a formidable wedge separating the paper from the public it intended to represent. It is not surprising, then, to find that response letters published in the paper (in part to prove its importance as a shaper of opinion) were almost exclusively written either by non-Afghans or by Afghans residing abroad. Ordinary Afghans, the defense of whose reputation the paper had made its mission, were conspicuously absent in its pages. The sporadic occasions when the paper offered a glimpse of the Afghan population's existence beyond the abstract notion of a Muslim Afghan nation were when Afghans were berated. Tarzi lamented the Afghans' lack of proper public manners, including Afghan men's tendency to urinate in public or children's habit of using foul language.[6] Elsewhere we find references to the Hindu community, the recent converts of Nuristan, and the Mangal tribal rebellions.[7] Even though these reports provide a glimpse of the reality of a country that was far from pacified or unified, the actual purpose of the articles was to overcome and even deny such disunity.

Even though *Seraj al-Akhbar* was an avowedly nationalist newspaper, defining its purpose as a medium of Afghan self-expression, perusing its pages we would look in vain for an accurate depiction of Afghanistan as the politically unstable country it was in this period. Though absent in *Seraj al-Akhbar,* glimpses of this reality are seen elsewhere—for example, in the rival publications of British India, chiefly the *Pioneer* newspaper.[8] We know about the existence of such rival reports because *Seraj al-Akhbar* regularly published refutations of them. These reports included local uprisings in Khost and Herat, and an early assassination attempt against King Habibullah. *Seraj al-Akhbar* republished these accounts and then refuted them in detail, but it is through such refutations that we find out that Afghan traders traveling to India acted as the informants who provided this uncensored information to Indian newspapers. Tarzi was dismissive of such informants, accusing them of trading lies in return for "a cup of tea and a toke from the hookah."[9] In this peculiar cycle of information transmission, what was dismissed as cheap and nonsensical bazaar news by the first Afghan news editors served as the information base for the more established and professionalized newspapers of British India. The distance that separated the paper from the very people it represented is reflected in this example, given the fact that it was the work of Afghan informants that undermined their country's one and only newspaper. More importantly, as the subsequent assassination of King Habibullah in 1919 and the tribal uprisings of 1928 were later to reveal, the Afghan informants' bazaar news ultimately turned out to be a more accurate reflection of the situation in Afghanistan.

While Indian newspaper reports described a country where religious minorities were discriminated against and local strongmen oppressed the kingdom's subjects to the point of leaving them little choice but to rebel, the Afghanistan that appeared in *Seraj al-Akhbar* was quite the opposite. *Seraj al-Akhbar* presented a land that was steadily taking steps toward modernization, introducing roads and electricity, cars and telephones, and setting up orphanages and printing presses.[10] Numerous images of such modernization projects were published, particularly in the newspaper's second year. The fact that the king himself was a keen photographer explains the ready availability of such photographs, as well as the fact that an advertisement about a photo competition was printed in the paper.

Seraj al-Akhbar represented Afghanistan exclusively through images of the state, the royal family, and the military leadership, whose photographs appeared regularly alongside pictures of iconic modernization projects, such as an iron bridge, a hydroelectricity project, new government buildings, and military parades. In all such reports, the role of the foreign experts who oversaw the projects was often reduced to a nominal mention of their names, thus presenting modernization as an essentially Afghan success story.

Culturally, the country was represented through the medium of the Persian language, with Pashto beginning to appear only in the fourth year of publication, and through poetry, not prose (or, hence, news). The first poem, entitled "A Pashto Poem without Pashto letters," implied that the absence of the necessary equipment (in this case Pashto letters) in the printing press's typeset prevented Pashto from being printed.[11] But we also know from an essay published in 1913 that linguistic issues were deemed too politically sensitive to be discussed in a public forum such as *Seraj al-Akhbar*.[12] So, at the end of an essay about the origins of the Pashto language, Tarzi pointed out that he was aware that writing about Pashto encouraged his critics to accuse him of ethnic nationalism.[13] What we find here is an early, tentative attempt at dealing with yet another key Afghan paradox: even though the monarchs who led the country were ethnically Pashtun, they belonged culturally to the Persianate realm. As an established language of bureaucracy, Persian dominated the media for decades, and in contemporary Afghanistan it is only now beginning to be balanced out by Pashto and Turkish media outputs.

That the linguistic diversity of Afghanistan, home to approximately thirty languages, was hardly represented in *Seraj al-Akhbar* is even more striking given the fact that its editor, Tarzi, was a polyglot who ran a translation bureau, lending the paper the capacity to translate from a variety of foreign languages, including Turkish, Urdu, Arabic, French, and English. Once again we find that translation was easier than printing in the country's own languages, with even so key a language as Pashto not being an exception to this rule.

Seraj al-Akhbar's geographic scope was equally limited, with news from Afghanistan chiefly pertaining to protocol articles about royal visits and ceremonies that took place alternatively in Kabul or Jalalabad, the royal winter residence. *Seraj al-Akhbar* represented an ideal and even utopian image of Afghanistan, a country that chiefly existed in the imagination of its editor-in-chief. The fact that few Afghans could read the paper and respond to its content meant that inevitably its interactions were with subscribers who lived outside of Afghanistan and knew that the Afghan public played little part in the paper's debates and definition of the Afghan nation. The small group of elite Afghans who took an interest in the paper included royal princes, one of whom, Amanullah, became king in 1919. Through accounts of the king's daughter, Princess India, we learn that Amanullah's attention to the paper was of such intensity that he regularly attended printing sessions. Prince Enayatullah also founded his own printing press, publishing Tarzi's literary works and translations of Jules Verne's French novels from their Turkish editions. Later, Tarzi's intellectual relationship with the princes was further cemented by the marriage of his two daughters to Prince Enayatullah and Prince Amanullah. Given such royal support, Amanullah's coronation in 1919 could be interpreted as the promising victory of modern printed news over its oral rivals, the traditional sources of information represented by religious sermons and bazaar news. The victory turned out to be short-lived. Amanullah, the son-in-law of the founding father of modern Afghan media, was brought down in 1928 by a rebellion triggered by a rumor of his wife's immorality during her European tour, perhaps the most notorious example of the traditional sources of information transmission. Needless to say, the actual reasons for the king's downfall were more complex, but in the popular Afghan imagination the rumor continues to be credited with having triggered the downfall. The circumstances of the rumor are important because they reveal that the distribution of the printed newspaper and traditional oral information were not fully separated and at times interacted with each other. The rumor here pertains to the story that photographs printed in foreign newspapers, showing the Afghan queen unveiled, were distributed to the eastern border tribes, who then took offense and rebelled to protect what they perceived as a threat to Islamic values pertaining to women. The accuracy of the rumor has never been established, but its persistence until this day is testimony to the power of what Tarzi derided as "cheap and nonsensical bazaar news," which the first Afghan newspapers intended to counterbalance with the authority of the printed word. A precedent having been set by the rumor's spread in 1928, perceived offenses to Islamic values have remained a powerful trigger of public unrest, often resulting in censorship due to public pressure expressed by religious scholars, the traditional custodians of the informal, oral sources of information. Throughout the Afghan media's history, the only points where oral culture has interacted with and reacted to print materials have pertained to perceived offenses to Islam.

From this overview of the early history of Afghan media development, we can draw the conclusion that some of the key characteristics of contemporary Afghan media emerged with the inception of modern printed news media in the late nineteenth and early twentieth centuries. These characteristics include an overreliance on translated materials; limited geographical coverage of the country; the dominance of Persian as the language of the media; and the inability to reflect hard and factual news due to censorship, ideological considerations, geographical inaccessibility, and security concerns. Against this backdrop, subsequent Afghan news outlets found themselves in competition with their regional and international rivals, regularly losing potential audiences to their competitors.[14] The fact that Afghans share their languages with economically more powerful and culturally more productive nations of the region— Iran and Turkey to the west, India and Pakistan to the east—has further exacerbated this problem through a reliance on imported printed matter and eventually cross-border radio and television programming. Moreover, the history of modern Afghan media was shaped by translators rather than reporters. As a consequence, the media emerged through a translated engagement with the outside world rather than through internal dynamics, with local information sources and even languages largely ignored as sources of news.

Experimenting with Freedom of Speech

A brief period of political liberalization began with the adoption of the Afghan constitution in 1964. This constitution granted freedom of speech, lifting state censorship and so resulting in the emergence of a number of what at first promised to be independent newspapers. These political reforms were the culmination of the gradual and cautiously conducted process of modernization that resulted in the opening of the country to foreign development workers in 1957 and the expansion of public education. The latter is of key importance because Kabul University students were the main target readers of the new newspapers of the 1960s. The relative expansion of literacy and the opening of the country to development projects were significant changes. But it is equally true that by the 1960s the conditions of Mahmud Tarzi's time persisted in much of the country, particularly in rural regions where most of the population lived. In terms of media development, traditional oral sources of information distribution coexisted and at times interacted with new print outlets, a situation that Afghanistan had in common with other Muslim-majority societies such as Pakistan and Iran.

It was also in this brief liberalization period that for the first time in the country's history the ideological diversity of the country's literate elite manifested itself in public through print. The key architects of modern Afghan media in earlier times were intelligentsia translators whose careers often culminated in diplomatic postings; their counterparts in the 1960s were leftist political agitators who used newspapers as a means of mass mobilization for revolution. Leftist newspapers in particular stand out in this period, championing political journalism and experimenting with the limits of the freedom of speech that was offered to them by the very government they criticized in their newspapers. Three newspapers in particular merit scrutiny here because they reveal significant sociopolitical changes that had taken place since the country's opening in 1957. The first was the leftist, openly pro-Soviet newspaper called *Khalq* (a Pashto term, meaning "the masses"). It drew considerable attention, not only because of its usage of Marxist terminology, but also through its high circulation of 20,000 issues. Judged against the size of the population, this figure may appear insignificant, but in the absence of a developed printing market, publishing was a highly costly venture and so the circulation numbers raised questions about the source of the paper's funding. If suspicions were raised at the time, evidence for them emerged much later with the publication of the memoirs of the Soviet defector Vasili Mitrokhin. If his account is to be trusted, the Soviet politburo not only financed *Khalq* but even suggested the original idea of its publication. Perhaps even more significantly, Mitrokhin's account claimed that the paper's editor-in-chief, Nur Muhammad Taraki (1917–1979), had earlier served as a KGB informant.[15] Looking back at both *Shams al-Nahar*'s and *Seraj al-Akhbar*'s battles against cheap "bazaar news," in *Khalq* we find the figure of the informal informant elevated to the position of editor-in-chief of a newspaper funded by a foreign state.

Khalq's connections to external ideologies and founders rather than a local Afghan public was not limited to its source of funding. It also revealed itself in its style, content, and vocabulary, which showed a remarkable resemblance to the Persian publications of the pro-Soviet Tudah party in Iran.[16] Whereas earlier the first Afghan newspapers had emerged in reaction to the outside world, what we find by the mid-1960s is the outside world, in the shape of the Soviet Union, actively financing and shaping an Afghan newspaper that presented itself as an avant-garde, leftist, and authentically local news outlet. Pushing the boundaries of freedom of speech by printing ideologically pro-Soviet articles, the paper found itself banned after only six issues. Even so, the short term of its publication allowed the Soviet Union's influence on the small group of Afghan university graduates to reveal itself in full. The invasion of Afghanistan by the Red Army more than a decade later allows us to understand the apparent temerity of *Khalq,* not as a reflection of such media-makers' self-confidence, but as a sign of defiance that drew upon its editors' having forged an alliance with a superpower. The most provocative newspaper of the time was therefore also the least "authentic" and "independent."

Eslah (Reform), another leftist newspaper published in the 1960s, achieved notoriety after it published a cartoon of a man whom readers identified as the Prophet Muhammad. It depicted a man standing in front of the reception desk of a hotel with a group of veiled women behind him and being told by the receptionist that the hotel had no room for a man with ten wives. Such deliberate provocation is interesting, not only because it shows the extent to which leftist newspapers experimented with the limits of freedom of speech, but also because of what was triggered by publication of such controversial materials. The protests that took place in 1969 in reaction to the cartoon and in 1970 against a "blasphemous" poem show that the print sphere of the literate and the sphere of traditional oral culture interacted with each other and that, if considered blasphemous, the content of a newspaper published in Kabul could reach the provinces and trigger large-scale public reaction.[17] The 1969 and 1970 protests against "blasphemous" content printed in leftist newspapers therefore echo the 1928 rumor and rebellion that brought down King Amanullah. In both cases, offensive images (a cartoon of the Prophet, a photo of an unveiled queen) printed in newspapers reached the provinces and triggered reactions among a public otherwise unaffected by the print media. In contrast to 1928, the monthlong 1970 protest was curbed effectively, preventing it from growing into something more politically significant and destabilizing. The enabling factor that allowed for the print content to reach places outside Kabul was the Afghan National Assembly, a key product of the 1964 constitution. It was an MP from the Assembly who took the paper back to his province and so triggered the protests. In terms of content, the publication of a cartoon of the Prophet obviously was a much greater offense to Muslim sensitivities than the earlier printing of the unveiled queen's photograph, and as such had a greater potential for inciting a rebellion. By curbing the protests, the Afghan state of the mid-1960s proved itself to be in far better control than its predecessor of 1928. The power of traditional sources of information transmission, then, was variable and conditional, increasing or decreasing in relation to the state's power and position with regard to freedom of speech.

Representing the Maoist branch of the Afghan left, *Sho'la-ye Jawed* (Eternal Flame) broke new ground by experimenting with more modern forms of journalism, such as visiting economically deprived neighborhoods and interviewing their people and presenting an accurate—albeit ideologically colored—image of the ordinary public. These were the same Afghans who were earlier berated by *Seraj al-Akhbar* for their lack of proper manners. But in the 1910s as in the 1960s, widespread illiteracy meant that the very people who appeared in the newspapers were also those who were the least affected by the paper's content. If anything, the articles on ordinary Afghans served as means to trigger political discussions between the state and the leftist political parties who used their newspapers as a platform for communication and influence with the government. These debates were therefore largely conducted in the absence of the very people whose situation was used as evidence to criticize the government.

The brief era of political liberalization in the mid-1960s was marked by a diversification of the type of political journalism that had been first launched with *Seraj al-Akhbar* in 1911. The leftist print media scene was championed by activists and agitators who pursued the goal of a socialist revolution, some of them acting with covert Soviet assistance. Vocal but limited in numbers, these papers not only broke social taboos but also disseminated leftist avant-garde poetry, on one occasion publishing a controversial poem in which the traditional format of religious panegyric was used to sing praises not of Muhammad but of Lenin, one of the iconic figures of atheism. This too was a continuation of an earlier tradition that began with *Seraj al-Akhbar*'s publication of poems in traditional formats but with radically contemporary themes such as coal, bridges, and gymnastics. The 1960s therefore still represented a considerable degree of continuity with their predecessors. Print media were dominated by a small group of literate Afghans from among whom the newspapers drew their readers and writers alike. As in the early twentieth century, the 1960s newspapers presented themselves as the voices of the masses while in reality they were a reflection of the utopian fantasies and ideological loyalties of their editors-in-chief. In both periods, the only instance of interaction between the printed paper and the illiterate public was marked by conflict and hostility formulated through the language of religion. In 1928 such hostility ultimately brought down the state, but in the mid-1960s the state's greater control revealed itself in its ability to curb the protests against "blasphemous" content published in leftist newspapers. The desire to replicate the media advances that took place outside of Afghanistan's borders that had triggered the emergence of the first two newspapers in the 1870s and 1910s also reappeared in the 1960s, but this time in the more consolidated form of the transnational political ideologies of communism and political Islamism.

Because both the government and the print media underwent their first experience of freedom of speech in the 1960s, the period was one of experimentation, though it was frequently interrupted by state-imposed bans and closures. With the end of the constitutional monarchy in 1973, state censorship was resumed and political media-makers of the 1960s were gradually sidelined. They reemerged in April 1978, however, using a military coup d'état as a shortcut for advancing the political careers of former newspaper editors. One of the first institutions the new government brought under its control was Radio Afghanistan, which the coup protagonists used to broadcast their take-over of power. Even so, the infrastructural underdevelopment of Afghanistan meant that in much of the country it still took weeks, even months, for the news of the 1978 coup in Kabul to reach Afghans in faraway provinces. With the exception of the brief period of liberalization in the mid-1960s, the Afghan media of the 1960s through 1980s is closely comparable to that of its Turkish counterpart. In both countries the media were controlled by the state, serving to promote its ideological definition of a cohesive national identity. Technological advances reached Afghanistan later than in its regional counterparts, and so until 1978 radio was the sole nonprint news medium. Launched in 1927, Radio Afghanistan played a key role in defining and promoting what constituted official Afghan "national" culture, its purpose being to reflect national unity rather than represent actual diversity. In doing so, the media made official the preexisting traditional distinctions that separated high culture from popular taste. To gain nationwide fame, access to and recognition by Radio Afghanistan was crucial for Afghan musicians, folk or classical, male or female. Its concentration on high culture meant that the language spoken on Radio Afghanistan was closer to the written language, having little in common with the way Afghans spoke in their daily interactions. Just as earlier the gap of illiteracy forced a wedge between ordinary Afghans and the printed language of newspapers, Radio Afghanistan's control of culture created a similar boundary, separating official culture from its popular counterparts.

Perhaps the most striking media-related incident of the 1970s pertained to the end of President Muhammad Daud's rule, in 1978. The incident is little known because it is buried in the pages of the memoirs of the Afghan deputy foreign minister of the time, Abdul Samad Ghaus. Describing the week that led to the April 1978 communist coup that paved the way for the Soviet occupation in 1979, the minister described in his memoirs how a week prior to the coup, the BBC World Service's Persian service had aired a commentary announcing that a military coup was imminent in Kabul. The memoir recounts how the deputy minister printed the report and presented it to President Daud, who dismissed it, saying that the BBC sometimes got it wrong. The reliability of Ghaus's account has not been established. But truthful or otherwise, it voices an echo of the much older paradox we have seen, where media outlets operating outside of Afghanistan were often regarded as having access to more timely and accurate information on Afghanistan than domestic news periodicals operating inside the country. In the 1910s, *Seraj al-Akhbar* published refutations of a report published in British India of an assassination attempt targeting King Amanullah; seven decades later, in Ghaus's testimony, we find the BBC playing a similar role of accurately predicting from abroad a political event of huge significance within Afghanistan.[18]

The Soviet invasion of 1979 marked a new phase in the development of Afghan media. In the 1980s the official Afghan media were heavily influenced by a Soviet style of journalism, while Moscow also provided much of the media's technical equipment.[19] The ideological concerns that had ultimately prevented *Seraj al-Akhbar* and the newspapers of the 1960s from projecting an accurate image of the country that allowed ordinary Afghans to see themselves reflected in the media were elevated in the 1980s to the position of state ideology, further widening the gap between the public and the media. The culmination of this disconnect also marked the beginning of a period in which Afghan listeners increasingly turned to the BBC World Service. Airing programs in shortwave had allowed the BBC to bypass the twin problems of illiteracy and geographical inaccessibility, gaining it large numbers of listeners in rural Afghanistan. In doing so, the BBC managed to succeed where its Afghan counterparts had failed through much of their history. A desire to reach the general public—variously referred to as *ra 'aya* (subjects), *mellat* (nation), or *Khalq* (masses)—had existed from the inception of modern media in Afghanistan. Ultimately, though, it was the BBC's technological capacity and censor-free reporting that allowed it to not only reach but also appeal to the otherwise inaccessible majority of provincial and rural Afghans. Judging by a survey conducted in 2010, in Afghanistan the BBC still draws the bulk of its listeners from among such rural Afghans, a public whose loyalty it had first won three decades earlier.[20]

Another critical development of the 1980s was the emergence of unofficial and highly dispersed exile media, which since then have led a parallel existence to the official media. A thorough examination of the period's parallel internal/external media developments is beyond the scope of this chapter, but for present purposes the most significant change was the geographic dispersal of around five million Afghan refugees, who set up diasporic communities all across the globe. *Seraj al-Akhbar*'s formulation of the Afghan national identity had taken shape without interaction with the very people it defined, but from the 1980s onward the public's absence was even more pertinent, manifesting itself physically with the emigration of Afghans to Iran, Pakistan, western Europe, Canada, Australia, and the United States. In the early twentieth century, modern media had emerged in Afghanistan from a desire to join the developed countries of the world; by the end of the century, the Afghan mass exodus of the 1980s and 1990s made Afghans members of this wider world, closing the circle of interaction that had begun a century earlier with the first newspaper-mediated reports of events in Europe and America. From these communities of global Afghans, the key shapers of the contemporary Afghan media have emerged.

Continuity and Change since 2001

What is striking about the mediascape of the post-2001 period is the fact that we find considerable changes from the past as well as continuity with historical precedent. In theoretical terms, we find all of William A. Rugh's classificatory categories for Arab media coexisting simultaneously in Afghanistan along with overlaps with specific developments in other Muslim-majority societies, such as Turkey or the Gulf states.[21] The picture that emerges is of a highly dispersed mediascape that does not neatly fit into Rugh's distinct categories of mobilization, loyalist, or diverse media systems, but shows a simultaneous coexistence of all these categories. The diffused nature of the post-2001 media in Afghanistan is a mirror image of its politics, with a conflicting set of players moving the media in the opposing directions of cohesive nation-building and ethnonationalist identity creation. Radical structural departures from the past have occurred in the sphere of audiovisual media, while print and online media remain rooted in the literate sphere of influence. Politically, sharp geographical disparities persist, with the degree of freedom of speech varying radically, being almost fully observed in the capital and nearly nonexistent in faraway provinces controlled by political strongmen only nominally loyal to Kabul. All this is happening in a society in which the return of exile communities has brought with it shifts in linguistic identity-marking, exacerbating preexisting ethnic divisions and resulting in linguistic battles being played out in the increasingly diverse and fragmented media.

A notable shift since 2001 has been the commercialization of audiovisual media. Media producers treat the public as consumers whose tastes dictate the popularity or demise of television shows and even stations. This transformation is a direct result of the mass exodus of Afghans, which over the last three decades has allowed for the creation of a new diasporic business class from among whom the key media-shapers have emerged. These new figures include the owners of the two most popular privately owned television stations, Tolo and Ariana, which belong to this global Afghan business class, equally at home in Kabul, New York, and Dubai. Given that a century earlier, the founding figure of modern Afghan media, Mahmud Tarzi, was also a returnee from political exile, it is tempting to draw comparisons with those contemporary counterparts. However, in contrast to Mahmud Tarzi, Ehsan Bayat and Saad Mohseni are not members of the traditional literary and political elite. A businessman and a banker, respectively, Bayat and Mohseni belong to an international commercial elite, and this particular background explains why they were able to make productive use of the free-market conditions and freedom-of-speech laws that were instituted in Afghanistan after 2001. This ability has allowed them to transform a televised medium, which historically only the state had the financial means to support, into profitable private business ventures.

The commercialization of the audiovisual media as exemplified by Tolo and Ariana has had multiple and probably unplanned side effects, crucially the lifting of the barriers that separated high culture from popular culture. The media debuts of amateur artists, musicians, and journalists, whose styles have developed in the absence of a state-controlled definition of high culture, has since become a point of contention, with the established artistic, literary, and religious classes frequently taking offense at what they perceive as a lowering of artistic or moral standards by such television stations. The situation is reminiscent of the way the popular genre of Rai music struggled to find acceptance in the equally state-controlled cultural milieus of Morocco, Algeria, and Tunisia.[22]

The lifting of the state's or intelligentsia's control over what were traditionally perceived as publically acceptable languages, accents, and gender-voices has led to a far fuller public display of the diversity of Afghans. Chiefly noticeable is the manner of speaking of returnee Afghans, many of whose language has been shaped by the diasporic experience of growing up in Iran and Pakistan. Returnees from Iran mostly supply the Persian-medium journalist community, whose usage of what is perceived as Iranian Persian vocabulary has often raised questions of political loyalty. Such linguistic struggles have frequently taken place between the Ministry of Culture and Information and the journalist community, regularly leading to bans and dismissals. The politically loaded issue of the dominance of Dari-Persian in the media has met with the establishment of three television channels broadcasting exclusively in Pashto. Returnees from Pakistan, in turn, have since 2001 stood out for fluency in Urdu: when groups of young men are interviewed on Kabul's streets, Urdu speakers are heard on Afghan television as often as Pashto or Persian speakers. Ultimately, instead of creating a standardized language and pronunciation, the commercialization of popular audiovisual media has led to an accurate reflection of a public that does not possess the set of fully standardized national languages that appear in the 2004 constitution as Afghanistan's four official languages.

Since 2001 the outside world has played a complex role in enabling audiovisual media to break away from the restrictions of the past. The fact that these conditions were accompanied by military intervention has complicated this role. As a result of military operations, regions affected by insurgency remained inaccessible even in 2012 and often could not be covered by journalists. At the same time, the full use of freedom of speech by audiovisual media has at times led to criticism by international armed forces, who regard reporting of the views of Taliban commanders as propaganda. Similarly, because the international community helped finance some of the new television stations, the stations have been accused of serving foreign agendas. Such tensions are arguably the inevitable side effects of a democratization process that is accompanied by a military occupation. Still, the fact that the post-2001 media-shapers no longer come from the traditional political and literary elite is a significant change from the past; for the first time, the media can appeal to the public rather than attempt to reshape or redefine them according to ideological definitions of the state.

The above outline pertains only to television stations operating from Kabul. In the capital city the commercialization of audiovisual media has introduced international formats like cooking programs, foreign soap operas, and talent shows. In contrast, in the border provinces of the north, television stations are owned and controlled by local strongmen. Taking the example of Aina TV, which is owned by the former Uzbek warlord Rashid Dostum, what we see is the use of audiovisual media for the promotion of ethnic identity formulations that are local and global at the same time.[23] Hence, Aina TV broadcasts programs in Uzbek as well as in Turkish, often relaying films and documentaries produced by Turkish companies. The promotion of such pan-Turkic linguistic identity markers aside, Aina TV has often broken social taboos, as when broadcasting a Britney Spears concert on the anniversary of the mujahedin's victory and so setting itself apart from the more conservative, religious television channels also owned by former warlords. Compared to how, years before, television stations celebrated the anti-Soviet victory by broadcasting solemn and sometimes religious programs, Aina TV's provocative showing of Britney Spears was reminiscent of the attempts to break socioreligious taboos by the leftist newspapers of the 1960s. Aina TV, therefore, shows how post-2001 audiovisual media development has been far from homogeneous and marked by geographic disparities in agenda and content. While Kabul-based television stations often managed to make full use of freedom of speech, their provincial counterparts operated in a political sphere marked by the censorship and authoritarianism that shaped the Afghan media for much of its history. It is here that we find all four of Rugh's classifications of the Arab media coexisting simultaneously in Afghanistan. This coexistence is explained by the fact that, unlike many of its Muslim-majority counterparts, Afghanistan has never been rendered a coherent nation-state and so continues to exist as a collection of diverse political entities only nominally subservient to the state. Such regional differences have, under conditions of media deregularization, led to the simultaneous emergence of widely diverging media scenes, from the socially liberal (and secular) media of the north to the virtually nonexistent and socially conservative media of the south, with Kabul being a unique media island of relative political liberty and product diversity.

As exemplified by Tolo and Ariana, a key part of the success of the audiovisual media has been their ability to bypass the Afghan public's mass illiteracy through their audiovisual output, lending the twenty-first century media great resonance with traditional oral culture. Because mass illiteracy has persisted, developments in print media have radically diverged from the audiovisual media. Newspaper ownership is not a financially rewarding investment, because there is no visible market for printing in Afghanistan. Contemporary newspapers continue their earlier function as platforms of communication between political parties and the government, with the international community having since 2001 been added to the list of political entities to be addressed. Because the government and the international NGOs have their offices in Kabul, most of the newspapers have also been published in the capital city. Just like in earlier years, when the financial costs of printing led to suspicions of extra-national loyalties, as exemplified in the case of Soviet funding of *Khalq,* the commonly known fact that a majority of printed media are funded by international aid has somewhat undermined the independent image of the newspapers, a problem shared with audiovisual media outlets. Newspaper pages continue to be dominated by translations of Afghan-related news items taken from international newspapers, such as the *New York Times* and the *Guardian.*

The introduction of the Internet (access to which is very limited in Afghanistan) has meant that major newspapers also chose to publish online, and in doing so have come to draw much of their readership from the literate Afghan public in diaspora.[24] Their international online readership recalls the readership of *Seraj al-Akhbar* in the 1910s, as does the new newspapers' championing of political journalism. For the bulk of the population, however, the physical "newspaper" itself often serves mainly the practical purposes of wrapping shopping purchases and lighting fires, rather than intellectual engagement with their editorial stance. According to a widespread joke, the most popular newspaper published in Karzai's Afghanistan is the ISAF publication—the strong foreign paper on which it is printed is excellent for wrapping French fries. Yet local derision aside, in spite of their limited number of readers, some of the more critical post-2001 papers have been outspoken enough to find themselves censored and ultimately closed down. Once again, this too is reminiscent of the radical newspapers of the 1960s, while the fact that papers can be effectively banned shows that their key interlocutor is the Afghan state rather than the public.

Conclusions

Founded by intelligentsia translators rather than reporters, with the newspapers of the late nineteenth and early twentieth centuries the Afghan media emerged as expressions of a desire to become part of the developed world, on the one hand, and to respond to reports on Afghanistan published in the rival newspapers of British India, on the other. Despite being published in Afghan cities, local newspapers were unable to report on developments on the ground in the country. This inability was due to censorship, mass illiteracy, and the absence of an efficient communications infrastructure. Nonetheless, by the early twentieth century the second Afghan newspaper, *Seraj al-Akhbar* (1911–1919), was published regularly for eight years and became a model emulated by subsequent generations of Afghan newspaper editors, even though it relied on foreign newspapers for its reporting of international news.

A brief period of liberalization inaugurated by the 1964 constitution triggered the publication of radical newspapers affiliated with various leftist political parties. In this period, the ideological diversity of the Afghan intelligentsia was for the first time made public in print, revealing strong pro-Soviet leanings. In contrast to their predecessors, the newspaper editors of the 1960s were political activists and agitators who used newspapers for the political mobilization of the masses. Yet the newspapers' main interlocutor remained the Afghan state rather than the public. This ultimately resulted in the closure of the key radical leftist newspapers, inaugurating an era of censorship that persisted through to the end of the century.

The post-2001 media emerged after three decades of wars, a period during which there was a mass exodus of Afghan refugees across the globe and Taliban rule over Afghanistan. The end of the Taliban media ban in 2001 launched a new period of media liberalization. Television has been an especially important growth area. A significant structural change of the post-2001 media has been the successful commercialization of audiovisual media, making Afghan viewers part of a global community of consumers of international television formats. A mirror image of Afghanistan's political situation, post-2001 media development is marked by geographic and social disparities. Print is still rooted in its traditional role as a platform of communication between political entities and the Afghan state rather than the public. The audiovisual media are in turn marked by geographical divides separating Kabul and the provinces, rather than joining the country into a unified national mediascape. Privately owned television stations in Kabul are largely free; their provincial counterparts are controlled by local strongmen only nominally loyal to the central state. As a result, the post-2001 media are moving in multiple and contradictory directions, with the agendas of nation building and ethnic consolidation alternatively promoted by television stations in different parts of Afghanistan.

13 / Women and the Drug Trade in Afghanistan

Fariba Nawa

I n a dusty district two hours from the Iranian border in Ghoryan, Herat Province, repatriating Afghan refugees squatted on street corners begging for drug money to feed their opium or heroin addiction. Widows sat at home mourning the loss of their husbands and sons who died as mules smuggling drugs to Iran. Iranian authorities shot them dead as they tried to pass, or they became caught in the crossfire of competing armed traffickers. The surviving women feared that drug lords would come to collect on the loans incurred from the opium their men took with them. They also begged to survive, but instead of paying for food, they had to pay back their husbands' debts. Some of them will sell their daughters as brides. In the same district, the drug lords have built gaudy, four-story homes dubbed opium palaces. Many members of the Ghoryan police take cuts from poppy farmers and traffickers, and a few times a year they round up the farmers who did not pay them and burn their eradicated crops in public.[1] Residents with a plot of land plant poppy because it is the most profitable crop, even if they must plant it in their front yard.

Ghoryan, with a population of 54,000, is a border district drowning in opium, an example of the plight of other villages along the borders that Afghanistan shares with six neighboring countries.

My travels from 2000 to 2007 in Pakistan, Iran, and most provinces in Afghanistan showed the various ways drugs have changed people's lives and how mistakes by the international community have caused more problems than solutions. I follow the chain that links the actors in the poppy trade, including farmers, smugglers, counternarcotics police, and addicts. The roles become nebulous when the police are also the smugglers. The latest trend in drugs is the participation of women in smuggling and their increased addiction to opium. In this narco-state, women play a part in every link of the drug chain, from farmer to smuggler to addict. Most of them are clear victims of a drug industry that preys on the weakest and poorest, but some have been able to change their lives for the better with the cash earned from the poppy business. I will attempt to unravel the complexity of the roles that women play in a worldwide illicit business. This chapter will also discuss the debate to drive poppy out and the multifaceted approaches to resolving the issue.

A Brief History of Drugs in Afghanistan

Illicit drugs are responsible for Afghanistan's survival and destruction. The opium trade makes up 30 to 50 percent of the GDP; Colombia's cocaine trade at its height accounted for 5 percent.[2] The country supplies more than 90 percent of the globe's demand for illegal opiates. The Afghan opium trade is worth $4 billion and is a major funder for the Afghan government and their opponents, the Taliban.[3] The impact in Afghanistan has left thousands better off than they were before poppy farming became the main staple of agriculture in the 1980s, and has left tens of thousands of others in debt or dead. Neighboring countries also suffer the consequences as their criminals reap the benefits. Iran has the highest addiction rate in the world: 1 in 17 Iranians are addicts.[4] Pakistan and the Central Asian countries have also seen an increasing number of addicts and their government officials corrupted with drug money. Afghan heroin, the refined product of opium, is in highest demand in Europe and Asia. Russia has lost twice as many people to Afghan opiates—thirty thousand deaths by overdose in 2009—than soldiers in the ten-year Afghan–Soviet war.[5] Ninety percent of the heroin in the United Kingdom comes from Afghanistan. A small percentage, roughly 10 to 15 percent, makes it to the United States and Canada, while Mexico's black-tar heroin dominates North American streets.[6] The concern for the United States is not their addicts—it's the Taliban who finance their war with opium profits. Estimates of Taliban and al-Qaida income from the trade are sketchy but range from $70 million to $400 million a year.[7]

For centuries opium has been traded along the ancient Silk Road. Poppies were cultivated mainly for medicinal use and also consumed locally. In the late nineteenth century, when Afghanistan's modern boundaries were demarcated, communities on the border, including Pashtun groups that the Afghan ruler had resettled in places like Ghoryan, turned to smuggling. Opium and hashish were among the commodities, such as green tea and spices, that they smuggled on donkeys or in sacks on their backs to avoid taxes. In the twentieth century, Afghans found a growing market in Iran for opiates and other narcotics. In 1958, King Muhammad Zahir outlawed the cultivation and consumption of opium but did not implement the ban—perhaps because it was a contained problem. Afghanistan produced a hundred tons of opium consistently to meet Iran's demand. Cannabis farming was even more popular: 30 percent of the hashish consumed globally was cultivated in Afghanistan.[8] In the 1960s and early 1970s, Afghanistan was on the hippie trail, and tourists traveled there, in part, to smoke hashish. Counternarcotics policies did not challenge drugs until 1971, when the United States confronted hashish-trafficking syndicates in Kabul. In 1973, in one of the last royal decrees before Daud Khan ousted King Zahir, the ban on opium and hashish was reissued, and forced eradication cleared out the cannabis farms. But Afghanistan's economy did not depend on drug exports. The communist coup of 1978 and the subsequent Soviet invasion changed the drug trade.

As in Laos, Burma, Vietnam, Colombia, and other parts of the world, illicit drugs began to finance war in Afghanistan. The other common link with these countries is that they were drawn into proxy wars between the United States and the Soviet Union. The United States encouraged, and in some cases helped, anticommunist guerillas to sell drugs in exchange for arms. In Afghanistan, the CIA chose to support the most radical guerilla leader, Gulbuddin Hekmatyar, a known trafficker, against the Soviets.[9] Pakistanis who had become experienced in farming and smuggling opium helped Afghans learn the techniques. Seeds were loaned to poor Afghan farmers to start the process. If they made a profit, they could pay back the loan and keep some of the profit. If there was no harvest, farmers still had to repay the loan in cash. If they did not have the cash, they bartered their belongings, their property, or their daughters.

In Helmand, mujahedin commander Mullah Nasim forced farmers to grow opium. An American-funded project to industrialize farming in the Helmand River Valley in the 1950s had damaged the soil to a point that poppy became one of the few crops that yielded a harvest there. Moreover, the mujahedin and their cohorts discovered the lucrative benefits of heroin. As poppy farming took root across the country, in the east in Nangarhar, and in the north in Badakhshan and Balkh, Afghanistan eventually turned into a one-stop shop for drugs: cultivating and processing opium into heroin and trafficking. Once the Soviets left, the mujahedin and then the Taliban continued to reap the profits. In 2000 the Taliban imposed a ban on cultivation in response to a flooded global opium market and in an attempt to gain international recognition. But the Taliban continued to process and traffic drugs.

When the Taliban banned poppy farming, they sent soldiers into the fields. They had a hold over the country similar to Saddam's hold over Iraq, and people obeyed out of fear for their lives. The Taliban also used their influence with local elders to convince them to stop farming. International and Afghan experts on narcotics control are still impressed and baffled by how effective the Taliban campaign was. By contrast, in the last ten years $2 billion already spent and millions more allocated to stop poppy farming have not achieved what the Taliban did. But the farmers were not provided with any alternatives, which sent them further into debt.

After the 2001 American-led war ousted the Taliban, the drug trade boomed to a record high. In 2007 the United Nations reported about eight thousand tons of opium output.[10] Despite the official government ban, those in the Karzai government, which includes many of the mujahedin, and the Pakistani-supported insurgency were already deeply entrenched in the drug trade. The United States and United Kingdom fattened the pockets of known traffickers, like Haji Bashir Noorzai, now in a U.S.

prison on drug charges, who provided intelligence on the Taliban.[11] The neoconservatives in the Pentagon were adamant that the fight against the drug trade should not undermine the so-called war on terrorism. The problem is that the terrorists and the drug dealers are one and the same.

Furthermore, the battle against drugs is complicated by the fact that many of those who benefit the most from the drug trade are the same people who now run Afghanistan's provinces, with Western support. The Afghan president's half brother Ahmed Wali Karzai, as well as General Daud Daud, former director of counternarcotics, were accused of being smugglers who controlled large swaths of territory.[12] They were both assassinated in 2011—Daud in a bombing in Takhar, and Wali Karzai in a shooting by a close ally in Kandahar. Karzai's anticorruption chief served time for selling narcotics to U.S. Drug Enforcement Administration agents in Las Vegas. Ali Jalali, the most respected interior minister in Karzai's administration, quit in part because he could not convince the U.S.-led Coalition and Karzai to get tougher on drug dealers inside the government.

Counternarcotics efforts that aggravated the problem included eradication of poppy farms. In 2002 the British were assigned the lead among the Coalition and NATO to rid opium from Afghanistan. From April to June 2002, the British compensated farmers $300 a hectare for eliminating their crops. Boxes of cash were flown into the eastern and southern part of the country and distributed to local authorities to hand out to farmers. Authorities ripped out the soil with their tools and tractors. About 4,500 hectares of poppy harvest were destroyed. But many of the governors pocketed the money instead of giving it to the farmers, and farmers continued to plant poppy, according to the Dutch-based Transnational Institute, which studies drugs in Afghanistan.[13]

In the spring of 2004 the American company DynCorp paid $5 a day to dozens of Afghan troops to eradicate poppy fields. A year later, they plunged into one of the most dangerous areas, the poppy fields in the district of Maiwand in Kandahar Province. As DynCorp supervisors watched, the Afghan troops—armed with bush hogs, knives, and tractors—slashed the ripe poppy stalks. A group of three hundred villagers gathered at the site, shouting in protest, but the crowd dispersed after the police fired warning shots. Meanwhile, about twenty-five miles from where DynCorp was monitoring the poppy slashers, some six hundred demonstrators descended on Kandahar City to protest the eradication. The farmers shouted that their livelihoods were being destroyed without any compensation. The protest degenerated into violence, and ended in tragedy. Local police—which DynCorp points out had not yet been trained—fired into the crowd and killed twelve people.

The eradication program, which had been unpopular from its inception, halted after this incident, but it picked up again in the spring of 2006. Nonetheless, poppy cultivation steadily grew between 2001 and 2007. One of the Afghan supervisors of the eradication program said he expected the negative reaction. "A person is about to eat dinner and when he's about to take the first bite, you take the morsel out of his mouth. That's what we did and we got what we deserved," he told me in Kabul.[14]

Farmers, in turn, work with middlemen who buy their raw opium. A small amount of opium was processed inside the country in the 1980s—most was transported to Pakistan, Turkey, and the Gulf for refinement—but as the business boomed, so did the number of laboratories. No definite data exist about the number of labs, because many of them are mobile. The UN reports that two-thirds of the opium is refined into morphine base and heroin inside the country now.[15] Chemists are brought in from Turkey and Pakistan to refine opium into heroin. When I was in Takhar Province in the north, no one spoke of opium. Everyone dealt in "powder," which is the local term for heroin. A kilo of opium may cost $300, but the same amount in heroin can be as high as $3,000.[16]

Russian authorities say 175 drug syndicates are actively involved in trafficking Afghan opiates.[17] Mafias based in Pakistan, Turkey, Albania, and Nigeria buy and sell Afghan heroin, which includes the purest form, called "China white." Big trucks can easily cross borders with heroin and opium, but that is not necessary because tons of opium are exported from Kabul airport to Dubai on commercial flights.[18]

But drugs have also played an indirect role in the development of the country, because drugs are 40 to 60 percent of the GDP.[19] Drug money may be reinvested in construction projects. Actually, there are a handful of what Afghans call "good" drug lords—like Haji Barat, who has built clinics and roads with his money in the north in Badakhshan. But most drug barons are nothing like Barat. While each drug vendor I got to know had a complex set of beliefs, most were concerned with their own well-being and their family's. They made other people's lives miserable to make their own better. They believe that as long as the consumers of Afghan opiates are infidels, they are morally justified in selling drugs. What they failed to admit is that Afghans and other Muslims worldwide are also becoming addicts.

Afghanistan traditionally had a minute number of addicts, mostly among individuals of Turkmen ethnicity who spent inhumane hours weaving carpets. They smoked opium to treat the pain in their fingers. They gave it to their children and women. But ironically, now the culture of addiction is dictated by the neighboring countries, and the Afghans who are working there as refugees are importing the problem back to Afghanistan. Drug pushers are encouraging addiction because they recruit addicts to become couriers to cross the border—the most dangerous job—in return for a kilo of heroin to consume. The UN reported in June 2010 that a million Afghans, 8 percent of the population, are addicts; thousands of these are women and children.[20]

Afghan Women in Modern History

The journey of Afghan women in the drug trade predictably intertwines with the tragedy of war. The trajectory of change for Afghan women dates back to Malalai, an Afghan heroine from Kandahar who in 1880 joined the men in the battlefield in the second Anglo-Afghan war. The stories I heard as a child about Malalai invoked patriotism. "She offered her veil as a flag after the flag bearer was killed and shamed the Afghan men who were tired of fighting to keep fighting," my maternal grandfather, Sayed Akbar Hossaini, recounted in one of his bedtime stories. Malalai died in the battle, but her name lived on in the girls' schools named after her. Her fury, strength, and unveiling for the greater cause symbolized a shift from the typical life of an Afghan woman behind compounds taking care of her family. Furthermore, the fact that she was from Kandahar, an area that strictly observes the seclusion of women under Pashtunwali tribal codes, made her even more of an idol. Unfortunately, she was just an exception, and few in Afghan society would accept a woman with those characteristics now.

The quest for women's rights in Afghanistan has not followed a course of steady progress and has largely been limited to urban areas, specifically Kabul City. In the late nineteenth century Amir Abdul Rahman (r. 1880–1901) gave women the right to refuse marriage to their husband's brother when they were widowed, and the right to inherit property, and he raised the age of marriage. Inspired by the reform agendas of Reza Shah of Iran and Ataturk of Turkey, King Amanullah Khan (r. 1919–1929) and his wife Queen Soraya pushed in the 1920s for women's liberation, which upset conservative Afghan society. Amanullah discouraged the veil, pushed for individual rights, wanted to make education for women mandatory, and called for an end to polygamy and the payment of bride price. The first organization to protect women and the first woman's publication were founded during Amanullah's reign.[21] But the implementation of his policies reached as far as the capital, and his insistence on women's liberation was one of the main reasons he was ousted from power in 1929. Women's reactions to these ideas could not be measured because no one asked them; the radical policies were ordained from the royal family, whose ideas were far removed from the majority of Afghanistan. Many of the women at the time, like my step-grandmother, Bibi Gul, felt uncomfortable with these new ideas, especially the removal of the veil. My grandmother viewed wearing the veil as an act of piety, and its removal was sinful to her. Clerics and tribal chiefs protested the liberation of women as a disgrace to their entire clan's honor. Amanullah's successor, Nadir Shah (r. 1929–1933), appeased the conservatives and rescinded some of Amanullah's laws. He closed down the only woman's newspaper and stayed clear of radical change for women.

But his son King Zahir (r. 1933–1973), with the help of his cousin Daud Khan, established basic human rights for Afghan women under the 1964 constitution, including the right to vote, the right to an education, and the right to unveil. My mother, Sayed Begum Nawa, 75, remembers the late 1960s and early 1970s as the golden age for Afghans, men and women. "I was teaching, working for the first time in Herat, and it was probably the best time in my life. I had the freedom to wear what I want and all the cities seemed to be opening up to women. Maybe because our men had jobs and security. They were also happier," she says. Although the reforms were more gradual than during Amanullah's time, the hinterlands remained isolated. The villages continued to be deprived of the freedoms and education that city women had.

When the communists seized control of the country, they tried to enforce gender reforms again. They decreed compulsory education for women, established the minimum legal age for marriage of women at 16, and eliminated bride price. Their efforts were met with violence. The first uprising against the communist government occurred in Herat in the spring of 1979 after the communists ordered mandatory literacy classes for women. The efforts of the communist regime benefited women in Kabul, but the women who took advantage of liberal reforms were branded communists and targeted by the conservative mujahedin. A member of the mujahedin on a bicycle assassinated the headmistress of my Herat girls' school with a gunshot to her head because she was accused of being a communist. Fearing for their lives, women reappeared in the burqa and stopped going to school, and many stopped working. Those in the villages lost their sons and husbands, the breadwinners of their families, in war—Afghanistan has one million war widows.[22] Women had to become the providers as well as the caretakers. The most desperate became beggars; others became drug smugglers or prostitutes.

Once the mujahedin wrested control from the communists, many commanders raped and forced women to become their wives.[23] In 1994, when the Taliban marched through the southern provinces, they promised to protect women—that translated into confining them to their home, shutting down girls' schools, and forbidding women to work in most jobs. As Afghan men suffered the consequences of war—physical disability, joblessness, homelessness—they took out their frustration on the women. The emasculation of Afghan men has led to the worst domestic violence against women—one man cut off his wife's nose, many beat their wives to death.[24]

Progress for women in the Karzai years has been limited but visible, and although long-term reforms are elusive, education and job opportunities have extended to the villages. The media and women's access to satellite television and cell phones have opened doors to a virtual place where women can escape war and gain knowledge about the rest of the world. Women have taken advantage of the opportunity to work and go to school. According to a February 2010 UNICEF survey, women make up 70 percent of all manufacturing workers and 44 percent of agricultural workers. The number of girls who attended high school doubled from 2007 to 2008 to more than 136,000. Twenty-seven percent of the Afghan Parliament, 68 out of 249 seats, are women. Unfortunately, the numbers that show the continued destitution of women has grown worse. An estimated 60 to 80 percent of girls are forced into marriages. An Afghan woman dies in childbirth every 29 minutes; for those who survive, the average life expectancy for a woman is 43 years. While 39 percent of men can read and write, only 12 percent of the women 15 years or older are literate.[25]

Western aid and projects that single out women tend to backfire. One of the failures of the international organizations is the lack of cultural understanding in advocating gender reform. Afghan women tend to view themselves as part of a family, a unit, rather than an individual, and when programs aim to help only women, they isolate the men and increase the burden on women. Jobs only for women that men are also capable of doing should be open to both genders, because when Afghan men are left jobless, their sense of honor and dignity is questioned in society. "How can you sit at home while your womenfolk are working," I heard a taxi driver in Kabul ask one of his male passengers who shared that his wife worked as a baker while he remained jobless. The men usually do not do the housework. Women return from work to cook, clean, and take care of their children.

Similar to the mujahedin, the Taliban assassinate women who work with the government or foreign organizations. Several have been killed in Kandahar, one was a policewoman named Malalai who helped victims of domestic violence. Women resist in tragic ways—the Afghan health ministry reports that an average of 2,400 Afghan women self-immolate every year.[26] The ministry lists depression from war, forced marriages, abuse, and displacement as reasons women set themselves on fire. But Afghan women also survive in creative ways, their resilience a testament to human tenacity.

Women and Drugs

Gandomi Soltanzi is a widow in her 60s who lives in Ghoryan, the district bordering Iran in Herat Province. She has lost two sons and her husband to opium smuggling. Iran executed her husband and one son for trafficking, another son disappeared in the mountains of Afghanistan traveling with a truckload of opium, and her last son is addicted and roams the streets in Iran begging for money. One of her daughters self-immolated after her husband was also killed smuggling opium. Now Gandomi lives with one daughter, Aabi, and her two grandchildren. There are no men to support them. Aabi's husband died of a stomach illness. Gandomi weaves wool into yarn and collects bushes of thorn in the desert in her tattered shoes. She sells the yarn to carpet weavers and thorn to shepherds to use as fuel, eking out a meager living. "My family has smuggled opium for seven generations. We were shepherds but that didn't always help us survive. We would take a few kilos of opium in sacks on our shoulders across the border and get a sack of flour in return from the big dealers. Nobody was killed and few were jailed. Now my whole family has been destroyed because of this work," she told me in 2003.

Gandomi stands up to the cronies whom drug lords send to harass her daily. Her son had borrowed opium, and the drug lords demanded the opium or the several thousand dollars it was worth from her now. She opens the door and repeats the same thing to one man with a beard who bangs on her door every morning. "I don't have anything to give you. You've already taken the carpet." The man threatens to burn down her house and kill the rest of her family. But Gandomi finds the will and strength to continue working. She looks to her grandsons for hope as they laugh and play in her dust-filled yard with her daughter, Aabi. Gandomi is one of hundreds of widows in a similar predicament, deep in drug debt and fearful of ruthless lenders. It is a blessing that she does not have virgin daughters, she says, because then she would have to barter them in marriage to settle her opium debt.

The Afghan Independent Human Rights Commission (AIHRC) branch in Kandahar says it received reports of sixty-nine cases of murder and self-immolation of women from Helmand and Kandahar in 2006, several of them linked to opium marriages.[27] Hundreds of families are forced to sell their daughters to pay off debts. They are usually young, and their husbands are double their age and married with children. Those forced to give their daughters may get arrested for taking money from a smuggler, so they do not complain to the authorities and may even keep it a secret. Girls resist by running away or suicide. In November 2006,

Nasima, a member of the women's council in Grishk, Helmand, snatched the Kalashnikov of a policeman guarding a meeting of the council and shot herself dead. She ended her life at 25 years old after a year of living with a husband she had been sold to in 2005. He was an opium smuggler to whom her father owed a large opium debt; he had a wife and four children. Nasima married him but could not tolerate his daily beatings.[28]

The practice of settling debts and disputes with virgin brides is not new. It has been tribal custom to trade women in marriage for various issues, including forgiveness of murder as well as debt. My family neighbor, Mr. Jawan, in Herat, was an opium smuggler since the 1950s, like the rest of his tribe, and two of his attractive sisters were bartered as opium brides decades ago. But what has changed is the number of girls forced into opium marriages. No statistics exist to illustrate the rise in this practice, but anecdotes across the country show the increase. In Nangarhar, forced government eradication of farms exacerbated the problem. In 2004 one father gave his daughter's hand to a blind man who had lent him $1,600 in advance for his opium harvest. When the government destroyed his crop, he had nothing but his 17-year-old girl for payback. "I will be serving my blind husband to the end of my life," the girl told an Afghan reporter in Jalalabad, Nangarhar. "I am an Afghan girl and have to respect my father's choice even though I disagree with it."[29] The explanation for why opium lenders accept women as payment is given by Payenda Gul, a farmer in Nangarhar who also sold his daughter, 17, to a divorced man who was 38 years old. "When you have an agreement with an opium dealer, nothing but the opium can be paid but they cannot refuse the daughters. It is a way in which a dealer can find a wife for himself or for a son. The son may be disabled or he may be growing older and not had a wife. It is easy to present him with a pretty girl."[30] Sharifa Shahab, an official with the International Commission on Human Rights, told the Institute for War and Peace Reporting that most of these cases go unreported and the girls may commit suicide or end up as drug addicts.[31]

Until the drug boom in the 1980s, addiction among Afghan women was limited to Turkmen women who weave carpets. Different surveys cite varying numbers on how many women are addicted, and they do not specify how many are women and how many are children. All the surveys agree that the number of women hooked on opium and heroin

is consistently rising. Many of these women, like the men, are returning refugees from Iran and Pakistan. The husbands, brothers, and other
male relatives became addicts on the job—they smoked heroin to work
more hours and make more money. But they ended up spending that
money on more heroin and brought their habit home. Their children and
women became users, and entire families in Afghanistan have become
drug abusers. One family I visited in the historic neighborhood of Deh
Afghanan in Kabul described how they became addicted in refugee
camps in Pakistan. Mahbooba, a wife and mother of five children, lived
in Peshawar for ten years. "My husband was in construction, laying bricks
all day long in Peshawar. He would come home tired and in pain. We had
a neighbor in the camp who offered him some opium to ease his pain. He
began smoking the opium in the house. Then the opium was not enough.
So the neighbor offered him heroin. The heroin made him feel so ener-
getic and good that he worked two days in a row and didn't complain.
But he needed more and more as time went by. My teeth were hurting
and I decided to use opium as a painkiller too. Then day by day, I became
interested in the heroin he was smoking. My teenage sons who were fruit
vendors also began using the drugs. Instead of eating dinner, we smoked.
When we moved back to Kabul after the Taliban left, we found new dealers. My husband works all day and we smoke the money, eating as much
as we need to survive. I would like to quit but I think it's too late."

Mahbooba and her family returned to their bullet-riddled home and
do not have to pay rent. Counselors at Nejat Center, one of forty-three
treatment centers in Afghanistan, say a large percentage of families at Deh
Afghanan are addicts.[32] The neighborhood was deserted during the civil
war between the mujahedin in the 1990s, and families repatriated only
after 2001. The counselors make home visits and hand out methadone to
addicts. They try therapy and various other methods of outpatient treatment with the women, but there are more addicts than the center has the
capacity to serve. The impact of addiction unravels the basic unit that has
given Afghans their resiliency to survive four decades of war: the family.
Mahbooba says her relatives do not contribute to a collective family fund.
Each working member spends money on their own addiction, and she
begs once a week on the streets to find money for food. Mahbooba's own
addiction has damaged her role as the matriarch of the seven-member

family. "My children do not respect me or listen to me. They judge me for becoming addicted. They say I should've stopped them and their father from being addicted. I wish I had, but nothing's stronger than heroin," she said, crying, as she sat on a crumbling stairway outside her house. The addicts are the poppy trade's most tragic consequence, their addiction an extremity of the human condition that, like war, is an abyss of hopelessness and death. They are the last link in the chain of the poppy trade, which begins with a colorful flower, white, purple, or red, spread across the fields of Afghanistan.

At the root of the trade are Afghan farmers. Yet, of the $4 billion generated from illicit drugs in Afghanistan, farmers receive only 20 percent, while traffickers, kingpins, and their political connections snatch the other 80 percent.[33] The Afghan Ministry of Counter Narcotics estimates that 245,000 farming households of the 30 million Afghans remain dependent on farming opium in Afghanistan.[34] Poppy is a cash crop, and the farming households who plant poppy tend to live on debt, basing their livelihood on the following year's harvest. The profits are ten times more than wheat, the staple of most farmers, but families who plant poppy only use one-third of their land for the crop—one-third is for wheat or rice, and the last third is left fallow. When they have a good opium harvest, the benefits give them access to credit, cash, land, and labor, and the women involved in the process become beneficiaries. Women have been active in farming throughout the country's history, but the labor-intensive nature of poppy cultivation has made women an indispensable part of agriculture in Afghanistan. Their roles on farms are many, including weeding, planting the seeds, lancing the opium from the pod, and providing meals for migrant laborers who work on their family land.

Though women laborers complain of back and leg pain and an extra workload added to their caretaking and household activities, they also admit that they have improved their lives through poppy farming. Bibi Deendaray, 55, a widow from Kandahar, told UN researchers that for eleven years she has been a landowning poppy farmer who supports twenty people. She shares a portion of her land with a male farmer who is responsible for the bulk of the labor while she oversees the work. Bibi says she expects her harvest to bring in six kilos of opium, which she can sell for $3,000. "The more poppy fields you have, the more status you have in the community. People respect you and they loan you as much money as you want," she says.[35]

Poppy profits have transformed the lives of thousands of women-led households throughout the country. Poppy gives women cash and status. They can prepare healthier meals and buy newer clothes. Women also use poppy money to find alternative means of employment for themselves and their families. Parween, a farmer I interviewed in the northeastern province of Badakhshan, used opium cash to buy her son a car to drive as a taxi, she bought herself and her daughter a carpet frame and sells the carpets they weave, and for the first time in the family's life, they can have three full meals a day, complete with rice and meat. But Parween did not have the bribe to pay officials not to eradicate her field. The government eradication plan in 2004 destroyed her poppy harvest, and Parween told me she plans to farm potatoes the following year. "At least we have the taxi and carpets to keep us going," she said. The shift from a poppy economy to other livelihoods is precisely what the international community wants to focus on with poppy farmers. Although Parween is upset by the eradication, alternative livelihood experts see her situation as a success story because she has weaned herself from opium farming.

Women who work on the farms usually do so inside walled compounds because of the societal restrictions that require the seclusion of women. In a rare instance in Argu district in Badakhshan, I met an Uzbek woman who scored the poppy pods on land exposed on the main highway. Her burgundy scarf hid her face from view, and when I approached her, she admitted that she was ashamed to be working on the farm alongside men. "I have to because we do not have enough people to do this but when I'm done here at sunset, I have to go prepare a meal and take care of my children. I also take care of the animals. I'm so tired, my entire body hurts," she told me.

The woman said her family life minimally improved with opium cash but at the expense of her physical and mental health. "I'd rather be taking care of my children and home. This is not work I want to be doing." This woman's case is similar to those surveyed by the UN in 2000 in Nangarhar, who complain of ailments from being overworked and overburdened with doing both housework and farm work. The UN also concludes that women who work on the poppy farms do not have the time to transfer other traditional skills to their daughters, such as embroidery, carpet weaving, and sewing. Their daughters grow up without skills that could earn them a licit income in their adulthood.[36]

A UN report based on numerous interviews with women farmers in 2004 concluded that "opium cultivation could not offer sustainable solutions to women for either their economic needs, nor increased rights for women," despite the short-term benefits.[37] However, the UN report fails to recognize that opium cash can lead to upward mobility, effecting a considerable break in a cycle of poverty in the long term, like it did for Parween, the female farmer in Badakhshan. The moral argument that opium is a harmful substance that leads to addiction and death is just, but it is important to understand that poppy benefits not only evil traffickers but impoverished farmers who can reinvest poppy funds into legal means of livelihood.

The women who benefit the most from poppy are involved in smuggling and trafficking. There is limited research on these women, but it is a growing population. Women can smuggle small packets of opium and heroin because they are not targeted for searches as often. More drug lords and kingpins are hiring women, especially widows, to become mules. The monetary return for the women may pay for a month's room and board—$100 for a border run from Afghanistan to Tajikistan—but the risk to their life is much greater.[38] Women, like the men, can get caught in the crossfire of other smugglers, or neighboring countries can capture them. Once imprisoned, they can become victims of rape and torture. Most of the women I spoke to were caught by the Afghan police when trying to cross over from or to Pakistan. Zadrana, a Kuchi farmer, was convicted for planting and trafficking two kilos of opium and sentenced to a year in prison, where I met her in Kabul. Zadrana had six more months of her yearlong sentence. With raisin-wrinkled brown skin and coal-rimmed eyes, Zadrana had one leg for walking. The other was disabled from an unidentified illness. She crawled or held onto the wall as she walked. Zadrana was a widow with two sons and a 5-year-old daughter who suffered from a blindness that caused pain. The daughter, who lived with Zadrana in jail, sat next to her mother, holding her eyes and whimpering. Zadrana said the little girl inexplicably stopped seeing one day. She still saw shadows, and she cried from pain.

Zadrana owned two plots of land in Kondoz Province. She had decided to plant opium and sell the harvest to pay for an operation on her daughter's eyes. She scraped off the juice of the poppy bulbs, prepared it into gummy opium, and stuffed it in a plastic bag. Then she and one of her sons set off in a public bus heading south. Their destination was Pakistan through the Kandahar border. But halfway through her trip, in Chawk-e Arghandi, the police searched and found the opium. She confessed to smuggling but asked for part of her sentence to be forgiven. "I won't accept another six months in here. I don't deserve it and I won't do this again. It was out of desperation," Zadrana said.

Women smugglers can hide drugs well; they load a sack and wrap it around their stomachs to look pregnant, they swallow capsules full of heroin, like women in Colombia, and excrete it when they reach their destinations. They conceal it in their jewelry and private parts. The most famous case is of a woman smuggler captured in Kabul airport with a large amount of heroin. She was videotaped in conversation with Aminullah Amarkhil, who was then the Kabul airport police chief. She threatened to call contacts she had in the government who could get Amarkhil fired for capturing her and the drugs. A week later, Amarkhil lost his job. The attorney general accused him of corruption, but Amarkhil said he is being framed by drug dealers inside the government.[39]

The lines separating those who are clean and those who are corrupt have become blurred in Afghanistan, where all echelons of the government are involved in drugs. They either look the other way or get a cut from deals, which they sometimes arrange themselves. Women in the government may also be involved. At the same time, officials in both the Ministry of Interior and the Ministry of Counter Narcotics, which deals with policy-making, want to hire women to arrest women involved in various roles of the drug trade. Women are part of an elite counternarcotics force trained by Americans and the British; they carry guns, blow up heroin labs, and go on raids and search women in homes. Policewomen also serve on official checkpoints to search women in private cars and public buses. Many of these policewomen are widows as well and share a bond with the women they capture. Sakina, one of the policewomen who conducted searches on public buses in Kabul, told me she did not arrest some of the women she caught with drugs on board buses "because they are desperate and have no other way out." Thus law enforcement and counternarcotics have provided a livelihood for Sakina, a widow with four young children. "What do you think about the fact that opium is giving you and these widows you're arresting money for survival?" I asked her. "I'm on the right side of the law but yes, the truth is if there was no opium, I might not have this job," she said. She made $70 a month, which paid for rent and food.

Sakina the policewoman, Zadrana the smuggler, and Parween the opium farmer can be considered the beneficiaries of the heroin trade. In some small way this income has given them more status, respect, and a way out of a life that lists Afghan women at the bottom of a development chart among poor countries. If these women can take the money they earn from the drug trade and turn it into a legal economic opportunity, then they are victors in the losing battle against drugs. Meanwhile, Gandomi, the widow who owes drug lords opium money, Nasima, the bartered opium bride, and Mahbooba, the heroin addict, are clear victims of an illegal business run by ruthless drug lords and the mafia. They are trapped in the opium chain, dependent on its free-market capitalism.

It is too simplistic to dismiss the drug trade exclusively as a negative influence on Afghanistan. It is partly drug money that is being invested in reconstruction and the economy, and these women play a role in that process. These investments have led to the development of roads, schools, and clinics. The illegal drug trade breeds anarchy, but, paradoxically, it is a trade that could help with stability if channeled in the right direction.

Suggestions for Change

The current discussions in Washington, London, and Kabul all concentrate on prioritizing the Afghan drug trade as a top issue. One controversial idea that has received little attention is legalization. The Senlis Council, a European think tank, has been lobbying for the legalization of the poppy crop to be used for medicinal purposes, but where is the stable central government to monitor that process? Countries such as Turkey and India have legal poppy farms, but they also have the governments to regulate those farms.

A coherent, all-encompassing strategy focused on bringing security, giving poppy farmers alternatives to opium, and leveraging the funds of the drug criminals with influence in the government is needed. Finding alternatives to the poppy crop and stabilizing the country is the long-term answer. The first priority is to end the war. If the Taliban join the government with Pakistani backing, and security returns to Afghanistan, President Karzai will have to address corruption. For now, the answer is not in arresting or getting rid of the wealthy smugglers inside the government but rather convincing them to reinvest more of their funds in the development of the country instead of exporting it to the Gulf. After all, the U.S. state of Florida flourished with drug money. Afghan drug syndicates may take a generation or two to turn away from illegal smuggling and do business in legitimate commodities. Opium is the easiest crop to grow and the best moneymaker. The cultivation of opium requires little water, and traders come to the farmers—the farmers do not need to market their product. Legal lucrative crops such as Bulgarian rose oil, saffron, and black cumin can replace opium only if there are means to grow, transport, and sell the harvest. A counternarcotics strategy for farmers needs to include a budget for building irrigation canals and roads and finding markets for these alternative crops in due time. Once security has been established in an area and the police and local government are not taking part in the trade, then alternatives to poppy should be introduced. Otherwise, substitutes to poppy farming will fail, as they did in Helmand province in 2005 when the governor was directly involved in smuggling, and several aid workers trying to rid the province of poppy were ambushed and murdered. Americans wanted to quickly convince farmers to plant the alternative crops, so they paid cash for farmers and others unemployed in the area to build their own canals and roads, with few skilled laborers, on the front line of the latest battles between the Taliban and NATO.

The lesson was to give farmers time for the transition and to invest in anticorruption and security first, then hire skilled laborers locally and nationally to complete development projects that will jump-start a legal agricultural process. Because Iran and Pakistan present the closest markets, their needs should be targeted. Crops that are not highly profitable but are in demand in those neighboring countries, such as okra for Pakistan, should be planted. Once roads are built and transportation becomes easier, global markets can be considered in cultivating different crops.

The international community seems to be learning from their mistakes in battling the poppy trade in Afghanistan in the last nine years. Radical ideas like aerial poison spray is not a long-term solution and will not work. The Afghan government now is executing voluntary eradication. After the record harvest in 2007, the UN satellite poppy field survey showed a 31 percent drop in production to 5,500 tons, and the Afghan government announced that twenty of the thirty-four provinces were poppy-free in 2008.[40] The main reason for the slowdown is the market: an oversupply caused prices to fall. Hence, Afghan farmers took the government incentives not to plant poppy for a year or two until they can make money again. This is a short-term solution that will not stick.

For production to remain low, Afghanistan needs a stable government and viable economic opportunities. International support for substitute crops and employment for poppy farmers must increase to provide a way out of the poppy trap. The Afghan government needs to work with tribal elders, as they have done in the province of Nangarhar, to convince farmers to stop planting poppy. Poppy eradication should be limited to wealthy landowners, because targeting poor farmers only makes traffickers more money: when Karzai announced in 2005 that poppy would be eradicated, this prompted traders to hide their supplies, and prices soared from $90 to $1,000 a kilo.[41]

Some successful efforts have materialized to establish enforcement against drugs. A new jail for drug criminals was opened in 2006, and some of the cells are filled. New antidrug laws have been passed, and prosecutors and judges are being trained along with a special counternarcotics police. The United States has arrested four major Afghan kingpins, who are being tried in American courts. Intercepting heroin labs and big drug deals must become more effective. When I spent time with the counternarcotics agents, they relied on informants who were double agents. They would tell the government where the labs were located but would also tell the perpetrators when the police were coming to bust them. The lab workers escaped and took their supplies with them before the police arrived. The police ended up blowing up the equipment and had nothing to show for their dramatic explosions except bullet-riddled pots and pans. When I asked why they could not find trustworthy narcs, the police told me the drug dealers paid them more. Thus, another way to curb corruption is to increase the salaries for police and informants.

All these efforts to limit the influence of the drug trade in Afghanistan will take time, perhaps twenty years. There are no quick fixes or short-term answers that are sustainable. Perhaps the drug trade will find another home where lawlessness rules, but at least Afghanistan will get a break from its detrimental impact. Perhaps Gandomi's grandchildren can find work other than opium smuggling in Ghoryan.

Epilogue

Shahzad Bashir and Robert D. Crews

The spring of 2011 proved to be a precipitous time for two quite dissimilar men whose celebrity is identified closely with Afghanistan, Pakistan, and their common borderland. On April 17, the American television program *60 Minutes* ran a segment that called into question numerous claims made by Greg Mortenson in his bestselling book *Three Cups of Tea*. Widely regarded as a pioneer for the development of facilities for girls' education until this time, Mortenson was charged with falsifying the account of his experiences while mountaineering in Pakistan. A fortuitous turn into the wrong village in Baltistan, he had claimed, had led to his discovering a highly effective method for improving the lives of some Pakistanis. Among other revisions to the original story, he now acknowledged that the celebrated dramatic story in his book was a "compressed" version of events that occurred at different times over numerous trips to the region.[1] Mortenson's fall from grace provoked disappointment in the media and perhaps some schadenfreude on the part of those who might have envied his success.

On May 2, a fortnight after the CBS report on Mortenson, U.S. Navy SEALs tracked and killed Osama Bin Laden in the Pakistani city of Abbottabad. Shortly thereafter, Bin Laden's body was disposed off at sea, bringing to conclusion an American manhunt that began in 1998 and became a military priority of the first order following the iconic attacks on targets in New York and Washington, DC, on September 11, 2001. Bin Laden's death unleashed a brief euphoria in American public settings, although continuing accounts of a war effort at a stalemate nearly a decade after its inception displaced Bin Laden from front pages rather quickly. In the final analysis, the biggest effects of Bin Laden's death seem to have been the satisfaction of revenge on the part of some, and the availability of a trove of information from his hideout that is now subject to highly controlled and selective dissemination by the American government to further its political and military purposes.

Most readers of this book are likely to regard Mortenson and Bin Laden as belonging to entirely different categories of persons: the former is a humanitarian, however flawed, and the latter a belligerent activist willing to use all possible means to attack those he considered his enemies. The distinction is justifiable, but we believe there are benefits in putting the two together in a single frame as well. Both arrived in the Afghanistan-Pakistan borderland from afar. Both utilized the local landscape and peoples to make their names in their respective fields of influence. And both were principally concerned with addressing audiences far removed from the scenes of their operations in South Asia. The prominence given to Mortenson and Bin Laden in the worldwide media's portrayal of Af-Pak is indicative of the way the agency of individuals and communities that inhabit the borderlands have been written out of the stories of their own lives. Whether seen as naïve people in need of a savior from Montana, or as simpletons susceptible to brainwashing that may lead to suicide bombings, the locals seem to need foreigners to come and tell them what to do.

We hope that information and analyses presented in the essays in this volume provide a corrective to the mainstream media's portrayal of the Afghanistan-Pakistan borderland. Clearly, the unremitting emphasis on figures such as Mortenson and Bin Laden in such portrayals is not because there are no local stories and histories that should be of interest to those wishing to know more and act responsibly as world citizens.

Instead, the foregrounding of certain foreigners and the backgrounding of most locals are derivatives of the politics of production and dissemination of knowledge about the region on a worldwide scale. In the way it usually reaches us, such knowledge is always tied to the viewpoints and interests of major corporate actors such as states (Afghan, Pakistani, the U.S., etc.) and international and non-governmental agencies responsible for the flow of money, goods, and services in the region. Consequently, our sense of the lives of the people who inhabit the area never strays far from frameworks determined by the purviews and interests of these political and socioeconomic entities.

One major objective of this book has been to highlight this politics of knowledge and its real world repercussions by providing access to alternative frames of reference. We believe that knowledge and action—whether military, political, humanitarian, or developmentalist—are intimately interconnected and must be investigated in conjunction. This is clearly evident in the cases of Mortenson and Bin Laden. For instance, when called upon to explain the discrepancies between the narrative of his book and the account of locals, Mortenson provided the following written defense of his choice to reorder the past in his book:

> It is important to know that Balti people have a completely different notion about time. Even the Balti language—an archaic dialect of Tibetan—has only a vague concept of tenses and time. For example, "now" can mean immediately or sometime over the course of a whole long season. The concept of past and future is rarely of concern. Often tenses are left out of discussion, although everyone knows what is implied. And if a person is a day or a week late or early it doesn't matter. The Balti consider the western notion of time quite amusing.[2]

One does not have to be a professional linguist to shudder at the oversimplification and condescension reflected in this "culturalist" explanation. It is absurd to suggest that Balti has no precise mechanism for indicating tense because of its supposed "archaic" nature and that those who speak Balti are somehow predetermined in all their behavior to act according to the strictures of the grammar of their first language. Mortenson's claim that Baltis cannot tell the difference between "now" and "then" frees them from investment in their own past, present, and future, voiding the possibility that they may be regarded as historical subjects. Itself reminiscent of "archaic" civilizational debates of the nineteenth century, Mortenson's comment underscores his prerogative to reorder the telling of Balti lives. From Mortenson's perspective, the Baltis live in an ever-existing "present" that happens to be the frozen archaic time of the human species. Since Mortenson's philanthropic mission is to thaw the Baltis out of their present, which happens to be our past, rearranging the order of events with respect to his own encounter with them is subject to the needs of his own narrative and ambitions alone.[3]

Our main purpose here is not to criticize Mortenson's response on intellectual grounds, a task that is neither difficult nor worthwhile on its own. Rather, the greatest point of interest is the tremendous public success achieved by someone with Mortenson's perspective, which subsequently led to a sense of betrayal felt by those who had come to believe in him. The overwhelming popularity of *Three Cups of Tea* rested on the fact that it fully confirmed the overall media portrayal of the Afghanistan-Pakistan borderland, along with the crucial addition of casting an American in the role of a savior. The book not only enjoyed enviable sales figures, it led to highly successful fundraising for Mortenson's charity, and eventually brought Mortenson into the embrace of American occupying forces in Afghanistan. In July 2010, Elisabeth Bumiller of the *New York Times* reported that, "Mr. Mortenson—who for a time lived out of his car in Berkeley, Calif.—has also spoken at dozens of military bases, seen his book go on required reading lists for senior American military commanders and had lunch with Gen. David H. Petraeus, General McChrystal's replacement. On Friday he was in Tampa to meet with Adm. Eric T. Olson, the officer in charge of the United States Special Operations Command."[4] Clearly, the book struck a chord in terms of its ability to explain the region's realities to a wide set of audiences and also provided models for strategies that may be effective on the level of policy. By identifying themselves with Mortenson, American military officers could portray themselves as agents of universal human betterment rather than weapon-wielding foreigners.

Five days after the operation that killed Osama Bin Laden, the U.S. Department of Defense made available a number of videos said to have been recovered from the compound in Abbottabad where he may have lived since 2005. One of these shows a white-bearded Bin Laden sitting on the floor, wrapped in a shawl, watching satellite television. As he flips channels like suburbanites all over the world, we see images of Bin Laden himself in earlier times, on-screen guides for available programs, and Barack Obama. The scene reminds one strongly of Faisal Devji's argument that entities like al-Qaeda should be understood as modern movements for ethical self-fashioning for which modern media is a necessary enabling condition. For figures such as Bin Laden, the desire to be represented in the media, Devji suggests, is critical to their self-perception and parallels the proliferation of television reality shows, webcams, and surveillance equipment of all types during the past two decades.[5] The Pentagon official who introduced the video to reporters emphasized Bin Laden's white beard, said to indicate vanity on his part since it proved that he dyed his beard for making video pronouncements to the world. Moreover, the official was quoted: "Our takeaway is that he jealously guarded his own image."[6] There is some irony in the remark given that it was made in the context of the U.S. government addressing the media because of its obvious concern to manage its own image and make the best use of the media frenzy surrounding Bin Laden's death for its own purposes.

Bin Laden being taped watching his photos and action shots on international news channels; American intelligence officials watching the tape and selecting bits that can be aired to further their strategic interests; audiences worldwide watching the selections courtesy of international news channels and the internet. There is a circular pattern here that ties the politics of knowledge to political and military decision-making, whether that of Bin Laden and his associates or individual governments and alliances such as NATO. The circle excludes any sustained concern for the perspectives of the local population of the borderland, and, most critically, the flow of images has become so seamless that we are liable to forget that media dramas connect to the stories of millions of complex human lives. The coverage of politics and cultural and historical patterns pertaining to Afghanistan and Pakistan in this volume has aimed to disrupt the usual picture by providing access to perspectives other than those of global power holders.

Although we wish to highlight the local, our argument is not that this should be done at the expense of larger perspectives. In fact, we hope that the volume shows that today's local realities in Afghanistan and Pakistan are products of the interaction between agents ranging from international and national organizations to micro-level structures of authority. Contrary to its stereotypical portrayal as a land forgotten by time, the borderland can be considered a rather cosmopolitan meeting place of powers great and small throughout the modern period. As ground zero for great rivalries such as the Anglo-Russian great game, the still unresolved boundary dispute between Afghanistan and Pakistan, the U.S.-backed anti-Soviet insurgency, and the post-9/11 "global war on terror" (under George W. Bush) and the ongoing campaign against "violent extremism" (under Barack Obama), there is hardly any modern idea or weapon that has not had a significant impact on the region. But neither of these states nor their contested borderland has ever been an empty slate to be written upon by agents from the outside. Its substantial local populations have always been agents, affecting the plans of others in fundamental ways, and themselves being transformed by the new conditions that come to prevail with the change of circumstances. Based on this understanding, the exclusion of the local from our perception of the border region between Afghanistan and Pakistan amounts to a dire gap that needs filling, whether one's objective is to advocate for the rights of individuals or communities or pursue strategic military or political goals.

Notes

Introduction

1. See Roberto J. González, "Going 'Tribal': Notes on Pacification in the 21st Century," *Anthropology Today* 25, no. 2 (April 2009): 15–19; and, on the Afghan context, Richard Tapper, "Ethnic Identities and Social Categories in Iran and Afghanistan," in *History and Ethnicity,* ed. Elizabeth Tonkin, Maryon McDonald, and Malcolm Chapman (London:Routledge, 1989), 232–246.

2. David Kilcullen, "Taliban and Counter-Insurgency in Kunar," in *Decoding the New Taliban: Insights from the Afghan Field,* ed. Antonio Giustozzi (London: Hurst, 2009), 235.

3. See David B. Edwards, *Heroes of the Age: Moral Fault Lines on the Afghan Frontier* (Berkeley: University of California Press, 1996), 181; and B. D. Hopkins, "The Problem with 'Hearts and Minds' in Afghanistan," *Middle East Report,* no. 255 (Summer 2010): 24–29.

4. See Ayesha Jalal, *Partisans of Allah: Jihad in South Asia* (Cambridge, MA: Harvard University Press, 2008), 94–97.

5. Mukulika Banerjee, *The Pathan Unarmed: Opposition and Memory in the North West Frontier* (Karachi: Oxford University Press, 2000).

6. Scott Shane, "CIA Is Disputed on Civilian Toll in Drone Strikes," *New York Times,* August 12, 2011. On the politics of intelligence gathering, see

Kate Clark, "The Takhar Attack: Targeted Killings and the Parallel Worlds of US Intelligence and Afghanistan," Afghanistan Analysts Network (2011), http://aan-afghanistan.com/index.asp?id=1691. For an account of the human costs of drone attacks that rarely find any mention in Western media, see Muhammad Idrees Ahmad, "Gunboats and Gurkhas in the American Imperium," Al Jazeera, July 14, 2011, http://english.aljazeera.net/indepth/opinion/2011/07/20117145247361110.html.

7. For some details regarding this question, see Sumit Ganguly and David Fidler, *India and Counterinsurgency: Lessons Learned* (New York: Routledge, 2009).

1. Political Struggles over the Afghanistan-Pakistan Borderlands

1. "Remarks by the President in Address to the Nation on the Way Forward in Afghanistan and Pakistan," The White House, December 1, 2009, http://www.whitehouse.gov.

2. Marvin G. Weinbaum, "Pakistan and Afghanistan: The Strategic Relationship," *Asian Survey* 31, no. 6 (June 1991): 496; Husain Haqqani, *Pakistan: Between Mosque and Military* (Washington, DC: Carnegie Endowment for International Peace, 2005), 161–162.

3. Weinbaum, "Pakistan and Afghanistan," 496.

4. For more on the term *neo-Taliban,* see Amin Tarzi, "The Neo-Taliban," in *The Taliban and the Crisis in Afghanistan,* ed. Robert D. Crews and Amin Tarzi (Cambridge, MA: Harvard University Press, 2008), 274–310.

5. Vartan Gregorian, *The Emergence of Modern Afghanistan* (Stanford, CA: Stanford University Press, 1969), 132; for the concept of Afghanistan serving as "curtain," see Amin Tarzi, "The Judicial State: Evolution and Centralization of the Courts in Afghanistan, 1883–1896" (PhD diss., New York University, 2003), 101–103.

6. M. E. Yapp, introduction to *The Life of Abdur Rahman Amir of Afghanistan, G.C.B., G.C.S.I.,* ed. Sultan Mohamed Khan, 2 vols. (Karachi: Oxford University Press, 1980), 1:xi–xii.

7. Mir Muhammad Siddiq Farhang, *Afghanistan dar panj qarn-e akhir,* 2 vols. (Qom: Isma'iliyan, 1992), 1:667; Ludwig W. Adamec, *Afghanistan's Foreign Affairs to the Mid-Twentieth Century* (Tucson: University of Arizona Press, 1974), 92–93; Sana Haroon, *Frontier of Faith: Islam in the Indo-Afghan Borderland* (New York: Columbia University Press, 2007), 104–113.

8. For texts of the treaties, see Percy Sykes, *A History of Afghanistan,* 2 vols. (New Delhi: Munshiram Manoharlal, 2002), 2:355–369.

9. D. G. Tendulkar, *Abdul Ghaffar Khan: Faith Is a Battle* (New Delhi: Gandhi Peace Foundation, 1967), 424; see also Haroon, *Frontier of Faith,* 176–179.

10. Zahir Tanin, *Afghanistan dar qarn-e bistum, 1900–1996* (Tehran: Erfan, 2005), 92–93.

11. *Pakhtunistan Day* (Hove, Sussex: Key Press, 1949), 29. The booklet anonymously printed by the Afghan Embassy in London states that the purpose of its publication "is to outline the causes which led to the setting up of the Constitution of the State of Pakhtunistan."

12. Rahman Pazhwak, "An Article on Pakhtunistan: A New State in Central Asia" (London: Royal Afghan Embassy, 1960), 7.

13. Selig S. Harrison, *In Afghanistan's Shadow: Baluch Nationalism and Soviet Temptations* (New York: Carnegie Endowment for International Peace, 1981), 141.

14. For more on the beginnings of the Baloch insurgency in Pakistan, see ibid.

15. Azmat Hayat Khan, *The Durand Line: Its Geo-Strategic Importance* (Islamabad: PanGraphic, 2000), 188–189; Farhang, *Afghanistan dar panj qarn-e akhir,* 1:667–669.

16. Farhang, *Afghanistan dar panj qarn-e akhir,* 1:668.

17. Weinbaum, "Pakistan and Afghanistan," 496.

18. Khurshid Hasan, "Pakistan-Afghanistan Relations," *Asian Survey* 2, no. 7 (September 1962): 17.

19. S. M. M. Qureshi, "Pakhtunistan: The Frontier Dispute between Afghanistan and Pakistan," *Pacific Affairs* 30, nos. 1–2 (Spring–Summer, 1966): 106; Khan, *The Durand Line,* 232–233.

20. Haqqani, *Pakistan,* 167.

21. Ibid., 159.

22. Weinbaum, "Pakistan and Afghanistan," 499.

23. Ibid., 498.

24. Haider A. H. Mullick, *Pakistan's Security Paradox: Countering and Fomenting Insurgencies,* Joint Special Operations University Report 09-9 (Hurlburt Field, FL: JSOU Press, 2009), 30.

25. Ahmed Rashid, *Taliban: Militant Islam, Oil and Fundamentalism in Central Asia* (New Haven: Yale University Press, 2000), 187.

26. Mullick, *Pakistan's Security Paradox,* 33.

27. Amin Tarzi, "Afghanistan: Border Dispute Takes Toll on Security," RFE/RL, January 8, 2007, http://www.rferl.org/content/article/1073855.html.

28. Weinbaum, "Pakistan and Afghanistan," 505.

29. Shuja Nawaz, *FATA—A Most Dangerous Place: Meeting the Challenge of Militancy and Terror in the Federally Administered Tribal Areas of Pakistan* (Washington, DC: Center for Strategic and International Studies, 2009), 12.

30. M. Din, "The Frontier Problem," *Military Digest,* no. 12 (April 1954): 8.

31. Nawaz, *FATA—A Most Dangerous Place,* 36.

32. Robert Birsel, "Afghan-Pakistani Border Pact Seen Key to Trust," http://www.afghanistannewscenter.com/news/2006/october/oct42006.html.

2. The Transformation of the Afghanistan-Pakistan Border

1. In 1893 the Durand Line was traced on purely military grounds by a British commission, dividing the local tribes between the British Empire and Afghanistan. Afghanistan never recognized the Durand Line as an international border and for this reason voted against the admission of Pakistan in the United Nations after the partition.

2. The formal trade is around $2 billion, the contraband probably higher; Matthew Green, "Islamabad and Kabul Urged to Improve Ties," *Financial Times,* December 6, 2010.

3. Social capital is defined here more in the sense of Pierre Bourdieu, *Practical Reason: On the Theory of Action* (Stanford, CA: Stanford University Press, 1998), than of Robert D. Putnam, ed., *Democracies in Flux: The Evolution of Social Capital in Contemporary Society* (Oxford: Oxford University Press, 2002). Resources are understood according to Giddens; see William J. Sewell, "A Theory of Structure: Duality, Agency, and Transformation," *American Journal of Sociology* 98, no. 1 (1992): 1–29. Resources are all that can produce or reproduce power (unequally shared). The rules produce the resources (the way in which they can be used in a given social context), and the rules without resources disappear. The dynamics of social systems stem in particular from the fact that the rules are numerous and contradictory, a fact that the actors make creative use of.

4. Peter Jackson, Philip Crang, and Claire Dwyer, eds., *Transnational Spaces* (Routledge: London: 2004).

5. The field is a system of interactions between collective or individual actors of the same nature competing or collaborating around common stakes. See Pierre Bourdieu, *Rules of Art: Genesis and Structure of the Literary Field* (Stanford, CA: Stanford University Press, 1996). The transnational space is defined here as a territory where the rules of interaction are distinctive. We seek to distinguish here a concept of field, which explains the regular and sometimes competing interactions between the actors, from the larger notion of sector—which in the Weberian tradition refers to all-encompassing activities (economic, religious, political, aesthetic, intellectual, etc.), and whose definition rests upon conceptual categories.

6. Ahmad Iqbal, "A Mirage Misnamed Strategic Depth," *Al-Ahram Weekly,* no. 392 (August 27–September 2, 1998).

7. The Afghan state tried to develop governmental madrasas to compete with both private and foreign ones. But the civil war basically put an end to this effort. Iran is playing a similar role for Shia religious scholars, most of them being trained in Iran.

8. Leon Poullada, *Reform and Rebellion in Afghanistan, 1919–1929: King Amanullah's Failure to Transform a Tribal Society* (Ithaca, NY: Cornell University Press, 1973).

9. Kamal Matinuddin, *The Afghan Phenomenon: Afghanistan, 1994–1997* (Karachi: Oxford University Press, 1999), 17.

10. Gilles Dorronsoro, *Revolution Unending: Afghanistan, 1979 to the Present* (New York: Columbia University Press, 2005).

11. Robert D. Blackwill, "A De Facto Partition for Afghanistan," *Politico.com,* July 7, 2010, http://dyn.politico.com/printstory. cfm?uuid=AACEE164-18FE-70B2-A8E30566E50DFB3A.

3. Religious Revivalism across the Durand Line

Thanks to Nile Green, Robert Crews, and Ayesha Jalal for their comments on earlier versions of this paper.

1. For the role of religious leaders in the early nineteenth century, see Christine Noelle, *State and Tribe in Nineteenth-Century Afghanistan: The Reign of Dost Muhammad Khan (1826–1863)* (Richmond, Surrey: Curzon, 1997), 276–280. For the late nineteenth century, see Ashraf Ghani, "Islam and State Building in a Tribal Society," *Modern Asian Studies* 12, no. 2 (1978): 269–284; and David Edwards, *Heroes of the Age: Moral Fault Lines on the*

Afghan Frontier (Berkeley: University of California Press, 1996). For Amanullah's reign, see Senzil Nawid, *Religious Response to Social Change in Afghanistan, 1919–1929: King Aman-Allah Khan and the Afghan Ulama* (Costa Mesa, CA: Mazda, 2000); and Leon Poullada, *Reform and Rebellion in Afghanistan, 1919–1929* (Ithaca, NY: Cornell University Press, 1973). For the post-1930 period there is little compelling ethnographic or historical work on the intersections of state power and religious leadership and discourse.

2. It should be noted that almost all the historical studies of religious leadership in Afghanistan have focused on the eastern and southern Pashtun regions (including Kabul, Kandahar, Ningrahar, Khost, and Jalalabad), where the largest number of mullah/ulama-led revolts occurred. This has somewhat obscured the historic role of the religious leadership across the rest of Afghanistan.

3. The overwhelming involvement of ulama, mashaykh, and sayyids as independent representatives of the people in the 1924 Loya Jirga is a good example of this. See M. J. Hanifi, "Editing the Past: Colonial Production of Hegemony through the Loya Jerga in Afghanistan," *Iranian Studies* 37, no. 2 (2004): 309–311; and Sana Haroon, *Frontier of Faith* (London: Hurst, 2007), 104–124.

4. Bukhari Mulla to Mahmudul Hasan, August 4, 1916. Iqbal Shaidai Collection, National Archives Islamabad.

5. Obaidullah Sindhi, *Zati Dairi* (Lahore: Al-Mahmud Academy, 1994), 60; Nawid, *Religious Response*, 77; Mir 'Ali Jan Khan, Abdul Raziq Khan [*sic*] and Muhammad Sarvar Khan, *Siraj al-Ahkam fi Mu'amalat al-Islam* (Kabul: Matba'-i Shahi, Dar al-Saltanah, 1909); Afghanistan Digital Library, NYU Libraries [Hereafter ADL].

6. Moreover, the Afghan minister of education, Sardar Faiz Khan, was on extremely "informal terms" with Muhammad Bashir of the Jama'at-e Mujahedin, who was in Kabul at that time (Abdul Karim Chamarkandi, *Sarguzasht-i Mujahid*, (Lahore: Idara-e Matbu'at-e Sulaimani, 1981), 143.

7. One of the members of the Jama'at wrote in a letter that the deputation to Kabul had received a warm welcome and Sardar Nasrullah Khan granted members of the Jama'at annual allowances of up to four hundred rupees per head. Hussain Ahmed Madni, *Naqsh-i Hayat* (Karachi: Bait al-Tauhid, 1953), chap. 5.

8. May Schinasi, *Afghanistan at the Beginning of the Twentieth Century* (Naples: Istituto Universitario Orientale, 1979), 186.

9. Sindhi, *Zati Dairi,* quoted in Madni, *Tehrik-i Reshmi Rumal* (Lahore: n.p., 1966), 167; and North-West Frontier Province Political Diaries, 20 January 1917.

10. Quoted in Ludwig Adamec, *Afghanistan, 1900–1923* (Berkeley: University of California Press, 1967), 110.

11. Ibid.

12. Letter from Amanullah Khan to Haji Mulla Abdul Razzaq, no date, in appendix to Muhammad Wali Zalmai, *Mujahed-i Afghan* (Kabul: Da Pashto da Ta'mim aw Indishaf sangah, 1967), 60–61.

13. See intercepted letters of Mulla Bashir sent "in Afghan Government Service" in 1934, in "Maulvi Abdul Rahim" file 2258, NWFP Special Branch 419/88.

14. See, for example, the list of approved textbooks for study of *fiqh* (Islamic legal thought) at the School of Judges, *Kulliyat va Istilihat-i Fiqha-ya: Silsila Talifat Maktab Dar al-Quzat al-Amaniyah* (Kabul: Matba-i Huruf-i Mashinkhanah, 1922); ADL.

15. Textbooks and principles of study were laid out for teaching Persian reading and writing, religious knowledge, math, and writing in schools. The principles to be studied in religion were "Tauhid, namaz, rozah, zakat, Hajj": see *Nizamnamah Makatib-i Khanagi* [The Edict on (regulation of) Private Schooling] (Kabul: Matba'-e Vizarat-e Mu'arif, 1923), 5–6; ADL.

16. Noelle, *State and Tribe,* 278; Khan, *Siraj al-Ahkam fi Mu'amalat al-Islam.*

17. May Schinasi has talked about the role of the Indians in Afghanistan in the sphere of publishing, arguing that their knowledge of Persian, English, and Urdu, and often Arabic and Pashtu, meant that they could translate articles for the new Afghan newspapers that were the pride of Habibullah and Amanullah's administrations (Schinasi, *Afghanistan at the Beginning of the Twentieth Century,* 188–189).

18. *Ittihad-e Mashriqi,* February 18, 1925, reproduced in the NWFP Intelligence Bureau Diaries, March 5, 1925.

19. Madni, *Naqsh-i Hayat,* 607–608.

20. *Firman* from Habibullah Khan to Maulana Saif al-Rahman, 1336 HS (1918), Saif al-Rahman Collection (hereafter SRC), p. 137.

21. Sa'id al-Rahman, "Unpublished biography Maulana Saif al-Rahman," n.d., SRC; and Firman dated 25/1/1337 [October 1919], SRC, p. 136.

22. Draft letter, Maulana Saif al-Rahman to Amir (Amanullah), n.d., SRC, p. 59–61.

23. Saif al-Rahman's undated handwritten notes, SRC, pp. 1–4.

24. Letter from Ministry of Education to Maulana Saif al-Rahman, 21 Hamal 1301 [April 11, 1923]. He tested them on their knowledge of the *Muwata* of Imam Muhammad, an important Hanifi text authored by one of the students of Imam Abu Hanifa. SRC, p. 130.

25. Ministry of Law to Saif al-Rahman, April 11, 1923; November 23, 1923; and n.d., SRC pp. 128–130.

26. Invitation to Saif al-Rahman, 28/1/1311 HS [1932], SRC, p. 134.

27. Ibid.; and invitation to Saif al-Rahman, 25/9/1353 [1935], SRC, p. 135.

28. Notes on the judgments passed on Malik Ayub etc., n.d., SRC, p. 45.

29. SRC, p. 84.

30. See for example Haqir Fakhruddin Rasul's letter to Maulana Saif al-Rahman, 14 Hamal 1301 HS [1922], SRC p. 176. Rasul asks Saif al-Rehman to intercede with the Amir on his behalf.

31. Abdul Satar Sirat, "Sharia and Islamic Education in Modern Afghanistan," *Middle East Journal* 23, no. 2 (1969): 217–219, 1.

32. I am uncertain of the exact date of the creation of the Jam'iyat al-'Ulama Afghanistan. Hanifi ("Editing the Past," 312–313) states that its creation was approved in Amanullah Khan's 1924 Loya Jirga, whereas Dupree says that it was created by Nadir Shah in 1931 (Louis Dupree, *Afghanistan* [Karachi: Oxford University Press, 1997], 108). The constitution of 1931 defined the state religion as Islam according to Hanafi sharia; the constitution of 1964 stated that the state defined appropriate religious interpretation according to the Hanafi school of law (ibid., 574–579).

33. *Miramnameh wa Surat Tadvir Majlis Jam'iyat al-Ulama Afghanistan,* (Kabul: Matb'ua 'Umumi Sarkari, 1348 [1928-1929]), pp. 3–4. Afghanistan Digital Library, NYU Libraries.

34. Ghulam Sakhi was one such young man. See Ghulam Sakhi to Saif al-Rahman, 17 Akrab 1315 [1936], SRC, p. 236.

35. Qazi Sayyid Mujaddid Governor Shinwar to Saif al-Rahman, 13 Qus 1300 [1921] and 1301 [1922], SRC, pp. 202–203, 200–201.

36. His family says that, later in his life, Abdul Aziz received an appointment as a mufti of Kabul. This story was verbally recollected to me by Shireen Taj, daughter of Abdul Aziz and granddaughter of Saif al-Rahman in Islamabad, March 10, 2011.

37. Amanullah Khan had given Saif al-Rahman a house, gardens, cultivating lands, and an annual stipend of about 3,500 Afghan rupees a month. Firman Amanullah Khan, 19 Rajab 1337 [14 April 1919], SRC, p. 16.

38. Petition, 27 Rajab 1350 HQ [December 7, 1931], SRC, p. 87; and letters from Saif al-Rahman and then Sa'id al-Rahman to Ministers of State, undated, SRC, pp. 26, 30, 50; letter from Prime Minister to Saif al-Rahman denying him the right to sell his land, 23 Asad 1323 HS [1944], SRC, p. 138.

39. Many thanks to Robert Crews for this term, defined through his works "Empire and the Confessional State: Islam and Religious Politics in Nineteenth-Century Russia," *American Historical Review* 108, no. 1 (2003), and *For Prophet and Tsar: Islam and Empire in Russia and Central Asia* (Cambridge, MA: Harvard University Press, 2006), and his suggestions for its particular applicability to the role of the ulama in twentieth-century Afghanistan.

40. See David Edwards, *Genelogies of the Afghan Jihad* (Berkeley: University of California Press, 2002), 215–217. Also Sirat, "Sharia and Islamic Education," 217–219 (the author of this article was himself dean of the faculty of Islamic Law but left Afghanistan in 1975 and taught Islamic Law in Mecca for many years).

41. List of books borrowed from al-Afghani, al-Hijaz, November 14, 1939, SRC, p. 85; letter from Muhammad Masif in Jeddah to Aziz al-Rahman saying that the writer sends the book *Mukhtasar-al Sawa'iq* as a gift, 21/11/1356 [January 22, 1938], SRC, p. 197; and Saif al-Rahman to the King of the "government and country of Islam," n.d. Shaikh Sanussi was in Mecca in 1937 when Saif al-Rahman performed Hajj (Ali Salih Karrar, *The Sufi Brotherhoods in the Sudan* [London: Hurst, 1992], 53).

42. Saif al-Rahman to the editor of *Shuban al-Muslimin,* n.d., SRC, p. 114. The editor had links to Maulana Taqiuddin Hilali, a Moroccan scholar who translated the Quran into English.

43. For a discussion on the debates among the ulama on the issue of sharia, see Muhammad Qasim Zaman, *The Ulama in Contemporary Islam* (Princeton: Princeton University Press, 2002), 94–110.

44. Alamgir M. Serajuddin, *Muslim Family Law, Secular Courts and Muslim Women of South Asia* (Karachi: Oxford University Press, 2011), 13–14.

45. Zaman, *Ulama in Contemporary Islam,* 102–108.

46. Some good examples of these are: Shams al-Haqq Afghani, *Ulum al-Quran* (Lahore: Maktaba Ashrafiya, 1980?); Yusuf Binori's popular commentary on the principles expounded in the Quran, *Ulum al-Quran* (Karachi: ?, 1976); Mufti Muhammad Shafi's commentary on the significance of Hajj, *Ahkam-i Hajj* (Karachi: Darul Isha'at, 1972) and his Urdu translation of the Quran with extensive commentary *Ma'arif al-Quran* 8 vols. (Karachi: Idarat al-Ma'arif, 1969-73). This last text is discussed by Qasim Zaman, *The Ulama*, p. 56.

47. Excerpt from Maulana Abdul Qayyum Haqqani's personal notes on meetings held and "Glimpses of Some Gatherings of Maulana Abdul Haqq and Leaders of the *Jihad*," reproduced in Abdul Haqq Abdul Qayyum Haqqani, *Sahbatay ba Ahl-i Haq* (Nowshehra: Idarat al-'Ilm Va al-Tahqiq, 1998), 358–364.

48. Haqqani, *Sahbatay*, 307–309.

49. Ibid., 216–217.

50. Sultan Mahmud Zia, introduction to Maulana Masud Azhar, *Khutbat-i Jihad* (Karachi: Maktabah Hasan, 2007), 11. This compilation in two volumes was first published in 1994.

51. Abdul Qayyum Haqqani, *Islami Inqilab ka Fikri Laeh Aml* (Akora Khattak: Dar al-'Ulum Haqqaniyya, 1991), 182.

52. Ministry of Education Pakistan, "Pakistan Education Statistics 2007–2008," http://www.moe.gov.pk/Pakistan%20Education%20Statistics%2007-08.pdf.

53. This was one of the first Deobandi monthly journals. It began printing at least as early as 1986.

54. List of Deobandi journals published by Institute of Policy Studies Islamabad, http://www.ipsurdu.com/index.php?option=com_content&view=article&id=472&Itemid=315.

55. For example, Abdul Haqq's sermons and essays on the divinity of God and love for the Prophet (1970), the importance of religious schools (1970), and the necessity for personal observation of the five pillars of Islam (1967), compiled in *Da'wat-i Haqq*. ed. Sami' al-Haqq (Akora Khattak: Dar al-'Ulum Haqqaniyya, 2000); and Mufti Mahmud's speeches, including those denouncing Ahmadi interpretations of Islam (1953) and speeches in parliament (1964), published as *Khutbat-i Mahmud,* ed. Muhammad Ismail Shujabadi (Lahore: Maktaba Khatam-i Nubuwwat, 1997).

56. See Obaidullah Sindhi, *Zaati Dairi;* Abu Salman Sindhi, ed., *Makatib Maulana Obaidullah Sindhi* (Lahore: al-Mahmud Academy, 1994); Ghulam Rasul Mehr, *Sayyid Ahmad Shahid* (Karachi: Shaikh Ghulam 'Ali and Sons, n.d.). Also treatises by Deobandis such as Muhammad Miyan and Maulana Madni, who had supported the movement.

57. "The Enforcement of Sharia Act, 1991," Act X of 1991.

58. Swat is an extraconstitutional territory governed directly by the governor of Khyber Pakhtunkhwa Province. This movement, carried forward by Mulla Fazlullah after 2001, eventually led to the passage of the

Nizam-e Adl bill in the provincial parliament in 2009; this bill established that the laws of sharia would govern the territories of Swat under the supervision of district qazis. Qazis had to be qualified judges, but the ordinance established that those who had completed a course in sharia would be given preference in these roles. For a discussion of the class and power dynamics that underpin religious politics in contemporary Swat, see also Robert Nichols, "Class, State and Power in the Swat Conflict," in *Beyond Swat,* ed. Magnus Marsden and Ben Hopkins (London: Hurst and Co., forthcoming).

59. Perhaps a rethinking of politics, as Qasim Zaman urges, is necessary.

4. Taliban, Real and Imagined

1. Due to limitations of space and context, this chapter does not address discourses circulating through the English and Urdu and Dari media of Pakistan and Afghanistan, respectively, that impinge greatly on the media world of the Pashto language community on either side of the border.

2. Compare Shah Mahmoud Hanifi, *Connecting Histories in Afghanistan: Market Relations and State Formation on a Colonial Frontier* (Stanford: Stanford University Press, 2011).

3. See Muzaffar Alam, *The Languages of Political Islam* (Chicago: University of Chicago Press, 2004); Rosalind O'Hanlon, "Kingdom, Household and Body: History, Gender, and Imperial Service under Akbar," *Modern Asian Studies* 41, no. 5 (2007): 889–923.

4. Cf. Muhammad 'Arif Gharwal, *Gharǝne Sandare* (Kabul: Afghanistan Academy of Sciences, n.d.), 104–105.

5. See David Edwards, *Heroes of the Age* (Berkeley: University of California Press, 1996); James Caron, "Cultural Histories of Pashtun Nationalism" (PhD diss., University of Pennsylvania, 2009), esp. chap. 4.

6. Muhammad Wali Zalmay, *Da Kandahar Mashahir* (Kabul: Ministry of Information and Culture, 1970).

7. Caron, "Cultural Histories," chap. 4; Edwards, *Heroes of the Age,* chap. 4; Sana Haroon, *Frontier of Faith* (New York: Columbia University Press, 2007).

8. Ajmal Khattak, *Qissa Zama da Adabi Zhwand* (Charsadda: Riaz Book Agency, 2005), 104–105 (my translation).

9. Ajmal Khattak, "Jannat," translated by Aziz Akhmad (unpublished).

10. Zakariya Mlatar, *Taliban aw da Paxto Shi'r* (Peshawar[?]: n.p., 1986), pp. *jim–dal.* (my translation).

11. Asef Bayat, *Life as Politics: How Ordinary People Change the Middle East* (Stanford: Stanford University Press, 2010), 137.

12. Ibid., 153.

13. See John Lee Anderson and Thomas Dworzak, *Taliban* (London: Trolley, 2003).

14. See David Edwards, "Words in the Balance: The Poetics of Political Dissent in Afghanistan," in *Russia's Muslim Frontiers: New Directions in Cross Cultural Analysis,* ed. Dale Eickelman (Bloomington: Indiana University Press, 1993), 114–129.

15. Abdul Salam Zaeef, *My Life with the Taliban,* ed. and trans. Alex Strick van Linschoten and Felix Kuehn (New York: Columbia University Press, 2010).

16. Recounted by 'Alam Gul Sahar, "Par Paxto Shi'r da Jagare Aghize," http://www.larawbar.com/detail.php?id=12632.

17. Zaeef, *My Life with the Taliban,* 43.

18. Ibid.

19. I thank my onetime Pashto faculty for both of these vocabulary items, and for their textured explanations of why they are so important.

20. See Zaeef, *My Life with the Taliban,* 57–65.

21. Qarib al-Rahman Sa'id, commissioned by Lutfullah Sadiq, *Qissa da Talib Jan* (Peshawar: Zeb Art, 2007?).

22. See http://www.youtube.com/watch?v=uoozZbAkOP8 ; posted by "Talib Gul" on December 1, 2009.

23. See http://www.youtube.com/watch?v=zfNIYOwnOko&feature=rela ted; posted by "islamafghanTK" on August 20, 2006.

24. See http://www.youtube.com/watch?v=6Y7KzfJLuGY; posted by "pakhtoonhalek" on January 26, 2009.

5. Quandaries of the Afghan Nation

1. The 1979 population estimate is from the World Bank through Google, http://www.google.com/publicdata?ds=wb-wdi&met=sp_pop_totl&idim=country:AFG&dl=en&hl=en&q=afghanistan+population+statistics. The current CIA numbers are revealed at http://www.cia.gov/library/publications/the-world-factbook/geos/af.html. The *CIA World Factbook* notes: "(28,395,716 [a July 2009 estimate]) is a significantly revised figure;

the previous estimate of 33,609,937 was extrapolated from the last Afghan census held in 1979, which was never completed because of the Soviet invasion; a new Afghan census is scheduled to take place in 2010."

2. In my view, Afghans, Pashtuns, and Pathans are separable because each group comes to textual light and social life in different historical contexts, and each group has its own dynamic historical relationship to Pashto and other languages, including Persian and Indian and Turkic languages. See Shah Mahmoud Hanifi, "A History of Linguistic Boundary Crossing within and around Pashto," in *Beyond Swat: History, Society and Power along the Afghanistan-Pakistan Frontier*, ed. Magnus Marsden and Ben Hopkins (London: Hurst, 2012; New York: Columbia University Press, 2012).

3. Ganda Singh, *Ahmad Shah Durrani: Father of Modern Afghanistan* (1959; Lahore: Tariq, 1981).

4. See Louis Dupree, *Afghanistan* (1973; New Delhi: Rama, 1994), esp. p. 333 for one version of the name change based upon Mir Ghulam Ghobar's *Ahmad Shah Baba-ye Afghan* (Kabul: n.p., 1943), which, as the name implies, is the first to apply the title *Baba* to Ahmad Shah.

5. Ahmad Shah's Pashto poetry exists in manuscript form at the British Library and has been published twice in Kabul and once in Peshawar. For English translations of part of Ahmad Shah's Diwan, see Henry George Raverty, *Selections from the Poetry of the Afghans: From the Sixteenth to the Nineteenth Century, Literally Translated from the Original Pushto; with Notices of the Different Authors, and Remarks on the Mystic Doctrine and Poetry of the Sufis* (1867; Peshawar: De Chapzai, 1981).

6. For Nadir Shah Afshar, see Laurence Lockhart, *The Fall of the Safavi Dynasty and the Afghan Occupation of Persia* (Cambridge: Cambridge University Press, 1958); and Ernest Tucker, *Nadir Shah's Quest for Legitimacy in Post-Safavid Iran* (Gainseville: University Press of Florida, 2006).

7. For the official histories of Nadir Shah Afshar and Ahmad Shah Abdali/Durrani, see, respectively, Mahdi Khan Astarabadi, *Tarikh-i Jahangusha-ye Nadiri* (1765–1766; Bombay: Matbaʻ-i Haidari, 1875), and Mahmud b. Ibrahim al-Husaini, *Tarikh-i Ahmad Shahi*, 2 vols., ed. D. Saidmuradov (c. 1773; Moscow: Izd-vo Nauka, 1974).

8. ʻAziz al-Din Wakili Fufolzai, *Timur Shah Durrani*, 2 vols. (Kabul: Anjuman-e Tarikh-e Afghanistan, 1967).

9. Faiz Muhammad Katib, *Siraj al-Tawarikh*, 3 vols. (Kabul: Matbaʻ-i Hurufi-ye dar al-Sultana-ye Kabul, 1913–1915). Folio 9 describes Ahmad's birth and early life. Robert D. McChesney's translation of *Siraj al-Tawarikh*

will soon appear on the Afghanistan Digital Library website, http://afghanistandl.nyu.edu/.

10. I am adopting the "knowing the country" phrase from Chris Bayly, "Knowing the Country: Empire and Information in India," *Modern Asian Studies* 27, no. 1 (1993): 3–43.

11. For the unsustainable view that Afghanistan has "no experience with colonialism," see, for example, Thomas J. Barfield, "On Local Justice and Culture," *Connecticut Journal of International Law* 437 (2002): 436–443. A wide range of colonial consequences are demonstrated very clearly in two recent works on nineteenth-century Afghanistan: B. D. Hopkins, *The Making of Modern Afghanistan* (London: Palgrave Macmillan, 2008); and Shah Mahmoud Hanifi, *Connecting Histories in Afghanistan: Market Relations and State Formation on a Colonial Frontier* (Stanford: Stanford University Press, 2011).

12. For Ahmad Shah's correspondence with the British, see Singh, *Ahmad Shah Durrani*, 374–384.

13. Sir William Jones and Henry Vansittart, "On Descent of the Afghans from the Jews," in *Asiatic Researches Comprising History and Antiquities, the Arts, Sciences, and Literature of Asia,* by the Asiatic Society, vol. 2 (1790; New Delhi: Cosmo, 1979): 54–61.

14. Mountstuart Elphinstone, *An Account of the Kingdom of Caubul, and Its Dependencies in Persia, Tartary, and India,* 2 vols. (1815; Karachi: Indus, 1992), esp. vol. 1, bk. 2, chaps. 1 and 4.

15. Hopkins, *The Making of Modern Afghanistan,* esp. chap. 2.

16. Hanifi, *Connecting Histories;* and Hanifi, "Henry George Raverty and the Colonial Marketing of Pashto," in *Knowing India: Colonial and Modern Constructions of the Past,* ed. Cynthia Talbot (New Delhi: Yoda Press, 2011).

17. Ashraf Ghani, "Disputes in a Court of Sharia, Kunar Valley, Afghanistan, 1885–1890," *International Journal of Middle Eastern Studies* 15, no. 3 (1983): 353–367.

18. Shah Mahmoud Hanifi, "Impoverishing a Colonial Frontier: Cash, Credit, and Debt in Nineteenth-Century Afghanistan," *Iranian Studies* 37, no. 2 (2004): 1–20.

19. Rather than continually increasing and diversifying, the engagement of Pashto has been episodic, uneven, and generally limited in each state setting. In Afghanistan the state has had an amplified engagement with Pashto during the 1930s and 1940s, 1980s, and the contemporary post-2001 era. See Shah Mahmoud Hanifi, "A History of Linguistic Boundary Crossing within

and around Pashto," in *Beyond Swat: History, Society and Power along the Afghanistan-Pakistan Frontier,* ed. Magnus Marsden and Ben Hopkins (London: Hurst, 2012; New York: Columbia University Press, 2012).

20. A. Rahman Pazhwak, *Afghanistan (Ancient Aryana): Brief Review of the Political and Cultural History and the Modern Development of the Country* (Hove, England: Key Press, 1955).

21. Louis Dupree, Nancy Hatch Dupree, and A. A. Motamedi, *The National Museum of Afghanistan* (Kabul: Afghan Air Authority and Afghan Tourist Organization, 1974).

22. Warwick Ball, "The Archaeology of Afghanistan: A Reassessment and Stock-Taking," in *Art and Archaeology of Afghanistan: Its Fall and Survival,* ed. Juliette Van Krieken-Pieters (Leiden: Brill, 2006). See also http://www. nationalgeographic.com/mission/afghanistan-treasures/index.html.

23. Abdul Rahman, *Kalimat Amir al-Bilad fi al-Targhib ila al-Jihad* (Kabul: Dar al-Saltanah, 1886–1887), available at http://afghanistandl.nyu. edu/search/?start=0&sort=title.sort&q=jihad.

24. David B. Edwards, "Mad Mullahs and Englishmen: Discourse in the Colonial Encounter," *Comparative Studies in Society and History* 31, no. 4 (1989): 649–670.

25. Hanifi, *Connecting Histories.* Also see entries for "Kabul Jan" on YouTube and Facebook.

26. For attention to the Persianification of Pashto words (such as the Persian *elmar* for the Pashto *lmar* or sun in state medallions from Amanullah's reign, 1919–1929), the Pashtoification of Persian words (e.g., *wuluswalai* for *wulus*) and the imposition of fresh Pashto words in the state bureaucracy (the Pashto *shahgalai* for all civil servants, for example) and other such linguistic matters, see Shah Mahmoud Hanifi, "Representations of Social Class in Afghanistan," in *Power Hierarchies and Hegemony in Afghanistan: State Building, Ethnic Minorities and Identity in Central Asia,* ed. Shah Mahmoud Hanifi (London: Tauris, forthcoming).

27. Anthony Hyman, "Nationalism in Afghanistan," *International Journal of Middle East Studies* 34, no. 2 (2002): 299–315. Note the citation problem in footnote 4 on page 301, which describes the futility and collapse of a Pashto language initiative on Dupree's authority.

28. David Price, *Anthropological Intelligence: The Deployment and Neglect of American Anthropology in the Second World War* (Durham, NC: Duke University Press, 2008).

29. Louis Dupree, *Afghanistan* (Princeton: Princeton University Press, 1973).

30. Shah Mahmoud Hanifi, "Comparing Regimes of Colonial Knowledge in Afghanistan, 1809–2009 " (unpublished paper).

31. Nancy Hatch Dupree, "Louis Dupree: An American Lover of Afghanistan," *Central Asia* 33 (1993): 119–130. For more on Louis Dupree's legacy, see M. Nazif Shahrani, "Louis Dupree: A Tribute," *Refuge: Canada's Periodical on Refugees* 9, no. 1 (1989): 3. See also Louis Dupree's obituary, read into the U.S. Congressional Record on May 2, 1989, which speaks of his influence on policy, including through covert organizations not limited to the Central Intelligence Agency: http://www.jezail.org/02_essays/01fr_dupree.html.

32. Louis Dupree, "Ethnography of Afghanistan," *Encyclopaedia Iranica,* http://www.iranica.com/articles/afghanistan-iv-ethnography.

33. For Nancy Dupree as "Honorary Grandmother of Afghanistan," along with Air Force Reserve Major Jo Danner, see http://www.embassyofafghanistan.org/12.12newsgrand.html. For David B. Edwards, see his *Heroes of the Age: Moral Fault Lines on the Afghan Frontier* (Berkeley: University of California Press, 1996); and Edwards, *Before Taliban: Genealogies of the Afghan Jihad* (Berkeley: University of California Press, 2002). One of the most important inheritances David Edwards received from Louis Dupree, with the support of Nancy Dupree, is a collection of photographs taken between 1949 and 1989; these are an important part of the Williams Afghan Media Project site, which contains thousands of images of the country; see http://contentdm.williams.edu/wamp/web/information.htm. For Milton Bearden, see Bearden, "Curse of the Khyber Pass," *National Interest,* March 12, 2009, http://www.nationalinterest.org/Article.aspx?id=20940. Bearden is also mentioned in Aram Roston, "How the US Funds the Taliban," *The Nation,* November 12, 2009.

34. For Louis Dupree's legacy in the Human Terrain System Project, see http://zeroanthropology.net/2009/11/05/reality-check-for-the-human-terrain-system-marilyn-dudley-flores-responds/.

35. Hanifi, "Henry George Raverty."

6. How Tribal Are the Taliban?

This chapter further develops thoughts laid out in Thomas Ruttig, *The Other Side: Dimensions of the Afghan Insurgency: Causes, Actors—and Approaches* to *Talks,* Thematic Report 01/2009 (Kabul/Berlin: Afghanistan Analysts Network, July 2009). It builds on presentations given at a workshop organized by the Abbasi Program in Islamic Studies at Stanford University, December 3, 2009, and at the Jamestown Foundation's 2009 Terrorism Conference "The Changing Strategic Gravity of Al Qaeda," December 9, 2009.

1. See Thomas Ruttig, "Implications of Mullah Baradar's Arrest," *AAN Blog,* February 16, 2010, http://www.aan-afghanistan.org/index.asp?id=646; Thomas Ruttig, "The Taliban Arrest Wave in Pakistan: Reasserting Strategic Depth?," *CTC Sentinel* 3, no. 3 (March 2010): 5–7.

2. In *The Other Side,* I argued that "reconciliation" is more than just talks between the government and the Taliban: it needs to be a broader concept that encompasses all of Afghan society.

3. The best article on Pashtunwali is still Lutz Rzehak, "Das Paschtunwali—Traditionelle Normen, Wertvorstellungen und Bräuche der Paschtunen," *Asien, Afrika, Lateinamerika* 15, no. 5 (1987): 821–832, now available in an updated and English version: Lutz Rzehak, "Pashtunwali—tribal life and behavior among the Pashtuns", Kabul/Berlin: Afghanistan Analysts Network, Thematic Report 1/2011 (March 2011), http://www.aan-afghanistan.org/index.asp?id=1567. Surprisingly, there does not seem to be a comprehensive English-language book or article dealing with the types of Pashtunwali among Pashtun tribes in Afghanistan as such, apart from the colonial (and Pakistan-focused) "standard" books like Olaf Caroe, *The Pathans: 550 BC–AD 1957* (New York: St. Martin's Press, 1958). A number of recent papers concentrate on the jirga aspect mostly and deal with Pashtunwali only at their periphery. One source also refers to "*nirkhi,*" arbiters, in such jirgas. Christian Sigrist, "Pashtunwali—Das Stammesrecht der Pashtunen," in *Revolution in Iran und Afghanistan,* ed. Kurt Greussing und Jan-Heeren Grevemeyer (Frankfurt am Main: Syndikat 1980), 264.

4. *Acephalous* means "with no centralized authority," also called "regulated anarchy." Christian Sigrist, *Regulierte Anarchie: Untersuchungen zum Fehlen und zur Entstehung politischer Herrschaft in segmentären Gesellschaften Afrikas* (Olten: Walter, 1967). *Watan* also is a blurry term. It can stand for the whole nation/country but also for the narrower area of origin (a valley, etc.).

5. Mark Bradbury, *Becoming Somaliland* (London: Progressio, 2008), 13–15, citing Virginia Luling, "Genealogy as Theory, Genealogy as Tool: Aspects of Somali 'Clanship,'" *Social Identities* 12, no. 4 (2006): 471–485.

Endogamous and *exogamous* are relative terms. As a rule, marriage among Afghans is endogamous, i.e., within the broader community. Often, however, cousin marriage is preferred—to save costs and to keep the property (land, etc.) together. In contrast, exogamous marriage is a means to create political and business alliances.

6. I put some of those terms in quotations because these categories are fluid. A "subtribe" here is, in a purely descriptive way, just a group of people that is considered (or considers itself) part of a larger tribe. The Pashtuns altogether do not form a single "tribe" ("the Pashtun tribe" as media often say) but something a category higher. Some call it a "nation" or "nationality," a "people" (in German, *Volk*) or an "ethnic group." Afghan terms used for it (*qaum, mellat,* etc.) are also blurred. There are different tribes *among* the Pashtuns. Qais Abdul Rashid is the ancestor of all Pashtuns. He and his sons Sarban, Baitan, and Gharghasht, as well as the "adopted" Karlan, are forefathers of the major Pashtun "confederations." The ones most important in Afghanistan, the Durrani and the Ghilzai, go back to Sarban and Baitan, respectively. See Akbar S. Ahmed, *Millennium and Charisma among Pathans: A Critical Essay in Social Anthropology* (London: Routledge and Kegan Paul, 1976), 7.

7. The same line was not often taken by "ordinary" Taliban with whom I talked during my stay in Kabul in 2000–2001 under the Taliban regime. They eagerly told me which tribe they belonged to.

8. Often referred to as "Achakzai," the Dari form. The Dari language lacks the Pashtun consonant 'ts' (cf. *tsenga ye,* "How are you?") in Pashto or *Cäsar* or *Zitrone* in German). The Sur(i) who ruled northern India in the sixteenth century, for example, were probably absorbed by the local population. In this chapter, the phrase "southeastern region" is used for the three provinces of Loya Paktia, and "southern region" for Kandahar, Helmand, Uruzgan, and Zabul. The latter region is referred to as the "southwestern region" by some.

9. The Babozai case also is of political relevance: one wife of Mullah Muhammad Omar reportedly is a Babozai from Oruzgan Province. (Mullah Omar's family is from Zabul originally and belongs to the Hotak tribe, with the exact subtribe unknown. He himself was born in the Dehrawud district of Oruzgan, to which the family had migrated; with his stepfather he moved further south to Kandahar Province. Most Hotak and Nurzai currently support the Taliban. See Abdul Awwal Zabulwal, "Taliban in Zabul: A Witness

Account," in *Decoding the New Taliban: Insights from the Afghan Field*, ed. Antonio Giustozzi (London: Hurst and Co., 2009), 180. Often these "tribal confederations" are understood as purely genealogical. But as the Babozai case illustrates, they are also influenced by politics. An Afghan source importantly points to the fact that the Durrani also emerged as a *political* confederation, called *gund* (party), "put together" by a *pir* in the reign of Ahmad Shah Abdali (later, Durrani) for a concrete political reason. Muhammad Omar Rawand Miakhel, *De Pashtano Qabilo Shujre au Mene* [The Lineages and Dwellings of the Pashtun Tribes] (Kabul: Maiwand 1999), 217.

10. Author's interviews in Kandahar, February and September 2009.

11. Examples of different *nirkh* systems are given in Sigrist, "Pashtunwali," 264–275 (for the tribes of Paktia); and The International Legal Foundation, *The Customary Laws of Afghanistan: A Report by the International Legal Foundation* (2004), http://www.usip.org/files/file/ilf_customary_law_afghanistan.pdf. When the jirga was composed of different tribal groups, it had to be decided in advance whose *nirkh* would be used. It often could be that of a third tribal group.

12. Ahmed, *Millennium and Charisma*, 76. See also Palwasha Kakar, *Tribal Law of Pashtunwali and Women's Legislative Authority*, http://www.law.harvard.edu/programs/ilsp/research/kakar.pdf. Ahmed, the original source, describes *nang* and *qalang* for *Pakistani* Pashtuns. It can be assumed, however, that the principle also works among Afghan lowland Pashtuns, like many Durrani, because the pattern of land ownership is similar.

13. Author's interviews in Kandahar, 2008 and 2009.

14. For more about the Haqqani network, see Thomas Ruttig, "Loya Paktia's Insurgency: The Haqqani Network as an Autonomous Entity in the Taliban Universe," in Giustozzi, *Decoding the New Taliban*, 57–88.

15. Rozi Khan had rushed to help a friend who was attacked at night by unrecognizable gunmen he thought were Taliban but turned out to be Australian Special Forces who thought that Rozi Khan was a talib.

16. A contemporary source reports that by 1989, "the word shura is not used in Dari-speaking areas to refer to local-level consultative bodies" and that "more likely . . . the . . . word 'majlis'" would be used, that shuras were mainly "formed by commanders for the purpose of coordinating military operations" (with some expanding into administration of areas) and "largely" consisted "of members of *one* tanzeem" (my emphasis). That is, the word *shura* has had a rather late career. The same authors underline that

shuras, jirgas, and majlis were "not a democratic 'one man [*sic!*] one vote' situation" and that the "consensus" decision was often a "majority" vote in reality because "some persons were more influential and/or more persuasive than others." Lynn Carter and Kerry Connor, *A Preliminary Investigation of Contemporary Afghan Councils* (Peshawar: Agency Coordinating Body for Afghan Relief, ACBAR, 1989), 2–3, 10.

17. While working with the UN in the southeastern region in 2003 and during later trips to those areas, I became aware of examples from Ghazni (Andar, Muqur) and Paktia (Zurmat).

18. Thomas Barfield, Neamat Nojumi, and J. Alexander Thier, *The Clash of Two Goods: State and Non-State Dispute Resolution in Afghanistan* (Washington, DC: U.S. Institute for Peace, 2006), 2; *Afghanistan Human Development Report, 2007* (Kabul: Center for Policy and Human Development, 2007), 9, 10.

19. The leaders of the insurgent "Haqqani network," Jalaluddin and Serajuddin Haqqani, are Dzadran.

20. During a visit to Gardez in August 2009, I witnessed attempts of various Mangal shuras to claim authority over the whole tribe vis-à-vis UNAMA.

21. See Ruttig, "Loya Paktia's Insurgency," 68–69; Susanne Schmeidl and Masood Karokhail, "The Role of Non-State Actors in 'Community-Based Policing': An Exploration of the Arbakai (Tribal Police) in South-Eastern Afghanistan," *Contemporary Security Policy* 30, no. 2 (2009): 324–326.

22. Interestingly, one contemporary source describes the first revolts as nonideological but mainly driven by reasons resembling the current insurgency—i.e., arbitrary arrests and misuse of power by government officials to settle personal scores. The PDPA government initially even had won the support of many tribes by organizing jirgas. See David Busby Edwards, "Origins of the Anti-Soviet Jihad," in *Afghan Resistance: The Politics of Survival*, ed. Grant M. Ferr and John G. Merriam (Lahore: Vanguard Books, 1988), 24, 32–34.

23. The seven major Sunni tanzim that were officially recognized by Pakistan, and therefore were exclusively entitled to receive Western and Arab aid, were Hizb (Hekmatyar), Hizb (Khales), Jam'iyat (Rabbani), Harakat (Nabi Muhammadi), Ittehad (Sayyaf), Nejat (Mujaddedi), and Mahaz (Gailani).

24. Olivier Roy witnessed "Tolaba fronts" in Oruzgan, Zabul, and Kandahar in the summer of 1984. The former chief of Pakistan's army staff,

General Aslam Beg, said that he was part of an "experiment" to establish "Taliban forces" in liberated territories of Kunar in 1985–1986. Christina Lamb visited a "Mullahs front" established a year earlier in Kandahar that involved later Taliban leaders Mullah Razzaq, Mullah Borjan and Maulawi Pasanai in 1998 and was told that it had bases in "Arghandab, Malajat, and Zabul." The first-ever Taliban front is reported by Zabulwal from Zabul already in 1979. See Olivier Roy, "Die Taliban-Bewegung in Afghanistan," *Mahfel*, no. 45 (1995): 8, translated from *Afghanistan-Info*, no. 36 (1995); "Taliban schon seit 1985/86?," *Mahfel*, no. 45 (1995): 5, translated from *The News* (Pakistan), March 3, 1995; Christina Lamb, *The Sewing Circles of Herat: My Afghan Years* (London: HarperCollins, 2002), pp. 51–65; Zabulwal, "Taliban in Zabul," in Giustozzi, *Decoding the New Taliban*, 181.

25. In its original meaning, this term *shirk* stands for "idolatry" and "polytheism," but in a figurative sense it is also used for "factionalism."

26. *The News* (Pakistan), March 3, 1995, quoted and translated from "Taliban schon seit 1985/86?"

27. In Zabul, an early Taliban front seems to have fragmented along tribal lines (coinciding with tanzim lines) fairly soon, however. See Martine van Bijlert, "The Battle for Afghanistan: Militancy and Conflict in Zabuland Uruzgan," Washington, DC: The New America Foundation (September 2010), http://www.newamerica.net/publications/policy/the_battle_for_afghanistan_zabul_and_uruzgan.

28. The rank given to mullahs differs, though, from tribe to tribe. In many Pashtun tribes, mullahs participate in the jirga. In some they even act "as custodians of *pashtunwali*," in others they are "careful not to interfere in these matters." See Sana Haroon, *Frontier of Faith: Islam in the Indo-Afghan Borderland* (London: Hurst, 2007), 68; Olivier Roy, *Islam and Resistance in Afghanistan* (Cambridge: Cambridge University Press, 1986), 36.

29. This practice actually was started, but on a much lower level, by Amir Dost Muhammad Khan (reigned r. 1826–1863). See Haroon, *Frontier of Faith*, 38.

30. Ibid., 89.

31. Thomas Ruttig, *Institutionen ohne Demokratie: Strukturelle Schwächen des Staatsaufbaus in Afghanistan und Ansätze für eine politische Stabilisierung* (Berlin: Stiftung Wissenschaft und Politik, 2008), 18–21.

32. Sébastien Trives, "Afghanistan: Tackling the Insurgency, the Case of the Southeast," *Politique étrangère* 1 (2006): 5–6.

33. Ibid., 3; Tom Coghlan, "The Taliban in Helmand: An Oral History," in Giustozzi, *Decoding the New Taliban,* 137; and Antonio Giustozzi, *Koran, Kalashnikov, and Laptop: The Neo-Taliban Insurgency in Afghanistan* (New York: Columbia University Press, 2008), 44–45.

34. My Afghan Analysts Network colleague Martine van Bijlert has introduced these local Afghan terms, *majburi* and *na-raz,* into the literature. See van Bijlert, "Unruly Commanders and Violent Power Struggles: Taliban Networks in Uruzgan," in Giustozzi, *Decoding the New Taliban,* 160–161. I prefer them to David Kilcullen's terminology "accidental guerillas" and Sean D. Naylor's "auxiliary" Taliban. See Kilcullen, *The Accidental Guerrilla: Fighting Small Wars in the Midst of a Big One* (Oxford: Oxford University Press 2009); and Naylor, "The Waiting Game: A Stronger Taliban Lies Low, Hoping the U.S. Will Leave Afghanistan," *Armed Forces Journal,* February 1, 2006. Officially the Taliban refer to themselves as the Islamic Movement of the Taliban *(De Talibano Islami Ghurdzang or Tehrik)* and the Islamic Emirate of Afghanistan *(De Afghanistan Islami Emarat).* In these terms, there is no reference to Pashtuns. In areas with growing Taliban influence in the northeast, the Taliban also increasingly attract non-Pashtuns, particularly Uzbeks and perhaps even Tajiks.

35. "Kandahari" means that they are from the southern or southwestern region, with its center in Kandahar but also including the provinces of Helmand, Zabul, and Nimruz. The hitherto independently acting local Wahhabi groups in Kunar and Nuristan reportedly have recently sworn allegiance to Mullah Omar as well. See Thomas Ruttig, "On Kunar's Salafi Insurgents," *AAN Blog,* January 14, 2010, http://www.aan-afghanistan.org/index.asp?id=570.

36. However, the Haqqanis were already known for recruiting commanders and fighters from other tribes during the anti-Soviet resistance period.

37. The layha is a book of rules for the Taliban fighters. It was issued by the movement's leadership in mid-2009 and is now in its third edition. De Afghanistan Islami Emarat Dar-ul-Ensha, *De Talibano lepara layha,* not dated (circa May 2009), articles 37, 38, and 39, pp. 41–43.

38. *Paktiawal* is a general term for the tribes from Greater Paktia. Some authors inadequately describe the Taliban as a predominantly Ghilzai movement, probably a projection bolstered by government-linked Durrani strongmen in southern Afghanistan. See Thomas H. Johnson and M. Chris Mason, "Understanding the Taliban and Insurgency in Afghanistan," *Orbis* 51, no. 1 (Winter 2007): 4.

39. Maulawi Wakil Ahmad Mutawakkil, *Afghanistan au Taliban* [Afghanistan and the Taliban] (Kabul: Baryalai Pohantun, 1384 [2005]), 33; author's interview with his former deputy, in Kabul, May 2008.

40. Mansur replaced Agha Jan Mo'tasem, a Kandahari Sayyid, who was in this position.

41. "Afghanistan 'Agrees Taliban Deal,'" BBC, July 27, 2009; Ben Arnoldy, "Short-Lived Cease-Fire with Taliban Dims Prospects for Broader Deals," *Christian Science Monitor,* July 27, 2009; author's interviews, Kabul, August 2009.

42. Email conversation with analyst Carlo Calabrese, January 2010.

43. Alissa Rubin, "Taliban Overhaul Their Image in Bid to Win Allies," *New York Times,* January 20, 2010.

44. "Interview with Shireen Mazari," *The Leaders,* February13, 2007, http://www.spf.org/the-leaders/library/15.html.

45. For example, see my article from Khost, "US-Truppen machen, was sie wollen," *Tageszeitung,* February 24, 2009.

46. Ghulamreza Fazlinaiem and Nick Miszak, "Mullah Omar Wants You! Taliban Mobilisation Strategies or Motivations of Joining the Insurgency," in *Afghanistan, 1979–2009: In the Grip of Conflict* (Washington, DC: Middle East Institute, 2009).

47. Examples witnessed by the author were (1) the role of the Ministry of Defense commander for the southeastern zone, General Gul Haidar—an ally of then defense minister Fahim—during the Ahmadzai-Dzadran rivalry over the Paktia governorship; and (2) difficulties in obtaining funds for schools in Paktia—locally interpreted as purposely holding back money by then education minister Qanuni, another NA leader, in 2002–2003.

48. This term is not specific enough. In Europe, this has a chauvinistic undertone. *National* would fit better, and many Afghans therefore often take "national" *(melli)* to be almost synonymous with *patriotic,* another word disliked by many in Europe.

49. "National-Islamist" is used by analogy with the term "national communists," a label found in the literature for the pre-1989 Yugoslav or Romanian communists, with their ideological congruence with Moscow that did not preclude divergent national interests.

50. One former high-ranking Talib and *'alem,* when asked in 2009 about the religious base of the movement, replied with emphasis: "We are not Wahhabi, we are Hanafi." "Taliban Leader Urges Afghans to Boycott 'Deceptive Elections,'" *Afghan Islamic Press* (Peshawar), December 7, 2008.

51. *De Afghanistan Islami Emarat,* 57; "Taliban Can't be Bracketed with Pashtuns: Analysts," *Pajhwok Afghan News* (Kabul), November 2, 2007.

52. Bernt Glatzer, "Zum politischen Islam der afghanischen Taliban," in *Sendungsbewusstsein oder Eigennutz: Zu Motivation und Selbstverständnis islamischer Mobilisierung,* ed. Dietrich Reetz (Berlin: Das Arabische Buch, 2001), 173–182.

53. Giustozzi, *Koran, Kalashnikov, and Laptop,* 12. See also Ruttig, *The Other Side,* 18–20.

54. Karen Armstrong, "Die goldene Regel: Das religiose Ideal des Mitgefühls und die Überwindung des Egoismus," *Lettre International,* no. 84 (2009): 72.

55. Documents of the United Nations Assistance Mission in Afghanistan (UNAMA) and the Policy Action Group (PAG) seen by the author.

56. Ahmed Rashid, *Taliban: Islam, Oil and the New Great Game in Central Asia* (London: Yale University Press, 2000), 41.

57. "Afghan Clerics' Decisions Delivered to Osama: Taliban Envoy," *People's Daily* (China), September 28, 2001.

58. De Afghanistan Islami Emarat Dar-ul-Ensha, *De Talibano lepara layha,* 37–38.

59. According to Taliban ex-foreign minister Mutawakkil, there needs to be consensus in the rahbari shura itself when decisions are taken.

60. See, for example, Giustozzi, *Koran, Kalashnikov, and Laptop,* 13.

61. Dadullah even stated that he wanted to take revenge for Zarqawi's death. See "Mullah Dadullah Vows to Avenge Zarqawi's Death," *Afghan Islamic Press* (Peshawar), June 9, 2006; also, Ruttig, "Loya Paktia's Insurgency," 75.

62. "Taliban Sack Military Commander," BBC, December 29, 2007.

63. *De Afghanistan Islami Emarat,* 45; *"Ameer Al-Mu'meneen Mullah Mohammad Omar Mujahid about the Pleasure of Eid al-Fitr,"* http://www. afghanvoice.com/index.php/news/news-in-english/237-ameer-al-mumeneen-mullah-mohammad-omar-mujahid-about-the-pleasure-of-eid-al-fitr.

64. Jason Burke, "Misreading the Taliban," *Prospect Magazine,* no. 152 (November 2008).

65. "Statement of the Islamic Emirate of Afghanistan on the Occasion of the Eighth Anniversary of the American Attack on Afghanistan," October 7, 2009, http://www.nefafoundation.org/miscellaneous/nefaTalib8anniv1009. pdf; and "Statement of the Leadership Council of the Islamic Emirate of

Afghanistan regarding the London Conference," http://www.alqimmah.net/showthread.php?t=13721.

66. After heavy losses on the leadership level and the transition to what some authors call "leaderless jihad"—i.e., with quasi-autonomous "national" groups that, as "franchises," copy al-Qaida's ideology and strategy and only occasionally have real contact with its leadership—al-Qaida's main approach is to "hijack" national movements, like the Pakistani and Afghan Taliban and al-Shabaab in Somalia. On its own, without them, al-Qaida can carry out only limited operations.

67. Vahid Brown, "The Facade of Allegiance: Bin Ladin's Dubious Pledge to Mullah Omar," *CTC Sentinel* 3, no. 1 (January 2010): 4–5.

68. I owe the inspiration for "phasing" the Taliban to Boris Wilke's presentation at the conference of the German Arbeitsgemeinschaft Afghanistan in Bonn on March 27, 2010.

69. During those years, two international consortiums, led by the U.S. company Unocal and Argentinian Bridas, competed to establish pipelines connecting Central Asian oil and gas fields with ports in South Asia through Afghanistan. Semi-official Taliban delegations visited the United States, Germany, Switzerland, and other countries. Charlie Santos, a UN representative in Afghanistan who also was a consultant on energy questions, said on February 15, 1995, "The advance of the Taliban positively influences the peace process." See Thomas Ruttig, "Taliban stehen vor Kabul, UN-Plan in Scherben," *Mahfel*, no. 44 (1995), 3. Saudi Arabia and the UAE later withdrew the recognition.

70. Giustozzi, *Koran, Kalashnikov, and Laptop,* 13–14, 38, 236.

71. Quoted in Anne Stenersen, "Blood Brothers or a Marriage of Convenience? The Ideological Relationship between al-Qaida and the Taliban," paper presented at ISA's 50th Annual Convention (New York, February 15–18, 2009), http://www.allacademic.com//meta/p_mla_apa_research_citation/3/1/2/5/2/pages312525/p312525-1.php; "Transcript: Afghan Taliban Spokesman Discusses War," CNN (online, May 5, 2009), http://www.cnn.com/2009/WORLD/asiapcf/05/05/afghan.taliban.transcript/.

72. The ban on TV, satellite phones, and the use of computer during the Taliban regime should be understood as an attempt to control information rather than as a general rejection of these technologies as such: the Taliban watched TV, and Foreign Minister Mutawakkil operated a computer in his office.

73. Rudolph Peters, "Erneuerungsbewegungen im Islam vom 18. bis zum 20. Jahrhundert und die Rolle des Islams in der neueren Geschichte: Antikolonialismus und Nationalismus," in *Der Islam in der Gegenwart*, ed. Werner Ende and Udo Steinbach (Frankfurt am Main: Büchergilde Gutenberg, 1989), 120.

74. For the latest publicly available compilation of what is known, see Bill Roggio, "The Afghan Taliban's Top Leaders," *The Long War Journal*, February 23, 2010. This list, however, contains nineteen names as "known active members of the Quetta shura" (the rahbari shura), while most other sources speak of ten to twelve members.

75. Those names do not appear on Ahmed Rashid's lists of the original "Leadership Council" and of the original members of the Taliban movement. See Rashid, *Taliban*, 220, 222–225.

76. Giustozzi, *Koran, Kalashnikov, and Laptop*, 37–38.

77. In some cases those who did not comply with ISI instructions were handed over to the United States as "irreconcilable." A similar approach seems to have applied in the recent arrests in Pakistan of Mullah Baradar and others.

78. "Afghan Taliban Name New Deputy Leaders after Arrest," BBC, March 23, 2010. Mullah Akhtar Muhammad Mansur is not related to Abdul Latif Mansur from Paktia.

79. Here, even Antonio Giustozzi cannot point to too many examples. See his *Between Patronage and Rebellion: Student Politics in Afghanistan*, AREU Briefing Paper Series (February 2010), 13. In another incident, after an attack against a NATO convoy in Kabul, a teacher was among the arrested. Rahim Faiez, "Afghans: 7 Arrests in Deaths of Army Colonels," Associated Press (May 24, 2010). *Hizb* is traditionally more active on campuses than the Taliban. Giustozzi speaks of no organized Taliban activity among students in Kabul and Herat, while there is some at Nangarhar University in Jalalabad, mainly carried out by students "from Wardak Province, Logar Province and the southern region."

80. "Taliban Have Expanded Their Influence across Afghanistan: NATO Official," *Daily Times* (Pakistan), December 28, 2009. This means that shadow governors exist in all provinces. A lack in one province may be because the Taliban might not recognize all of the newly established provinces.

81. With the limitation that the rahbari shura seems to be exclusively Pashtun now, after the disappearance from it of Sayyid Ghias al-Din,

the only non-Pashtun in the original leadership council, an Uzbek from Faryab who was a commander—and this is the *andiwali* link—of *Harakat-e Inqilab-e Islami.*

82. See their "Open Letter of the Islamic Emirate of Afghanistan to Shanghai Summit," October 14, 2009, http://www.revolutionmuslim.com/index.php?option=com_content&view=article&id=306:open-letter-of-the-islamic-emirate-of-afghanistan-to-shanghai-summit&catid=11:revolutionary-media&Itemid=15. See also an interview with Agha Jan Mo'tasem, "Islamic Emirate of Afghanistan: Dialogue with an Official of the Political Committee of the Islamic Emirate of Afghanistan," March 29, 2009, http://www.blogfrommiddleeast.com/?new=52984.

83. "Open Letter of the Islamic Emirate of Afghanistan to Shanghai Summit."

84. See also their contacts with the International Committee of the Red Cross, which, among others, provides first-aid training to insurgents. "Red Cross in Afghanistan gives Taliban first aid help," BBC, May 26, 2010.

85. One author states that "political and social segmentation" was one factor for the *stability* of the "Afghan empire," enabling it to withstand colonialist onslaughts. He also points to the fact that segmentation does not contradict the emergence of a central government. See Jan-Heeren Grevemeyer, *Afghanistan: Sozialer Wandel und Staat im 20. Jahrhundert* (Berlin: Verlag für Wissenschaft und Bildung, 1990), 11. An example of a minor breakaway group is the "moderate Taliban party" Jam'iyat-e Khuddam al-Forqan, founded in January 2002, which was blocked by Kabul and remains at the political fringes. Another group that temporarily split off (in 2003) was Jaish al-Muslimin, which, in fact, was more of a criminal franchise and returned to the Taliban's fold in June 2005.

86. Z. Zewar, *De Pashto adabiato tarikh: Osenei daura* (*History of Pashto Literature: The Current Period*) (Kabul: Academy of Sciences of the Democratic Republic of Afghanistan 1360 [1981]), 83; Habibullah Rafi, "De Pashto tserene au palene markazuna" (Centers of Pashto Studies and Preservation), *Jumhuri Palwasha* (Kabul:1355 [1976]): 5–7.

87. Quote from his presentation at the Wilton Park Workshop "Understanding the Pashtun Context: Afghanistan and Pakistan" (London, October 15, 2009). See also Bernt Glatzer, "The Pashtun Tribal System," in *Concept of Tribal Society,* ed. G. Pfeffer and D. K. Behera (New Delhi: Concept Pub. Co, 2002), 265–282.

88. For further details, see Mathieu Lefèvre, *Local Defence in Afghanistan: A Review of Government-backed Initiatives* (Kabul: Afghanistan Analysts Network, 2010).

89. Bradbury, *Becoming Somaliland,* argues that this has worked in Somaliland. However, in Afghanistan the utilization of pseudotribal mechanisms, as in the Community/Local Defense Initiative and, earlier, the Afghan Auxiliary National Police and the Afghanistan Social Outreach Program, shows a poor understanding of the highly heterogeneous Pashtun society. Rather, such mechanisms are an expression of the desperate search for an exit strategy caused by the deteriorating situation in Afghanistan. They run the risk of exacerbating existing intratribal conflicts rather than remedying them, not least because they are usually linked to lavish funding.

7. Ethnic Minorities in Search of Political Consolidation

1. For a broader discussion on ethnicity and ethnic conflicts in Afghanistan, see Conrad Schetter, *Ethnizität und ethnische Konflikte in Afghanistan* (Berlin: Reimer, 2003).

2. English translation quoted according to International Constitutional Law Project Information, http://servat.unibe.ch/icl/af00000_.html.

3. Most field studies took place in the southwestern parts of Afghanistan where the Baloch have compact settlements and where I was engaged in the development of a writing system for the Balochi language of Afghanistan and in the edition of a Balochi-Pashto-Dari-English dictionary (published in Kabul in 2007). In 2008, representatives of a Baloch splinter group in the northeastern province of Takhar invited me to their place to study their language, culture, and history. It was evident that they wanted me to find out how much they had in common with other Baloch in Afghanistan and outside. Other material was collected during dialect studies in Balkh Province in spring 2010.

4. While I was engaged in the development of a writing system for the Balochi language in Afghanistan during the last six years, all involved persons agreed that schooling in the Balochi language would be introduced for the Brahui as well. Furthermore, the publication of the first dictionary of the Balochi language of Afghanistan was sponsored by Karim Brahui, the former minister of tribal and frontier affairs, who is a Baloch of the Brahui branch himself. He did so because the authors of the dictionary

appealed to his ethnic feeling and to his responsibility as a Baloch minister. Nevertheless, the Brahui, obviously, regarded it as necessary or useful to be mentioned as a separate group in addition to the Baloch when the text of the new constitution of Afghanistan was adopted.

5. The term *tribe* was preferred in a translation published by the Afghan embassy in Washington, DC: "The nation of Afghanistan shall be comprised of Pashtun, Tajik, Hazara, Uzbek, Turkman, Baloch, Pachaie, Nuristani, Aymaq, Arab, Qirghiz, Qizilbash, Gujur, Brahwui and other tribes." See The Embassy of Afghanistan in Washington, DC, http://www.embassyofafghanistan.org/constitution.html. At least three different terms *(Völkerschaften, Ethnien, ethnische Gruppen)* were used in the German translation that was done by the Max Planck Institute for Comparative Public Law and International Law, http://www.mpil.de/shared/data/pdf/verf_dt3.pdf.

6. The idea of a continuum is based upon the definition of "ethnic groups" given by Erwin Orywal, "Ethnische Identitäten—Konzept und Methode," in *Die ethnischen Gruppen Afghanistans: Fallstudien zu Gruppenidentitäten und Intergruppenbeziehungen,* ed. Erwin Orywal (Wiesbaden: Reichert, 1986), 74.

7. For a description of the socioeconomic situation among the Baloch of southwestern Afghanistan up to the Saur revolution of 1978, see Erwin Orywal, *Die Baluč in Afghanisch-Sıstan: Wirtschaft und sozio-politische Organisation in Nımruz, SW-Afghanistan* (Berlin: Reimer 1982).

8. See Daniel Balland and Augustin de Benoist, "Nomades et semi-nomades Baluč d'Afghanistan," *Revue géographique de L'Est* 22, nos. 1–2 (1982): 117–144 ; and Pierre Centlivres, "L'Histoire récente de l'Afghanistan et la configuration ethnique des Provinces du Nord-Est," *Studia Iranica* 5, no. 2 (1976): 255–267.

9. Among many others I'd like to mention the book *Baloch kai ant?* [Who are the Baloch?] (Kabul: Zuwan-u labzank-ai put-u pal-ai bunja auganistan-ai ulumi akadimi, 1360 [1981–1982]), which was written in Balochi by the leading Baloch intellectual of Afghanistan, Abdul Rahman Baloch, alias Pahwal. See, too, the material of a conference on Balochi culture held in Kabul in 2009, Abdul Sattar Purdeli, ed., *Zaban wa farhang-e balochha-ye afghanestan. Majmu'a-ye maqalat-e sampoziyum* (Kabul: Regional Studies Center of Afghanistan, 1388 [2009–2010]); and a much-discussed book on the same subject written both in Balochi and in Persian by Abdul Sattar Purdeli, *Chint pahlok sha balochani zindagi pahlistana: Chand goli az*

farhang-e porbar-e baloch (Kabul: Regional Studies Center of Afghanistan, 1387 [2008–2009]).

10. Thus a young man from Zaranj, who took part in one of the colloquiums on the development of Balochi language because he was working as a speaker in the local Balochi radio program, introduced himself to me as Pashtun.

11. Beyond common words of Persian or Arabic origin there were only some coincidental analogies in the phonetic adaptation of some words. Thus in Balochi a word that is pronounced *draush* denotes a mark made with an awl in the ears of animals. The Baloch of Takhar call this sign *drosh*. However, both words undoubtedly originate from the Persian word *darafsh*, which originally denotes the awl by which these marks are made.

12. This assessment is based upon preliminary dialect studies carried out in the spring of 2010, when language samples were recorded with a dozen informants. More-detailed dialect studies, which will also include inquiries on relevant terminology, are planned for the future.

13. A comprehensive collection of such epic songs that had been recorded among eastern Baloch was published with English translation by Longworth Dames, *Popular Poetry of the Baloches,* 2 vols. (London: Royal Asiatic Society, 1907). See also Lutz Rzehak, "Das belutschische Epos von Šay Murad und Āno (Materialien aus dem Nachlaß von Alexander L. Grünberg)," *Strany i narody Vostoka,* vol. 30 (St. Petersburg: Peterburgskoe vostokovedenie, 1988), 149–186.

14. An example from a book about the history and culture of the Baloch of Afghanistan: "The Baloch are this ancient and honorable nation in our beloved homeland Afghanistan which has performed glorious deeds in all periods of history" (Baloch, *Baloch kai ant,* 1).

15. Purdeli, *Chint pahlok sha balochani zindagi pahlistana,* 39, 119.

16. This information was given by the present Baloch representative from Nimroz in the Afghan parliament during an interview taken by the author on October 15, 2008, in Kabul.

17. The original Balochi name is *balochi labzankai karwan organaizeshn.*

18. The original Dari name is *sazman-e farhangi-ye ensejam wa madafe'-e hoquq-e balochha-ye afghanestan.*

19. This information was given by the present Baloch representative from Nimroz in the Afghan parliament during an interview taken by the author on October 15, 2008, in Kabul.

8. Red Mosque

This chapter first appeared in *Public Culture* 20, no. 1 (Winter 2008): 19–26, copyright 2008 Duke University Press. All rights reserved. Reprinted by permission of the publisher.

1. Tom Lasseter, "Transcript from Tom Lasseter's interview with Abdul Rashid Ghazi," *Dallas Morning News,* July 10, 2007.

2. Ibid.

3. Ibid.

9. Madrasa Statistics Don't Support the Myth

The findings, interpretations and conclusions expressed in this chapter are those of the authors and do not necessarily represent the views of the World Bank, its executive directors, or the governments they represent.

1. In 2010 the North West Frontier Province was renamed Khyber Pakhtunkhwa. FANA has formally now been given the status of a province and is named Gilgit-Baltistan. We don't have these numbers in our data.

2. See Tahir Andrabi, Jishnu Das, Asim Ijaz Khwaja, and Tristan Zajonc, "Religious School Enrollment in Pakistan: A Look at the Data, 2006," *Comparative Education Review* 50, no. 3 (August 2006): 446–477.

3. For details, see http://www.leapsproject.org.

4. Tahir Andrabi, Jishnu Das, and Asim Ijaz Khwaja, "A Dime a Day: The Possibilities and Limits of Private Schooling in Pakistan," *Comparative Education Review* 52, no. 3 (August 2008): 329–355.

5. See LEAPS report, 2007 at http://www.leapsproject.org.

10. Will Sufi Islam Save Pakistan?

I am particularly indebted to Shahzad Bashir and Robert Crews for their guidance in helping me shape an account that connects recent developments in Pakistan to international policy discussions without sacrificing historical depth. I am also grateful to Faisal Devji for his close reading of this version and for his insightful comments. Patrick and Emile Chabal ensured that my ideas were conveyed in language within reach of the educated nonspecialist.

1. Heritage Foundation, *Reviving Pakistan's Pluralist Traditions to Fight Extremism,* by Lisa Curtis and A. H. Mullick, May 4, 2009, http://www.

heritage.org/Research/Reports/2009/05/Reviving-Pakistans-Pluralist-Traditions-to-Fight-Extremism.

2. Not to be confused with the name recently adopted by the banned Sunni sectarian group, the Sipah-e Sahaba—Pakistan (SSP).

3. World Organization for Resource Development and Education (WORDE), "Traditional Muslim Networks: Pakistan's Untapped Resource in the Fight against Terrorism," Report of the WORDE Initiative, http://www.worde.org/publications/worde_reports/traditional-muslim-networks-pakistans-untapped-resource-in-the-fight-against-terrorism/; "Understanding the Socio-Political Dynamics of Pakistan," by Hadieh Miramadi, Mehreen Farooq, and Waleed Ziad, May 2010, http://www.worde.org/programs/understanding-the-socio-political-dynamics-of-pakistan/. See also Zeyno Baran, "Understanding Sufism and Its Potential Role in US Foreign Policy," Nixon Center Conference Report, March 2004, http:/Zia al-Haq/www.hudson.org/files/publications/Understanding_Suffism.

4. Indeed, Western interest in Sufism had already found expression in the plethora of New Age spiritual movements that predated 9/11 and the current preoccupations of Western policymakers. The enthusiasm reserved for the ideas of the Sufi mystic Idries Shah (1924–1996) in some Western literary circles, the international appeal of Sufi devotional music popularized by the Pakistani singer Nusrat Fateh Ali Khan (1948–1997), and Western fascination with the works of the thirteenth-century Sufi master Jalaluddin Rumi are testimony to this long-standing Western interest in Sufism. They also point to some fascinating connections between New Age spirituality, Sufism, and the hypermodern lifestyles of the urban West in which current conversations about the politics of knowledge involving local Sufi saints and Washington think tanks appear to be almost irrelevant. I am indebted to Faisal Devji for sharing these observations with me.

5. Cheryl Benard, *Civil-Democratic Islam: Partners, Resources and Strategies*, RAND, 2003, http://www.rand.org/pubs/monograph_reports/2005/MR1716.pdf.

6. A. Rabasa, C. Benard, L. Schwartz, and P. Sickle, *Building Moderate Muslim Networks*, RAND Centre for Middle East Public Policy, 2007, http://www.rand.org/pubs/monographs/2007/RAND_MG574.pdf.

7. Parvez Musharraf, "A Plea for Enlightened Moderation," *Washington Post*, June 1, 2004, http://www.washingtonpost.com/wp-dyn/articles/A5081-2004May31.html. "Enlightened moderation" and its ideologues have

recently received some scholarly attention. See Gilles Boquerat and Nazir Hussain, "Enlightened Moderation: Anatomy of a Failed Strategy," in *Pakistan: From the Rhetoric of Democracy to the Rise of Militancy,* ed. Ravi Kali (London: Routledge, 2011), 177–193; and for a more opaque reading, Sadaf Aziz, "Making a Sovereign State: Javed Ghamidi and 'Enlightened Moderation,'" *Modern Asian Studies* 4, no. 3 (2011): 597–629.

8. The Ahl-e Hadith (lit. Followers of the Tradition) represent adherents of a nineteenth-century conservative movement who are skeptical of the value of subscribing to any one of the main four established Sunni schools *(mazhab)* of Islamic law. In modern times they have made common cause with various Salafi movements, which seek to restore the purity of Islam by rejecting all sources of law except the Quran. Deobandis, by contrast, though conservative, subscribe broadly to the rules of Sunni Hanafi *mazhab.*

9. For a discussion of the polemics of "moderation," especially in the context of Afghanistan, see Robert Crews, "Moderate Taliban?," in *The Taliban and the Crisis of Afghanistan,* ed. Robert Crews and Amin Tarzi (Cambridge, MA: Harvard University Press, 2008), 238–273.

10. "Sufism to Be Promoted," *Dawn,* October 13, 2006, http://archives. dawn.com/2006/10/13/nat15.htm. See also "Pakistan: Sufism Promoted to Improve Image," *Religioscope,* October 14, 2006, http://religion.info/english/ articles/article_270.shtml.

11. "Government to Set Up Sufi Advisory Council," *Dawn,* June 7, 2009, http://archives.dawn.com/archives/145514.

12. Sarkis Pogossian, "Sufis and Neocons: The Global War on Terrorism's Strangest Bedfellows," *World War 4 Report,* July 1, 2009, http://www. ww4report.com/node/7502.

13. David Gilmartin, *Empire and Islam: Punjab and the Making of Pakistan* (Berkeley: University of California Press, 1988).

14. "Do not make every conjurer and juggler your *pir,* do not go for his charms and miraculous powers . . . the only sign of a saint is whether he follows the *sunnah* and the Shari'a of the Messenger of God"; quoted in Christian Troll, *Sayyid Ahmad Khan: A Reinterpretation of Islamic Theology* (Karachi: Oxford University Press, 1978/1979), 46.

15. Kathryn Ewing, *Arguing Sainthood: Modernity, Psychoanalysis, and Islam* (Durham: Duke University Press, 1997), 10, 254–255.

16. On Iqbal's shift toward "purism," see Farzana Shaikh, "Millat and Mazhab: Re-thinking Iqbal's Political Vision," in *Living Together Separately:*

Cultural India in History and Politics, ed. Mushirul Hasan and Asim Roy (Oxford: Oxford University Press, 2005), 365–388.

17. Sana Haroon, *Frontier of Faith: Islam in the Indo-Afghan Borderland* (London: Hurst, 2007), 175.

18. Sarah Ansari, *Sufi Saints and State Power: The Pirs of Sind, 1843–1947* (Cambridge: Cambridge University Press, 1992), 122.

19. Farzana Shaikh, *Making Sense of Pakistan* (New York: Columbia University Press, 2009).

20. Shaikh, *Making Sense of Pakistan;* and Leonard Binder, *Religion and Politics in Pakistan* (Berkeley: University of California Press, 1961), 116–154, 142–143.

21. Ewing observes that despite his hostility to the role of local Sufi pirs, it was Iqbal who opened the way for this new relationship by reinterpreting Sufism as the spiritual framework for a program of political action (Ewing, *Arguing Sainthood,* 69).

22. Ian Talbot, *Pakistan: A Modern History* (London: Hurst, 2005) 160.

23. Oskar Verkaaik, *Migrants and Militants: Fun and Urban Violence in Pakistan* (Princeton: Princeton University Press, 2004) 36.

24. Ibid., 38.

25. Qasim Zaman, *The Ulama in Contemporary Islam* (Princeton: Princeton University Press, 2002), 125–133.

26. Ansari, *Sufi Saints and State Power,* 151.

27. Richard Kurin, "Islamization: A View from the Countryside," in *Islamic Re-assertion in Pakistan,* ed. A. Weiss (Lahore: Vanguard, 1987), 115–128.

28. The major state-controlled daily, the *Pakistan Times,* in 1980 declared that saints "were not miracle mongers but educated luminaries" (cited in Ewing, *Arguing Sainthood,* 78).

29. Jamal Malik, *The Colonialization of Islam* (Delhi: Manohar, 1988). In August 2003, while in exile abroad, Bhutto became a member of Minhaj ul Quran, the Sufi-informed religious network founded by Shaikh Tahir ul Qadri, http://www.minhaj.org/english/tid/30/.

30. Talbot, *Pakistan,* 339–342.

31. Vali Nasr, "Islam, the State and the Rise of Sectarian Militancy," in *Pakistan: Nationalism without a Nation,* ed. Christophe Jaffrelot (London: Zed Press, 2001), 105.

32. Mumtaz Ahmad, "Tablighi Jamaat," in *The Oxford Encyclopedia of the Modern Islamic World,* vol. 4 (Oxford: Oxford University Press, 2001), 168.

33. Robert Rozenhal, "Reimagining the 'Land of the Pure': A Sufi Master Reclaims Islamic Orthodoxy and Pakistani Identity," in *Beyond Crisis: Re-Evaluating Pakistan,* ed. Naveeda Khan (London: Routledge, 2010), 131.

34. Ibid., 136. For a more extended discussion of Wahid Bakhsh's role in highlighting the relevance of Sufism for the definition of Pakistan's national identity, see Robert Rozehnal, *Islamic Sufism Unbound: Politics and Piety in Twenty-First Century Pakistan* (London: Palgrave Macmillan, 2009).

35. For a fine exposition of Qadri's ideas, see Mumtaz Ahmad, "Media-Based Preachers and the Creation of New Muslim Publics in Pakistan," in *Who Speaks for Islam?,* by the National Bureau of Asian Research, ARB Special Report no. 22, February 2010, pp. 9–12, http://www.nbr.org/publications/specialreport/pdf/Preview/SR22_preview.pdf.

36. "Prominent Muslim Cleric Denounces bin Laden," October 18, 2001, United Press International, http://archive.newsmax.com/archives/articles/2001/10/17/195606.shtml.

37. "Terrorism and Suicide Attacks," video press conference of Dr. Tahir ul Qadri, Minhaj ul Quran, December 5, 2009, http://www.minhaj.org/english/tid/9385/'Terrorism-and-Suicide-Attacks'-the-Press-Conference-of-Dr.-Tahir-ul-Qadri.html. See also "Pakistanis Mourn Military, Civilian Dead in Mosque Attack," *Washington Post,* December 6, 2009, http://www.washingtonpost.com/wp-dyn/content/article/2009/12/05/AR2009120503001.html.

38. The formal launch of Qadri's massive fatwa in London was attended by prominent Muslim British MPs and leaders of the Muslim Council of Britain and the Quilliam Foundation. The last two, though often at odds with each other over doctrinal matters, are closely involved in the British government's counter-radicalization program aimed at young British Muslims. See Minhaj ul Quran, "Historical Launching of Fatwa against Terrorism," March 2, 2010, http://www.minhaj.org/english/tid/9959/Historical-Launching-of-Fatwa-Against-Terrorism-leading-Islamic-authority-launches-fatwa-against-terrorism-and-denounces-suicide-bombers-as-disbelievers-Anti-terror-Fatwa-launched.htm.

39. Christian Caryl, "Sheikh to Terrorists: Go to Hell," *Foreign Policy,* April 14, 2010, http://www.foreignpolicy.com/articles/2010/04/14/sheikh_to_terrorists_go_to_hell?page=full.

40. Some have even pointed to the party's preference for a markedly "irrational" approach to Islam, based on reports that President Asif Ali Zardari

had taken to ordering the daily ritual sacrifice of a black goat to ward off the "evil eye," and to employ the services of a pir, who is said to have taken up residence at the president's house in Islamabad. See *Dawn*, April 21, 2010, http://www.dawn.com/wps/wcm/connect/dawn-content-library/dawn/the-newspaper/front-page/19a-resident-pir-at-the-presidency-140-hh-06.

41. Philip Jones, *The Pakistan People's Party: Rise to Power* (Karachi: Oxford University Press, 2003), 288–289. See also Verkaaik, *Migrants and Militants*, 36.

42. *Daily Times* (Lahore), March 26, 2008, http://www.dailytimes.com.pk/default.asp?page=2008%5C03%5C26%5Cstory_26-3-2008_pg12_5.

43. Other important Sufi figures in the party include the current minister for commerce and senior member of the PPP, the Makhdoom of Hala (in Sind), Amin Faheem—a mystic poet, *sajjida nashin,* and spiritual leader of the Sarwari Jama'at, a local Sufi order.

44. "Can Sufi Islam Counter the Taliban?," BBC News, February 14, 2009, http://news.bbc.co.uk/1/hi/world/south_asia/7896943.stm.

45. Haroon, *Frontier of Faith*, 33–64.

46. Raheel Khan, "The Battle for Pakistan: Militancy and Conflict in Khyber," Counterterrorism and Strategy Initiative Policy Paper, New America Foundation, April 2010, pp. 3–4, http://counterterrorism.newamerica.net/sites/newamerica.net/files/policydocs/khyber_1.pdf. See also Imtiaz Gul, *The Most Dangerous Place: Pakistan's Lawless Frontier* (London: Penguin, 2010), 72–73.

47. WORDE, "Traditional Muslim Networks," 19.

48. For a classic account of the political antecedents of the ANP and its ideology of nonviolence, see Mukulika Banerjee, *The Pathan Unarmed: Opposition and Memory in the North West Frontier* (Oxford: James Currey, 2000).

49. Qalandar Bux Memon, "The Bad Sufi," *Dawn,* January 26, 2010, http://www.dawn.com/wps/wcm/connect/dawn-content-library/dawn/news/pakistan/03-the-bad-sufi-ss-02.

50. "US Puts Up $149,000 for Sufi Shrines' Preservation," *Daily Times* (Lahore), April 22, 2010.

51. Memon, "The Bad Sufi."

52. They include the writer and Sufi specialist Ayeda Naqvi. See "Can Sufi Islam Counter the Taliban?"

53. In contrast to the common perception of Sufi pirs as agents of the status quo and the law (such as it is), the *qalandar,* in his defiance of the

law, can embody "a subaltern resistance to a dominant social and political order." See Ewing, *Arguing Sainthood,* 205.

54. Ayesha Siddiqa, "Faith Wars," *Dawn,* February 14, 2009, http://www.dawn.com.pk/wps/wcm/connect/dawn-content-library/dawn/the-newspaper/columnists/faith-wars-yn.

55. "Pakistan Clerics Accuse Punjab Leaders of Taliban Link," BBC News, July 5, 2010, http://news.bbc.co.uk/1/hi/world/south_asia/10511046.stm.

11. The Politics of Pashtun and Punjabi Truck Decoration

The material in this article appeared in different form in Jamal J. Elias, *On Wings of Diesel: Trucks, Identity and Culture in Pakistan* (Oxford: Oneworld, 2011).

1. Government of Pakistan, "Pakistan Transport Plan Study" (2006), Final Report, Japan International Cooperation Agency (JICA) and National Transport Research Centre (NTRC), Ministry of Communications, Government of Pakistan, March, section 2.2.2 (1), fig. 2.2.6; *Pakistan Statistical Yearbook, 2003,* 214ff, 223, 228; Government of Pakistan, "Economic Survey 2008–09" (2009), Finance Division Economic Advisor's Wing, Islamabad, Pakistan, table 14.4, p. 211.

2. For more on the place occupied by truck decoration in the art cultures of Pakistan, see Jamal Elias, *On Wings of Diesel: Trucks, Identity and Culture in Pakistan* (Oxford: Oneworld, 2011), chap. 10.

3. My use of the term *hybridization* follows Néstor García Canclini, who succinctly defines it as follows: "I understand for hybridization socio-cultural processes in which discrete structures or practices, previously existing in separate form, are combined to generate new structures, objects, and practices. In turn, it bears noting that the so-called discrete structures were a result of prior hybridizations and therefore cannot be considered pure points of origin." N. García Canclini, *Hybrid Culture: Strategies for Entering and Leaving Modernity,* trans. C. L. Chiappari and S. L. López (Minneapolis: University of Minnesota Press, 1995), xxv. My discussion of truck decoration and truck culture is strongly influenced by the writings of Bourdieu, particularly in his use of the concept of *habitus,* defined as "systems of durable, transposable *dispositions,* structured structures predisposed to function as structuring structures, that is, as principles of the generation and structuring of practices and representations which can be

objectively 'regulated' and 'regular' without in any way being the product of obedience to rules." Pierre Bourdieu, *Outline of a Theory of Practice*, trans. Richard Nice (Cambridge: Cambridge University Press, 1977; rpt. 2006), 72.

4. See Elias, *On Wings of Diesel*, chaps. 6 and 7; and Jamal J. Elias, "On Wings of Diesel: Spiritual Space and Religious Imagination in Pakistani Truck Decoration," *Res* 43 (2003): 187–202.

5. See Elias, *On Wings of Diesel*, 186ff.

6. Marie-Bénédicte Dutreux, "La Peinture des camion en Afghanistan" (PhD diss., Paris I, Sorbonnes, Section Arts Plastiques, 1978), 166.

7. For more examples of images of partridges on trucks, as well as shifts in the representation of Shii symbols, see Elias, *On Wings of Diesel*, 162ff.

8. For more on the commemoration of Husayn's martyrdom in Pakistan, see Vernon J. Schubel, *Religious Performance in Contemporary Islam: Shi'i Devotional Rituals in South Asia* (Columbia: University of South Carolina Press, 1993).

9. For more on the Tablighi Jama'at, see Yoginder Sikand, *The Origins and Development of the Tablighi-Jama'at (1920–2000)* (New Delhi: Orient Longman, 2002); M. Khalid Masud, ed., *Travellers in Faith* (Leiden: Brill, 2000); Barbara D. Metcalf, "Living Hadith in the Tablighi Jamaat," *Journal of Asian Studies* 52 (1993): 584–608.

10. Iftikhar Dadi, "Ghostly Sufis and Ornamental Shadows: Spectral Visualities in Karachi's Public Sphere," *Comparing Cities: The Middle East and South Asia,* ed. Martina Rieker and Kamran Ali (Oxford: Oxford University Press, 2009), 159–193.

11. Kajri Jain, *Gods in the Bazaar: The Economies of Indian Calendar Art* (Durham, NC: Duke University Press, 2007), 319.

12. The Afghan Mediascape

1. *Shams al-Nahar,* no. 1, March 1873, 2.

2. Ibid.

3. *Seraj al-Akhbar Afghaniya,* no. 1, October 1911, 1.

4. Ibid., no. 1, September 1912, 2.

5. A. C. Jewett, *An American Engineer in Afghanistan, from the Letters and Notes of A. C. Jewett,* ed. Marjorie Jewett Bell (Minneapolis: University of Minnesota Press, 1948), 112, 223.

6. *Seraj al-Akhbar,* no. 3, November 1911, 8; no. 4, November 1911, 8.

7. Ibid., no. 22, August 1912, 2; no. 14, April 1912, 1, 5–6.

8. Ibid., no. 15, May 1912, 8.

9. Ibid., no. 18, June 1912, 6.

10. Ibid., no. 14, April 1912, 6

11. Ibid., no. 3, October 1914, 9.

12. Ibid., no. 9, January 1913, 9.

13. Ibid., no. 9, January 1913, 11.

14. *Anis,* no. 14, July 1931, 3.

15. Christopher M. Andrew and Vasili Mitrokhin, *The World Was Going Our Way: The KGB and the Battle for the Third World* (New York: Basic Books, 2005), 387.

16. Louis Dupree, *Afghanistan* (Princeton: Princeton University Press, 1973), 601.

17. David B. Edwards, *Before Taliban: Genealogies of the Afghan Jihad* (Berkeley: University of California Press, 2002), 208.

18. A. S. Ghaus, *The Fall of Afghanistan: An Insider's Account* (Virginia: Pergamon-Brassey's International Defense Publishers, 1988), 195.

19. *Assisting the Democratic Republic of Afghanistan in Strengthening the Mass Media,* Cold War International History Project, Woodrow Wilson International Center for Scholars.

20. *Afghan Media in 2010: Synthesis Report,* USAI and Altai Consulting, October 2010. p. 59, http://www.altaiconsulting.com/docs/media/2010/Afghan%20Media%20in%202010.pdf.

21. William A. Rugh, *Arab Mass Media: Newspapers, Radio, and Television in Arab Politics* (Westport, CT: Praeger, 2004), 23; K. Hafez, ed., *Mass Media, Politics, and Society in the Middle East* (Cresskill, NJ: Hampton Press, 2001).

22. Michael Drewett and Martin Cloonan, eds., *Popular Music Censorship in Africa* (Aldershot, UK: Ashgate, 2006), 207.

23. For examples from Turkey, see Dale F. Eickelman and Jon. W. Anderson, eds., *New Media in the Muslim World: The Emerging Public Sphere* (Bloomington: Indiana University Press, 2003), 181.

24. According to a recent survey, 98 percent of Afghans have never used the Internet. See, for example, *Afghanistan in 2010: A Survey of the Afghan People,* Asia Foundation (2010), 156, http://asiafoundation.org/country/afghanistan/2010-poll.php.

13. Women and the Drug Trade in Afghanistan

1. Author interviews with officials and residents in Ghoryan, July 2003. Some names in this chapter have been changed to protect the identities of interviewees.

2. Gretchen Peters, *Seeds of Terror: How Heroin Is Bankrolling the Taliban and al Qaeda* (New York: St. Martin's Press, 2009), 186; Adam B. Kushner, "The Truth about Plan Colombia," *Newsweek,* January 3, 2009.

3. Colum Lynch, "U.N. Finds Afghan Opium Trade Rising," *Washington Post,* June 27, 2008.

4. Robert Tait, "Iran Faces Up to Its Most Lethal Threat—Drugs," *Guardian,* October 27, 2005.

5. Victor Ivanov, "Proposals for the Elimination of Afghan Drug Production," a talk presented at the Moscow conference on counternarcotics, June 2010.

6. McClatchy Newspapers, "Afghanistan Heroin Finds Way to US Streets," *The State,* January 7, 2007.

7. Eric Schmitt, "Many Sources Feed Taliban War Chest," *New York Times,* October 18, 2009.

8. Interview with counternarcotics specialist Matthew DuPee of Naval Post Graduate School, December 2010.

9. Peter Dale Scott, "America's Afghanistan: The National Security and a Heroin-Ravaged State," *Asia-Pacific Journal,* May 17, 2009.

10. UN Office for Drugs and Crime, *Afghanistan: 2007 Annual Opium Poppy Survey,* August 2007, IV.

11. Scott, "America's Afghanistan."

12. Dion Nissenbaum, "Afghan Report Links President's Brother to Illegal Land Grabs," *Anchorage Daily News,* June 23, 2010; Tom Lasseter, "Afghan Drug Trade Thrives with Help, and Neglect, of Officials," McClatchy Newspapers, May 11, 2009.

13. Author interview with official from Transnational Institute, December 2005.

14. Author interview with Afghan supervisor of eradication program, Kabul, 2005.

15. UN Office on Drugs and Crime, *Illicit Drug Trends in Afghanistan,* June 2008, 6.

16. Author interviews with Drug Enforcement Administration agents, 2005.

17. Ivanov, "Proposals for the Elimination of Afghan Drug Production."

18. Bilal Sarwary, "Afghan Officials Accused on Drugs," BBC News, January 6, 2006.

19. Jonathan Burch, "Afghan Opium Crop May Rise after 'Cash Bonanza,'" Reuters, January 20, 2011.

20. "Around One Million Afghans Suffer from Drug Addiction, UNODC Reports," UN Office on Drugs and Crime website, June 22, 2010, http://www.unodc.org/unodc/en/frontpage/2010/June/around-one-million-afghans-suffer-from-drug-addiction-unodc-survey-shows.html; Aunohita Mojumdar, "Mothers, the Hidden Addicts of Afghanistan," Independent, December 12, 2010.

21. Ann Jones, "In Afghanistan, a Woman's Place Is at the Peace Table," Los Angeles Times, January 13, 2011.

22. UN Development Fund for Women, "Women in Afghanistan Fact Sheet 2010," http://www.unifem.org/afghanistan/media/pubs/factsheet/10/index.html.

23. Author interviews with Afghan women who admitted to having been raped, Herat, 2000.

24. Aryn Baker, "Afghan Women and the Return of the Taliban," Time, July 29, 2010.

25. UN Development Fund for Women, "Women in Afghanistan Fact Sheet 2010."

26. "Suicide Rate Soars among Afghan Women," People's Daily Online, August 1, 2010, http://english.peopledaily.com.cn/90001/90777/90851/7088366.html.

27. "Girls and Women Traded for Opium Debts," UN Integrated Regional Information Networks, January 23, 2007, http://www.rawa.org/temp/runews/2007/01/23/girls-and-women-traded-for-opium-debts.phtml.

28. Ibid.

29. Haytullah Gaheez, "Daughters Sold to Settle Debts," Institute for War and Peace Reporting, November 16, 2005, http://iwpr.net/report-news/daughters-sold-settle-debts.

30. Ibid.

31. Ibid.

32. Author interviews with Nejat Center counselors, Kabul, 2005; Niamatullah Zafarzaoi, "Number of Drug Addicts on the Rise in Kabul," Pajhwok Afghan News Service, June 1, 2010.

33. Barnett Rubin and Jake Sherman, *Counter Narcotics to Stabilize Afghanistan: The False Promise of Crop Eradication* (New York: Center on International Cooperation, February 2008), 6.

34. "Afghanistan Opium Survey 2009," Afghan Ministry of Counter Narcotics, December 2009, 9.

35. UN Office for the Coordination of Humanitarian Affairs—Integrated Regional Information Network, "Afghanistan: Interview with Female Opium Farmer," http://208.106.251.104/Report.aspx?ReportID=25856; see the film *Bitter-Sweet Harvest: Afghanistan's New War,* August 2004, http://208.106.251.104/Film/?id=4101.

36. UN Office on Drugs and Crime, *The Role of Women in Opium Poppy Cultivation in Afghanistan* (Islamabad: UNODCP, June 2000), 37.

37. UN Integrated Regional Information Networks, *In-Depth: Bitter-Sweet Harvest: Afghanistan's New War: Afghan Women and Opium,* Nairobi, August 2, 2004, http://www.irinnews.org/InDepthMain.aspx?InDepthId=21&ReportId=62950.

38. Author interviews with Afghan smugglers in Takhar, July 2006.

39. Sarwary, "Afghan Officials Accused on Drugs."

40. Office of National Drug Control Policy, "Summary of Findings," http://web.docuticker.com/go/docubase/27210.

41. Barnett R. Rubin and Omar Zakhilwal, "A War on Drugs or a War on Farmers?," *Wall Street Journal,* January 11, 2005.

Epilogue

1. http://gregmortenson.blogspot.com/2011/04/greg-mortensons-response-to-allegations.html.

2. http://gregmortenson.blogspot.com/2011/04/greg-mortensons-response-to-allegations.html.

3. The simple effort of going through webpages on the internet should disabuse one of the notion that Baltis have no sense of their own place in history (see, for example, the extensive list of resources provided on the website maintained by Kenneth Iain MacDonald: http://www.utsc.utoronto.ca/~kmacd/Kar-i/HTML/kklinks.htm). For a reflection on the centrality of history to contemporary Balti identities see Shahzad Bashir, "Resisting Assimilation: Encounters with a Small Islamic Sect in Contemporary Pakistan," in *Engaging South Asian Religions: Boundaries, Appropriations*

and Resistances, ed. Peter Gottschalk and Mathew Schmalz (Albany: SUNY Press, 2011), 173–190.

4. Elisabeth Bumiller, "Unlikely Tutor Giving Military Afghan Advice," The *New York Times,* July 17, 2010, http://www.nytimes.com/2010/07/18/world/asia/18tea.html.

5. See Faisal Devji, *Landscapes of the Jihad: Militancy, Morality, Modernity* (Ithaca: Cornell University Press, 2005).

6. Elisabeth Bumiller, "Videos From Bin Laden's Hide-Out Released," *The New York Times,* May 7, 2011, http://www.nytimes.com/2011/05/08/world/asia/08intel.html?_r=1.

Recommended Readings

The editors recommend, in addition to the work of the contributors to this book, these texts on the history and politics of Afghanistan and Pakistan.

Banerjee, Mukulika. *The Pathan Unarmed: Opposition and Memory in the North West Frontier.* Karachi: Oxford University Press, 2000.

Barfield, Thomas. *Afghanistan: A Cultural and Political History.* Princeton: Princeton University Press, 2010.

Canfield, Robert L., and Gabriele Rasuly-Paleczek, eds. *Ethnicity, Authority, and Power in Central Asia: New Games Great and Small.* London: Routledge, 2011.

Deol, Jeevan, and Zaheer Kazmi, eds. *Contextualising Jihadi Thought.* New York: Columbia University Press, 2012.

Edwards, David B. *Before Taliban: Genealogies of the Afghan Jihad.* Berkeley: University of California Press, 2002.

Giustozzi, Antonio, ed. *Decoding the New Taliban: Insights from the Afghan Field.* London: Hurst, 2009.

González, Roberto J. *American Counterinsurgency: Human Science and the Human Terrain.* Chicago: Prickly Paradigm Press, 2009.

Green, Nile. "The Trans-Border Traffic of Afghan Modernism: Afghanistan and the Indian 'Urdusphere'," *Comparative Studies in Society and History* 53, no. 3 (2011): 479-508.

Hopkins, Benjamin, and Magnus Marsden, eds. *Fragments of the Afghan Frontier*. London: Hurst, 2012.

Iqtidar, Humeira. *Secularizing Islamists? Jama'at-e-Islami and Jama'at-ud-Da'wa in Urban Pakistan*. Chicago: University of Chicago Press, 2011.

Jalal, Ayesha. *Partisans of Allah: Jihad in South Asia*. Cambridge, MA: Harvard University Press, 2008.

Khan, Naveeda, ed. *Beyond Crisis: Re-evaluating Pakistan*. London: Routledge, 2010.

Maley, William, ed. *Fundamentalism Reborn? Afghanistan and the Taliban*. New York: New York University Press, 2001.

Marsden, Magnus. *Living Islam: Muslim Religious Experience in Pakistan's North-West Frontier*. Cambridge: Cambridge University Press, 2005.

Rashid, Ahmed. *Taliban: Militant Islam, Oil and Fundamentalism in Central Asia*. New Haven: Yale University Press, 2000.

Rubin, Barnett R. *The Fragmentation of Afghanistan: State Formation and Collapse in the International System*. New Haven: Yale University Press, 1995.

Semple, Michael. *Reconciliation in Afghanistan*. Washington, DC: U.S. Institute of Peace Press, 2009.

Zaeef, Abdul Salam. *My Life with the Taliban*. Edited by Alex Strick van Linschoten and Felix Kuehn. New York: Columbia University Press, 2010.

Zaman, Muhammad Qasim. *The Ulama in Contemporary Islam: Custodians of Change*. Princeton: Princeton University Press, 2002.

Contributors

Nushin Arbabzadah is a research scholar at UCLA's Center for the Study of Women. She is the author of *From Outside In: Refugees and British Society* (2007) and editor of *No Ordinary Life: Being Young in the Worlds of Islam* (2007). She is the co-editor, with Nile Green, of *Afghanistan in Ink: Literature between Diaspora and Nation* (forthcoming). She writes regularly for *The Guardian* online.

Tahir Andrabi is Professor of Economics at Pomona College. He has published widely on education in Pakistan and is the principal investigator on the Learning and Educational Achievement in Pakistan Schools (LEAPS) project and on a National Academy of Sciences/Higher Education Commission, Pakistan, grant to evaluate recovery from the 2005 earthquake.

Shahzad Bashir is Lysbeth Warren Anderson Professor in the department of Religious Studies and Director of the Abbasi Program in Islamic Studies at Stanford University. He is the author of *Messianic Hopes and Mystical Visions: The Nurbakhshiya between Medieval and Modern Islam* (2003), *Fazlallah Astarabadi and the Hurufis* (2005), and *Sufi Bodies: Religion and Society in Medieval Islam* (2011).

James Caron is a Lecturer in Islamicate South Asia in the Department of the Languages and Cultures of South Asia at the School of Oriental and African Studies. He has done field work in Kabul and Peshawar and specializes in the social and cultural history of Afghanistan. He teaches courses on modern Afghanistan, Pakistan, and Islam in South Asia.

Robert D. Crews is Associate Professor of History and Director of the Center for Russian, East European, and Eurasian Studies at Stanford University. He is the author of *For Prophet and Tsar: Islam and Empire in Russia and Central Asia* (2006) and co-editor, with Amin Tarzi, of *The Taliban and the Crisis of Afghanistan* (2008).

Jishnu Das is a Senior Economist in the Development Research Group at The World Bank, where his research has focused on education and health. He is also a Visiting Scholar at The Center for Policy Research, New Delhi.

Faisal Devji is Reader in Modern South Asian History and Fellow of St. Antony's College, Oxford University. He is the author of *Landscapes of the Jihad: Militancy, Morality, Modernity* (2005), *The Terrorist in Search of Humanity: Militant Islam and Global Politics* (2008), and *The Impossible Indian: Gandhi and the Temptation of Violence* (2012).

Gilles Dorronsoro is a Visiting Scholar at the Carnegie Endowment. He is the author of *Revolution Unending: Afghanistan, 1979 to the Present* (2005) and *La révolution afghane, des communistes aux Taleban* (2000), and editor of *La Turquie conteste: Mobilisations sociales et régime sécuritaire* (2005). The author of numerous articles on Afghanistan, Turkey, and South Asia, he co-founded and edits the *South Asian Multidisciplinary Academic Journal* and the *European Journal of Turkish Studies*.

Jamal J. Elias is Class of 1965 Term Professor of Religious Studies at the University of Pennsylvania. He is the author of *On Wings of Diesel: Trucks, Identity and Culture in Pakistan* (2011); *The Throne Carrier of God: The Life and Thought of 'Ala' ad-dawla as-Simnani* (1995) and *Islam* (1999); co-author of *Interpreting the Self: Autobiography in the Arabic Literary Tradition* (2001); and editor and translator of *Death before Dying: Sufi Poems of Sultan Bahu* (1998), and *Key Themes for the Study of Islam* (2010).

Shah Mahmoud Hanifi is Associate Professor of History at James Madison University. He is the author of *Connecting Histories in Afghanistan: Market Relations and State Formation on a Colonial Frontier* (2008) and editor of *Power Hierarchies and Hegemony in Afghanistan: State Building, Ethnic Minorities and Identity in Central Asia* (forthcoming).

Sana Haroon teaches in the Department of Social Sciences, IBA Karachi, and is Malathy Singh Visiting Lecturer and Postdoctoral Associate at Yale University. She is the author of *Frontier of Faith: Islam in the Indo-Afghan Borderland* (2007).

Asim Ijaz Khwaja is Sumitomo-FASID Professor of International Finance and Development and the faculty chair of the Master in Public Administration / International Development program at the Harvard Kennedy School of Government. His work explores education, development, finance, political economy, and institutions. In 2009 he was selected as a Carnegie Scholar to conduct research on the Hajj.

Fariba Nawa is a journalist whose work has appeared in the *Sunday Times of London, Mother Jones, The Village Voice, The Christian Science Monitor,* and other publications. She also reports for radio, including National Public Radio. She is the author of *Afghanistan, Inc.* (2006) and *Opium Nation: Child Brides, Drug Lords and One Woman's Journey through Afghanistan* (2011).

Thomas Ruttig was trained in Afghanistan Studies at Berlin's Humboldt University and is currently a Co-Director and Senior Analyst of the Afghanistan Analysts Network (Kabul and Berlin). His many essays and media appearances can be found at the AAN website (http://aan-afghanistan.com/).

Lutz Rzehak is Associate Professor of the Central Asian Seminar of the Institute of Asian and African Studies at Humboldt University. He is the author of *Tadschikische Studiengrammatik* (1999) and *Vom Persischen zum Tadschikischen* (2001). He has translated and edited an Afghan memoir, *Die Taliban im Land der Mittagssonne* (2004), and collaborated on the publication of a Balochi-Pashto-Dari-English dictionary published in Kabul (2007).

Farzana Shaikh is Associate Fellow of the Asia Programme, Chatham House. Her numerous publications include *Community and Consensus in Islam: Muslim Representation in Colonial India, 1860–1947* (1989; 2012), *Islam and Islamic Groups: A Worldwide Reference Guide* (1992), and *Making Sense of Pakistan* (2009).

Amin Tarzi is Director of Middle East Studies at Marine Corps University. He has published widely on security issues in South Asia and the Middle East and is co-editor of *The Taliban and the Crisis of Afghanistan* (2008) and editor of *The Iranian Puzzle Piece: Understanding Iran in the Global Context* (2009).

Acknowledgments

An edited volume is a collaborative project by definition, and our foremost gratitude goes to colleagues who have written the essays. We greatly appreciate their interest in the project and their patience while responding to editorial queries and suggestions. Anonymous colleagues who undertook to review the manuscript provided invaluable advice for streamlining the volume and helping us make its varied elements cohere into a whole. At Harvard University Press, Joyce Seltzer offered brilliant guidance on the structure and conception of the manuscript. Her vision shaped the book in innumerable ways. We also thank Brian Distelberg, who expertly handled the many practicalities of the publishing process. Don Pirius was very kind to draw excellent maps and tables, and Wendy Nelson skillfully improved the text through her outstanding editing.

This book culminates a journey that began as a workshop entitled "Alienated Nations, Fractured States: Afghanistan and Pakistan," sponsored by the Abbasi Program in Islamic Studies at Stanford University in December 2009. Special thanks go to Burçak Keskin-Kozat, the Associate Director of the Abbasi Program, for helping to formulate the workshop's intellectual goals as well as managing practical details in an exemplary manner. We thank the workshop's other sponsors: the Center for International Security and Cooperation; the Center for South Asia; the Center for Russian, East European, and Eurasian Studies; and the Department of History. Stanford colleagues

Aishwary Kumar, Parna Sengupta, and Stephen Stedman generously aided us by chairing the sessions and leading discussions.

We are most grateful to our families for the encouragement, invaluable support, and forbearance on their part that made it possible for us to complete this project. The topic of this book matters to us deeply as both an academic endeavor and a matter of global citizenship aimed at humane understandings of the lives addressed in its contents. We wish to dedicate the book to the ordinary people of Afghanistan and Pakistan, whose complex realities, we hope, are reflected in the treatments provided by our contributors.

Index

Abdali, Ahmad Shah. *See* Durrani
An Account of the Kingdom of Caubul (Elphinstone), 90
Achakzai, Mahmud Khan, 211
Afghani, Sayyid Jamal al-Din, 128
Afghan Independent Human Rights Commission (AIHRC), 246–247
Afghanistan, 83–101; NATO in, 2; U.S. in, 2, 96; Pashtuns in, 3–4, 22–23, 41, 86, 95; Baloch in, 4, 139–151, 292n3; Islam in, 9, 19, 52, 270n2; Soviet Union in, 9, 23–24, 56, 113; tribes in, 10–11, 41, 293n5; media in, 13, 215–235; newspapers in, 13, 215–226; television in, 13, 230–233; women in, 13, 236–256; humanitarian aid for, 14; NGOs in, 14, 233; al-Qaida in, 18, 124; India and, 22, 271n17; nationalism in, 33, 87–97; political parties in, 34; Taliban in, 34, 36, 75–76, 102–135; Deobandi in, 45–53; Britain and, 47–48, 84, 89–93; jihadists in, 53–57; Pashto language in, 63, 95; population of, 85; refugees from, 85; origins of, 87–93; ethnicity in, 136–152; marriage in, 148, 243, 245, 282n5; freedom of speech in, 222–229; Internet in, 233, 303n24; literacy in, 245; madrasas in, 269n7

Afghanistan Peace and Reconciliation Program (APRP), 103, 134
Afghan Ministry of Counter Narcotics, 249
Afghan National Assembly, 22, 225
Afghan National Museum, 94
Afghan National Police, 112
Af-Pak, 2, 3, 4, 6, 8, 17–29, 30–44, 162, 258
Afshar, Nadir Shah, 87–88
Agha Khan Institute, 94
Ahl-e Hadith, 38, 297n8
Ahl-e Sunnat, 189
Ahl-e Sunnat al-Jama'at, 174

317

International Security Assistance
Force (ISAF), 109, 233
Internet, 120, 129, 233, 289n72, 303n24
Inter-Services Intelligence (ISI), 33,
120, 290n77
Iqbal, Muhammad, 177–178, 204–205
Iran, 14, 88, 145, 230, 236, 238, 254
Iraq, 207–209
ISAF. *See* International Security
Assistance Force
ISI. *See* Inter-Services Intelligence
Islah (newspaper), 94
Islam, 31, 43, 45–59, 92, 157, 202–204;
in Afghanistan, 9, 19, 52, 270n2; in
Pakistan, 9, 11–12, 23–24, 33, 189–
191; Taliban and, 79, 114, 130–131;
Pashtuns and, 121. *See also* Shiites;
Sufism; Sunnis
Islamabad, 163
Islamic Emirate of Afghanistan (IEA),
61, 117, 124–125, 126
Islamic law, 4, 52. *See also* Hanafi law;
Jafari law; Sharia
*Islamic Revolution and Its Philosophi-
cal Underpinnings*, 56
Ittehad-e Mashriqi (newspaper), 49

Jabha (district), 116
Jafari law, 88
Jaish al-Muslimin, 291n85
Jaish-e Muhammad, 56
Jalil, Mullah, 129
Jamal, Qudratullah, 129
Jama'at al-da'wa al-Quran wa al-
sunna, 38
Jama'at-e Islami, 34, 53, 155
Jama'at-e Mujahedin, 46, 57
Jami'a 'Arabiyya, 51
Jam'iyat al-'Ulum al-Islamiyah, 38
Jam'iyat-e 'Ulama-e Islam (JUI), 35,
37, 39, 54–55, 183, 211

Jam'iyat-e 'Ulama-e Pakistan (JUP),
176, 189
Jam'iyat Imam Bukhari, 38
Al Jazeera, 155
Jewett, A. C., 218
Jihadists, 30, 32–37, 53–57, 94–95,
123–124, 125
Jinnah, Muhammad Ali, 177, 178,
204–205
Jirga, 103–104, 110–111, 283n16,
284n22
Jirgadar (those with knowledge of
jirga), 104
Jogezai, Nawab Taimur Shah, 210, 213
Jones, William, 90, 93
JUI. *See* Jam'iyat-e 'Ulama-e Islam
JUP. *See* Jam'iyat-e 'Ulama-e
Pakistan

Kabul University, 52, 223
Kafer Baloch (ingrate Baloch), 148
Kafirstan, 217
Kamal Khan dam, 150–151
Kandahari, 117–118, 146, 286n35
Kandahari Taliban, 116, 117
Kappa (tents), 147
Karokhel, 42
Karzai, Ahmed Wali, 240
Karzai, Hamid, 100, 103, 108, 130,
134, 150, 244–245, 255
Karzai family, 43, 79, 108
Kashmir, 23, 34, 206
Kaumi (tribal organization), 145
Khales, 39, 41, 116, 284n23
Khalq (newspaper), 223–224, 233
Khan (tribal leader), 104
Khan, Abdul Ghaffar, 21, 33
Khan, Abdul Qadeer, 209–210
Khan, Ayub, 180, 205
Khan, Daud, 243
Khan, Habibullah, 20, 47, 49, 219

Operation Bluestar, 154
Operation Silence. *See* Red Mosque
Organization of the Young Muslim.
  See Sazman-e Jawan-e Musulman
Oruzgan, 41, 109, 117
Ottoman Empire, 40

Pak, Sayyid Musa, 186, 188
Pakhtunistan, 21–26
Pakhtuns, 5
Pakistan, 6, 7, 18, 24, 40–41, 145,
  208, 230, 254; Islam in, 9, 11–12,
  23–24, 33, 189–191; education in,
  12; Sufism in, 12, 174–191; truck
  decoration in, 12–13, 192–214;
  India and, 14–15; Kashmir and, 23,
  206; indirect rule in, 32; jihadists in,
  33, 34, 35; madrasas in, 36, 37–39,
  114–115, 162–173; political parties
  in, 36; Taliban and, 37, 124; Sharia
  in, 53–57; Red Mosque in, 153–161
Pakistan Awami Tehrik, 184
Pakistan People's Party (PPP), 176,
  182, 185–186, 205
Paktia, 111, 112, 115
Paktiawal, 117–118, 286n38
Paktika, 115
Pamiri language, 136, 138
Panjshiris, 121
Pari (fairy), 195
Partridges, 196–199
Pasaband, 113
Pashto language, 9–10, 63, 76–80,
  90–92, 95, 136, 144, 146, 279n26; in
  madrasas, 36; Taliban and, 62–70;
  U.S. and, 97; in media, 229
Pashtunistan, 21–26, 121
Pashtuns, 9, 19–20, 24, 26, 40–41,
  46, 87, 98–99, 102, 121, 282n6; in
  Afghanistan, 3–4, 22–23, 41, 86,
  95; counterinsurgency and, 3–4;

smuggling by, 30–31, 238; refugees,
  31; in NWFP, 35; in Iran, 88; Taliban
  and, 104–113, 121; tribes of, 104–113;
  truck decoration and, 192–214
Pashtunwali, 91, 104, 107, 281n3
Patak-salari (rule by checkpoint), 75
PDPA. *See* People's Democratic Party
  of Afghanistan
Pech Valley, 113
People's Democratic Party of Afghan-
  istan (PDPA), 19, 23–25, 108, 109,
  284n22
Persian language, 90–91, 136,
  142–144, 215, 229, 231, 279n26
Peshawar Seven, 113
Petraeus, David, 2, 260
Pioneer (newspaper), 219
Piri-muridi, 177
Pirs (spiritual masters), 174, 177,
  300n53
Pisrand (clan), 145
Polygamy, 243
Popolzai, 42, 108, 136
Portraits, on truck decoration,
  204–213
PPP. *See* Pakistan People's Party
Pradai (stranger), 114–115
Prasun language, 138
Provincial Reconstruction Teams
  (PRTs), 42
Provisional Government of India in
  Exile, 47
PRTs. *See* Provincial Reconstruction
  Teams
Punjab, 36, 97, 163, 183, 188, 192–214

Qabila, 139
Qadri, Maulana Muhammad Ajmal,
  189
Qadri, Muhammad Tahir ul, 184–185
Qadri, Noor ul Haq, 187

Silk Road, 238
Sind, 188
Sindhi, Obaidullah, 47, 57
Sistan, 139
60 Minutes, 257
Smuggling, 30–31, 236, 238, 251–252
Soltanzi, Gandomi, 245–246
Soraya, 243
South Waziristan, 37, 40
Soviet Union, 2, 9, 23–24, 56, 113, 228, 238–239. *See also* Russia
Spears, Britney, 232
Spingiri (whitebeards), 104, 110
Srinagar, 155
Sufi Advisory Council (SAC), 191
Sufism, 93; in Pakistan, 12, 174–191; Western interest in, 296n4
Suicide bombers, 109, 123, 124
Sunnis, 34, 37, 88, 122, 147–148, 156, 182, 202, 284n23
Suroz (stringed instrument), 143
Swat, 168–169, 274n58

Tablighi Jama'at, 37–38, 183–184
Tajikistan, 14
Takhallus (surname), 109
Takhar, 141–147, 151
Taliban, 1, 3, 7, 9, 17, 60–82, 289n69, 290n79; literature and, 10, 62–70; Neo-Taliban, 19, 102, 127–128; Durand Line and, 26; al-Qaida and, 26, 125; in Afghanistan, 34, 36, 75–76, 102–135; Sharia and, 36, 123, 131; Khyber Pakhtunkhwa and, 37; Pakistan and, 37, 124; as Sunnis, 37, 122; in NWFP, 38; Dar al-'Ulum Haqqaniyya and, 39; tribes and, 41–42, 102–125; mujahedin and, 61, 114, 126; Pashto language and, 62–70; music and, 71; Islam and, 79, 114, 130–131;

Pashtuns and, 104–113, 121; origins of, 113–119; madrasas and, 114–115, 163; Leadership Council of, 116, 124, 128, 130; ideology of, 119–131; Internet magazine of, 120; jihadists and, 123–124; development phases of, 126–127; technology and, 128; internet and, 129, 289n72; ethnicity and, 137; Sufism and, 187; drug trade and, 238, 239; women and, 243; *tanzim* and, 285n27; television and, 289n72
Taliban Ulama Council, 122
Tamil Tigers, 127
Tanzim (organization), 113, 119, 283n16, 284n23, 285n27
Taraki, Nur Muhammad, 224
Tarun (pact), 111
Tarzi, Amin, 8–9
Tarzi, Mahmud, 217–218, 230
Tayifa (clan), 139, 145
Tazkiras (biographical directories), 64, 80
Tehrik-e Nifaz-e Shariat-e Muhammadi, 55, 211
Tehrik-e Taliban-e Pakistan (TPP), 4, 17, 37, 211
Television, 13, 230–233, 289n72
Terrorism, 17, 19, 27, 262
Three Cups of Tea (Mortenson), 6, 257
Tiga (moratorium), 104
Tokhi, 117
Tolaba fronts, 284n24
Tolo (television station), 230, 233
Topaki (foot soldier), 76
Topak-salari (rule by rifle), 75
Tora (courage), 104
Transnational space, 31–32, 44, 269n5
Tribal Solidarity Council, 111
Tribes: in Af-Pak, 3; in Afghanistan, 10–11, 41, 293n5; in FATA, 40;